PostgreSQL 10 High Performance

Expert techniques for query optimization, high availability, and efficient database maintenance

Ibrar Ahmed
Gregory Smith
Enrico Pirozzi

BIRMINGHAM - MUMBAI

PostgreSQL 10 High Performance

Commissioning Editor: Amey Varangaonkar
Acquisition Editor: Namrata Patil
Content Development Editor: Amrita Noronha
Technical Editor: Jovita Alva
Copy Editor: Safis Editing, Vikrant Phadke
Project Coordinator: Shweta H Birwatkar
Proofreader: Safis Editing
Indexer: Rekha Nair
Graphics: Jisha Chirayil
Production Coordinator: Nilesh Mohite

First published: April 2018

Production reference: 1300418

Published by Packt Publishing Ltd.
Livery Place
35 Livery Street
Birmingham
B3 2PB, UK.

ISBN 978-1-78847-448-1

www.packtpub.com

I want to thank my wife Michela for helping and supporting me, and I want to dedicate this book to my father.

- Enrico Pirozzi

`mapt.io`

Mapt is an online digital library that gives you full access to over 5,000 books and videos, as well as industry leading tools to help you plan your personal development and advance your career. For more information, please visit our website.

Why subscribe?

- Spend less time learning and more time coding with practical eBooks and Videos from over 4,000 industry professionals

- Improve your learning with Skill Plans built especially for you

- Get a free eBook or video every month

- Mapt is fully searchable

- Copy and paste, print, and bookmark content

PacktPub.com

Did you know that Packt offers eBook versions of every book published, with PDF and ePub files available? You can upgrade to the eBook version at `www.PacktPub.com` and as a print book customer, you are entitled to a discount on the eBook copy. Get in touch with us at `service@packtpub.com` for more details.

At `www.PacktPub.com`, you can also read a collection of free technical articles, sign up for a range of free newsletters, and receive exclusive discounts and offers on Packt books and eBooks.

Contributors

About the authors

Ibrar Ahmed is a senior database architect in an Enterprise PostgreSQL company. He started his development career in 1999. He has contributed to the PostgreSQL community, the company's PostgreSQL fork, and other open source communities such as Google Chrome. He also has experience in MySQL, Oracle, MongoDB and Hadoop (Hive, Hbase, Spark). He is a major contributor in integrating other databases with PostgreSQL. He also authored *PostgreSQL Developer's Guide*. He has a master's in computer science (1999) and MS in computer engineering (2015), and is finalizing his PhD.

Gregory Smith is a chief PostgreSQL evangelist in Charleston, South Carolina, for Crunchy Data Solutions. He's been providing database advice to clients in industries such as manufacturing, finance, and web development for 20 years. He has contributed feature additions to every PostgreSQL version since 8.3. He's also the creator of a growing set of add-on tools for the database, currently including PgTune, pgbench-tools, peg, and 2warm.

Enrico Pirozzi, EnterpriseDB certified on implementation management and tuning, with a master's in computer science, has been a PostgreSQL DBA since 2003. Based in Italy, he has been providing database advice to clients in industries such as manufacturing and web development for 10 years. He has been training others on PostgreSQL since 2008. Dedicated to open source technology since early in his career, he is a cofounder of the PostgreSQL Italian mailing list, PostgreSQL-it, and of the PostgreSQL Italian community site, PSQL.it.

About the reviewer

Feng Tan is from China. He is a member of the China PostgreSQL User Group Association and a special expert in the PostgreSQL branch of China OSS (Open Source Software) Promotion Union. He is one of the translators of *PostgreSQL 9 Administration Cookbook Chinese Edition*, as well as a technical reviewer of *PostgreSQL High Performance Cookbook English Edition*.

He was a PostgreSQL DBA at SkyMobi for more than 6 years, maintaining over 100 PostgreSQL instances. He likes to share PostgreSQL technology a lot and has posted over 500 tech blogs.

Srivathsava Rangarajan is a lead software engineer at a publicly traded financial company in downtown Chicago. He was introduced to PostgreSQL after an interesting start in the NoSQL world of CouchDB and Cassandra. Impressed with PostgreSQL's robustness, he is now its avid advocate for the right applications and co-organizes the Chicago PostgreSQL User Group to help in its adoption. He loves data and helps spread the understanding of data structures, domains, and data models to foster healthier interactions with databases.

Packt is searching for authors like you

If you're interested in becoming an author for Packt, please visit `authors.packtpub.com` and apply today. We have worked with thousands of developers and tech professionals, just like you, to help them share their insight with the global tech community. You can make a general application, apply for a specific hot topic that we are recruiting an author for, or submit your own idea.

Table of Contents

Preface

PostgreSQL has become an increasingly viable database platform to serve as storage for applications, from classic corporate database use to the latest web apps. But getting the best performance from it is not an easy subject to learn. You need just the right combination of thumb rule to get started, solid monitoring, and maintenance to keep your system running as well as suggestions for troubleshooting, and add-on tools to add the features the core database doesn't try to handle on its own. This book is an update of the book *PostgreSQL 9.6 High Performance*.

Who this book is for

This book is aimed at intermediate to advanced database administrators who are using, or planning to use, PostgreSQL. Portions will also interest systems administrators looking to build or monitor a PostgreSQL installation, as well as developers interested in advanced database internals that impact application design.

What this book covers

Chapter 1, *PostgreSQL Versions*, introduces how PostgreSQL performance has improved in the most recent versions of the database. It makes a case for using the most recent version feasible, in contrast to the common presumption that newer versions of any software are buggier and slower than their predecessors.

Chapter 2, *Database Hardware*, discusses how the main components in server hardware, including processors, memory, and disks, need to be carefully selected for reliable database storage and a balanced budget. In particular, accidentally using volatile write-back caching in disk controllers and drives can easily introduce database corruption.

Chapter 3, *Database Hardware Benchmarking*, moves on to quantifying the different performance aspects of database hardware. Just how fast are the memory and raw drives in your system? Does performance scale properly as more drives are added?

Chapter 4, *Disk Setup*, looks at popular filesystem choices and suggests the trade-offs of various ways to lay out your database on disk. Some common and effective filesystem tuning tweaks are also discussed.

Chapter 5, *Memory for Database Caching*, digs into how the database is stored on disk and in memory, and how the checkpoint process serves to reconcile the two safely. It also suggests how you can actually look at the data being cached by the database to confirm that what's being stored in memory matches what you'd expect to be there.

Chapter 6, *Server Configuration Tuning*, covers the most important settings in the postgresql.conf file, what they mean, and how you should set them. The settings that may cause you some trouble if you change them are pointed out too.

Chapter 7, *Routine Maintenance*, starts by explaining how PostgreSQL determines which rows are visible to which clients. The way visibility information is stored requires a cleanup process named VACUUM to reuse leftover space properly. Common issues and general tuning suggestions for it and the ever-running autovacuum are covered. Finally, there's a look at adjusting the amount of data logged by the database, and using a query log analyzer on the result to help find query bottlenecks.

Chapter 8, *Database Benchmarking*, investigates how to get useful benchmark results from the built-in pgbench testing program included with PostgreSQL.

Chapter 9, *Database Indexing*, introduces indexes in terms of how they can reduce the number of data blocks read to answer a query. That approach allows for thoroughly investigating common questions such as why a query is using a sequential scan instead of an index in a robust way. In this chapter, we present new PostgreSQL 10 index types.

Chapter 10, *Query Optimization*, is a guided tour of the PostgreSQL optimizer, exposed by showing the way sample queries are executed differently based on what they are asking for and how the database parameters are set. This chapter also covers the new way to perform searches in multi-core mode.

Chapter 11, *Database Activity and Statistics*, looks at the statistics collected inside the database, and which of them are useful for finding problems. The views that let you watch query activity and locking behavior are also explored.

Chapter 12, *Monitoring and Trending*, starts with how to use basic operating system monitoring tools to determine what the database is doing. Then, it moves onto suggestions for trending software that can be used to graph this information over time.

Chapter 13, *Pooling and Caching*, explains the difficulties you can encounter when a large number of connections are made to the database at once. Two types of software packages are suggested to help connection poolers, to better queue incoming requests, and caches which can answer user requests without connecting to the database.

Chapter 14, *Scaling with Replication*, covers approaches for handling heavier system loads by replicating the data across multiple nodes, typically a set of read-only nodes synchronized to a single writable master. This chapter also covers the new logical replication method.

Chapter 15, *Partitioning Data*, explores how data might be partitioned into subsets usefully, such that queries can execute against a smaller portion of the database. The approaches discussed include the standard single-node database table partitioning and the new declarative partition method.

Chapter 16, *Avoiding Common Problems*, discusses parts of PostgreSQL that regularly seem to frustrate newcomers to the database. Bulk loading, counting records, and foreign key handling are some examples. This chapter ends with a detailed review of which performance-related features have changed between each version of PostgreSQL from 8.1 to 10.3. Sometimes, the best way to avoid a common problem is to upgrade to a version in which it doesn't happen anymore.

To get the most out of this book

In order for this book to be useful, you need at least access to a PostgreSQL client that is allowed to execute queries on a server. Ideally, you'll also be the server administrator. Full client and server packages for PostgreSQL are available for most popular operating systems at http://www.postgresql.org/download/. All the examples here are executed on Command Prompt, usually running the psql program. This makes them applicable to most platforms. It's straightforward to do many of these operations using a GUI tool for PostgreSQL instead, such as the pgAdmin program. Some scripts that are written in the bash scripting language are provided.

Download the example code files

You can download the example code files for this book from your account at www.packtpub.com. If you purchased this book elsewhere, you can visit www.packtpub.com/support and register to have the files emailed directly to you.

You can download the code files by following these steps:

1. Log in or register at www.packtpub.com.
2. Select the **SUPPORT** tab.
3. Click on **Code Downloads & Errata**.
4. Enter the name of the book in the **Search** box and follow the onscreen instructions.

Once the file is downloaded, please make sure that you unzip or extract the folder using the latest version of:

- WinRAR/7-Zip for Windows
- Zipeg/iZip/UnRarX for Mac
- 7-Zip/PeaZip for Linux

The code bundle for the book is also hosted on GitHub at https://github.com/ PacktPublishing/PostgreSQL-10-High-Performance. In case there's an update to the code, it will be updated on the existing GitHub repository.

We also have other code bundles from our rich catalog of books and videos available at https://github.com/PacktPublishing/. Check them out!

Download the color images

We also provide a PDF file that has color images of the screenshots/diagrams used in this book. You can download it here: http://www.packtpub.com/sites/default/files/ downloads/PostgreSQL10HighPerformance_ColorImages.pdf.

Conventions used

There are a number of text conventions used throughout this book.

CodeInText: Indicates code words in text, database table names, folder names, filenames, file extensions, pathnames, dummy URLs, user input, and Twitter handles. Here is an example: "The sync here is to try and flush all the data to the disk before we just blow away the caches."

A block of code is set as follows:

```
for each outer row:
  for each inner row:
    if join condition is true:
      output combined row
```

Any command-line input or output is written as follows:

```
EXPLAIN ANALYZE SELECT * FROM orders WHERE customerid IN (SELECT customerid
FROM customers WHERE customerid=1000 OR customerid=2000);
```

Bold: Indicates a new term, an important word, or words that you see onscreen. For example, words in menus or dialog boxes appear in the text like this. Here is an example: "HD Tune includes a **Random Access** test that gives its results in terms of the standard IOPS figure, at various block sizes."

Warnings or important notes appear like this.

Tips and tricks appear like this.

Get in touch

Feedback from our readers is always welcome.

General feedback: Email feedback@packtpub.com and mention the book title in the subject of your message. If you have questions about any aspect of this book, please email us at questions@packtpub.com.

Errata: Although we have taken every care to ensure the accuracy of our content, mistakes do happen. If you have found a mistake in this book, we would be grateful if you would report this to us. Please visit www.packtpub.com/submit-errata, selecting your book, clicking on the Errata Submission Form link, and entering the details.

Piracy: If you come across any illegal copies of our works in any form on the Internet, we would be grateful if you would provide us with the location address or website name. Please contact us at copyright@packtpub.com with a link to the material.

If you are interested in becoming an author: If there is a topic that you have expertise in and you are interested in either writing or contributing to a book, please visit authors.packtpub.com.

Reviews

Please leave a review. Once you have read and used this book, why not leave a review on the site that you purchased it from? Potential readers can then see and use your unbiased opinion to make purchase decisions, we at Packt can understand what you think about our products, and our authors can see your feedback on their book. Thank you!

For more information about Packt, please visit packtpub.com.

PostgreSQL Versions ^1

PostgreSQL certainly has a reputation. It's known for having a rich feature set and very stable software releases. The secure stance that its default configuration takes is simultaneously praised by security fans and criticized for its learning curve. The SQL-specification conformance and data integrity features allow only the strictest ways to interact with the database, which is surprising to those who come from a background working with looser desktop database software. All of these points have an element of truth to them.

Another part of PostgreSQL's reputation is that it's slow. This, too, has some truth to it, even today. There are many database operations where the right thing takes longer to do than the alternative. As the simplest example of this, consider the date February 29, 2009. With no leap year in 2009, that date is only valid as an abstract one. It's not possible for this to be the real date of something that happened. If you ask the database to store this value into a standard date field, it can just do that, the fast approach. Alternatively, it can check whether that date is valid to store into the destination field, note that there is no such date in a regular calendar, and reject your change. That's always going to be slower. PostgreSQL is designed by, and intended for, the sort of people who don't like cutting corners just to make things faster or easier, and in cases where the only way you can properly handle something takes a while, that may be the only option available.

However, once you have a correct implementation of something, you can then go back and optimize it. That's the mode PostgreSQL has been in for the last few years. PostgreSQL usually rises above these smaller issues to give excellent database performance. Parts of it have the sort of great design that outperforms simpler approaches, even after paying the overhead that complexity can introduce. This is a fairly recent phenomenon though, which explains quite a bit about the perception that PostgreSQL is a slower database than its competitors. In this chapter, we will cover the following topics:

- Performance of historical PostgreSQL releases
- PostgreSQL or another database?

- PostgreSQL tools
- PostgreSQL application scaling life cycle
- Performance tuning as a practice

Performance of historical PostgreSQL releases

In November 2005, PostgreSQL 8.1 was released. It included a number of internal architectural changes, some of which aimed to improve how fast the database would run on a multiprocessor system with many active clients. The result was a major improvement in the ability of the database to scale upwards to handle a heavy load. Benchmarks on modern hardware really highlight just how far that version leapfrogged earlier ones. You can find an excellent performance comparison of versions 8.0 through 8.4 from György Vilmos at `http://suckit.blog.hu/2009/09/29/postgresql_history`. This shows exactly how dramatic these improvements have been.

This test gives a **transactions per second** (TPS) figure that measures the total system speed, and you can run it in either a read-only mode or one that includes writes. The read-only performance improved by over four times from 8.0 to 8.1 and more than doubled again by 8.3:

Version	Peak read-only TPS	# of clients at peak
8.0.21	1256	4
8.1.17	5620	14
8.2.13	8109	18
8.3.7	13984	22
8.4.1	13546	22

The rise in the number of clients at the peak load gives us an idea of how well the database internals handle access to shared resources. The area 8.1 in particular included a significant upgrade. Performance improved similarly on the write side, with almost an 8 times gain between 8.0 and 8.3:

Version	Peak write TPS	# of clients at peak
8.0.21	361	2
8.1.17	873	10
8.2.13	1358	14
8.3.7	2795	18
8.4.1	2713	12

The small decrease in performance from 8.3 to 8.4 in both these tests is due to some subtle retuning of the database to improve its worst-case performance. More statistics are collected in 8.4 to improve complicated queries, at the expense of slightly slowing the sort of trivial ones tested here.

These improvements have been confirmed by other benchmarking results, albeit normally not covering such a wide range of versions. It's easy to see that any conclusion about PostgreSQL performance reached before late 2005, when 8.1 shipped, is completely out of date at this point. The speed improvement in 2008's 8.3 release was an additional large leap. Versions before 8.3 are not representative of the current performance and there are other reasons to prefer using that one or a later one too.

Choosing a version to deploy

Because of these dramatic gains, if you have an older PostgreSQL system you'd like to make faster, the very first thing you should ask yourself is not how to tweak its settings, but instead if it's possible to upgrade to a newer version. If you're starting a new project, 8.3 is the earliest version you should consider. In addition to the performance improvements, there were some changes to that version that impact application coding that you'd be better off to start with to avoid needing to retrofit later.

Chapter 16, *Avoiding Common Problems*, includes a reference guide to what performance-related features were added to each major version of PostgreSQL from 8.1 through 10.0. You might discover that one of the features only available in a very recent version is compelling to you, and therefore you have a strong preference to use that one. Many of these version-specific changes are also highlighted throughout the book.

Upgrading to a newer major version

Until very recently, the only way to upgrade an existing PostgreSQL version to a newer major version, such as going from 8.1.X to 8.2.X, was to dump and reload. The and/or programs are used to write the entire content of the database to a file, using the newer versions of those programs. That way, if any changes need to be made to upgrade, the newer dumping program can try to handle them. Not all upgrade changes will happen automatically though. Then, depending on the format you dumped in, you can either restore that just by running the script it generates or use the program to handle that task. pg_restore can be a much better alternative in newer PostgreSQL versions that include a version with parallel restore capabilities.

 If you are using a system that doesn't easily allow you to run more than one system with PostgreSQL version at a time, such as the current RedHat Linux RPM packages, getting both old and new versions of PostgreSQL installed on your system at the same time can be difficult. There are some changes to improve this situation under development for PostgreSQL 9.0 and 10.0. Make sure to check the feasibility of running more than one version at once as part of planning an upgrade.

Dumping can take a while, and restoring can take even longer. While this is going on, your database likely needs to be down, so that you don't allow any changes that won't then be migrated over by the dump. For large databases, this downtime can be both large and unacceptable.

The most demanding sites prefer near-zero downtime, to run 24/7. There, a dump and reload is never an acceptable option. Until recently, the only real approach available for doing PostgreSQL upgrades in those environments has been using statement replication to do so. Slony is the most popular tool for that, and more information about it is available in Chapter 14, *Scaling with Replication*. One of Slony's features is that you don't have to be running the same version of PostgreSQL on all the nodes you are replicating to. You can bring up a new node running a newer PostgreSQL version, wait for replication to complete, and then switch over once it matches the original.

Another tool used for the asynchronous primary/secondary replication is Londiste from SkyTools. One of the benefits of Londiste over the streaming replication that's in the core of PostgreSQL is that Londiste can replicate a single database or a table from a database. Streaming replication will create an exact copy of the database server. Londiste provides more granularity for replication which makes it ideal for our migration. It allows us to move databases from several servers to one unified server.

Now, there is another way available that works without needing any replication software. A program originally called `pg_migrator` is capable of upgrading from 8.3 to 8.4 without the dump and reload. This process is called in-place upgrading. You need to test this carefully, and there are both known limitations and likely still unknown ones related to less popular PostgreSQL features. Be sure to read the documentation of the upgrade tool very carefully. Starting in PostgreSQL 10.0, this module is included with the core database, with the name changed to `pg_upgrade`. `pg_upgrade` is a native PostgreSQL command and must be offline. While all in-place upgrades have some risk and need careful testing, in many cases, these will take you from 8.3 or 8.4 to 10.0 and hopefully beyond.

The PostgreSQL development community is now moving to an online replication approach, for example the `pg_logical` extension for PostgreSQL providing much faster replication than Slony, Bucardo or Londiste, as well as cross-version upgrades

Upgrades to PostgreSQL 8.3+ from earlier ones

The major internal changes to 8.3 make it impossible to upgrade from any earlier version past it without dumping the entire database and reloading it into the later one. This makes 8.3 a doubly important version milestone to cross. Not only is it much faster than 8.2, once your data is in 8.3, you can perform in-place upgrades from there.

Going from an earlier version to PostgreSQL 8.3 or later can be a difficult change. Some older applications rely on non-character data types being transparently cast to the type, a behavior removed from 8.3 for a variety of reasons. For details, see `http://www.postgresql.org/docs/8.3/static/release-8-3.html`.

While there's always a chance that upgrading your database version can introduce new issues, it is particularly likely that applications written against an earlier version will need to be updated to work against 8.3 or later. It is possible to work around this issue by manually adding back the automatic typecasting features that were removed. However, fixing the behavior in your application instead is a more robust and sustainable solution to the problem. The old behavior was eliminated because it caused subtle application issues. If you just add it back, you'll both be exposed to those and need to continue doing this extra cost additional step with every new PostgreSQL release. There is more information available at https://www.endpoint.com/blog/2010/01 on this topic and on the general challenges of doing a major PostgreSQL upgrade.

Minor version upgrades

A dump/reload, or the use of tools such as pg_upgrade, is not needed for minor version updates, for example, going from 8.4.1 to 8.4.2. These simply require stopping the server, installing the new version, and then running the newer database binary against the existing server data files. Some people avoid ever doing such upgrades once their application is running for fear that a change in the database will cause a problem. This should never be the case for PostgreSQL.

The policy of the PostgreSQL project described at http://www.postgresql.org/support/versioning states very clearly:
While upgrades always have some risk, PostgreSQL minor releases fix only frequently-encountered security and data corruption bugs to reduce the risk of upgrading.

You should never find an unexpected change that breaks an application in a minor PostgreSQL upgrade. Bug, security, and corruption fixes are always done in a way that minimizes the odds of introducing an externally visible behavior change, and if that's not possible, the reason why and the suggested workarounds will be detailed in the release notes. What you will find is that some subtle problems, resulting from resolved bugs, can clear up even after a minor version update. It's not uncommon to discover that the reporting of a problem to one of the PostgreSQL mailing lists is resolved in the latest minor version update compatible with that installation, and upgrading to that version is all that's needed to make the issue go away.

Migrating from PostgreSQL 9.x to 10.x – a new way to work

Starting from version 9, it is possible to migrate a complete cluster (users and databases) using `pg_upgrade`. It is useful to migrate from a minor version to a major version, for example from PostgreSQl 9.6 to PostgreSQL 10. This way to work is safe and faster than dump/restore, because `pg_upgrade` migrates PostgreSQL pages in a binary way and it's not necessary rebuild any indexes.

As mentioned above, another approach may be to use pglogical, pglogical is a logical replication system implemented entirely as a PostgreSQL extension. Fully integrated, it requires no triggers or external programs. This alternative to physical replication is a highly efficient method of replicating data using a publish/subscribe model for selective replication. Using pglogical we can migrate and upgrade PostgreSQL with almost zero downtime

PostgreSQL or another database?

There are certainly situations where other database solutions will perform better. For example, PostgreSQL is missing features needed to perform well on some of the more difficult queries in the TPC-H test suite (see `Chapter 8`, *Database Benchmarking*, for more details). It's correspondingly less suitable for running large data warehouse applications than many of the commercial databases. If you need queries along the lines of some of the very heavy ones TPC-H includes, you may find that databases such as Oracle, DB2, and SQL Server still have a performance advantage worth paying for. There are also several PostgreSQL-derived databases that include features making them more appropriate for data warehouses and similar larger systems. Examples include Greenplum, Aster Data, and Netezza.

For some types of web applications, you can only get acceptable performance by cutting corners on the data integrity features in ways that PostgreSQL just won't allow. These applications might be better served by a less strict database, such as MySQL or even a really minimal one, such as SQLite. Unlike the fairly mature data warehouse market, the design of this type of application is still moving around quite a bit. Work on approaches using the key/value-based NoSQL approach, including CouchDB, MongoDB, and Cassandra, are all becoming more popular at the time of writing this. All of them can easily outperform a traditional database, provided you have no need to run the sort of advanced queries that key/value stores are slower at handling. PostgreSQL also natively supports and indexes the Json data type for a NoSQL data approach.

PostgreSQL 10.x and NoSQL

Starting from version 9.4, PostgreSQL has the `jsonb` field and it can be used as a NoSQL system. `jsonb` fields are indexable fields, and starting from version 10.x, new operators and functions are present in PostgreSQL that allow deleting, modifying, or inserting values into `jsonb` values, including at specific path locations.

PostgreSQL as HUB

Starting from version 9.3, PostgreSQL has **foreign data wrapper (fdw)** support. With fdw, PostgreSQL can connect to many external **database management system (DBMS)**, and it can see foreign tables (for example, MySQL or Oracle tables) as local tables. Some of the best know fdws are:

- Oracle
- MySQL
- Informix
- Firebird
- SQLite
- CSV files
- Sybase
- Microsoft SQL Server
- MongoDB
- Cassandra

The complete list is available at `https://wiki.postgresql.org/wiki/Foreign_data_wrappers`.

PostgreSQL tools

If you're used to your database vendor supplying a full tool chain with the database itself, from server management to application development, PostgreSQL may be a shock to you. Like many successful open source projects, PostgreSQL tries to stay focused on the features it's uniquely good at. This is what the development community refers to as the PostgreSQL core: the main database server, and associated utilities, that can only be developed as a part of the database itself. When new features are proposed, if it's possible for them to be built and distributed out of core, this is the preferred way to do things. This approach keeps the database core as streamlined as possible, as well as allowing those external projects to release their own updates without needing to synchronize them against the main database's release schedule.

Successful PostgreSQL deployments should recognize that a number of additional tools, each with their own specialized purpose, will need to be integrated with the database core server to build a complete system.

PostgreSQL contrib

One part of the PostgreSQL core that you may not necessarily have installed is what's called the `contrib` modules (it is named after the directory they are stored in). These are optional utilities shipped with the standard package, but that aren't necessarily installed by default on your system. The `contrib` code is maintained and distributed as part of the PostgreSQL core, but not required for the server to operate.

From a code quality perspective, the `contrib` modules aren't held to quite as high a standard, primarily by how they're tested. The main server includes heavy regression tests for every feature, run across a large build farm of systems that look for errors and look for greater performance and greater stability. The optional `contrib` modules don't get that same level of testing coverage. However, the code itself is maintained by the same development team, and some of the modules are extremely popular and well tested by users.

A list of all the `contrib` modules available can be found at at `http://www.postgresql.org/docs/current/static/contrib.html`.

Finding contrib modules on your system

One good way to check whether you have `contrib` modules installed is to see if the program is available. That's one of the few `contrib` components that installs a full program, rather than just the scripts you can use. Here's a Unix example of checking for `pgbench`:

```
$ pgbench -V
pgbench (PostgreSQL) 10.0
```

If you're using an RPM or DEB packaged version of PostgreSQL, as the case would be on many Linux systems, the optional package contains all of the `contrib` modules and their associated installer scripts. You may have to add that package using `yum`, `apt-get`, or a similar mechanism if it wasn't installed already. On Solaris, the package is named `SUNWpostgr-contrib`.

If you're not sure where your system's PostgreSQL `contrib` modules are installed, you can use a filesystem utility to search. `locate` works well for this purpose on many Unix-like systems, as does the `find` command. The file search utilities available on the Windows Start menu will work. A sample file you could look for is `pg_buffercache.sql`, which will be used in the upcoming chapter `Chapter 5`, *Memory for Database Caching*, on memory allocation. Here's where that might be on some of the platforms that PostgreSQL supports:

- RHEL and CentOS Linux systems will put the main file you need into `/usr/share/pgsql/contrib/pg_buffercache.sql`
- Debian or Ubuntu Linux systems will install the file at `/usr/share/postgresql/version/contrib/pg_buffercache.sql`
- Solaris installs it into `/usr/share/pgsql/contrib/pg_buffercache.sql`
- The standard Windows one-click installer with the default options will always include the `contrib` modules, and this one will be in `C:\Program Files\PostgreSQL/version/share/contrib/pg_buffercache.sql`

Installing a contrib module from source

Building your own PostgreSQL from source code can be a straightforward exercise on some platforms if you have the appropriate requirements already installed on the server. Details are documented at `http://www.postgresql.org/docs/current/static/install-procedure.html`.

After building the main server code, you'll also need to compile contrib modules by yourself too. Here's an example of how that would work, presuming that your PostgreSQL destination is /usr/local/postgresql, and that there's a directory there named source you put the source code into (this is not intended to be a typical or recommended structure you should use):

```
$ cd /usr/local/postgresql/source
$ cd contrib/pg_buffercache/
$ make
$ make install
/bin/mkdir -p '/usr/local/postgresql/lib/postgresql'
/bin/mkdir -p '/usr/local/postgresql/share/postgresql/contrib'
/bin/sh ../../config/install-sh -c -m 755 pg_buffercache.so
'/usr/local/postgresql/lib/postgresql/pg_buffercache.so'
/bin/sh ../../config/install-sh -c -m 644 ./uninstall_pg_buffercache.sql
'/usr/local/postgresql/share/postgresql/contrib'
/bin/sh ../../config/install-sh -c -m 644 pg_buffercache.sql
'/usr/local/postgresql/share/postgresql/contrib'
```

It's also possible to build and install all the contrib modules at once by running / from the directory.

 Note that some of these have more extensive source code build requirements. The uuid-ossp module is an example of a more challenging one to compile yourself.

Using a contrib module

While some contrib programs such as pgbench, are directly executable, most are utilities that you install into a database in order to add extra features to them.

As an example, to install the module into a database named abc, the following command line would work (assuming the RedHat location of the file):

```
$ psql -d abc -f /usr/share/postgresql/contrib/pg_buffercache.sql
```

You could instead use the pgAdmin III GUI management utility, which is bundled with the Windows installer for PostgreSQL, instead of the command line:

1. Navigate to the database you want to install the module into.
2. Click on the SQL icon in the toolbar to bring up the command editor.
3. Choose **File/Open**. Navigate to `C:\Program Files\PostgreSQL/version/share/contrib/pg_buffercache.sql` and open that file.
4. Execute using either the green arrow or **Query/Execute**.

You can do a quick test of the module installed on any type of system by running the following quick query:

```
SELECT * FROM pg_buffercache;
```

If any results come back, the module was installed. Note that `pg_buffercache` will only be installable and usable by database superusers.

pgFoundry

The official home of many PostgreSQL-related projects is pgFoundry.

pgFoundry only hosts software for PostgreSQL, and it provides resources such as mailing lists and bug tracking, in addition to file distribution. Many of the most popular PostgreSQL add-on programs are hosted there:

- Windows software allowing access to PostgreSQL through .NET and OLE
- Connection poolers, such as pgpool and pgBouncer
- Database management utilities, such as pgFouine, SkyTools, and PgTune

While sometimes maintained by the same people who work on the PostgreSQL core, pgFoundry code varies significantly in quality. One way to help spot the healthier projects is to note how regularly and recently new versions have been released.

PGXN

Another site where it is possible to find many PostgreSQL-related projects is PGXN. PGXN is more recent than pgFoundry and it is possible to find recent extensions there.

The **PostgreSQL Extension Network (PGXN)** is a central distribution system for open source PostgreSQL extension libraries. It consists of four basic parts:

- **PGXN Manager**: An upload and distribution infrastructure for extension developers
- **PGXN API**: A centralized index and API of distribution metadata
- **PGXN Search**: This site is for searching extensions and perusing their documentation
- **PGXN Client**: A command-line client for downloading, testing, and installing extensions

The difference between pgFoundry and PGXN is that pgFoundry is about project management and PGXN is about distribution and exposure.

Additional PostgreSQL-related software

Beyond what comes with the PostgreSQL core, the `contrib` modules, and software available on pgFoundry, there are plenty of other programs that will make PostgreSQL easier and more powerful. These are available from sources all over the internet. There are actually so many available that choosing the right package for a requirement can itself be overwhelming.

Some of the best programs will be highlighted throughout the book, to help provide a short list of the ones you should consider early. This approach, where you get a basic system running and then add additional components as needed, is the standard way large open source projects are built.

It can be difficult for some corporate cultures to adapt to that style, such as ones where any software installation requires everything from approval to a QA cycle. In order to improve the odds of your PostgreSQL installation being successful in such environments, it's important to start introducing this concept early on. Additional programs to add components building on the intentionally slim database core will be needed later, and not all of what's needed will be obvious at the beginning.

PostgreSQL application scaling life cycle

While every application has unique growth aspects, there are many common techniques that you'll find necessary as an application using a PostgreSQL database becomes used more heavily. The chapters of this book each focus on one of the common aspects of this process. The general path that database servers follow includes the following steps:

1. Select hardware to run the server on. Ideally, you'll test that hardware to make sure it performs as expected too.
2. Set up all the parts of database disk layout: RAID level, filesystem, and possibly table/index layout on disk.
3. Optimize the server configuration.
4. Monitor server performance and how well queries are executing.
5. Improve queries to execute more efficiently, or add indexes to help accelerate them.
6. As it gets more difficult to just tune the server to do more work, instead reduce the amount it has to worry about by introducing connection pooling and caching.
7. Partition larger tables into sections. Eventually, really large ones may need to be split so that they're written to multiple servers simultaneously.

This process is by no means linear. You can expect to make multiple passes over optimizing the server parameters. It may be the case that you decide to buy newer hardware first, rather than launching into replication or partitioning work that requires application redesign work. Some designs might integrate caching into the design from the very beginning. The important thing is to be aware of the various options available and to collect enough data about what limits the system is reaching to decide which of the potential changes is most likely to help.

Performance tuning as a practice

Work on improving database performance has its own terminology, just like any other field. Here are some terms or phrases that will be used throughout the book; both of these terms will be used to refer to the current limitation that is preventing performance from getting better:

- Running a test to determine how fast a particular operation can run. This is often done to figure out where the bottleneck of a program or system is.

- Monitoring what parts of a program are using the most resources when running a difficult operation, such as a benchmark. This is typically to help prove where the bottleneck is, and whether it's been removed as expected after a change. Profiling a database application usually starts with monitoring tools, such as `vmstat` and `iostat`. Popular profiling tools at the code level include `gprof`, `OProfile`, and `DTrace`.

One of the interesting principles of performance tuning work is that, in general, you cannot figure out what bottleneck an application will next run into until you remove the current one. When presented with a system that's not as fast as someone would expect it to be, you'll often see people guessing what the current bottleneck is, or what the next one will be. That's generally a waste of time. You're always better off measuring performance, profiling the parts of the system that are slow, and using that to guess at causes and guide changes.

Let's say what you've looked at suggests that you should significantly increase `shared_buffers`, the primary tunable for memory used to cache database reads and writes. This normally has some positive impact, but there are potential negative things you could encounter instead. The information needed to figure out which category a new application will fall into, whether this change will increase or decrease performance, cannot be predicted from watching the server running with the smaller setting. This falls into the category of chaos theory: even a tiny change in the starting conditions can end up rippling out to a very different end condition, as the server makes millions of decisions and they can be impacted to a small degree by that change. Similarly, if is set too small, there are several other parameters that won't work as expected at all, such as those governing database checkpoints.

Since you can't predict what's going to happen most of the time, the mindset you need to adopt is one of heavy monitoring and change control.

 Monitor as much as possible, from application to database server to hardware.

Introduce a small targeted change. Try to quantify what's different and be aware that some changes you have rejected as not positive won't always stay that way forever. Move the bottleneck to somewhere else, and you may discover that some parameter that didn't matter before is now suddenly the next limiting factor.

There's a popular expression on the mailing list devoted to PostgreSQL performance when people speculate about root causes without doing profiling to prove their theories: *less talk, more gprof*. While gprof may not be the tool of choice for every performance issue, given it's more of a code profiling tool than a general monitoring one, the idea that you measure as much as possible before speculating as to the root causes is always a sound one. You should also measure again to verify that your change did what you expected too.

Another principle that you'll find is a recurring theme in this book is that you must be systematic about investigating performance issues. Do not assume your server is fast because you bought it from a reputable vendor; benchmark the individual components yourself. Don't start your database performance testing with application level tests; run synthetic database performance tests that you can compare against other people's first. That way, when you run into the inevitable application slowdown, you'll already know your hardware is operating as expected and that the database itself is running well. Once your system goes into production, some of the basic things you might need to do in order to find a performance problem, such as testing hardware speed, become impossible to take the system down.

You'll be in much better shape if every server you deploy is tested with a common methodology, which is exactly what later chapters here lead you through. Just because you're not a hardware guy, it doesn't mean you should skip over the parts here that cover things such as testing your disk performance. You need to perform work like that as often as possible when exposed to new systems—that's the only way to get a basic feel of whether something is operated within the standard range of behavior or if instead there's something wrong.

Summary

PostgreSQL has come a long way in the last five years. After building solid database fundamentals, the many developers adding features across the globe have made significant strides in adding both new features and performance improvements in recent releases. The features added to the latest PostgreSQL, 10.0, making replication and read scaling easier than ever before, are expected to further accelerate the types of applications the database is appropriate for.

The extensive performance improvements in PostgreSQL 9.x and 10.x in particular shatter some earlier notions that the database server was slower than its main competitors.

There are still some situations where PostgreSQL's feature set results in slower query processing than some of the commercial databases it might otherwise displace.

If you're starting a new project using PostgreSQL, use the latest version possible (your preference really should be to deploy version 8.3 or later).

PostgreSQL works well in many common database applications, but certainly there are applications it's not the best choice for.

Not everything you need to manage and optimize a PostgreSQL server will be included in a basic install. Be prepared to include an additional number of utilities that add features outside of what the core database aims to provide.

Performance tuning is best approached as a systematic, carefully measured practice.

In the following chapter, we will discuss the hardware best-suited for the PostgreSQL server.

2
Database Hardware

This chapter aims to help prioritize spending when planning out the purchase of a new server intended to run PostgreSQL. If you already have a running database server, then following the instructions in, Chapter 3, *Database Hardware Benchmarking*, and Chapter 8, *Database Benchmarking*, might be a more appropriate place to start. Ultimately, you may end up taking a few round trips alternating through that material and what's covered here. For example, if you benchmark your server and the disks seem slow, the background here might give you an idea of what hardware change you could make to improve that. Once that's done, it's back to benchmarking again; repeat until performance matches your expectations.

In this chapter, we will cover the following topics:

- Balancing hardware spending
- Reliable controller and disk setup

Balancing hardware spending

One of the reasons working with open source databases such as PostgreSQL can be so effective is that every dollar you save on software licensing can be put toward better hardware instead. The three main components you'll need to balance in your budget are CPUs, memory, and disks, with the disk controller as a related and critical part too.

vailable processors are bundling at least 2, and possibly as many as 22, cores
?U, making the core count the figure of merit for most database applications
and, wim i ostgreSQL 10.x, we can use multiple cores for every single query with the
mechanism called parallel query.

There are two basic decisions you need to make while deciding which CPU solution would
best match your database application:

- Which processor family? Nowadays, this normally boils down to choosing
  between the various 64-bit product lines from Intel or **Advanced Micro Devices
  (AMD)**, although there are some other less popular choices still floating around
  (Itanium, **Scalable Processor Architecture (SPARC)**, and so on).
- Do you get more cores or faster cores?

These choices are sometimes more tied together than you might think. Currently, Intel has
the lead in delivering individual processor cores that are the fastest around, often due to
faster transfers between the processor and system RAM. But the processors and related
parts are more expensive too. AMD still is competitive at providing more cores per dollar,
and their server class designs normally do a good job of making the best of the memory
available to each core. But if what you want is many more affordable cores instead, that's
where AMD is stronger. AMD also has a better history of making its fastest processors
available in configurations with many sockets, when you want to put more than two
physical CPUs into a single server.

The best way to figure out which class of database app you have—more cores or faster
cores—is to monitor an existing server using tools such as `top`. If there's a small number of
processes running, using a single CPU each, that's the sort of workload where faster cores
are better. That tends to happen if you have giant queries running in a batch fashion, for
example, when large quantities of data need to be sorted to deliver any single report. But if
all the CPUs are active with many more concurrent processes instead, then you'd likely
benefit better from more cores. That's normally what you'll see in applications with a larger
user count, such as databases backing web applications.

If you don't have the benefit of a working system to inspect, you can try to guess which
type of situation you're in by noting the limitations of the database. PostgreSQL does not
allow splitting a single query across more than one core, which is what's called a parallel
query by some other databases that support it. That means that if you have a single query or
a small number of queries that must run as fast as possible, the only way to do that is to
prioritize getting faster cores.

Another situation where having a faster core is a better choice is when you need to prioritize data loading for export situations. PostgreSQL's best performing data import method can easily become (but isn't always) limited by CPU performance, where that turns into the bottleneck for operations. While it's possible to split input files into pieces and load them in parallel, that's something you'll need to build or acquire yourself, rather than something the server knows how to do for you. Exporting a copy of the database using the utility is another example of something that can become CPU limited on some systems.

Memory

How much to prioritize memory for your application depends on the size of the working set of data needed to handle the most common operations. Generally, adding more RAM will provide a significant performance boost. There are a few situations where you'd be better served doing something else instead:

- If your data set is small enough to fit into a smaller amount of RAM, adding more won't help you much. You probably want faster processors instead.
- When running applications that scan tables much larger than what you can feasibly purchase as RAM, such as in many data warehouse situations, you might be better served by getting faster disks rather than more memory.

The normal situation where more memory helps most is when the data you access frequently will fit with the larger amount, but not with the smaller. This happens more often than you might think because of the way database B-tree indexes are stored. Even if you can't fit the entirety of a table, or even its index, in memory, being able to store a good-sized fraction of the index can mean that index-based data lookups will significantly speed up. Having the most popular blocks from the top of the tree structure cached is helpful even if you can't fit all the leaves into memory too.

Once you have an application running, you can usually get a better idea how memory is being used by looking inside the PostgreSQL buffer cache (and potentially inside the **operating system (OS)** one as well) and seeing what data it prefers to keep around. The section on using `pg_buffercache` in this book shows how to monitor that data.

Disks

While it's always possible to run into situations where the CPU in your database server is its bottleneck, it's downright likely that you'll run into a disk bottleneck—particularly if you only have a drive or two in the system. A few years ago, the basic two choices in hard drives were the inexpensive (also known as IDE) drives used in desktops, versus the more serious SCSI drives aimed at servers.

Both technologies have marched forward, and the current choice you're most likely to run into when configuring a database server is whether to use **Serial Advanced Technology Attachment (SATA)** or **Serial Attached SCSI (SAS)**. It's possible to find nearly identical drives available in both interfaces, and there are even drive controllers that allow attaching either kind of drive. Combined with a narrowing in the performance difference between the two, choosing between them is harder than ever.

The broad parameters of each technology are straightforward to compare. Here's the state of things at the time of writing:

- **SAS disks**:
    - **The maximum available RPM is higher**: 10,000 or 15,000
    - **Not as much drive capacity**: 73 GB to 1 TB, 1 TB to 8 TB are popular sizes
    - Cost per MB is higher
- **SATA disks**:
    - **Drives typically have a slower RPM**: 7200 is standard; some 10,000 designs exist, such as the Western Digital VelociRaptor
    - **Higher drive capacity**: 2 TB to 4 TB available
    - Cost per MB is lower

Generally, you'll find individual SAS disks to be faster even than SATA ones with similar specifications. In particular, you're likely to see better seek performance on random I/O due to faster drive mechanics in SAS, and sometimes a faster transfer rate from the disk too. Also, because the SAS drives have supported advanced features, such as command queuing for longer, it's more likely your OS will have matching support to take advantage of them.

RAID

The **Redundant Array of Inexpensive Disks (RAID)** approach is the standard way to handle both performance and reliability limitations of individual disk drives. A RAID array puts many disks, typically of exactly the same configuration, into a set that acts like a single disk, but with either enhanced performance, reliability, or both. In some cases, the extra reliability comes from computing what's called parity information for writes to the array. Parity is a form of checksum on the data, which allows it to be reconstructed even if some of the information is lost. RAID levels that use parity are efficient, from a space perspective, at writing data in a way that will survive drive failures, but the parity computation overhead can be significant for database applications.

The most common basic forms of RAID arrays used are as follows:

- **RAID 0**: This is also called stripping. Multiple disks are used at the same time, spreading reads and writes over each of them in parallel. This can be almost a linear improvement (two disks reading twice as fast as a single one), but a failure on any volume in the set will lose all the data.

- **RAID 1**: This is also called mirroring. Here, more copies of the same data are put onto multiple disks. This can sometimes improve performance—a good RAID 1 mirroring across two disks might handle two reads by sending one to each drive. Reads executed in parallel against both drives can effectively double average seeks per second. But generally, the reason for RAID 1 is redundancy: if a single drive fails, the system will continue operating using the other one.

- **RAID 10 or 1+0**: This first takes pairs of disks and mirrors them using RAID 1. Then, the resulting set is striped using RAID 0. The result provides both high performance and the ability to tolerate any single disk failure, without as many ways for speed to suffer in the average and worst case as RAID 5/6. RAID 10 is particularly appropriate for write-heavy environments, where the parity computation overhead of RAID 5/6 can cause disk performance to suffer. Accordingly, it's the preferred RAID level for high-performance database systems.

- **RAID 5**: This is also called stripped with parity. This approach sits midway between 0 and 1. You stripe data across multiple drives similarly to RAID 0, which improves read performance. But some redundant data is added to a parity drive. If one of the disks in the array is lost, the missing data can be recomputed from the ones left using that parity information. While this is efficient in terms of how little space is wasted relative to the tolerance for disk failures provided, write performance in particular can suffer in RAID 5.

- **RAID 6**: Similar to RAID 5, except with more parity information, enabling survival even with two disk failures. It has the same fundamental advantages and disadvantages. RAID 6 is an increasingly common way to cope with the fact that rebuilding a RAID 5 array after a disk loss can take a really long time on modern, high-capacity drives. The array has no additional fault tolerance during that period, and seeing a second drive failure before that rebuild finishes is not that unlikely when it takes many hours of intense disk activity to rebuild. Disks manufactured in the same batch are surprisingly likely to fail in groups.

To be fair, in any disk performance comparison, you need to consider that most systems are going to have a net performance from several disks, such as in a RAID array. Since SATA disks are individually cheaper, you might be able to purchase considerably more of them for the same budget than had you picked SAS instead. If you believe your application will get faster if it is spread over more disks, being able to buy more of them per dollar spent can result in an overall faster system. Note that the upper limit here will often be your server's physical hardware.

You only have so many storage bays or controllers ports available, and larger enclosures can cost more both up front and over their lifetime. It's easy to find situations where smaller numbers of faster drives, which SAS provides, is the better way to go. This is why it's so important to constantly benchmark both hardware and your database application, to get a feel of how well it improves as the disk count increases.

Drive error handling

Just because it's possible to buy really inexpensive SATA drives and get good performance from them, that doesn't necessarily mean you want to put them in a database server. It doesn't matter how fast your system normally runs at if a broken hard drive has taken it down and made the server unusable.

The first step towards reliable hard drive operation is for the drive to accurately report the errors it does run into. This happens through two mechanisms: error codes reported during read and write operations, and drive status reporting through the **SMART protocol**. SMART provides all sorts of information about your drive, such as its temperature and the results of any self-tests that have been run.

When they find bad data, consumer SATA drives are configured to be aggressive in retrying and attempting to correct that error automatically. This makes sense given that there's typically only one copy of that data around, and it is fine to spend a while to retry rather than report the data lost. But in a RAID configuration, as often found in a database environment, you don't want that at all. It can lead to a timeout and generally makes things more difficult for the RAID controller. Instead, you want the drive to report the error quickly, so that an alternate copy or copies can be used instead. This form of error handling change is usually the main difference in SATA drives labeled **enterprise** or **RAID edition**. Drives labeled that way will report errors quickly, where as the non-RAID versions will not. Having to purchase the enterprise version of a SATA hard drive to get reliable server error handling operation does close some of the price gap between them and SAS models. This can be adjustable in drive firmware.

Generally, all SAS disks will favor returning errors so data can be reconstructed rather than trying to self-repair.

Using an external drive for a database

External drives connected over USB or FireWire can be crippled in their abilities to report SMART and other error information, due to both the limitations of the common USB/FireWire bridge chipsets used to connect them and the associated driver software. They may not properly handle write caching for similar reasons. You should avoid putting a database on an external drive using one of those connection methods. Newer external drives using **external SATA (eSATA)** are much better in this regard, because they're no different from directly attaching the SATA device.

Hard drive reliability studies

General expected reliability is also an important thing to prioritize. There have been three excellent studies of large numbers of disk drives published in the last few years:

- **Google**: *Failure Trends in a Large Disk Drive Population*
- **Carnegie Mellon Study**: *Disk failures in the real world*
- **University of Wisconsin-Madison and Network Appliance**: *An Analysis of Data Corruption in the Storage Stack* `http://www.usenix.org/event/fast08/tech/full_papers/bairavasundaram/bairavasundaram.pdf` (long version) or `http://www.usenix.org/publications/login/2008-06/openpdfs/bairavasundaram.pdf` (shorter version)

The data in the Google and Carnegie Mellon studies don't show any significant bias toward the SCSI/SAS family of disks being more reliable. But the University of Wisconsin-Madison and Network Appliance study suggests "*SATA disks have an order of magnitude higher probability of developing checksum mismatches than Fibre Channel disks.*" That matches the idea suggested previously that error handling under SAS is usually more robust than on similar SATA drives. Since they're more expensive too, whether this improved error handling is worth paying for depends on your business requirements for reliability. This may not even be the same for every database server you run. Systems where a single master database feeds multiple slaves will obviously favor using better components in the master as one example of that.

You can find both statistically reliable and unreliable hard drives with either type of connection. One good practice is to only deploy drives that have been on the market long enough that you can get good data from actual customers on the failure rate. Newer drives using newer technology usually fail more often than slightly older designs that have been proven in the field, so if you can't find any reliability surveys, that's reason to be suspicious.

Drive firmware and RAID

In some disk array configurations, it can be important to match the firmware version of all the drives used for reliable performance. SATA disks oriented at consumers regularly have large changes made to the drive firmware, sometimes without a model number change. In some cases, it's impossible to revert to an earlier version once you've upgraded a drive's firmware, and newer replacement drives may not support running earlier firmware either. It's easy to end up with a situation where you can't purchase a replacement for a damaged drive even if the model is still on the market.

If you're buying an SAS drive, or one of the RAID oriented enterprise SATA ones, these tend to have much better firmware stability. This is part of the reason these drives lag behind consumer ones in terms of maximum storage capacity. Anyone who regularly buys the latest, largest drives available in the market can tell you how perilous that is—new drive technology is rather unreliable. It's fair to say that the consumer market is testing out the new technology. Only once the hardware and associated firmware has stabilized does work on the more expensive, business-oriented versions, such as SAS versions, begin. This makes it easier for the manufacturer to keep firmware revisions stable as new drive revisions are released—the beta testing by consumers has already worked out many of the possible bugs.

SSDs

The latest drive technology on the market right now is **solid state drives** (**SSDs**), also called flash disks. These provide permanent memory storage without any moving parts. They can vastly outperform disks with moving parts, particularly for applications where disk seeking is important—often the case for databases—and they should be more reliable too.

There are three major reasons why more databases don't use SSD technology yet:

- Maximum storage capacity is low, and databases tend to be big
- Cost of the storage you do get is fairly high
- Most SSD designs do not have a well designed write-cache on them

Due to how the erasing mechanism on an SSD works, you must have a write cache—typically a few kilobytes, to match the block size of the flash cells for them to operate in a way that they will last a long time. Writes are cached until a full block of data is queued up, then the flash is erased, and that new data written.

While small, these are still effectively a write-back cache, with all the potential data corruption issues any such design has for database use (as discussed in detail later in this chapter). Some SSDs include a capacitor or similar battery backup mechanism to work around this issue; the ones that do not may have very rare but still real corruption concerns.

Until SSD manufacturers get better at describing under exactly what conditions the write cache in their device can be lost, this technology remains an unknown risk for database use, and should be approached with caution. The window for data loss, and therefore database corruption, is very small, but it's often there. Also, you usually can't resolve that issue by using a controller card with its own battery-backed cache. In many cases, current generation cards won't talk to SSDs at all. And even if they can, the SSD may not accept and honor the same commands to disable its write cache that a normal drive would, because a working write cache is so central to the longevity aspects of the drive.

Disk controllers

One of the most critical aspects of PostgreSQL performance is also one of the easiest to overlook. Several hardware trends have made the disk controller seem less important now:

- Increasing CPU speeds and improved **direct memory access (DMA)** approaches make offloading disk work to a controller card seemingly less valuable. There is little chance that your controller will be any faster at previously expensive tasks such as RAID parity computation than your main system processor(s).
- Recent OS file system technology, such as Linux software RAID and ZFS, makes hardware RAID, with its often proprietary storage, seem less desirable.

Virtual machines and cloud deployments make the underlying disk hardware almost completely disconnected from the interface that your OS sees.

Faster drives, such as SSD, seem to eliminate the need for an intermediate intelligent controller.

Do not be fooled, however. When it comes to committing information into a database, spinning disk media and even flash media such as SSDs have some limitations that no amount of software cleverness can overcome.

Hardware and software RAID

When implementing a RAID array, you can do so with special hardware intended for that purpose. Many OSes nowadays, from Windows to Linux, include software RAID that doesn't require anything beyond the disk controller on your motherboard.

There are some advantages to hardware RAID. In many software RAID setups, such as the Linux implementation, you have to be careful to ensure the system will boot off of either drive in case of a failure. The BIOS provided by hardware cards normally takes care of this for you. Also, in cases where a failed drive has been replaced, it's usually easier to set up an automatic rebuild with a hardware RAID card.

When hard drives fail, they can take down the entire system in the process if they start sending bad data to the motherboard. Hardware RAID controllers tend to be tested for that scenario; motherboard drive controllers aren't necessarily.

The main disadvantage to hardware RAID, beyond cost, is that if the controller fails, you may not be able to access the drives anymore using a different controller. There is an emerging standard for storing the RAID metadata in this situation, the SNIA Raid **Disk Data Format** (**DDF**). It's not well supported by controller card vendors yet though.

The biggest advantage to hardware RAID in many systems is the reliable write caching they provide. This topic is covered in detail later in this chapter.

Recommended disk controllers

There are plenty of disk controllers on the market that don't do well at database tasks. Here are a few products that are known to work well with the sort of hardware that PostgreSQL is deployed on:

- LSI's MegaRAID line has been a source for reliable, medium performance SCSI, and now SAS/SATA, controllers for many years. They tend to have smaller cache sizes and their older products in particular were not always the fastest choice available, but their technology is mature and the drivers you get tend to be quite stable. The current SAS products perform extremely well in RAID 10, the usual preferred topology for databases. Its RAID 5 performance is still not very impressive.

- Dell has offered a rebranded LSI MegaRAID card as their **PowerEdge RAID Controller** (**PERC**) for some time now. The PERC6 is based on the LSI SAS design mentioned previously, as is its replacements, the PERC H700 and H800 (avoid the H200, which has no write cache at all). The PERC5 and earlier models tended to be slow, and the Dell customized firmware often didn't work as well as the ones in the genuine LSI models. These issues are all cleared up in the PERC6 and later models, which can easily clear 1 Gbps of reads from a properly configured 24-disk array.

- 3ware was one of the first companies to offer SATA RAID solutions, and they're particularly well known for providing excellent Linux drivers. Although some of the earlier 3ware models had unimpressive performance, the current 9690SA 9380 is a solid midrange performer if configured correctly. 3ware has gone through some company transitions; they were bought by AMCC, who were then bought by LSI. Eventually, you can expect that 3ware will be just another LSI line.

- HP provides a few RAID cards in their Smart Array series of products up to 12 Gbps SAS per physical link, or 6 Gbps SATA per physical link, including the P400, P600, and P800. The main difference between these cards is performance. The P800 is well respected as a card with high performance, while the P400 and P600 are considered at best medium speed performers.

- Emulex and QLogic provide the most popular high-performance cards for attaching Fibre Channel disk arrays to a server.
- Areca is a less well-known company than the rest on this list, but they've gained a following among fans of high-performance SATA cards; some models support SAS as well. Areca cards are featured in a few white-box vendor systems provided by resellers, for those who prefer not to deal with the big vendors mentioned previously. One concern with Areca is getting a management utility that is compatible with your system. The more expensive models that include a built-in management network port, what they call their out-of-band manager, are easiest to deal with here; just access the card over the network via its web console.

Driver support for Areca cards depends heavily upon the OS you're using, so be sure to check this carefully. Under Linux, for example, you may have to experiment a bit to get a kernel whose Areca driver is extremely reliable, because this driver isn't popular enough to get a large amount of testing. The 2.6.22 kernel works well for several heavy PostgreSQL users with these cards.

Typically, the cheapest of the cards you'll find in the preceding list sells currently for around USD 300. If you find a card that's cheaper than that, it's not likely to work well. Most of these are what's referred to as Fake RAID. These are cards that don't actually include a dedicated storage processor on them, which is one part that jacks the price up substantially.

Instead, Fake RAID cards use your system's CPU to handle these tasks. That's not necessarily bad from a performance perspective, but you'd be better off using a simple OS RAID (such as the ones provided with Linux or even Windows) directly. Fake RAID tends to be buggy, have low quality drivers, and you'll still have concerns about the volume not being portable to another type of RAID controller. They won't have a battery-backed cache, either, which is another major component worth paying for in many cases.

Prominent vendors of Fake RAID cards include Promise and HighPoint. The RAID support you'll find on most motherboards, such as Intel's RAID, also falls into the fake category. There are some real RAID cards available from Intel though, and they manufacture the I/O processor chips used in several of the cards mentioned previously.

Even just considering the real hardware RAID options here, it's impossible to recommend any one specific card because business purchasing limitations tend to reduce the practical choices. If your company likes to buy hardware from HP, the fact that Areca might be a better choice is unlikely to matter; the best you can do is know that the P800 is a good card, while their E200 is absent from the preceding list for good reason—it's slow. Similarly, if you have a big Dell purchasing contract already, you're likely to end up with a PERC6 or H700/800 as the only practical choice. There are too many business-oriented requirements that filter down what hardware is practical to provide a much narrower list of suggestions than what's been written here.

Attached storage – SAN and NAS

If you are connecting hard drives directly to your server through the motherboard or add-in cards, without leaving the case itself, that's referred to as Direct Attached Storage (DAS). The other alternative is to use an external interface, usually Fibre Channel or Ethernet, and connect a **Storage Area Network (SAN)** or **Network Attached Storage (NAS)** to hold the database disks. SAN and NAS hardware is typically much more expensive than DAS, and easier to manage in complicated ways. Beyond that, comparing the two is somewhat controversial.

 There are external drive arrays available that attach over SAS or eSATA cables, so they appear as direct attached storage even though they are technically external to the server chassis. Dell's PowerVault is a popular and relatively inexpensive example that is known to scale to 192 DAS drives.

An SAN or NAS (when SAN is used in this section, it's intended to refer to both) has a few clear advantages over direct storage:

- **Easier to use many drives**: It's hard to get direct storage to go much over 24 drives without moving into multiple external storage units, but that's only a medium-sized SAN that can be managed as a single component.
- **Read/write caching is often much larger**: 16 GB of cache is not unusual in a SAN, while direct storage will normally top out at closer to 1 GB. Also, SAN designs can include a way to dump even that large cache to disk cleanly in the event of any power failure, making it very hard to end up with a corrupted database in the process, no matter how long the outage.

- **SANs are easier to make redundant across multiple servers**: Typically, you'll have at least two Fibre Channel ports in a SAN, making it easy to connect to two systems if you want. Then, either server can access the data, as long as you partition access between the two properly.
- The management interface for a SAN will usually include fancier rebuild possibilities, and features such as snapshots that can make backup and mirroring operations much easier.

There are a few potential drawbacks as well:

- Performance can suffer compared to direct storage. Everything else being equal, going through the SAN/NAS interface (Fibre Channel, Ethernet, and so on) adds latency no matter what, and can introduce a write bottleneck too. This can really slow your system down if, for example, you're using an interface such as Gigabit Ethernet with many disks behind it. You can easily fill the network capacity long before you've reached the speed of all available drives in that case.
- SANs are very complicated. It's common to need to hire a consultant just to get the system working as you expect for your workload.
- Costs are much higher in terms of performance per dollar on a SAN compared to direct storage. If you really need the redundancy and management features a SAN provides, they can make perfect sense. This is particularly true if the SAN is so large, it's serving out work for many systems at once, which can make the whole system easier to cost justify.

If you want performance at a reasonable price, direct storage is where you'll end up at. If you need a SAN or NAS, the reasons why are likely related to your business rather than its performance.

If you follow the disk benchmarking practices recommended in this book, you should be able to nail down results quickly enough to make good performance a required component of the sales cycle for the SAN. Considering their price tag, you certainly can make the vendor of the SAN do some work as part of selling it if you benchmark before the system is completely paid for, in a standard way whose results aren't likely to be disputed. This can sidestep the need to hire an external consultant by leveraging the resources inside the vendor instead.

Reliable controller and disk setup

PostgreSQL uses a **write-ahead log** (**WAL**) to write data in a way that survives a database or hardware crash. This is similar to the log buffer or redo log found in other databases. The database documentation covers the motivation and implementation of the WAL at `https://www.postgresql.org/docs/current/static/wal-intro.html`.

To quote from that introduction:

"WAL's central concept is that changes to data files (where tables and indexes reside) must be written only after those changes have been logged, that is, after log records describing the changes have been flushed to permanent storage."

This procedure ensures that if your application has received commit for a transaction that transaction is on permanent storage, and will not be lost even if there is a crash. This satisfies the durability portion of the **atomicity, consistency, isolation, durability** (**ACID**) expectations that databases aim to satisfy.

The tricky part of the WAL implementation is the flushed to permanent storage part, which you might be surprised is going to take several pages to cover just in this chapter and which will reappear in later ones, too.

Write-back caches

The CPUs and memory in your server are quite fast compared to its disk drives. Accordingly, making the rest of the system wait for the disks, particularly when things need to be written out, can drag overall performance down heavily. Systems that wait for the disks to complete their writes before moving into their next task are referred to as having a write-through cache. While the data may be stored temporarily in a memory cache, until it's made it all the way through to the physical disk, any write an application requested isn't considered complete.

The normal solution to making that faster is to introduce a different type of write cache between the program doing the writing and disks. A write-back cache is one where data is copied into memory, and then control returns to the application that requested the write. Those writes are then handled asynchronously, at some future time dictated by the design of the write-back cache. It can take minutes before the data actually makes it to disk.

When PostgreSQL writes information to the WAL, and sometimes when it writes to the regular database files too, that information must be flushed to permanent storage in order for the database's crash corruption defense mechanism to work. So what happens if you have a write-back cache that says the write is complete, but it really isn't? People call these, and the result can be very bad:

 If you have a system with a write-back cache, and a system crash causes the content of that write-back cache to be lost, this can corrupt a PostgreSQL database stored on that drive and make it unusable. You can discover it takes expert intervention to even get the database to start again, and determining what data is damaged will be difficult.

Consider the case where you have committed a transaction. Details of that new transaction might be spread across two data blocks on the drive. Now, imagine that one of those made it to disk before the system crashed, but the other didn't. You've now left the database in a corrupted state: one block refers to a transaction that doesn't exist where it's supposed to in the other block.

Had at least all of the data blocks related to the WAL been written properly, the database WAL could correct this error after the crash. But the WAL protection only works if it can get honest information about whether information has been written to the disks properly or not, and the insincere write-back caches do not report that.

Sources of write-back caching

Servers are filled with write caches you need to be aware of:

- **Operating system write cache**: This cache can easily be gigabytes in size. Typically, you can flush data out of this cache by forcing a sync operation on the block that needs to be stored on disk. On POSIX systems (which includes all UNIX-like ones), this is done with the `fsync` or `fdatasync` calls. In some cases, it's possible to write directly in a `sync` mode, which is effectively a write followed by `fsync`. The `postgresql.conf` setting, `wal_sync_method`, controls which method is used and it's possible to disable this altogether to optimize for speed instead of safety.

- **Disk controller write cache**: You'll find a write cache on most RAID controller cards, as well as inside external storage such as a SAN. Common sizes right now are 128 MB to 512 MB 4 GB for cards, but gigabytes are common on a SAN. Typically, controllers can be changed to operate in the completely write-through mode, albeit slowly. But by default, you'll normally find them in write-back mode. Writes that can fit in the controller's cache are stored there, the OS is told the write is completed, and the card writes the data out at some future time. To keep this write from being lost if power is interrupted, the card must be configured with a battery. That combination is referred to as a **battery-backed write cache** (**BBC** or **BBWC**).
- **Disk drive write cache**: All SATA and SAS disks have a write cache on them, which, on current hardware, is 8 MB to 32/64 MB in size. This cache is always volatile; if power is lost, any data stored in there will be lost and they're always write-back caches if enabled.

How can you make sure you're safe given all these write-back caches that might lose your data? There are a few basic precautions to take:

- Make sure whatever filesystem you're using properly implements `fsync` calls, or whatever similar mechanism is used, fully. More details on this topic can be found in the `wal_sync_method`.
  documentation and in information about filesystem tuning in later chapters here.
- Monitor your driver controller battery. Some controller cards will monitor their battery health, and automatically switch from write-back to write-though mode when there is no battery or it's not working properly. That's a helpful safety measure, but performance is going to drop hard when this happens.
- Disable any drive write caches. Most hardware RAID controllers will do this for you, preferring their own battery-backed caches instead.

Disk controller monitoring

When you have a RAID controller card with a battery-backed cache, you probably expect you'll need to monitor the card to determine when disks fail. But monitoring controller battery health is an equally critical aspect of maintaining a reliable database system when you're using this technology. If the battery fails and you're using it in write-back mode, your writes are not safe. Similarly, if your power fails, you should prefer shutting the database server down after a few minutes of power loss to trying to keep it going. Integrating power monitoring via a UPS or similar mechanism should be part of your database server configuration, so that a short outage results in an orderly shutdown. Consider the purpose of the controller battery to protect yourself from really unexpected outages, like someone tripping over the power cord. Even if the manufacturer claims the controller battery will last through days of downtime, that's not a good reason to believe you'll actually be safe for an extended outage. You should consider the battery as something you'd prefer to only use for some number of minutes of protection. That may be the reality, particularly in a case where the battery is older and has lost much of its capacity, and some controller batteries don't start out with very much capacity. Be sure to run your own tests rather than blindly believing the manufacturer specifications; your data depends on it.

 Better RAID controllers will automatically disable write-back mode if their battery stops working normally. If performance suddenly drops on an older server, this is one potential cause.

Also, don't forget that every UPS has a battery that degrades over time as well. That's all the more reason to arrange an orderly shutdown of your server during a power outage, rather than optimistically presuming you can keep it running until power returns.

Disabling drive write caches

If your card doesn't disable all the drive write caches, or if you're using a software RAID approach, you'll need to turn the caches off yourself. The best way to do this is to see if it's possible to change the default write cache state using the utilities provided by the drive manufacturer.

You should be able to do this through software as well. Here is a sample session from a Linux system checking the write cache, toggling it off, confirming that the change took, and then toggling it on again:

```
# hdparm -I /dev/sda | grep "Write cache"
     * Write cache
# sudo hdparm -W 0 /dev/sda

/dev/sda:
 setting drive write-caching to 0 (off)
 write-caching =   0 (off)
# hdparm -I /dev/sda | grep "Write cache"
        Write cache
# hdparm -W 1 /dev/sda

/dev/sda:
 setting drive write-caching to 1 (on)
 write-caching =   1 (on)
```

Only the -W 0 configuration is completely safe for database use. The PostgreSQL WAL documentation suggests similar commands to use for other OSes.

Performance impact of write-through caching

If you don't have a battery-backed write cache, and therefore can't utilize a memory-based cache to accelerate fsync writes, commit performance on your database can be quite bad. The worst case here is where you have a single client that is issuing a commit after every statement it executes. The reality of how a hard drive works means that individual writes happen once each time the drive spins around.

Here are the measurements for the common drive speeds available right now, with the computed maximum commit rate:

Rotation speed	Rotation time (ms)	Max commits/second
5400	11.1	90
7200	8.3	120
10000	6.0	166
15000	4.0	250

It's important to realize how limiting this can be:

 If you have a common 7200 rpm hard drive, no single client can commit more than 120 transactions/second in any situation where all that's available is a write-back cache.

It doesn't matter how many disks you have in a RAID array, or how you configure your software. You must have hardware with a battery, enabling a non-volatile write-back cache, in order to safely exceed this limit.

Some PostgreSQL installs use a RAID controller card just for this purpose, to provide a BBWC, in **just a bunch of disks (JBOD)** mode, where no RAID is being done on the controller at all. Sometimes, disks are used directly, and others layer software RAID on top, which can have some advantages compared to hardware RAID.

If you have more than one client, you'll get more done per commit. It's normal to see >500 committed transactions per second if you have a larger number of clients all committing regularly, because each flushed disk write will include any queued-up commit requests from other clients, too. The other common technique here is to batch commits into larger pieces, perhaps going 1000 records at a time rather than a single one, in order to reduce the average impact of commit latency.

Another approach for accelerating systems that don't have a usable write cache is asynchronous commit, covered in `Chapter 6`, *Server Configuration Tuning*.

Summary

Building a database server with good performance is hard work. There are many individual components that are available in multiple quality levels and corresponding costs. Also, there are plenty of small details you must get right or you'll risk data corruption. Luckily, you don't have to start from scratch. Stick to common, well understood components with known good performance, while keeping an eye on reliability too, and you can build a well-balanced database server for a reasonable budget. Always make sure to run your own benchmarks on the result though. It's very easy to sabotage even good equipment with the wrong configuration when running a database.

Allocating your hardware budget between CPUs, memory, and disks is very application-dependent.

Carefully selecting and configuring your controller and disk caches is critical for reliable database operation.

Make sure you are monitoring components in your server that are likely to fail or have a known lifetime, particularly hard drives and the batteries in disk controller cards.

Any disk write caches in your system must be confirmed to properly support the write flushing mechanism the database uses, or database corruption can result.

The maximum rate at which database clients can commit transactions can be very low without a properly implemented write-back cache.

3
Database Hardware Benchmarking

After all the theory in the last chapter about what makes some systems perform well or poorly, you might be wondering just how your own system measures up. There are several reasons to always do your own hardware benchmarks. The first is simply to be systematic about your performance process. If you always measure things yourself, you'll get a better feel for what good and bad performance looks like, one that can help tip you off to even subtle problems.

Second, in the case of disks in particular, problems here are a very common underlying cause of database performance issues. If your disks are slow, and there are many ways that can happen, your database will likely be slow too. It's important when this happens to have accurate data on whether the problem is likely at the hardware or software level.

The goal of your basic hardware testing should be to look for large configuration errors, not to analyze every possible parameter. The sorts of problems you need to be most concerned about are really obvious, and detailed optimization is better done at the database application level.

In this chapter, we will look into the following topics:

- CPU and memory benchmarking
- Physical disk performance
- Disk benchmarking tools

CPU and memory benchmarking

The first thing worth testing on a new system is the speed of its memory, because if this is slow, both the CPU and disks will suffer accordingly. You might wonder why this is so important. It's because database work is intensive in both these areas. PostgreSQL works with database data in 8 KB pages, and it's constantly shuffling those around to system memory as needed to satisfy queries; looking through those pages for the specific rows needed is CPU-intensive. Even on benchmarks that focus on disk-heavy work, the speed of the underlying memory can have a surprisingly high impact on results.

Memtest86+

One of the most valuable tools in the PC hardware technician's bag is **Memtest86+**, a program whose primary purpose is to find intermittent errors on PC memory. It's a great way to burn-in new hardware and confirm that it works as expected.

You can download Memtest86+ directly from its website at `http://www.memtest.org/` and create a bootable CD to run the program. Note that it's now included as one of the boot options for many Linux distributions, both on the installer media and when starting the OS normally too. Any Ubuntu installer CD, for example, will include the Memtest86+ current when that version was released. Generally, if the program does not fully recognize your CPU hardware information, you probably need a newer version to make sure you're getting accurate results.

Once you've started it from a bootable CD, Memtest86+ reports the speed of the various memory at each of the cache levels it identifies. The most useful one is the Mbps value reported on the memory: line. This will be how fast memory access is to the main system RAM, and is good for confirming that performance matches baselines. It can be a quick way to confirm performance and stability if you're adjusting clocking on your memory or CPU to try and speed things up.

One problem with this program is that it requires local access to the system to run, which isn't always practical. And since Memtest86+ is only running a single process to test memory, its reported total speed number isn't really representative of the capabilities of modern processors. For that you'll need **STREAM**, which does run easily from a remote session too.

STREAM memory testing

STREAM is a memory bandwidth testing program that came from testing high-performance systems for scientific research. The program is hosted at `http://www.cs.virginia.edu/stream/`, and the website includes a variety of sample reports from the program, too.

The STREAM project provides some binaries for several platforms, even Windows, although the available Linux binary hasn't worked out well in my own testing. In addition, STREAM aims only to track the maximum bandwidth the system is capable of. You can find some benchmarks at `https://www.cs.virginia.edu/stream/peecee/Bandwidth.html`.

One of the things that you should be interested in for PostgreSQL use is how much memory bandwidth a single process can reach. If you are using a version of PostgreSQL <= 9.5 individual queries in PostgreSQL will only run on one CPU, if that number is low, you may be disappointed with how lone queries run, even on an otherwise idle server. To try and work on both these problems, for Linux systems, my `stream-scaling` script, available at `http://github.com/gregs1104/stream-scaling`, tries to automate a more comprehensive view of your memory performance. It downloads the program, measures the total amount of cache in all the system processors, and automatically compiles STREAM to use a value much larger than that. It then loops from a single active thread (presumably running on a single core) upward until it's using every processor on the server. Even if you're sold on this idea, it will take you a while to get your own library of references performance data assembled. A starting set from systems that I've confirmed results from myself is included on the site, and a few examples from there are included next.

STREAM and Intel versus AMD

The following table shows the reported STREAM speeds by processor/RAM for a few servers, as the number of cores utilized increases. All except the one Opteron model (featuring eight sockets of six core processors) are Intel systems. RAM included here is all **double data rate synchronous dynamic random access memory (DDR RAM)**. The main two standards in use in current hardware are DDR2 and DDR3, and the RAM DDR column shows which standard is used and what clock speed the memory is running at. The performance numbers shown for different total core counts are in units of Mbps:

Processor	Cores	Frequency (GHz)	RAM DDR	One core	Two cores	Four cores	All cores
T7200	2	2.00	2/667	2965	3084		3084
Q6600	4	2.40	2/800	4383	4537	4390	4390
Opteron 8431 (8 X 6)	48	2.40	2/800	4038	7996	13520	27214
Xeon E5506	4	2.13	3/800	7826	9016	9297	9297
i7 860	8	2.80	3/1600	9664	13096	14293	13231

This shows clear limiting of available bandwidth to a single core on all of the recent systems with many cores, relative to total system bandwidth. That particular problem has been more restrictive on AMD's systems than Intel's. Even though this large AMD system can achieve 27 Gbps when heavily tasked, a single process barely clears 4 Gbps.

This is exactly why there aren't more AMD processors included in this list. From mid-2008 to mid-2010, AMD lagged considerably behind Intel in terms of their memory technology on systems with small numbers of processor sockets. They've fallen out of favor with the purchasing I've been involved in as a direct result. Note the large memory speed jump for single core results starting with the Intel 5500 series processor. That represents the introduction of Intel's Nehalem architecture. That included a shift to faster DDR3 RAM, among other major memory improvements, and was what pushed Intel far ahead for a solid two years.

A detailed hardware benchmarking presentation can be found at
https://www.2ndquadrant.com/media/pdfs/talks/pg-hw-bench-2010.pdf.

CPU benchmarking

It's rather hard to find a CPU benchmark that is more representative of database performance more easily than by just using a database to do something processor-intensive. You can easily build some quick, PostgreSQL-oriented CPU tests using the database `psql` client and its `\timing` feature, which shows you how long each statement takes to run. Here's an example that just exercises the CPU and memory, by adding the first million integers together with the always handy `generate_series` set returning function:

```
\timing
SELECT sum(generate_series) FROM generate_series(1,1000000);
```

Here's another more complicated example that may use some disk accesses too, in addition to stressing CPU/memory; it depends on the amount of RAM in your server:

```
\timing
CREATE TABLE test (id INTEGER PRIMARY KEY);
INSERT INTO test VALUES (generate_series(1,100000));
EXPLAIN ANALYZE SELECT COUNT(*) FROM test;
```

Both the insertion time and how long it takes to count each value are interesting numbers. The latter also includes some CPU/memory-intensive work related to updating the hint bit values PostgreSQL uses to track transaction visibility information; see Chapter 7, *Routine Maintenance*, for more information about this.

Remember, the point of your CPU testing is not to map out a comprehensive view of its performance in every regard. What you should focus on is making sure the performance matches similar hardware, and, if this is an upgrade, ensuring that it exceeds the expectations you have from older systems.

Chapter 8, *Database Benchmarking*, will provide a more useful look at CPU capacity from a PostgreSQL perspective. Running a select-only test, using more clients than your system has cores, when all the data fits in RAM, is a very good way to see if your CPUs are delivering the expected performance. That's my preferred way to see how fast a new CPU I'm evaluating will work for real CPU and memory limited workloads. Just note that the pgbench in PostgreSQL versions before 9.0 can easily act as the bottleneck on results; more on this topic in that later Chapter 8, *Database Benchmarking*.

Sources of slow memory and processors

If your memory doesn't look to be as fast as it should be, or your CPU results look suspicious, there are a few common things to look for to figure out why.

Most memory is now designed to work in a dual-channel configuration, with pairs of memory put only into specific slots. If that's not done correctly, you'll halve memory speed by running in a single-channel setup. Memtest86+ can note when this is happening, and your BIOS may realize it if you look for the information.

Poor quality RAM can introduce a surprisingly large drop in system performance. And, just because you have fast memory in your server, that doesn't mean the motherboard is taking advantage of it. The defaults on some systems are quite conservative. Nowadays, your system should be looking up **serial presence detect** (**SPD**) information provided by your RAM to determine how fast it should run. But that doesn't always default to optimal performance, and manual tweaking of the memory timing may be required.

Recent high-performance PC RAM aimed at desktop systems uses a newer standard for the same purpose, the **Extreme Memory Profile** (**XMP**) protocol, to communicate the speed it's capable of running at to the system BIOS when you boot. But if your BIOS doesn't default to checking and using XMP, which some don't, your RAM will run at notably *non-extreme* speeds. You should be able to find out how fast your RAM is expected to run as a series of timing values.

The Intel i7 860 system mentioned before that uses DDR3-1600 has timing values of 8-8-8-24, for example. The motherboard did not run the RAM at those speeds until I'd adjusted several settings in it. Just because your hardware vendor should be taking care of all this for you doesn't mean it's safe to ignore this whole issue. It's easy for anyone to miss a step and ship a system with degraded performance.

A link to describe the details of RAM timings
is http://www.hardwaresecrets.com/understanding-ram-timings/.

Another problem that you can run into is using memory that doesn't work well with the clock speed of the processor you're using. Processors are often *locked* to certain multiplier possibilities that are relative to the speed the main system bus runs at. The motherboard ends up doing a complicated negotiation game between the processor and the RAM to find a common denominator speed to run everything at. For example, one of my older systems supported either DDR2-667 or DDR-800 RAM, running at a memory clock of 333 or 400 MHz. The system processor ran at 2.4 GHz, and only supported limited multiplier combinations. It turned out that if I used DDR2-667, the common frequency the motherboard settled on was running the memory bus at 300 MHz, with the CPU using an 8X multiplier. So the RAM was essentially 10% under clocked relative to its capabilities. Upgrading to DDR2-800 instead used a 400 MHz clock and a 6X CPU multiplier. That's a 33% jump in memory speed; just from using a better grade of RAM and better matching the CPU clock possibilities, the overall system performance improved proportionately.

In addition to getting the memory and multiplier details right, processor power management is an increasing source of issues when benchmarking hardware. Many OS now default to having modest or aggressive processor power management active by default. This is a surprisingly common issue on Linux, for example. The normal warning sign is that the processor is only shown as running at 1 GHz in `/proc/cpuinfo`, with correspondingly slow results on some benchmarks. Normally, you will need to adjust the Linux CPU governor setup to optimize for performance, rather than lower power use, at least for the duration of the benchmark. Exact details for how to adjust the governor vary by Linux distribution. You may want to return to optimizing for lower energy use at the expense of some performance afterwards, once you've confirmed that performance can be good when needed.

Physical disk performance

While a lot of high-level information about disk performance has been mentioned already, if you want to get useful benchmarks from drives, you'll need to know a bit more about their physical characteristics. This will drop back to theory for a bit, followed by examples of real measured disks that demonstrate common things you can expect to see.

Random access and input/outputs per second

Enterprise storage vendors like to talk in terms of **input/outputs per second** (**IOPS**). If you're buying a SAN, for example, expect to be asked *"how many IOPS do you expect in total and per spindle?"* and for measurements provided by the vendor proving good performance to be in this unit. This number represents typical disk performance on a seek-heavy workload and, unfortunately, it is a poor one to fixate on for database applications. Database applications are often complicated mixes of I/O with caching involved—sequential reads, seeks, and commits all compete—rather than always being seek-bound.

 Spindle is often used as a synonym for a single disk drive, and is used interchangeably here that way. It's more correctly used to only refer to a single section of a disk, the part that rotates. In this case, common use trumps correctness for most writing about this subject.

It's straightforward to compute IOPS for a single disk. You'll need to track down the manufacturer data sheet where they give the detailed timing specifications for the drive. The Seagate Momentus 7200.4 laptop drive used in the examples here has the following specifications:

- **Spindle Speed**: 7,200 RPM
- **Average latency**: 4.17 ms
- **Random read seek time**: 11.0 ms

This models the fact that every disk access on a drive requires:

- Seeking to the right track on the disk. That's the *random read seek time*.
- Waiting for the sector we want to read to show up under the read head. That's the *average [rotational] latency* time.

The *average latency* figure here represents rotational latency. That will always be exactly 1/2 of the rotation time of the drive. In this case, 7,200 RPM means one rotation happens every 1/120 of a second, which means a rotation every 8.33 ms. Since, in an average, you won't have to wait for a full rotation, that's halved to give an average, making for an expected rotation latency time of 4.17 ms. All 7,200 RPM drives will have an identical rotational latency figure, whereas seek times vary based on drive size, quality, and similar factors.

IOPS is simply a measurement of the average time for both those operations, the seek latency and the rotation latency, inverted to be a rate instead of an elapsed time. For our sample disk, it can be computed as follows:

```
Rotational latency RL = 1 / RPM / 60 / 2 = 4.17ms
Seek time S=11.0ms
IOPS = 1/(RL + S)
IOPS = 1/(4.17ms + 11ms) = 65.9 IOPS
```

Here are a few resources that discuss IOPS, including a calculator that you might find helpful:

- http://www.techrepublic.com/blog/the-enterprise-cloud/calculate-iops-in-a-storage-array/
- http://www.ryanfrantz.com/posts/calculating-disk-iops/

Remember that IOPS is always a worst-case scenario. This is the performance the drive is guaranteed to deliver, if it's being hammered by requests from all over the place. It will often do better, particularly on sequential reads and writes.

Sequential access and ZCAV

In many database situations, what you're also concerned about is the streaming sequential read or write rate of the drive, where it's just staying in one area instead of seeking around. Computing this value is complicated by the nature of how disks are built.

The first thing to realize about modern hard disks is that the speed you'll see from them depends highly on what part of the disk you're reading from. Disks spin at one speed all of the time, referred to as **constant angular velocity (CAV)**. A typical drive nowadays will spin at 7,200 RPM, and the actual disk platter is circular. When the disk read/write head is near the outside of the disk, the speed of the part passing underneath it is faster than on the inside. This is the same way that in a car, the outside edge of a tire travels further than the inside one, even though the actual rotation count is the same.

Because of this speed difference, manufacturers are able to pack more data onto the outside edge of the drive than the inside. The drives are actually mapped into a series of zones with different densities on them. There is a longer discussion of this topic at http://www.coker.com.au/bonnie++/zcav/ that also talks about using the **Zoned Constant Angular Velocity (ZCAV)** tool, which will be shown later.

The practical result is that the logical beginning part of the disk is going to be significantly faster than its end. Accordingly, whenever you benchmark a disk, you have to consider what part of that disk you're measuring. Many disk benchmark attempts give bad data because they're comparing a fast part of the disk, likely the first files put onto the disk, with ones created later that are likely on a slower part.

Short stroking

As disks have this very clear, faster portion to them, and capacities are very large. One observation you can easily make is that you should put the most important pieces of data on the early parts of the disk. One popular technique, named **short stroking**, limits the portion of the disk used to only include the fastest part, assuring you'll only be accessing its best area. Short stroking can be done just by adjusting the disk's partition table to only include the early part. You might partition the slower portion anyway, but just not use it regularly. Saving it for backups or migration use can be worthwhile. Occasionally, you can force short stroking using more physical means, such as a disk vendor or RAID controller tool that allows you to limit the capacity exposed to the OS.

Commit rate

As covered in `Chapter 2`, *Database Hardware,* how fast data can actually be committed permanently to disk is a critical performance aspect for database transaction processing. It's important to measure this area carefully. Speeds that are dramatically higher than expected are usually a sign that one of the write-caches has been put into a volatile write-back mode, which, as already explained, can result in data loss and database corruption. Some examples of how that can happen will be covered in `Chapter 4`, *Disk Setup.*

If you don't have any non-volatile caching available, the basic commit rate for a drive will be similar to its IOPS rating. Luckily, PostgreSQL will put multiple transactions into a physical commit if they aren't happening quickly enough.

PostgreSQL test_fsync

In a source code build of PostgreSQL, the `src/tools/fsync` directory contains a program named `test_fsync` that might also be included in some packaged versions. This aims to test the commit rate for each of the ways a given PostgreSQL install might commit records to disk. Unfortunately, this program doesn't give results consistent with other tests, and before PostgreSQL 9.0 it's in the wrong units (elapsed times instead of operations per second). Until it's improved a bit further, its output can't be relied upon.

pg_test_fsync is intended to give you a reasonable idea of what the fastest wal_sync_method is on your specific system, as well as supplying diagnostic information in the event of an identified I/O problem. However, differences shown by pg_test_fsync might not make any significant difference in real database throughput, especially since many database servers are not speed-limited by their WALs. pg_test_fsync reports the average file sync operation time in microseconds for each wal_sync_method, which can also be used to inform efforts to optimize the value of commit_delay.

INSERT rate

If you have the autocommit turned to on, each time you INSERT a record in a standard PostgreSQL install, it does a commit at the end. Therefore, any program that does a series of inserts in a loop and times them can measure the effective commit rate, presuming the records are small enough that true disk throughput doesn't become the limiting factor. It's possible to run exactly such a test using the pgbench tool shipped with PostgreSQL. You should be able to write your own similar test in any programming language you're familiar with that can issue PostgreSQL INSERT statements one at a time. Just make sure you don't batch them into a larger transaction block. That's the right approach if you actually want good performance, but not for specifically testing the commit rate using small transactions.

Windows commit rate

On the Windows platform, where sysbench and test_fsync will not be available, an INSERT test is really the only good option for testing the commit rate. Note that the PostgreSQL wal_sync_method needs to be set properly for this test to give valid results. Like most platforms, the Windows defaults will include unsafe write-back cache behavior.

Disk benchmarking tools

Now it's time to see some real disks measured. For the first few examples here, the drive being tested is a 320 GB Seagate Momentus 7200.4 3 Gb/s SATA, model number ST9320423AS. This is one of the fastest 2.5" laptop drives on the market, and its more detailed access time specifications were given in the IOPS section before. The results shown are from an installation on a Lenovo Thinkpad T60 with an Intel Core 2 Duo T7200 running at 2.0 GHz.

We'll start with the HD Tune program running on Windows, because its graphs are extremely nice and it measures almost everything you'd hope for. Its graphs demonstrate several aspects of general disk performance more clearly than the command-line tools for UNIX systems covered later.

HD Tune

A great tool for the sort of basic disk benchmarking needed for databases on Windows system is HD Tune, available at http://www.hdtune.com/. The program is free for a trial period, with a slightly limited feature set, and is modestly priced to purchase. The free features are sufficient for database hardware validation.

Here is what the output from HD Tune looks like running the basic transfer rate benchmark on this disk:

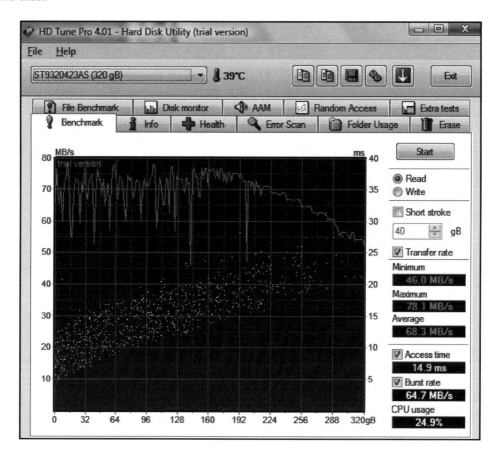

These are respectable results from a single drive of any sort, particularly a laptop one. The left axis and the upper line graph is charting Mbps at that point on the disk. The right axis label is in milliseconds, and the scattered dots in the middle and bottom are showing the access time along points in the drive. Note how the transfer speed falls and the access speed rises as you move further along the logical part of this disk, into the slower ZCAV zones.

An average of 68.3 Mbps is in the middle range of what you'll see on drives as this book is being written. High performance desktop SATA or SAS drives will do better, while some desktop and most laptop drives will do worse. The real-world seek access time of 14.9 ms is a similarly average value, and you can see it matches the drive specification.

There's one thing really odd about this graph though. Note how the early part, from 0 to 192 GB, is both flat on top and somewhat jagged. Both of those are warning signs that something is wrong. If you look at the Bonnie++ ZCAV results later, you'll see what the drive's performance really looks like. The performance should be dropping evenly from the very beginning, and the graph should be smoother. When you see a flat top where a ZCAV decline should be, normally that means the rate is being limited by some bottleneck other than the drive speed itself. This sort of issue is exactly why it's worthwhile becoming familiar with what drives look like when performing well, so you can spot the ones that aren't.

Short stroking tests

HD Tune includes a particularly easy-to-use short stroking test feature that shows you how performance would change if you were only using a portion of the disk.

For our sample, the first 160 GB were obviously the fastest parts, making that a reasonable short-stroked restriction:

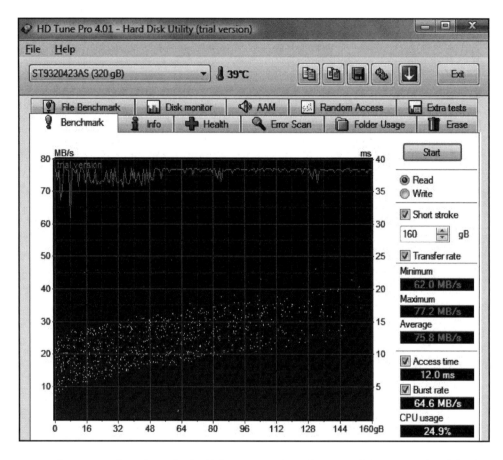

You can see that not using the whole disk range using short stroking considerably decreases worst-case seek time, which makes it particularly appropriate for applications that are more concerned about worst-case latency than disk capacity. And, in some cases, you may discover that SATA disks with very high capacities end up being much closer in performance to more expensive SAS disks just by applying this technique. For example, the first 100 GB of a 1 TB SATA drive is extremely fast, due to how dense that information is on the drive. You might be surprised at how well it compares with, say, a 143 GB SAS drive even with a higher rotation speed.

IOPS

HD Tune includes a **Random Access** test that gives its results in terms of the standard IOPS figure, at various block sizes:

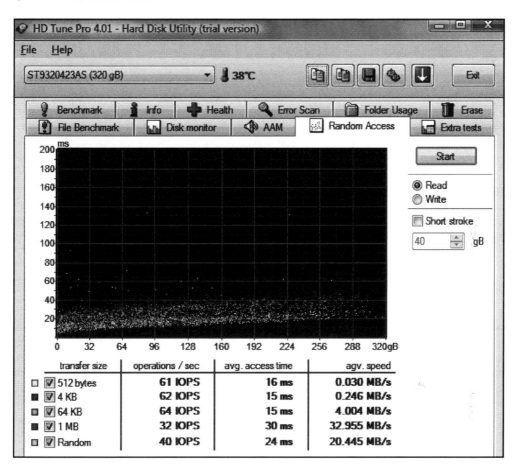

This is not far from the computed value derived previously for this drive: 69.5 IOPS.

The average speed computed number here (the poorly labeled **avg. speed** column) is always a good one to note when doing seek-based tests. It's easiest to explain what that means with a database-specific example. Consider that PostgreSQL reads in blocks of 8 KB each. Based on what we have seen, we could expect about **64 IOPS** out of this drive as its worst-case performance, doing nothing but random seeks, at that block size. This turns into a total transfer rate of:

```
64 IO/S * 8KB/IO * (1 MB / 1024 KB) = 0.5Mbps
```

That's what **avg. speed** is showing: the computed transfer speed for various block sizes.

This is the real world of disk performance. While you might think a disk is capable of 60 Mb/s or more of transfers, on a truly random workload, you might get 0.5 MB or less. This is a laptop disk, but only seeing 1 to 2 Mbps on completely random tasks is typical for desktop and server class drives too.

With enough practice, on a UNIX system, it's even possible to stare at the output from `vmstat` and `iostat`, see how busy the drives are and the actual read/write block counts, and make a rough estimate of the seek versus sequential workload breakdown from those numbers. If the drives are always busy, but only getting 0.5 Mbps, it has to be almost all seek. If they're busy half the time and getting 30 Mbps, that's probably a sequential read hitting a bottleneck on the processing side of things.

Unpredictable performance and Windows

Serious database administrators have a strong historical bias toward using UNIX-like systems for their servers. The first examples here are using Windows instead because the graphs produced are easier to read, and therefore better for introducing the concepts of this section. But doing so reminded me why Windows is not the preferred database hosting OS for so many people.

Getting useful benchmark results requires the system to be quiescent: free of other programs running that would spoil the results of what is intended to be measured. When booting into Windows Vista to generate these results, I discovered the `TrustedInstaller` process was hogging a considerable amount of CPU and disk resources. It turned out Windows Update had decided it was time to install the next major Vista Service Pack; it was downloading pieces in the background, and pushing me toward the upgrade at every opportunity. It was two hours later before I had completed all the background activity it compelled me to take care of, and had an idle system capable of running these tests.

Disk throughput in case of sequential read and write

dd is a standard UNIX utility that's capable of reading and writing blocks of data very efficiently. To use it properly for disk testing of sequential read and write throughput, you'll need to have it work with a file that's at least twice the size of your total server RAM. That will be large enough that your system cannot possibly cache all of the read and write operations in memory, which would significantly inflate results. The preferable block size needed by dd is to use 8 KB blocks, to match how the database is going to do sequential read and write operations. At that size, a rough formula you can use to compute how many such blocks are needed to reach twice your RAM size is as follows:

$$blocks = 250,000 * (gigabytes\ of\ RAM)$$

Once you know that number, the following simple commands will time writing out a file large enough to not fit in the OS RAM cache, and then read the results back:

```
time sh -c "dd if=/dev/zero of=bigfile bs=8k count=blocks && sync"
time dd if=bigfile of=/dev/null bs=8k
```

As this will run for a while without displaying anything interesting, you can watch vmstat or iostat during the test (in another Terminal) to see what's happening. The vmstat's bi and bo (block in and out) numbers will match the current read/write rate. You should also note the CPU percentage required to reach the peak rate. Displayed CPU percentages are often relative to the total CPU capacity of the system. So if you have four CPUs, and you're seeing 25% overall CPU usage, that could be a single CPU running at 100%.

Once the times are reported, you can then divide the file size in MB (=1024 * GB) by the number of seconds of runtime, and get a Mbps write and read score.

Recent dd versions, on Linux at least, will report a Mbps value at the end of their run. Note that the value reported will be a bit inflated, because dd will report it is finished before the actual blocks are all flushed to disk. This is why the previous recipe includes a sync at the end—this makes sure the time reported includes that overhead. The raw transfer rate reported by dd will usually be a bit higher than what you compute when taking this into account.

The dd numbers you'll see should closely match the Bonnie++ block output/input numbers, as demonstrated in the next section. If you intend to eventually run Bonnie++, there's little sense in performing this test too. Using dd is mainly helpful for UNIX systems where you don't want to install anything just to test the disks out, including ones that don't have the development tools to build additional software installed.

Bonnie++

The standard program used to run a simple disk I/O benchmark on a UNIX-like system is bonnie++. In its default configuration, it will create a file (or set of files) twice as large as the physical RAM in the server, to prevent the entire test from being cached in RAM, then read that whole file back in again. The main virtue of the program is that you can just run it from a directory on the volume you want to test and it usually does the right thing without further input.

Here's a full example of downloading bonnie++, building it, running it, and getting an HTML report from it:

```
$ wget http://www.coker.com.au/bonnie++/bonnie++-1.03e.tgz
$ tar xvfz bonnie++-1.03e.tgz
$ cd bonnie++-1.03e/
$ ./configure
$ make
$ ./bonnie++ -f -n 0 | tee `hostname`.bonnie
$ chmod +x ./bon_csv2html
$ cat `hostname`.bonnie | grep "," | ./bon_csv2html > `hostname`.htm
```

You'll want to do this on the disk you want to test, or to run the bonnie++ program from where you compiled it while in a directory on the test disk. Note that the program won't run as root. You'll need to make the directory you're running it in owned by a regular user and then log in as that user before running it.

The preceding example runs the program with two command-line options you will likely want to always use:

- n 0: Skip file creation test
- -f: Fast mode, skip per-character I/O tests

Neither of those tests are very informative nowadays. What you really want are the sequential block read and write numbers, as well as the seeks result.

You'll have two files come out of this. If you use the suggested file naming convention shown in the example, a full set of results will be in a file named after your hostname with the extension .bonnie. Without the fast mode enabled, it looks like the following (one run exactly as above will have less information), again from our sample laptop disk:

```
Version 1.03e ------Sequential Output------ --Sequential Input- -Random-
                -Char- -Block-  -Rewrite- -Char-   -Block-  -Seeks-
Machine Size K/s %CP K/s %CP K/s %CP K/s %CP K/s %CP /s %CP
meddle    4G 44754 96 58386 24 30439 12 52637 97 71059 19 232.8 0
```

The CREATE tests were deleted from the preceding output to save some space, and reformatted a bit to fit better into the width of the page here. The results will also be summarized in a list of comma-separated values that look like the following:

```
meddle,4G,44754,96,58386,24,30439,12,52637,97,71059,19,232.8,0,16,11349,36,
+++++,+++,+++++,+++,+++++,+++,+++++,+++,+++++,+++
```

The values showing up with + characters are tests that didn't produce useful output. This comma-delimited part can be sent through a program named bon_csv2html to produce a HTML formatted version of the results, which is much easier to read. In the preceding full example, that gets redirected to a file named after your host with the extension .htm.

If you did happen to compute just by running the program with its default parameters, you will want to ignore the per-character and create results, and look at the block output/input ones instead.

The random seeks number reported by Bonnie++ is not a simple read-only seek test. Here's its actual description from the manual:

"The test runs SeekProcCount processes (default 3) in parallel, doing a total of 8000 random seek reads to locations in the file. In 10% of cases, the block read is changed and written back."

This actually makes it a mixed read/write test, which is really more useful for something like a database simulation anyway. Note that the duration of this test 8000 seeks is short enough that powerful systems nowadays with large caches can easily give inflated results here, at intermittent times. You might see 500 seeks/second on one run, followed by 2000/second on the next. It's important to confirm the seek figure using additional tools that run longer.

Bonnie++ 2.0

The preceding results were generated with Bonnie++ 1.03e, the most recent version from the stable release series at this point. If you have a terabyte or larger drive, you'll need 1.03e at a minimum to get useful results; the earlier 1.0 releases don't handle that right. And currently, development is nearly complete on an updated Bonnie++ 2.0. There are already plenty of systems where the V1 Bonnie++ results aren't very useful. Ideally, you'd default to trying the snapshots of the experimental V2 releases (currently at 1.96 and 1.97.3) and only fall back to the 1.0 series if that doesn't work for you, but, as described in the next section, that may not always be practical. I normally end up needing to use both.

Here's a command line that works with version 1.97 and provides a faster and more accurate test than the earlier versions:

```
bonnie++ -f -n 0 -c 4
```

In addition to the flags described in the previous version, this turns on the following new option: concurrency, which uses four processes at once.

Tests here suggest very high values for concurrency fail to deliver any incremental improvement, but going from one up to two, three, or four can improve results in a multi-core system.

Bonnie++ ZCAV

Just like HD Tune, Bonnie++ has a utility, a separate binary named ZCAV, that will track transfer rate across the disk. It produces a simple text file you can save to a file:

```
./zcav -f/dev/sda > sda.zcav
```

You will probably need to run this program as root as it accesses the whole drive. You can convert the program's output to a graph using the gnuplot software.

 Unfortunately, results from ZCAV on the experimental branch using version 1.96 haven't been usable in my own tests. I find myself needing to drop back to the 1.03e version for ZCAV to work properly. Hopefully this gets sorted out before the official version 2.0 is released.

There are some examples of ZCAV results on the Bonnie++ site; here's the output showing performance on the sample laptop used for all the examples so far:

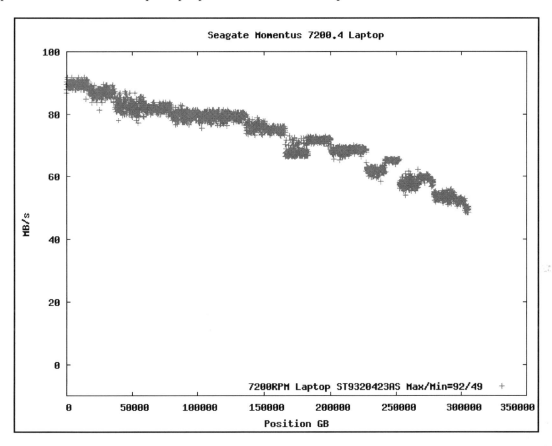

And this is the script that produced it:

```
unset autoscale x
set autoscale xmax
unset autoscale y
set autoscale ymax
set xlabel "Position GB"
set ylabel "Mbps"
set key right bottom
set title "Seagate Momentus 7200.4 Laptop"
set terminal png
set output "laptop-zcav.png"
plot "laptop.zcav" title "7200RPM Laptop ST9320423AS Max/Min=92/49"
```

The ZCAV software didn't produce any of the max/min data or titles shown on that graph; those were all manually edited to make a nicer graph after extracting the values from the raw text file. This is an example of how the Linux tools can give the same quality of basic results as something like Windows, but you have to put a bit more work into it.

There is one positive aspect to this extra work: the bottleneck on the early part of the disk seen on the Windows results isn't there. Performance peaks at 92 Mbps and falls slowly and steadily through all the transfer zones on the disk in the classic ZCAV pattern. Now that you see exactly what this sort of graph is supposed to look like, if you revisit the HD Tune once again, it should be obvious why I immediately suspected a problem when seeing it—the shape just wasn't right. This is exactly the same system, just booted into Ubuntu Linux instead of Windows Vista. That strongly suggests that whatever was limiting the Windows transfer rate to 78 Mbps, and therefore flattening the left side of the graph, was just some sort of Vista software problem.

This particular issue, noticing that something might be wrong with the disk configuration just because it didn't look right compared to similar hardware seen in the past, is exactly why it's worthwhile even for database administrators to become familiar with hardware benchmarking basics. A more serious problem of this type could easily throttle database performance, and without knowing it's the hardware to blame, much time could be wasted attacking that problem from the database side.

sysbench

While initially targeted as a MySQL tool, the `sysbench` program is also valuable for testing low-level aspects of performance that impact databases, ones that apply equally well to PostgreSQL. It even supports running read-only tests against PostgreSQL databases too, a feature not demonstrated here. Its use in this chapter is just for its low-level hardware tests.

 These specific `sysbench` tests should be considered secondary to the ones already shown. If you have confirmed that the sequential read, write, and seek speeds are good with Bonnie++, and know commit rates are good from doing `INSERT` tests with PostgreSQL, you really don't need this data too. It's mainly useful as an alternate way to do more thorough and specific seek and commit rate tests, and is not recommended as your primary testing tool.

Here's an example of downloading and compiling without support for any database, the only way it will be used here:

```
$ wget
http://sourceforge.net/projects/sysbench/files/sysbench/0.4.10/sysbench-0.4
.10.tar.gz/download
$ tar xvfz sysbench-0.4.10.tar.gz
$ cd sysbench-0.4.10/
$ ./configure --without-mysql
$ make
$ sysbench/sysbench --test=cpu run
```

This shows an example of running the simplest test available, the one for CPU speed. The results that test gives are not very useful for comparing modern processors, but it does confirm the program is working quickly.

> The choice of 0.4.10 instead of the latest version available right now (0.4.12) is deliberate. Changes made since 0.4.10 have introduced compilation issues on several platforms, and the software isn't very well maintained in that regard. You may discover that it takes more work on the steps that build for your system than shown here.

Once you've compiled the program, you don't even need to install it onto your system. It will run fine from a local build in your home directory.

pgbench

pgbench is a simple program for running benchmark tests on PostgreSQL. It runs the same sequence of SQL commands over and over, possibly in multiple concurrent database sessions, and then calculates the average transaction rate (transactions per second). By default, pgbench tests a scenario that is loosely based on TPC-B, involving five SELECT, UPDATE, and INSERT commands per transaction. However, it is easy to test other cases by writing your own transaction script files.

By default, pgbench will create the tables:

- pgbench_history
- pgbench_tellers
- pgbench_accounts
- pgbench_branches

with the number of rows shown as follows:

```
$ /pgbench -U postgres -i testdb
NOTICE:  table "pgbench_history" does not exist, skipping
NOTICE:  table "pgbench_tellers" does not exist, skipping
NOTICE:  table "pgbench_accounts" does not exist, skipping
NOTICE:  table "pgbench_branches" does not exist, skipping
creating tables...
100000 of 100000 tuples (100%) done (elapsed 2.71 s, remaining 0.00 s)
vacuum...
set primary keys...
done.

testdb=# select count(*) from pgbench_accounts ;
 count
--------
 100000
(1 row)
```

If you want to increase this default value, you have to execute:

```
pgbench -U postgres -i testdb -s 5
creating tables...
100000 of 500000 tuples (20%) done (elapsed 2.56 s, remaining 10.23 s)
200000 of 500000 tuples (40%) done (elapsed 5.48 s, remaining 8.23 s)
300000 of 500000 tuples (60%) done (elapsed 8.28 s, remaining 5.52 s)
400000 of 500000 tuples (80%) done (elapsed 11.18 s, remaining 2.80 s)
500000 of 500000 tuples (100%) done (elapsed 14.16 s, remaining 0.00 s)
vacuum...
set primary keys...
done.
```

This will create *10000*5* rows, as shown next:

```
testdb=# select count(*) from pgbench_accounts ;
 count
--------
 500000
(1 row)
```

This is the startup point:

```
$ pgbench -U postgres -c 10 -j 2 -t 100 testdb
starting vacuum...end.
transaction type: <builtin: TPC-B (sort of)>
scaling factor: 5
query mode: simple
number of clients: 10
```

```
number of threads: 2
number of transactions per client: 100
number of transactions actually processed: 1000/1000
latency average = 245.346 ms
tps = 40.758688 (including connections establishing)
tps = 40.829789 (excluding connections establishing)
```

In this scenario, it seems that our startup point is 40.758688 database transactions per second.

Seek rate

Unlike the rest of the tests sysbench is used for in this chapter, the seek rate test requires a three-step process where test files are created, the test is run, and then those files are cleaned up. You also have options for how many threads to keep active, how large the file should be, and what read/write mode to use. The following script shows how to run a seek test with the most commonly changed portions as environment variables:

```
#!/bin/sh
PREFIX="$HOME/sysbench-0.4.10"
THREADS=1
GBSIZE=4
MODE=rndrd
$PREFIX/sysbench/sysbench --test=fileio --num-threads=$THREADS --file-
num=$GBSIZE --file-total-size=${GBSIZE}G --file-block-size=8K --file-test-
mode=rndrd --file-fsync-freq=0 --file-fsync-end=no prepare
$PREFIX/sysbench/sysbench --test=fileio --num-threads=$THREADS --file-
num=$GBSIZE --file-total-size=${GBSIZE}G --file-block-size=8K --file-test-
mode=rndrd --file-fsync-freq=0 --file-fsync-end=no run --max-time=60
$PREFIX/sysbench/sysbench --test=fileio --num-threads=$THREADS --file-
num=$GBSIZE --file-total-size=${GBSIZE}G --file-block-size=8K --file-test-
mode=rndrd --file-fsync-freq=0 --file-fsync-end=no cleanup
```

Removing test files

Unlike the Bonnie++ seek test, which aimed at just twice your total RAM by default, you can easily make this test span a large portion of the disk instead. Any seek results should always include what portion of the disk the seeking took place over. To get useful results from larger disks, you might want to use hundreds of GB worth of data on this test, instead of just the *2 * RAM* that Bonnie++ uses for its seek testing.

fsync commit rate

It's possible to use `sysbench` to measure how fast commits can be flushed to disk, using the standard `fsync` call just like the database defaults to. Note that in this case, the file size being used is `16384` bytes, even though PostgreSQL block writes are 8192 bytes. The version tested here didn't work correctly with the block size reduced that far, and as the actual amount of bytes doesn't impact the commit rate until it becomes much larger anyway, that's not worth worrying about. The following is a Linux-specific script that includes disabling, and then re-enabling, the drive's write cache, but the basic `sysbench` call can be used on any platform the program runs on:

```
#!/bin/sh
DRIVE="/dev/sda"
PREFIX="$HOME/sysbench-0.4.10"
# Disable write cache
hdparm -W 0 $DRIVE
echo fsync with write cache disabled, look for "Requests/sec"
$PREFIX/sysbench/sysbench --test=fileio --file-fsync-freq=1 --file-num=1 --
file-total-size=16384 --file-test-mode=rndwr run
# Enable write cache (returning it to the usual default)
hdparm -W 1 $DRIVE
echo fsync with write cache enabled, look for "Requests/sec"
$PREFIX/sysbench/sysbench --test=fileio --file-fsync-freq=1 --file-num=1 --
file-total-size=16384 --file-test-mode=rndwr run
```

On a standard 7,200 RPM drive, spinning 120 times per second, and therefore limited to that as its maximum commit rate, the version with the write cache disabled would look like this:

```
104.81 Requests/sec executed
```

The cached version, meanwhile, will likely show thousands of commits per second.

Complicated disk benchmarks

There are many more complicated disk benchmark programs available:

- **IOzone**: `http://www.iozone.org/` allows testing for all sorts of disk scenarios.
- **Fio**: `http://freshmeat.net/projects/fio/` lets you completely script exactly what benchmark scenario you want to run. Many samples are available at `http://wiki.postgresql.org/wiki/HP_ProLiant_DL380_G5_Tuning_Guide`.
- **pgiosim**: `http://pgfoundry.org/projects/pgiosim/` simulates very specific types of PostgreSQL workloads.

There are a few issues that make all of these less useful than the tools covered here. The first is that these are complicated tools to set up and interpret the results of. Correspondingly, when you do find a problem, if it involves a hardware vendor issue, there's no way they will trust or attempt to replicate the things discovered via these tests. dd, Bonnie++, and HD Tune on their respective platforms are known to be simple, reliable, and easy to interpret tools. If you can show your vendor a problem using one of those tools, there's little they can do to wiggle out of that. Even sysbench is a bit more complicated than you'd want to rely on in a vendor dispute. Simplicity and transparency with your vendor is much more important for doing basic database performance testing than being able to test more complicated scenarios.

And really, if your goal is eventually to tune a database application, tuning exercises should primarily be done at that level anyway. Once you're sure the basic hardware works as expected, move right on to database-level tests and see if tuning changes have any impact. That's much more likely to find out the real issues that do and don't matter than these complicated synthetic disk benchmarks.

Sample disk results

Here's a summary of what was measured for the laptop drive tested in detail previously, as well as a desktop drive both alone and in a RAID array as a second useful data point:

Disks	Seq read	Seq write	Bonnie++ seeks	sysbench seeks	Commits per sec
Seagate 320GB 7200.4 laptop	71	58	232 @ 4GB	194 @ 4GB	105 or 1048
WD160GB 7200RPM	59	54	177 @ 16GB	56 @ 100GB	10212
3X WD160GB RAID 0	125	119	371 @ 16GB	60 @ 100GB	10855

Note how all the seek-related information is reported here relative to the size of the area being used to seek over. This is a good habit to adopt. Also note that in the laptop rate, two commit rates are reported. The lower value is without the write cache enabled (just under the rotation rate of 120 rotations/second), while the higher one has it turned on, and is therefore providing an unsafe, volatile write cache.

The other two samples use an Areca ARC-1210 controller with a 256 MB battery-backed write cache, which is why the commit rate is so high, yet still safe. The hard drive shown is a 7200 RPM 160 GB Western Digital SATA drive, model WD1600AAJS, remember that a battery-backed cache helps ameliorate the cost of disk write, especially in terms of block sizes and frequency. The last configuration there includes three of that drive in a Linux Software RAID 0 stripe. Ideally, this would provide 3X as much performance as a single drive. It might not look like this is quite the case from the read/write results: those represent closer to a 2.1X speedup. But this is deceiving, and once again it results from ZCAV issues.

Using the tool to plot speeds on both the single drive and RAID 0 configurations, you get the following curves:

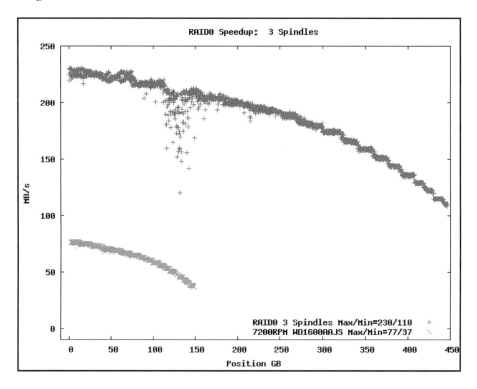

The figures derived from the raw data max and min transfer speed numbers are almost exactly tripled, as follows:

- *3 X 37=111 MB* theoretical min; actual is 110 MB
- *3 X 77=231 MB* theoretical max; actual is 230 MB

That's perfect scaling, exactly what you'd hope to see when adding more disks to a RAID array. This wasn't clearly doing the right thing when only looking at average performance, probably because the files created were not on exactly the same portion of the disk to get a fair comparison. The reason why ZCAV issues have been highlighted so many times in this chapter is because they pop up so often when you attempt to do fair comparison benchmarks of disks.

Disk performance expectations

So what are the reasonable expectations for how your disks should perform? The last example shown demonstrates how things should work. Any good drive nowadays should have sequential transfers of well over 50 Mbps on its fastest area, with 100 Mbps being easy to find. The slowest part of the drive will be closer to half that speed. It's good practice to try and test an individual drive before building more complicated arrays using them. If a single drive is slow, you can be sure an array of them will be bad too.

The tricky part of estimating how fast your system should be is when you put multiple drives into an array.

For multiple disks in a RAID 1 array, the sequential read and write speed will not increase. However, a good controller or software RAID implementation will use both drives at once for seeking purposes, which might as much as double measurements of that rate.

When multiple drives are added to a RAID 0 array, you should get something close to linear scaling of the speeds, as shown in the previous section. Two 50 Mbps drives in RAID 0 should be at least close to 100 Mbps. It won't be perfect in most cases, but it should be considerably faster than a single drive.

Combinations like RAID 10 should scale up sequential reads and writes based on the number of drive pairs in RAID 0 form, while also getting some seek improvement from the RAID 1 mirroring. This combination is one reason it's preferred for so many database disk layouts.

If you're using RAID 5 instead, which isn't recommended for most databases, read speeds will scale with the number of drives you use, while write speeds won't increase.

Sources of slow disk and array performance

Most of the time, if you meet expectations for sequential read and write speeds, your disk subsystem is doing well. You can measure seek time, but there's little you can do to alter it besides add more disks. It's more a function of the underlying individual physical drives than something you can do anything about. Most problems you'll run into with slow disks will show up as slow read or write speeds.

Poor quality drivers for your controller can be a major source of slow performance. Usually, you'll need to connect the same drives to another controller to figure out when this is the case. For example, if you have a SATA drive that's really slow when connected to a RAID controller, but the same drive is fast connected directly to the motherboard, bad drivers are a prime suspect.

One problem that can significantly slow down read performance in particular is not using sufficient read-ahead for your drives. This normally manifests itself as writes being faster than reads, because the drive ends up being idle too often while waiting for the next read request to come in. This subject is discussed more in `Chapter 4`, *Disk Setup*.

Conversely, if writes are very slow relative to reads, check the write caching policy and size of your controller if you have one. Some will prefer to allocate their cache for reading instead of writing, which is normally the wrong decision for a database system. Reads should be cached by your OS and the database; it's rare they will ask the controller for the same block more than once, but it's quite likely your OS will overflow the write cache on a controller by writing heavily to it.

RAID controller hardware itself can also be a bottleneck. This is most often the case when you have a large number of drives connected, with the threshold for what large means dependent on the speed of the controller. Normally, to sort this out, you'll have to reduce the size of the array temporarily and see if the speed drops. If it's the same even with a smaller number of drives, you may be running into a controller bottleneck.

The connection between your disks and the rest of the system can easily become a bottleneck. This is most common with external storage arrays. While it might sound good that you have a gigabit link to a networked array over Ethernet, a fairly common NAS configuration, if you do the math, that's at most 125 Mbps, barely enough to keep up with two drives, and possible to exceed with just one. No way will that be enough for a large storage array. Even Fiber Channel arrays can run into their speed limits and become a bottleneck for high sequential read speeds if you put enough disks into them. Make sure you do a sanity check on how fast your drive interconnect is relative to the speed you're seeing.

It's also possible for a disk bottleneck to actually be somewhere on the CPU or memory side of things. Sometimes, disk controllers can use quite a bit of the total system bus bandwidth. This isn't as much of a problem for modern PCI Express controller cards that use the higher transfer rates available, but you do need to make sure the card is placed in a slot and configured so it's taking advantage of those. Monitoring overall system performance while running the test can help note when this sort of problem is happening; it will sometimes manifest as an excessive amount of CPU time being used during disk testing.

Poor or excessive mapping of your physical disk to how the OS sees them can also slow down results by more than you might expect. For example, passing through Linux's **Logical Volume Manager** (**LVM**) layer can cause a 10-20% speed loss compared to just using a simple partition instead. Other logical volume abstractions, either in hardware or software, can lower your performance too.

One performance aspect that is overrated by storage vendors in particular is aligning filesystem blocks with those of blocks on physical storage, or with the stripes of some RAID array configurations. While, theoretically, such a misalignment can turn a single physical block write into two when blocks straddle a stripe boundary, you'll really need to have quite a system before this is going to turn into your biggest problem. For example, when doing random database writes, once the disk has done a seek to somewhere, it makes little difference whether it writes one or two blocks once it arrives. By far the biggest overhead was the travel to the write location, not the time spent writing once it got there. And since it's easy to have your bottlenecks actually show up at the block level in the OS or controller, where strip splits aren't even noticed, that makes this problem even less likely to come up. Alignment is something worth investigating if you're trying to get good performance out of RAID 5, which is particularly sensitive to this problem. But for most systems using the better performing RAID levels, trying to tune here is more trouble than it's worth. Don't be surprised if a storage vendor, particular one defending an underperforming SAN, tries to blame the performance issues on this area though. You'll likely have to humor them by doing the alignment just to rule that out, but don't expect that to change your database performance very much.

The length of this list should give you an idea of why doing your own testing is so important. It should strike you that there are a whole lot of points where a disk configuration can go wrong in a way that slows performance down. Even the most competent vendor or system administrator can easily make a mistake in any one of these spots that cripples your system's disk speed, and correspondingly how fast the database running it will get work done. Would you believe that even excessive vibration is enough to considerably slow down a drive nowadays? It's true!

Summary

Doing your own hardware benchmarking serves two complementary purposes. Knowing how fast your current systems are relative to one another, and being able to evaluate a candidate new server via the same measurements, are extremely valuable for helping nail down where the bottlenecks in your hardware are located.

Second, the difference between reality and your hardware vendor's claims or reputation can be quite large. It is not safe to assume that your system is fast because you bought it from a reputable vendor. You should not assume a SAN is properly configured when delivered simply because it's a very expensive item and you were told it's already optimized for you. Systems are complicated, odd hardware interactions are inevitable, and not everyone involved in sales is going to be completely honest with you.

At the same time, you don't need to be a benchmarking expert to do useful hardware validation tests. It's actually counterproductive to run really complicated tests. If they don't give expected results, it will be hard to get your vendor to acknowledge the result and replicate the issue where it can be resolved. It's better to stick with the simplest possible, industry-standard tests for benchmarking, rather than attempt to do really complicated ones. If it takes a complicated test requiring hours of custom application setup to show a performance problem, the odds your vendor is going to help resolve that issue are low. Much more likely, your application will be blamed.

If, on the other hand, you can easily replicate the problem using the UNIX standard command in a few minutes, it's difficult to refute that the lowest levels of hardware/software are to blame.

Finally, doing some heavy benchmarking work when a new server arrives will do one additional thing: put some early stress on the hardware while it's still new. It's always better to deploy a system that's already gotten a workout to prove itself.

Always run your own basic hardware benchmarks on any system you intend to put a database on. Simpler tests your vendor can replicate if you run into a problem are better than complicated ones.

Memtest86+, STREAM, sysbench, HD Tune, dd, and Bonnie++ are all useful tools for measuring various aspects of system performance. Disk drive testing needs to be very sensitive of how disk speed changes over the surface of the drive. IOPS is a common way to measure disk and disk array performance, but it's not very well matched to the requirements of database applications.

Speeds on a seek-heavy workload can be much slower than you might expect based on a disk's sequential read/write performance. The commit rate needs to be measured to confirm that the caching levels you believe to be are active really, since that impacts database reliability. Complicated tests are better done using benchmarks of real database applications, rather than focusing on synthetic disk tests.

After selecting suitable hardware and benchmarking the hardware, the next task is to select the OS and the filesystem for the database. The scope of the next chapter is to discuss the different kinds of filesystems, as well as the pros and cons of that filesystem. Disk setup and configuration are also part of the next chapter.

4
Disk Setup

Most **operating systems (OSes)** include multiple options for the filesystem used to store information onto the disk. Choosing between these options can be difficult, because it normally involves some tricky speed versus reliability trade-offs. Similarly, how to set up your database to spread its components across many available disks also has trade-offs, with speed, reliability, and available disk space all linked. PostgreSQL has some features to split its database information over multiple disks, but the optimal way to do that is very much application dependent.

In this chapter, we will go through the following topics:

- Maximum filesystem sizes
- Filesystem crash recovery
- Linux filesystems
- Solaris and FreeBSD filesystems
- Disk layout for PostgreSQL

Maximum filesystem sizes

One of the topics discussed for each filesystem is how large a volume can you put on it. For most of them, that number is 16 TB, a shared artifact of using 32-bit numbers to represent filesystem information. Right now, it's quite easy to exceed 16 TB in a volume created with a moderately sized array of 1 TB or larger hard drives. This makes this number an increasingly problematic limit.

There are three levels of issue you can run into here:

- The data structures of the filesystem itself don't support large volumes
- Tools used to create and manipulate the filesystem do not handle large sizes
- The disk partitioning scheme needed to boot the **operating system (OS)** doesn't handle large volumes

The last of those is worth spending a moment on, since that problem is mostly independent of the filesystem-specific details of the first two.

Most PC hardware on the market, with the notable exception of Apple Intel macOS X systems, partition drives using the **Master Boot Record** (**MBR**) partitioning scheme. This only supports partition sizes up to 2 TB in size (`https://en.wikipedia.org/wiki/Master_boot_record`). Creating a larger partition that you can boot from will require a different partitioning scheme. One possibility is the **GUID Partition Table** (**GPT**) scheme, promoted by Intel as a part of their **Extensible Firmware Interface** (**EFI**) standard intended to replace the old PC BIOS booting methods. Apple is so far the main early adopter of EFI and GPT. See `http://en.wikipedia.org/wiki/GUID_Partition_Table` for more information about GPT partitions, their support in various OSes, and the backward compatibility possibilities available.

This area is not very well explored or supported yet. Proceed with caution if you expect to need greater than 2 TB volumes on PC hardware, even if your chosen filesystem obviously supports it. At a minimum, expect that you may need to have a smaller OS disk that you boot off, only using GPT partitioning on the data disks mounted after the OS has started.

Filesystem crash recovery

Filesystem writes have two major components to them. At the bottom level, you are writing out blocks of data to the disk. In addition, there is some amount of filesystem metadata involved too. Examples of metadata include the directory tree, the list of blocks and attributes associated with each file, and the list of what blocks on disk are free.

Like many disk-oriented activities, filesystems have a very clear performance versus reliability trade-off they need to make. The usual reliability concern is what happens in the situation where you're writing changes to a file and the power goes out in the middle.

Consider the case where you're writing out a new block to a file, one that makes the file bigger (rather than overwriting an existing block). You might do that in the following order:

1. Write data block
2. Write file metadata referencing use of that block
3. Add data block to the list of used space metadata

What happens if power goes out between steps 2 and 3 here? You now have a block that is used for something, but the filesystem believes it's still free. The next process that allocates a block for something is going to get that block, and now two files would refer to it. That's an example of a bad order of operations that no sensible filesystem design would use. Instead, a good filesystem design would:

1. Add data block to the list of used space metadata
2. Write data block
3. Write file metadata referencing use of that block

If there was a crash between steps 1 and 2 here, it's possible to identify the blocks that were marked as used, but not actually written to use fully yet. Simple filesystem designs do that by iterating over all the disk blocks allocated, reconciling the list of blocks that should be used or free against what's actually used. Examples of this include the `fsck` program used to validate simple UNIX filesystems and the `chkdsk` program used on FAT32 and **New Technology File System** (**NTFS**) volumes under Windows.

Journaling filesystems

The more modern approach is to use what's called a journal to improve this situation. A fully journaled write would look like this:

- Write transaction start metadata to the journal
- Write used space metadata change to the journal
- Write data block change to the journal
- Write file metadata change to the journal
- Add data block to the list of used space metadata
- Write data block
- Write file metadata referencing use of that block
- Write transaction end metadata to the journal

What this gets you is the ability to recover from any sort of crash the filesystem might encounter. If you didn't reach the final step here for a given write transaction, the filesystem can just either ignore (data block write) or undo (metadata write) any partially completed work that's part of that transaction. This lets you avoid long filesystem consistency checks after a crash, because you'll just need to replay any open journal entries to fix all the filesystem metadata. The time needed to do this is proportional to the size of the journal, rather than the old filesystem checking routines whose runtime is proportional to the size of the volume.

The first thing that should jump out at you here is that you're writing everything twice, plus the additional transaction metadata, and therefore more than double the total writes per update in this situation.

The second thing to note is more subtle. Journaling in the filesystem is nearly identical to how WAL works to protect database writes in PostgreSQL. So if you're using journaling for the database, you're paying this overhead twice. Writes to the WAL, itself a journal, are journaled, and then writes to the disk are journaled too.

Since the overhead of full journaling is so high, few filesystems use it. Instead, the common situation is that only metadata writes are journaled, not the data block changes. This meshes well with PostgreSQL, where the database protects against data block issues, but not against filesystem metadata issues.

Linux filesystems

Linux is a particularly good example to start with for discussing filesystem implementation trade-offs, because it provides all of the common options among its many available filesystems.

ext2

The oldest Linux filesystem still viable for use now, ext2, does not have any journaling available. Therefore, any system that uses it is vulnerable to long recovery times after a crash, which makes it unsuitable for many purposes. You should not put a database volume on ext2. While that might work theoretically, there are many known situations, such as any user error made during the quite complicated `fsck` process, which can break the write ordering guarantees expected by the database.

Rather than presuming that you need to start with ext2, a sensible approach is to start with standard ext3, switch to write back ext3 if the WAL disk is not keeping up with its load, and only if that, too, continues to lag behind consider dropping to ext2. Since the WAL writes are sequential, while ones to the database are often random, it's much harder than you might think to have the WAL be a bottleneck on your system, presuming you've first put it into its own disk(s). Therefore, using ext2 without proving it is necessary falls into the category of premature optimization—there is a downside and you should only expose yourself to it when needed. Only if the WAL is a measured bottleneck should you consider the faster but riskier ext2.

ext3

ext3 adds a journal kept in a regular file on top of the ext2 filesystem. If the journal is empty (which will be the case on a clean server shutdown), you can even open an ext3 filesystem in ext2 mode. It's backward compatible with ext2, and it's possible to convert a volume in either direction: ext2 to ext3, or ext3 to ext2.

There are three levels of journaling available in ext3, specified as options when mounting the filesystem:

- `data=writeback`: Data changes are not journaled at all. Metadata changes are journaled, but the order in which they are written relative to the data blocks is not guaranteed. After a crash, files can have extra junk at their end from partially completed writes, and you might have a mix of old and new file data.
- `data=ordered`: Metadata is journaled, but data changes are not. However, in all cases, the metadata writes only occur after the associated data has already been written, thus the name `ordered` name. After a crash, it is possible to get a mix of old and new data in the file, as in the writeback mode, but you'll never end up with a file of incorrect length. The main differences in the behavior here compared to fully journaled writes are when you're changing blocks already on disk, when there is a data change but no associated metadata change. In cases where the file is new or the block being written is at the end, expanding the size of the file, the behavior of ordered mode is functionally equivalent to journal.
- `data=journal`: Both file data and filesystem metadata are written to the journal before the main filesystem is touched.

Choosing between these three isn't as easy as it might appear at first. You might think that writeback mode is the fastest mode here in all cases. That's true, but on systems with a functional write cache in particular, the difference between it and ordered is likely to be quite tiny. There is little reason to prefer writeback from a performance perspective when your underlying disk hardware is good, which makes the exposure to risk even less acceptable. Amusingly, the usual situation in which the writeback mode is said to be safe for PostgreSQL use is one where the underlying writes involve a battery-backed write cache, but that's exactly the situation under which the penalty of ordered mode is the least expensive.

In short, there are very few reasons to ever use writeback for your main database. The main weakness of writeback mode is that files can sometimes be extended with garbage bytes; it is not an issue for the WAL files. Those are both extended to their full size before use and written to with checksumming that rejects incorrect data. Accordingly, writeback is an appropriate mode to consider for a filesystem that only holds WAL data. When pressed for speed improvements on WAL writes, writeback is preferred to using ext2 from an integrity point of view, because the minimal metadata journaling you will get in this mode will prevent long `fsck` recovery time after a crash.

For the database disks, the choices are ordered or journal. On simple benchmarks such as Bonnie++ (more on this in the XFS section), ordered will sometimes lose as much as half its throughput (relative to raw disk speed) because of the double writing that the journal introduces. However, that does not mean journal will be half as fast for your database writes! Like the WAL, the journal is written out to a contiguous portion of disk, making it mostly sequential writes, and the subsequent updates to the data blocks are then written later. It turns out that this behavior makes the journal model particularly well suited to the situation where there are concurrent reads mixed with writes, which is exactly the case with many database applications.

In short, journal should not be immediately discarded as an option just because it delivers poor results in synthetic workloads. If you can assemble a reasonable simulation of your application running, including realistic multi-user behavior, it's worth trying journal mode in addition to ordered. You shouldn't start there though, because in simpler workloads, ordered will be faster, and the additional integrity provided by journal mode is completely optional for a PostgreSQL database.

Note that switching to a different mode for your root filesystem isn't as easy as changing the mount options in the `/etc/fstab` file. Instead, you'll need to edit the bootloader (typically grub) configuration file and add the change as a kernel option like the following:

```
rootflags=data=journal
```

Because the root drive is mounted before, even the file is consulted.

One of the limitations of ext3 that is increasingly relevant with today's hard drive sizes is that on common Intel and AMD processors, an ext3 filesystem can only be 16 TB in size, and individual files are limited to 2 TB.

ext4

The evolutionary replacement for ext3, ext4 was announced as production quality as of Linux kernel 2.6.28. A variety of fixes involving delayed allocation were applied between that and version 2.6.30, but more importantly for PostgreSQL, some bugs involving `fsync` handling were not fully corrected until kernel 2.6.31.8/2.6.32.1. Kernel 2.6.32 is the first version that includes an ext4 version that should be considered for a production PostgreSQL database. This is the version that both RHEL 6 and Ubuntu 10.04 are using, in the first long-term release from each that includes ext4 support.

The 16 TB filesystem limit of ext3 theoretically does not exist for ext4, but as this is being written, the associated `mkfs` utility is still stuck at that limit. The *Ext4 Howto* article at `https://ext4.wiki.kernel.org/index.php/Ext4_Howto` is the definitive source for updates about progress in removing that limitation.

From the perspective of PostgreSQL, the main improvement of ext4 over ext3 is its better handling of write barriers and `fsync` operations. See the section about *Write barriers* in a while for more information.

XFS

Unlike ext3, XFS was designed by **Silicone Graphics, Inc (SGI)** for efficiently journaling from its beginning, rather than having journaling added onto an existing filesystem. As you might predict, the result is a bit faster than ext3, some of which is just from better efficiency in the journal implementation. However, part of this speed results from the fact that XFS only journals metadata, and it doesn't even have an option to try and order the data versus metadata writes. Accordingly, XFS is most like ext3's writeback mode. One critical difference is that in situations where garbage blocks may have been written to a file, the main concern with ext3 writeback, the journal playback in XFS will instead zero out these entries. Then, they are unlikely to be interpreted as real data by an application. This is sufficient to keep PostgreSQL from being confused if it tries to read them, as a zeroed block won't have the right header to look like either a WAL block or a database data block. Some consider this a major flaw of XFS in that it took what could have been a perfectly good copy of a block and erased it. The way PostgreSQL does its writes, such damage will be sorted out by the WAL sometimes. Just make sure you have the `full_page_writes` configuration parameter turned on.

How much faster is XFS? Running a simple test comparing ext3 in two of its modes versus XFS, it does quite a bit better. The following table shows some simple results, which are not indicative of the performance difference you'll see on general database applications. The results show the range appearing in three runs against a single SATA drive:

Filesystem	Sequential write (MB/s)	Sequential read (MB/s)
ext3 `data=ordered`	39-58	44-72
ext3 `data=journal`	25-30	49-67
XFS	68-72	72-77

It's clear that raw XFS performance has less variation than these two ext3 modes, and that its write performance is much faster. The writeback mode of ext3 wasn't included because it's not safe, due to its tendency to add non-zero garbage blocks to your files after a crash.

On systems with larger disk arrays, the delayed allocation feature of XFS, and its associated I/O scheduling, are aimed to provide larger writes that are likely better aligned with RAID stripe sizes. Combine delayed allocation with a generally more efficient design, and XFS's performance advantage over ext3 can really look compelling on huge volumes. To further improve performance on larger systems, there are several options available for adjusting XFS memory use for things such as the in-memory size of the metadata journal, as well as what its target pre-allocation size should be.

XFS has historically not been popular among Linux users or distributors. However, XFS easily handles files of over a million terabytes, making it the primary Linux solution currently available for files greater than 16 TB. This has resulted in XFS having a comeback of sorts in recent enterprise-oriented Linux distributions, where that file limit is one that administrators are increasingly likely to run into. RedHat's RHEL 5.4 release added preliminary XFS support specifically to address that need, and their RHEL 6 release treats it as a fully supported filesystem on par with ext3 and ext4.

Since it defaults to using write barriers (described in more detail later), XFS is also paranoid about drives with volatile write caches losing writes. To prevent that, it is aggressive in sending drive cache `flush` commands to the underlying disks. This is what you want for a PostgreSQL database running on XFS using regular hard drives that have their write cache turned on. However, if you have a non-volatile write cache, such as a battery-backed write controller, this cache flushing is wasteful. In that case, it's recommended to use the `nobarrier` option when mounting the XFS filesystem in order to disable its cache flushing.

Benchmarks

Here are some benchmarks from RedHat:

Filesystem	RHEL 3	RHEL 4	RHEL 5	RHEL 6	RHEL 7
ext2/3	1TiB (3.0) 2TiB (3.5+)	2TiB	2TiB	2TiB	2TiB
ext4	n/a	n/a	16TiB (5.6+)2	16TiB	16TiB
XFS 3	n/a	n/a	100TiB [8EiB]	100TiB [8EiB]	500TiB [8EiB]

Other Linux filesystems

There are a few other filesystem options for Linux that are not well explored for PostgreSQL; some recommendations are as follows:

- **JFS**: Performs similar to XFS but with less CPU usage. But it is considered less stable than the recommended choices here. It's also not as well supported by mainstream Linux distributors. It's hard to tell the ordering there—is it less stable merely because it's not a mainstream choice and gets less testing as a result, or are there fewer users because of the stability issues? Regardless, **journaled file system (JFS)** was never very popular, and it seems to be losing ground now.
- **ReiserFS**: After starting as the first journaling filesystem integrated into the Linux kernel, for some time, ReiserFS was the preferred filesystem for major Linux distribution SuSE. Since SuSE abandoned it in late 2006 for ext3, ReiserFS adoption has been shrinking steadily. At this moment, the current ReiserFSv3 is considered stable, but its replacement ReiserFSv4 has yet to even be merged with the mainline Linux kernel. The uncertain future of the filesystem limits interest in it considerably. This is unfortunate given that the transparent compression feature of ReiserFSv4 would be particularly valuable for some database workloads, such as data warehouses where large sequential scans are common.
- **Btrfs**: This Oracle sponsored filesystem is considered the future of Linux filesystems even by the primary author of ext4. At this point, the code development hasn't reached a stable release. In the future, when this does happen, this filesystem has some unique features that will make it a compelling option to consider for database use, such as its support for easy snapshots and checksums.

While each of these filesystems has some recognized use cases where they perform well compared to the other mainstream choices, none of these are considered compelling for database use in general, nor in PostgreSQL, due to the maturity issues at the time of writing. Btrfs in particular may change in that regard as, unlike the other two, it has a healthy development community working on it still.

Write barriers

Chapter 2, *Database Hardware*, already mentioned that most hard drives have volatile write caches in them, and this, for the WAL, can be a data integrity problem. The important requirement here is that when a file sync operation (fsync on UNIX) occurs, the filesystem must make sure all related data is written out to a non-volatile cache or disk itself. Filesystem journal metadata writes have a similar requirement. The writes for the metadata updates require that the journal updates are first written out to preserve proper ordering.

To support both of these situations, where something needs to be unconditionally written to the disk and to where an ordering is required, the Linux kernel implements what they call write barriers. The following is a quote from the kernel documentation on barriers:

All requests queued before a barrier request must be finished (made it to the physical medium) before the barrier request is started, and all requests queued after the barrier request must be started only after the barrier request is finished (again, made it to the physical medium).

This sounds comforting, because this requirement that data be on a physical medium matches what the database expects. If each database sync request turns into a write barrier, that's an acceptable way to implement what the database requires, presuming that write barriers work as advertised.

Drive support for barriers

In order to support barriers, the underlying disk device must support flushing its cache, and preferably a write-through mode as well.

SCSI/SAS drives allow writes (and reads) to specify **force unit access** (**FUA**), which directly accesses the disk media without using the cache—what's commonly called write-through. They also support a SYNCHRONIZE CACHE call that flushes the entire write cache out to disk.

Early IDE drives implemented a FLUSH CACHE call and were limited to 137 GB in size. The ATA 6 specification added support for larger drives at the same time it introduced the now mandatory FLUSH CACHE EXT call. That's the command you send to a drive that does what filesystems (and the database) want for write cache flushing currently. Any SATA drive in the market now will handle this call just fine; some IDE and the occasional rare early SATA drives available many years ago did not. Today, if you tell a drive to flush its cache out, you can expect it will do so reliably.

SATA drives that support **Native Command Queuing** (**NCQ**) also can handle FUA. Note that support for NCQ in Linux was added as part of the switch to the `libata` driver in kernel 2.6.19, but some distributions (such as Red Hat) have back ported this change to their version of the earlier kernels they ship. You can tell if you're using `libata` either by noting that your SATA drives are named starting with `sda`, or by running:

```
$ dmesg | greplibata
```

The exact system calls used will differ a bit, but the effective behavior is that any modern drive should support the cache flushing commands needed for the barriers to work. And Linux tests the drives out to confirm that this is the case before letting you enable barriers, so if they're on, they are expected to work.

Filesystem support for barriers

ext3 theoretically supports barriers when used with simple volumes. In practice, and for database purposes, they are not functional enough to help. The problem is that `fsync` calls are not correctly translated into write barrier in a form what will always flush the drive's cache. It's just not something built into ext3 in the right form, and if you are using Linux software RAID or the **Logical Volume Manager** (**LVM**) with ext3, barriers will not be available at all anyway.

What actually happens on ext3 when you execute `fsync` is that all buffered data on that filesystem gets flushed out in order to satisfy that call. You read that right cached data goes out every time `fsync` occurs. This is another reason why putting the WAL, which is constantly receiving `fsync` calls, onto its own volume is so valuable with ext3.

XFS does handle write barriers correctly, and they're turned on by default. When you execute a `fsync` call against a file on an XFS volume, it will just write out the data needed for that one file, rather than the excessive cache flushing that ext3 does. In fact, one of the reasons this filesystem has a bad reputation in some circles relates to how early it introduced this feature. It enabled barriers before either the drives available or the underlying device drivers always did the right thing to flush data out, which meant the barriers it relied upon for data integrity were not themselves reliable. This resulted in reports of XFS causing corruption, caused by bugs elsewhere in the software or hardware chain, but XFS was blamed for them.

ext4 also supports barriers, and they're turned on by default. And `fsync` calls are implemented properly as well. The end result is that you should be able to use ext4, leave drive caching on, and expect that database writes will be written out safely anyway. Amusingly, it was obvious that ext4 was finally doing the right thing in 2.6.32 because of the massive performance drop in PostgreSQL benchmarks. Suddenly, `pgbench` tests only committed a number of transactions per second that corresponded to the rotation speed of the underlying disks, rather than showing an inflated result from unsafe behavior.

General Linux filesystem tuning

Regardless of what filesystem you choose, there are some general Linux tuning operations that apply.

Read-ahead

The first parameter you should tune on any Linux installation is device read-ahead. When doing sequential reads that seem to be moving forward, this feature results in Linux asking for blocks from the disk ahead of the application requesting them.

This is the key to reaching full read performance from today's faster drives. The usual symptom of insufficient read-ahead is noting that write speed to a disk is faster than its read speed. The impact is not subtle; proper read-ahead can easily result in a 100% or larger increase in sequential read performance. It is the most effective filesystem adjustment to make on Linux if you want to
see benchmarks like the bonnie++ read speed jump upwards. This corresponds to a big increase in large sequential I/O operations in PostgreSQL too, including sequential scans of tables and bulk operations such as COPY imports.

You can check your current read-ahead using this command:

```
$ blockdev --getra /dev/sda
```

The default is 256 for regular drives, and may be larger for software RAID devices. The units here are normally 512 bytes, making the default value equal to 128 KB of read-ahead. The normal properly tuned range on current hardware normally works out to be 4096 to 16384, making the following change:

```
$ blockdev --setra 4096 /dev/sda
```

A reasonable starting point. If you run bonnie++ with a few read-ahead values, you should see the sequential read numbers increase as you tune upwards, eventually leveling off. Unfortunately, read-ahead needs to be set for each drive on your system. It's usually handled by putting a `blockdev` adjustment for each device in the `rc.local` boot script.

The Linux read-ahead implementation was developed with PostgreSQL as an initial target, and it's unlikely you will discover increased read-ahead detuning smaller reads as you might fear. The implementation is a bit smarter than that.

File access times

Each time you access a file in Linux, a file attribute called the file's last access time (**atime**) is updated. This overhead turns into a steady stream of writes when you're reading data, which is an unwelcome overhead when working with a database. You can disable this behavior by adding `noatime` to the volume mount options in `/etc/fstab`, as in this example:

```
/dev/sda1 / ext3noatime,errors=remount-ro 0 1
```

There are two additional levels of access time updates available in some Linux kernels: `nodiratime` and `relatime`, both of which turn off a subset of the `atime` updates. Both of these are redundant if you use the preferred `noatime`, which disables them all.

Read caching and swapping

Linux will try to use any extra RAM for caching the filesystem, and that's what PostgreSQL would like it to do. When the system runs low on RAM, the kernel has a decision to make. Rather than reducing the size of its buffer cache, the OS might instead swap inactive disk pages out. How often to consider this behavior is controlled by a tuneable named `swappiness`. You can check the current value on your system (probably 60) by looking at `/proc/sys/vm/swappiness` and the easiest way to make a permanent adjustment is to add a line to `/etc/sysctl.conf` like the following:

```
vm.swappiness=0
```

A value of 0 prefers shrinking the filesystem cache rather than using swap, which is the recommended behavior for getting predictable database performance. However, you might notice a small initial decrease in performance at high memory usage. The things that tend to be swapped out first are parts of the OS that are never used, and therefore never missed. So, evicting them for buffer cache space is the right move in that specific case. It's when you run so low on memory that more things start getting swapped out that the problems show up. As is often the case, optimizing for more predictable behavior (avoiding swap) might actually lower performance for some cases (items swapped weren't necessary). Tuning for how to act when the system runs out of memory is not an easy process.

This change should be considered as part of setting up any Linux PostgreSQL server. A good practice here is to bundle it in with increasing the shared memory parameters to support larger values of `shared_buffers`, which requires editing the same `sysctl` file.

Write cache sizing

On the write side of things, Linux handles writes to the disk using a daemon named `pdflush`. It will spawn a number of `pdflush` processes (between two and eight) to keep up with the amount of outstanding I/O. `pdflush` is not very aggressive about writes, under the theory that if you wait longer to write things out, you will optimize total throughput. When you're writing a large data set, both write combining and being able to sort writes across more data will lower average seeking.

The main driver for when things in the write cache are aggressively written out to disk are two tuneable kernel parameters, as follows:

- `/proc/sys/vm/dirty_background_ratio`: Maximum percentage of active RAM that can be filled with dirty pages before `pdflush` begins to write them.
- `/proc/sys/vm/dirty_ratio`: Maximum percentage of total memory that can be filled with dirty pages before processes are forced to write dirty buffers themselves during their time slice, instead of being allowed to do more writes. Note that all processes are blocked for writes when this happens, not just the one that filled the write buffers. This can cause what is perceived as an unfair behavior where one `write-hog` process can block all I/O on the system.

The default here depends on your kernel version. In early 2.6 kernels, `dirty_background_ratio=10` and `dirty_ratio=40`. This means that a full 10% of RAM can be dirty before `pdflush` really considers it important to work on clearing that backlog. When combined with ext3, where any `fsync` write will force the entire write cache out to disk, this is the recipe for a latency disaster on systems with large amounts of RAM. You can monitor just exactly how much memory is queued in this fashion by looking at `/proc/meminfo` and noting how large the value listed for dirty gets.

Recognizing these defaults were particularly bad, in Linux kernel 2.6.22, both values were lowered considerably. You can tune an older kernel to use the new defaults like this:

```
echo 10 > /proc/sys/vm/dirty_ratio
echo 5 > /proc/sys/vm/dirty_background_ratio
```

And that's a common recipe to add to the `/etc/rc.d/rc.local` file on RHEL4/5 server installs in particular. Otherwise, the write stalls that happen when `dirty_ratio` is exceeded can be brutal for system responsiveness. The effective lower limit here is to set `dirty_ratio` to 2 and `dirty_background_ratio` to 1, which is worth considering on systems with more than 8 GB of RAM. Note that changes here will detune average throughput for applications that expect large amounts of write caching. This trade-off, that maximum throughput only comes with an increase in worst-case latency, is very common.

I/O scheduler elevator

One of the more controversial tunable Linux performance features, in that there are no universally accepted guidelines available, is that of the I/O scheduler choice. The name elevator is used due to how they sort incoming requests. Consider a real elevator, currently at the first floor. Perhaps the first person in requests the ninth floor, then the next person the third. The elevator will not visit the floors in the order requested; it will visit the third floor first, then continue to the ninth. The scheduler elevator does read and write sorting to optimize in a similar fashion.

You can set the default `elevator` scheduler at kernel boot time. Here's an example from a RedHat Linux system, changing the default `elevator` to the `deadline` option:

```
kernel /vmlinuz-2.6.18-128.el5 ro root=/dev/sda1 elevator=deadline
```

The exact location of the file where you have a similar kernel boot line depends on your Linux distribution and which boot loader you use. There are too many possibilities to list them all here; instructions for your Linux distribution on how to install a custom kernel should point you the right way.

And, as of Linux kernel 2.6.10, you can adjust the scheduler for individual devices without rebooting:

```
$ echo cfq> /sys/block/sda/queue/scheduler
$ cat /sys/block/sda/queue/scheduler
noop anticipatory deadline [cfq]
```

The four `elevator` choices are:

- `elevator=cfq`: **Completely Fair Queuing (CFQ)** tries to divide available I/O bandwidth equally among all requests. This is the default for most Linux installations.
- `elevator=deadline`: Deadline aims to provide something like real-time behavior, where requests are balanced so no one starves due to waiting too long for a read or write.
- `elevator=noop`: The no operation scheduler doesn't do any complicated scheduling; it handles basic block merging and sorting before passing the request along to the underlying device.
- `elevator=as`: Anticipatory scheduling intentionally delays I/O requests in the hope of bundling more of them together in a batch.

People seem drawn to this area as one that will really impact the performance of their system, based on the descriptions. The reality is that these are being covered last because this is the least effective tunable mentioned in this section. Adjusting the I/O scheduler in most cases has a minimal impact on PostgreSQL performance. If you want to improve read performance, adjusting read-ahead is vastly more important. And if you want to tweak write performance, adjusting the dirty cache writeback behavior is the primary thing to consider (after tuning the database to reduce how much dirty data it generates in the first place).

There are a few cases where the I/O scheduler can be effective to tune. On systems with a lot of device read and write cache, such as some RAID controllers and many SANs, any kernel scheduling just gets in the way. The OS is sorting the data it knows about, but that's not considering what data is already sitting in the controller or SAN cache. The `noop` scheduler, which just pushes data quickly toward the hardware, can improve performance if your hardware has its own large cache to worry about.

On desktop systems with little I/O capacity, the anticipatory schedule can be helpful to make the most of the underlying disk(s) by better sorting read and write requests into batches. It's unlikely to be suitable for a typical database server.

The other two options, CFQ and deadline, are impossible to suggest specific use cases for. The reason for this is that the exact behavior depends on both the Linux kernel you're using and the associated workload. There are kernel versions where CFQ has terrible performance, and deadline is clearly better because of bugs in the CFQ implementation in that version. In other situations, deadline will add latency exactly the opposite of what people expect when the system has a high level of concurrency. And you're not going to be able to usefully compare them with any simple benchmark. The main differences between CFQ and deadline only show up when there are many concurrent read and write requests fighting for disk time. Which is optimal is completely dependent on that mix.

Anyone who tells you that either CFQ or deadline is always the right choice doesn't know what they're talking about. It's worth trying both when you have a reasonable simulation of your application running, to see if there is a gross difference due to something like a buggy kernel. Try to measure transaction latency, not just average throughput, to maximize your odds of making the correct choice here. One way to measure query latency is to just enable logging query times in the database configuration, perhaps using `log_min_duration_statement`, then analyzing the resulting log files. But if the difference is difficult to measure, don't be surprised. Without a compelling reason to choose otherwise, you should prefer CFQ, as it's the kernel default and therefore much more widely tested.

Solaris and FreeBSD filesystems

While not identical, the common BSD heritage of Solaris and FreeBSD have much in common in terms of their respective filesystems, and both implement the same basic ZFS code as their current, most advanced filesystem. Choosing between the older UFS options and ZFS involves the usual performance and reliability tradeoffs found in so many other disk related options. In general, ZFS is particularly good at handling very large databases, while UFS can perform better on smaller ones. The feature sets are different enough that this may not be the deciding factor for your installation though.

Solaris UFS

The original **Unix file system (UFS)** implementation, also called the **Berkley Fast File System** or UFS1, originated in BSD UNIX. It later appeared in several commercial UNIX variations, including Solaris. The current Solaris UFS adds two major features not found in the original UFS: support for larger files and filesystems (up to 16 TB) and logging.

Logging here is again similar to the WAL database and the journaling used in Linux, and, like Linux's ext3 journal mode, there are known situations where having logging on turns out to be a performance improvement for UFS, because it turns what would otherwise be random writes into a series of sequential ones to the log. Logging is turned on by default on current Solaris releases; in ones before Solaris 9 (04/04) U6, it had to be specifically enabled by adjusting filesystem options /etc/vfstab to include it:

```
/dev/dsk/c0t0d0s1 /dev/rdsk/c0t0d0s1 / ufs 1 yes logging
```

In current versions where it's on by default, it can be disabled (which is not recommended) by using the no_logging mount option.

UFS is not tuned very well out of the box for PostgreSQL use. One major issue is that it only tries to cache small files, which means it won't do what the database expects on the anticipated large database files. And the maximum amount of RAM used for caching is a tiny 12% on SPARC systems and only 64 MB on Intel/AMD x64 systems. Reads and writes are not done in particularly large blocks either, which can be a problem for some workloads.

The last of those is the most straightforward to fix. When executing physical I/O, requests are broken up into blocks no larger than the maxphys parameter. This also serves as a limiter on read-ahead, and is therefore quite important to adjust upward. Normal practice is to adjust this to match the maximum allowed by the typical device drivers, 1 MB. The klustsize works similar for reads and writes to swap:

```
$ set maxphys=1048576
$ set klustsize=1048576
```

The code that stops UFS from caching larger files in memory is named freebehind. For PostgreSQL, you want this turned off altogether by setting it to 0, rather than trying to tune its threshold. The total size of the UFS filesystem cache, called the segment map, is set differently based on whether you're using a SPARC or x64 Solaris version.

On SPARC Solaris systems:

```
$ set freebehind=0
$ set segmap_percent=60
```

This size (60% of total RAM) presumes you're setting shared_buffers to 25% of total RAM and have a dedicated database server, so 85% of RAM is available for effective database cache. You might want a smaller value on some systems.

On Intel/AMD x64 Solaris systems:

```
$ setufs:freebehind=0
$ set segmapsize=1073741824
```

This example sets the cache size to 1 GB. You'll need to adjust this fixed value on each server based on the amount of RAM in your server, rather than being able to use a percentage.

Solaris systems allow turning off access time tracking using `noatime` as a mounting option, similar to Linux. This is a useful small optimization to enable.

A final Solaris—specific option to consider with UFS relates to the WAL writes. Since the WAL isn't read from, except after a crash, any RAM used to cache it is wasted. The normal way to bypass that is to use UNIX direct I/O, which doesn't go through the filesystem cache. But that isn't fully implemented in PostgreSQL on Solaris. If you separate out the `pg_wal` directory into its own filesystem, you can mount that using the `forcedirection` option to get optimal behavior here. This will quietly convert all the WAL writes to direct I/O that bypasses the OS cache.

FreeBSD UFS2

The FreeBSD community improved basic UFS in its own way, into what it calls UFS2. This also expanded filesystem capacity to far beyond 2 TB, although there are still some user tools that may not support this yet; be sure to investigate that carefully before presuming you can host a large database on FreeBSD.

Instead, implement a journal (Linux) or logging (Solaris). FreeBSD's solution to filesystem integrity issues during a crash and resulting long filesystem recovery times is a technique called soft updates. This orders writes such that the only type of integrity issue after a crash is blocks marked as used but not actually claimed by any file. After an unclean shutdown, the filesystem can be brought up almost immediately. What's called a background `fsck` then runs against a static snapshot of the filesystem, searching for unclaimed blocks to clean them up. This removes the overhead of journaling, while avoiding the worst of the traditional, non-journaled filesystem issues, including long integrity check times, that hold up booting after a crash. While not as common as journaling, this technique has been in use on FreeBSD for ten years already without major issues.

Given that PostgreSQL layers its own integrity checks on top of what the filesystem implements, UFS2 certainly meets the requirements of the database. You just need to be aware that the `fsck` activity related to the crash recovery will be a background activity competing with database reads and writes, and that might happen during the worst time, just after the server has started, when all of its caches are empty.

Just like on Linux, proper read-ahead significantly improves sequential read speed on FreeBSD. The parameter is sized using the filesystem block size, which defaults to 8 KB. The common useful range for this parameter is `32` to `256`. Adjust the value by adding a line to `/etc/sysctl.conf` like the following:

```
vfs.read_max = 32
```

To make this active, execute:

```
$ /etc/rc.d/sysctl start
```

The size of the write cache is set by the `vfs.hirunningspace` parameter. The guidelines in the FreeBSD handbook suggest only increasing this to, at most, a small number of megabytes. You may want to increase this value to something larger if you are using a system with a battery-backed write controller, where the kernel can likely dump much larger amounts of writes onto disk in a batch without significant latency issues.

ZFS

Few filesystems have ever inspired the sort of zealous advocacy fans of ZFS regularly display. While it has its weak points, in many respects, ZFS is a reinvention of the filesystem concept with significant advantages. One thing that's different about ZFS is that it combines filesystem and RAID capabilities into an integrated pair. The RAID-Z implementation in ZFS is a worthwhile alternative to standard RAID 5 and RAID 6 installations.

ZFS defaults to working in records of 128 KB in size. This is much larger than a PostgreSQL block, which can cause a variety of inefficiencies if your system is regularly reading or writing only small portions of the database at a time (like many **online transaction processing** (OLTP) systems do). It's only really appropriate if you prefer to optimize your system for large operations. The default might be fine if you're running a data warehouse that is constantly scanning large chunks of tables. But standard practice for ZFS database installations that do more scattered random I/O is to reduce the ZFS record size to match the database one, which means 8 K for PostgreSQL:

```
$ zfs set recordsize=8Kzp1/data
```

You need to do this before creating any of the database files on the drive, because the record size is actually set per file. Note that this size will not be optimal for WAL writes, which may benefit from a larger record size like the default.

One important thing to know about ZFS is that unlike Solaris's UFS, which caches almost nothing by default, ZFS is known to consume just about all the memory available for its **adaptive replacement cache** (**ARC**). You'll need to reduce those amounts for use with PostgreSQL, where large blocks of RAM are expected to be allocated for the database buffer cache and things like working memory. The actual tuning details vary, based on the Solaris release, and are documented in the *Limiting the ARC Cache* section of the *ZFS Evil Tuning Guide* at
`http://www.solaris-cookbook.eu/solaris/solaris-10-zfs-evil-tuning-guide/`
or `http://www.serverfocus.org/zfs-evil-tuning-guide`.

For FreeBSD, refer to `https://wiki.freebsd.org/ZFSTuningGuide` for similar information. One of the scripts suggested there, `arc_summary.pl`, is a useful one in both its FreeBSD and Solaris incarnations, for determining just what's in the ARC cache and whether it's using its RAM effectively. This is a potentially valuable tuning feedback for PostgreSQL, where the OS cache is used quite heavily, but such use is not tracked for effectiveness by the database.

ZFS handles its journaling using a structure called the intent log. High performance systems with many disks commonly allocate a dedicated storage pool just to hold the ZFS intent log for the database disk, in the same way that the database WAL is commonly put on another drive. However, there's no need to have a dedicated intent log for the WAL disk too.

Similar to XFS, if you have a system with a non-volatile write cache such as a battery-backed write controller, the cache flushing done by ZFS will defeat some of the benefit of that cache. You can disable that behavior by adjusting the `zfs_nocacheflush` parameter; the following line in `/etc/system` will do that:

```
setzfs:zfs_nocacheflush = 1
```

And you can toggle the value to 1 (no cache flushing) and back to 0 (default, flushing enabled) with the following on a live filesystem:

```
echozfs_nocacheflush/W0t1 | mdb -kw
echozfs_nocacheflush/W0t0 | mdb -kw
```

ZFS has a few features that make it well suited to database use. All reads and writes include block checksums, which allow ZFS to detect the sadly common situation where data is quietly corrupted by RAM or disk errors. Some administrators consider such checksums vital for running a large database safely. Another useful feature is ZFS's robust snapshot support. This makes it far easier to make a copy of a database you can replicate to another location, back up, or even to create a temporary copy you can then roll back to an earlier version. This can be particularly valuable when doing risky migrations or changes you might want to back out of.

Because of the robustness of its intent log and block checksum features, ZFS is one filesystem where disabling PostgreSQL's `full_page_writes` parameter is a candidate for optimization with little risk. It's quite resistant to the torn pages issue that makes that parameter important for other filesystems. There is also transparent compression available on ZFS. While expensive in terms of CPU, applications that do lots of sequential scans of data too small to be compressed by the PostgreSQL TOAST method might benefit from reading more logical data per physical read, which is what should happen if compression is enabled.

Windows filesystems

The choices for Windows are much easier, because there's only one of them that makes sense for a database disk (https://en.wikipedia.org/wiki/File_Allocation_Table)

FAT32

While generally deprecated at this point, it's still common for USB devices in particular to be formatted with the older FAT32 filesystem. Since FAT32 is not journaled, unclean shutdown requires running the `chkdsk` utility to recover from. Due to this and the lack of security on FAT32 files, the PostgreSQL installer does not support installing a database cluster directly onto a FAT32 volume. However, it's possible to install onto this filesystem if you manually run the `initdb` command after regular installation. However, this is not recommended for a reliable database configuration.

NTFS

Microsoft's flagship filesystem is NTFS. This filesystem uses non-ordered metadata journaling, similar to the writeback journal mode on Linux. This is generally reliable, but on rare occasions you might run into a volume that cannot be mounted in Windows without running the old `chkdsk` utility in a special mode as part of booting the system.

As described earlier, PostgreSQL installations on Windows using NTFS should prefer to set the following in the database configuration:

```
open_datasync=fsync_writethrough
```

This configures the filesystem to flush its WAL writes through any volatile disk write caches.

It's possible to create the functional equivalent of a symbolic link on NTFS called a filesystem junction. The junction utility available from `https://docs.microsoft.com/en-us/sysinternals/` allows these to be created. This lets NTFS volumes on Windows to relocate the `pg_wal` parameter, or other parts of the database tree, to another filesystem, and to use tablespaces too.

Theoretically, you can create an NFTS volume of 16 TB using the default cluster size of 4 KB, the same limit as most Linux deployments. It's even straightforward to create a volume with larger clusters though; at 64 KB, NTFS might support 256 TB volumes instead. As noted at the beginning of this chapter, partitioning such large volumes on PC hardware requires you create a GPT instead of using the older MBR approach, and that your version of Windows will understand the resulting partition scheme.

It's possible to turn on automatic compression of an NTFS volume, potentially valuable for the same reasons mentioned in the ZFS section. In practice, systems doing the sort of large queries that most benefit from this are not commonly practical on Windows anyway, due to its limitations in shared memory and connection capacity.

Adjusting mounting behavior

Similarly to the UNIX `noatime` parameter, it's possible to prevent NTFS from constantly updating when files were last accessed. Another useful tweak is to turn off the 8.3 filename generation that Windows does for backward compatibility with older applications. These behaviors are disabled as follows:

```
fsutil behavior set disablelastaccess 1
fsutil behavior set disable8dot3 1
```

Be careful when disabling the 8.3 filename generation in particular. One area where this has been known to cause problems is if the `%TEMP%` or `%TMP%` environment variables are using the short filenames to access their files. You may need to update these variables to refer to the full pathname instead.

Disk layout for PostgreSQL

Since PostgreSQL uses standard files for all its files, there are several parts of the database you can relocate to somewhere else just by moving the associated files and adding a symbolic link to the new location.

Symbolic links

Symbolic links (also called symlinks) are just entries in a filesystem directory that point towards another location. UNIX systems originally preferred to use what are called hard links, which link to the new location directly. The entry in the filesystem literally points to another spot on the disk. To make this easier to manage, the normal approach now is to use soft symlinks, which are easily visible. The most common thing to relocate using a symlink in PostgreSQL is the WAL transaction log. You can do this after the database cluster is created (but with the server down!), like the following:

```
$ cd $PGDATA
$ mv pg_wal /disk
$ ln -s /disk/pg_wal pg_wal
$ ls -l pg_wal
lrwxrwxrwx 1 postgrespostgres 11 2010-04-27 17:35 pg_wal -> /disk/pg_wal
```

Starting in PostgreSQL 8.3, it's possible to use the `--waldir`
parameter when running `initdb` to create the cluster. This doesn't work any differently; it will just create the soft symlink for you. The preceding technique is still quite common, and there's no reason to prefer one over the other besides what seems easier to you.

Tablespaces

The main unit of storage for a PostgreSQL database is the tablespace. Tablespaces are described accurately by their name: they're a space to put tables (and indexes) in. The idea is that every logical disk you want to use for a distinct purpose gets assigned a tablespace name, and then when you create a table, you refer that tablespace to put it there:

```
$ mkdir /disk/pgdata
$ psql
postgres=# CREATE TABLESPACE disk LOCATION '/disk/pgdata';
postgres=# CREATE TABLE t(i int) TABLESPACE disk;
```

Tablespaces are also implemented inside the database using symbolic links, and your OS needs to support them (or an equivalent, such as the NTFS junction) for this to work. Databases and tables are, by default, created in a virtual tablespace named pg_default. You can change that by setting the default_tablespace parameter in the server configuration. It's also possible to relocate an entire database by setting the parameter TABLESPACE when running CREATE DATABASE.

Database directory tree

With this background in mind, here are the major directories inside the PostgreSQL database structure that initdb creates:

- base: This is the location that holds pg_default, the default tablespace. The template databases and any additional ones created without an explicit tablespace assignment will all be placed here. The next chapter, Chapter 5, *Memory for Database Caching*, digs into the details of how the directory is organized into databases and tables.
- global: Holds the pg_global virtual tablespace. This is where system tables shared by all databases in a cluster, such as the database roles and other system catalog data, are stored.
- pg_xact: The transaction commit log data is stored here. This data is actively read from, by VACUMM in particular, and files are removed once there's nothing interesting in them. This directory is one of the reasons PostgreSQL doesn't work very well if you mount the database in a way that bypasses the filesystem cache. If reads and writes to the commit logs are not cached by the OS, it will heavily reduce performance in several common situations.

- `pg_stat_tmp`: This directory contains the files used to store database statistics. These files should never get very big, and if they do you'll see the database statistics process start to consume more resources.
- `pg_tblspc`: When you create a new tablespace, this directory is where the symbolic link created to manage that is saved.
- `pg_wal`: The database WAL used for crash recovery is stored here.
- `pg_subtrans`: Contains data related to sub transactions.
- `pg_multixact`: Contains multi-transaction status data. In situations where your application heavily uses shared row locks, use of this direction could be heavy.
- `pg_twophase`: Holds data related to two-phase commits.
- `pg_logical`: Subdirectory containing status data for logical decoding.
- `pg_replslot`: Subdirectory containing replication slot data.

Generally, the first thing people relocate onto their own disk is `pg_wal`. Then, they add more tablespaces to split out heavily accessed tables. Next, move temporary files. The directories containing transaction details are much less likely candidates to be split to their own disks, but applications where this has improved performance have been observed by PostgreSQL users.

Temporary files

There are a few situations where PostgreSQL saves temporary files, ones that are not critical to database operation. Tables created using CREATE TEMPORARY TABLE and their respective indexes are one source. Probably more importantly, when the database is doing a query that involves a sort operation, and the data exceeds work_mem, temporary files are created for that purpose. So, in situations where your users will be doing lots of sorting of large tables, as in a data warehouse, there can be quite a bit of activity going to disk for this purpose.

The `temp_tablespaces` database parameter allows relocation of all the temporary tables to one chosen from the list of additional tablespaces provided. If you put more than one tablespace on that list, which is used is selected at random when a transaction first does something that needs one. However, when a second or later bit of temporary storage is needed by a transaction, the database actually iterates over the list sequentially, therefore spreading activity more evenly across all the provided tablespaces.

By default, temporary objects are created in the default tablespace. They'll all appear in `base/pgsql_tmp` unless relocated. If you're not using temporary tables heavily, monitoring activity and disk space used in that directory can be used to estimate how heavy the sorting activity is on your database. This technique works even on earlier PostgreSQL releases that don't have the `log_temp_files` parameters. You can monitor disk space instead of relying on the logs for that information, and monitoring disk space used can be useful even if that's available, because it gives you an idea of how much concurrent sorting is happening. That can be hard to compute just from the log file entries.

One interesting property of temporary files is that they're prime candidates for storage even on less reliable drives, such as you might have your OS on. It's possible to safely, and sometimes quite usefully, put the temporary files onto a directory on your OS disks if they are underutilized. Just be careful because if those disks are lost, you'll need to recreate that empty tablespace on the OS drives of the replacement, or remove it from the `temp_tablespaces` list.

Disk arrays, RAID, and disk layout

Many people start their PostgreSQL tuning work by asking about how to spread the various pieces of the database across a large disk array. Recommending how to do that is really application-specific, and it's only after covering so much background the last few chapters that the right context is available to even discuss it.

If you have a really large number of disks available, a dozen or more, presuming that disk space needed for the database wasn't a problem, a good configuration would look like the following:

Location	Disks	RAID level	Purpose
/ (root)	2	1	OS
$PGDATA	6+	10	Database
$PGDATA/pg_wal	2	1	WAL
$PGDATA/pg_wal	2	1	WAL
Tablespace	1+	None	Temporary files

Here, we're presuming that you want every bit of important data to be redundant, and therefore are using the mirroring facilities of RAID 1 to do that. This gives a 3:1 ratio between database read/write throughput and that of the WAL, which is usually enough that activity to each will be balanced well. If you only have two pairs of drives for those (the database is on one pair and the WAL on another), it's likely the WAL will get considerably less activity than the database.

The leftover disk here from the hypothetical set of 12 would be assigned as a hot spare, something it's always a good idea to allocate. Given that arrays tend to be an even number of disks, pairing some temporary space with a hot spare can work out better than having two hot spares. Another typical use for a single leftover disk is to create a place to store non-critical backups and other working files, such as a database dump that needs to be processed before being shipped elsewhere.

Here's where things get tricky: what if, instead, the preceding was done like the following:

Location	Disks	RAID Level	Purpose
/ (root)	12	10	OS, DB, WAL

Would that perform better or worse than the manually split setup for the same number of disks shown previously? The answer to that is simple: there's no way to predict that. Having your data striped across so many disks is going to improve the average performance of every operation you do on this array. This setup is almost certainly better for a workload where random seeks are the norm. However, there are several database components that are not accessed randomly. The pg_wal parameter is only written to sequentially. Temporary files are not strictly sequential, but they're not heavily random either, and writes to the OS drive normally happen without the force of a sync operation forcing them to disk, which means that the OS is free to delay those writes for improved write combining and sorting, both of which reduce seeks.

Putting everything onto one big array will reduce the chance to take advantage of optimizations like that, because the cache flushing required to make the database happy is likely to force out plenty of other data too, particularly on ext3.

With that perspective, you can think about this a bit differently:

Function	Cache flushes	Access pattern
OS	Rare	Mix of sequential and random
Database	Regularly	Mix of sequential and random
WAL	Constant	Sequential
Temporary files	Never	More random as client count increases

The exact mix of sequential and random behavior for your database is completely application dependent, and how many concurrent users are involved impacts both database and temporary file patterns. Again, what your application is doing impacts whether temp files are even important. Any attempt to optimize disk layout that doesn't take into account the access pattern of your app, including concurrency, is unlikely to predict performance correctly.

And even if you do have enough information that you believe you can predict an optimal layout, the odds are still against you. To quote noted computer scientist Donald Knuth, "*the universal experience of programmers who have been using [performance] measurement tools has been that their intuitive guesses fail.*" You would be unwise to presume that you will be the lucky person who guesses correctly.

If you do split something out, make sure to measure the improvement to confirm whether you were right. Ideally, you'd be able to simulate that in a test environment before doing so on a production system. In the real world, most development servers have far fewer disks than the production ones, making that tough to simulate. One good place to try it is during acceptance testing of new production hardware. You should be doing general system burn-in and testing of any candidate replacement for a production database server. That's a great time to experiment with (and measure!) changes in application performance, including different disk configurations.

Disk layout guidelines

There are a few guidelines that can help you prune down the possible configurations:

- Avoid putting the WAL on the OS drive, because they have completely different access patterns and both will suffer when combined. Normally, this might work out fine initially, only to discover a major issue when the OS is doing things such as a system update or daily maintenance activity. Rebuilding the filesystem database used by the locate utility each night is one common source on Linux for heavy OS disk activity.
- If you have evidence you don't do any large sorting, the temporary files can be kept at their default location, as part of the database disk.
- On Linux systems running ext3, where `fsync` cache flushes require dumping the entire OS cache out to disk, split the WAL onto another disk as soon as you have a pair spare for that purpose.

Beyond those rough rules, it's hard to settle arguments between the *put everything in one big array and let the OS sort it out* versus *break out everything into individually assigned disks so the DBA can tune* crowds. As is the case with many types of database tuning, in order to really know for sure what works best here, you'll need to simulate both configurations, using a benchmark workload as similar as possible to your production workload.

As for which side I personally fall onto, I prefer to split things up. The reason for that is not because I expect it to perform better, but because it's unquestionably easier to quantify what an application is doing that way. Being able to measure the exact balance of data going to the database, WAL, and temporary disks is valuable, both for general optimization, as well as for finding bottlenecks in application design. I consider the value of being able to monitor to that level to be the tie-breaker between these schools of thought on database layout.

Remember that the hardware your application is currently running on is not necessarily going to be what it runs on forever. If I'm planning out a new server, and I can predict the WAL versus DB activity ratio based on measurements of the old system, that's not just guessing anymore, and the odds are much better it will be successful. But if the old system only has a large pile of disks, information gathered from them isn't nearly as useful in capacity planning for the future.

Summary

There aren't a lot of easy answers for what filesystem to use or how to arrange your disks. It's better to err on the side of paranoia, not performance, if you expect to keep your database intact under the sorts of odd things that will happen to it in production. And unfortunately, maximum reliability is usually slower too. The most valuable thing you can do is be systematic in how you test. Instrument what you're doing, benchmark whenever possible, and always try to collect reproducible examples of realistic workloads whenever they appear.

Filesystem crash protection is mostly commonly done by journaling writes, which adds overhead but makes recovery time after unclean shutdown predictable.

On Linux, the ext3 filesystem allows a wide variety of tuning possibilities for its journal. While not the best performer, its occasional problem spots are at least well understood. Both XFS and ext4 are at early production quality right now, and expected to become increasingly viable alternatives to ext3 in the near future.

Solaris and FreeBSD both have older UFS filesystems and the newer ZFS available. ZFS has several features that make it uniquely suited for large database installations.

The NTFS filesystem on Windows shares many fundamentals with the UNIX-based ones popular on other OSes.

Increasing read-ahead, stopping updates to file access timestamps, and adjusting the amount of memory used for caching, are common tuning techniques needed to get good performance on most OSes.

PostgreSQL allows relocating parts of the database through both symbolic links and creation of tablespaces.

The optimal way to arrange the components of a database across many available disks is heavily dependent on the specific application and usage pattern.

Memory for Database Caching

5

When you start a PostgreSQL server, it allocates a fixed-size block of shared memory through which all access to the information in the database passes. In addition, each client that connects to memory uses up their own bit of memory, expanding it as they use resources, such as sorting space and storing data about pending transactions to commit.

Some settings in the database can be adjusted by the clients after they connect. For example, the `work_mem` setting, a limiter on how much memory can be used for sorting, can be increased by a client after they connect. These allocations use non-shared memory, and tuning them is covered in the next chapter.

The major component to the shared memory used by the server is a large block allocated for caching blocks, read from and written to the database. This is set by a parameter named `shared_buffers`. Monitoring and optimizing how this memory is used is the major topic of this chapter. It is one of the most important parameters to get good performance, and one of the hardest to predict an optimum value for.

In this chapter, we will look into the following topics:

- Memory units in the `postgresql.conf` file
- Increasing Unix shared memory parameters for larger buffer sizes
- Crash recovery and the buffer cache
- Database buffer cache versus **operating system (OS)** cache
- Analyzing buffer cache content

Memory units in postgresql.conf

All of the shared memory settings and the starting client settings for the database are stored in the `postgresql.conf` file. In PostgreSQL 8.2, a change has greatly simplified memory settings. In earlier versions, you had to know the unit for each memory related setting; some were in units of 1 KB, and some 8 KB, which was difficult to keep track of.

Nowadays, you can still set values like that, but the preferred practice is to use a memory size instead. For example, if you wanted to set the `wal_buffers` value that controls how much memory to use for buffering WAL data, you can do that now with a line such as the following in the `postgresql.conf` file:

```
wal_buffers = 64 KB
```

If you use the `SHOW` command to display the value for this setting, it will write it similarly (although, it's possible that the value will get rescaled to display better). However, the database still converts this value into its own internal units, which, for this parameter, happens to be 8 KB blocks. It's helpful to be aware of this because you'll need to know the actual values to understand some of the internal information covered in this chapter.

The `pg_settings` view in the database can be used to see how that conversion happens. It's also helpful to know that the `current_setting()` function can be used to get the same basic information as `SHOW`, but in a way you can use in queries. You can combine these two to help see the relationship between the internal way in which the server stores parameters and what they actually represent:

```
$ psql
postgres=# show wal_buffers;
 wal_buffers
-------------
 64kB

postgres=# SELECT name,setting,unit,current_setting(name) FROM pg_settings
WHERE name='wal_buffers';
     name     | setting | unit | current_setting
--------------+---------+------+-----------------
 wal_buffers  | 8       | 8kB  | 64kB
```

Increasing Unix shared memory parameters for larger buffer sizes

When you use the `initdb` command to create a new PostgreSQL cluster, the server detects how large a shared memory block it can allocate by starting at a moderate value and decreasing it until the allocation is successful. This is necessary because on many platforms, including some very popular Unix ones, the default values for allocation of shared memory is very low. 32 MB or less is quite common, even on recent software, such as the constantly updated Linux kernels, and really small values are possible on older systems.

The default memory sizes in the `postgresql.conf` file are not optimized for performance or for any idea of a typical configuration. They are optimized solely so that the server can start on a system with low settings for the amount of shared memory it can allocate, because that situation is so common.

There are a variety of common errors you can get when a PostgreSQL server fails to start, documented at http://www.postgresql.org/docs/current/static/server-start.html, and the one related to shared memory parameters being too low looks like this on Centos 7:

```
feb 24 15:19:25 localhost.localdomain postmaster[1633]: 2018-02-24
15:19:25.548
feb 24 15:19:25 localhost.localdomain postmaster[1633]: 2018-02-24
15:19:25.554
feb 24 15:19:25 localhost.localdomain polkitd[589]: Unregistered
Authentication
feb 24 15:19:25 localhost.localdomain systemd[1]: postgresql-10.service:
main pr
feb 24 15:19:25 localhost.localdomain postmaster[1633]: 2018-02-24
15:19:25.572
feb 24 15:19:25 localhost.localdomain postmaster[1633]: 2018-02-24
15:19:25.572
feb 24 15:19:25 localhost.localdomain postmaster[1633]: 2018-02-24
15:19:25.572
feb 24 15:19:25 localhost.localdomain postmaster[1633]: 2018-02-24
15:19:25.572
feb 24 15:19:25 localhost.localdomain systemd[1]: Failed to start
PostgreSQL 10
```

The kernel resources documentation page at
http://www.postgresql.org/docs/current/static/kernel-resources.html goes over how to increase this parameter in detail for most platforms. If you have a system that supports the `getconf` command, which many Unix-like systems do, the following program will produce reasonable starting values by asking `getconf` for information about how much memory is in your system. Create a `shmsetup.sh` file with the following contents:

```
#!/bin/bash
# simple shmsetup script
page_size=`getconf PAGE_SIZE`
phys_pages=`getconf _PHYS_PAGES`
shmall=`expr $phys_pages / 2`
shmmax=`expr $shmall \* $page_size`
echo kernel.shmmax = $shmmax
echo kernel.shmall = $shmall
```

This sets the maximum shared block size to one half of total memory and outputs values suitable for a Linux `/etc/sysctl.conf` file. The following is an example from a system with 2 GB of physical RAM, run as root:

```
# ./shmsetup >> /etc/sysctl.conf
# sysctl -p
kernel.shmmax = 1055092736
kernel.shmall = 257591
```

Here, `shmmax` is the maximum size (in bytes) for a single shared memory segment, set to 1 GB, and `shmall` is the total amount of shared memory (in pages) that all processes on the server can use. The number of bytes in a page depends on the OS; 4096 is a common value. A more robust version of this program is included as one of this book's code samples, which handles this page math for you.

Kernel semaphores

While not a memory allocation figure, another occasional `sysctl` tweaking requirement for PostgreSQL is to increase the number of available systems, an object used for process communication.

The defaults on a recent Linux system look like this:

```
$ ipcs -l
...
------ Semaphore Limits --------
max number of arrays = 128
max semaphores per array = 250
max semaphores system wide = 32000
max ops per semop call = 32
max ops per semop call = 100
semaphore max value = 32767
...
```

One of the parts trimmed from the `icps` output also shows the shared memory limits, so you can also double-check them with it. Setting higher semaphore limits is done with a `kernel` parameter that combines the main four limits here into one line. The last shown `semaphore` maps into that format like this:

```
$ sysctl kernel.sem
kernel.sem = 250      32000 32     128
kernel.sem = 250      32000 100    128
```

All four of the values here might need to be increased on systems with a large number of processes, setting the same way as the increased shared memory sizes.

Estimating shared memory allocation

It's possible to predict how much memory the PostgreSQL server is expected to allocate given the server parameters. A table labeled *Configuration parameters affecting PostgreSQL's shared memory usage* near the bottom of `https://www.postgresql.org/docs/10/static/kernel-resources.htm` gives a rough estimate (last updated as of Version 8.3) of how much shared memory is allocated by the server. It looks like this:

Usage	Approximate shared memory bytes
Connections	*(1800 + 270 * max_locks_per_transaction) * max_connections*
Autovacuum max workers	*(1800 + 270 * max_locks_per_transaction) * autovacuum_max_workers*
Prepared transactions	*(770 + 270 * max_locks_per_transaction) * max_prepared_transactions*
Shared disk buffers	*(block_size + 208) * shared_buffers*
WAL buffers	*(wal_block_size + 8) * wal_buffers*
Fixed space requirements	770 kB

The first two lines are very similar because they're just accounting for the fact that the autovacuum workers each take up their own connection. You can just add `max_connections` + `autovacuum_max_workers` and use that as your true connection count to simplify this estimate a bit. Very little of this is likely to matter to you because all the other sizes are dwarfed by `shared_buffers` unless your client count is extremely high. Assuming a PostgreSQL 10.0 server, these are the default values for the settings involved here and assuming that you don't use `max_prepared_transactions` and assuming that if you want a `wal_buffers` based on `shared_buffers`. If you want to enable `max_prepared_transactions`, `max_prepared_transactions` must be equal to `max_connections`:

Parameter	Default value
`max_connections`	100
`max_prepared_transactions` (*)	0

`autovacuum_max_workers`	3
`shared_buffers`	128 MB
`wal_buffers (**)`	-1
`----- to remove`	8192
`-----to remove`	8

There's no default value you can assume for `shared_buffers`, because that value is detected at server cluster creation time. The default setting of `0` for `max_prepared_transactions` makes the prepared transaction space allocation go away altogether.

 Prepared transactions involve the two-phase commit features of the database, and have nothing to do with the much more common, prepared statements that are used for things such as preventing SQL injection.

To further simplify the memory estimate computation, you can just add in the autovacuum workers as clients (103 instead of 100). The main elements of the allocation estimate table then become:

Usage	Approximate shared memory bytes
Connections+AV workers	1.9 MB
Shared disk buffers	*8400 * shared_buffers*
WAL buffers	64 kB
Fixed space requirements	770 kB

That's about 2.8 MB plus whatever the `shared_buffers` amount comes out as. As a typical value for `shared_buffers` starts at 24 MB and, on PostgreSQL 10.0, this is 128 MB or more, it is obviously the dominant thing to be concerned about when estimating shared memory consumption.

A link useful for the configuration of the initial parameters of PostgreSQL is `http://pgtune.leopard.in.ua/`.

Inspecting the database cache

You can look inside the current content of the PostgreSQL `shared_buffers` database cache using the `pg_buffercache` module. This is one of the optional `contrib` modules available that ships with PostgreSQL; see *Chapter 1, PostgreSQL Versions*, for more information about making sure these are installed. An introduction to `pg_buffercache` is available as part of the PostgreSQL documentation at
`http://www.postgresql.org/docs/current/static/pgbuffercache.html`.

The information on how the database stores information in this chapter assumes you have this module installed, so that you can look at how blocks in shared memory change as you perform various activities. This is the best way to understand how the relevant database internals work. On a production server, using `pg_buffercache` may not be as vital, but it's extremely valuable for learning how the database works with its shared memory well enough to tune memory use.

 When hearing about a database block that is in memory, you'll sometimes hear that referred to as a page instead. It's normal to hear people speak of the database buffer cache being organized into 8 KB pages of memory. The only real distinction between these two terms, which are normally used interchangeably, is that a page in memory actually holds a block plus a small amount of overhead to identify what block it is—what's referred to as the buffer header.

Installing pg_buffercache into a database

The various parts of `pg_buffercache` include a library written in C and some SQL that handles viewing the information. While the buffer cache itself is shared among every database in the cluster, `pg_buffercache` can only show you really useful information related to the database you're currently connected to, and its SQL component needs to be installed in each database you want to monitor (but not the template ones) as well.

In order to install this utility or to use it, you will need to be connected to the database as its superuser. Here's a sample that installs `pg_buffercache` into a new database, presuming the RedHat Linux standard directory installation tree; substitute your own PostgreSQL installation directory here:

```
$ createdb pgbench
$ psql pgbench
$ pgbench=# create extension pg_buffercache;
CREATE EXTENSION
```

```
$ psql -d pgbench -f /usr/share/postgresql/contrib/pg_buffercache.sql
SET
CREATE FUNCTION
CREATE VIEW
REVOKE
REVOKE
```

You can confirm that the utility is working as expected by looking at how large your system `shared_buffers` is, and noting that the count of entries returned by `pg_buffercache` matches it:

```
$ psql
postgres=# SELECT name,setting,unit,current_setting(name) FROM pg_settings
WHERE name='shared_buffers';
      name       | setting | unit | current_setting
-----------------+---------+------+-----------------
 shared_buffers  | 3584    | 8kB  | 28MB
postgres=# select count(*) from pg_buffercache;
 count
-------
  3584
```

Note the small value here: `28MB`. This is from a Linux system running kernel 2.6.28 that has 8 gigabytes of RAM. Even on something that recent, the kernel defaults only allows under 32 MB of shared memory to be allocated.

There are several examples of useful reports you can produce with `pg_buffercache` by the end of this chapter.

Database disk layout

In order to fully interpret the information returned by utilities such as `pg_buffer_cache`, and therefore use that information to adjust memory sizing, it's helpful to know a bit about how databases are stored on disk. On Unix-like systems, typically, the `$PGDATA` environment variable on your system will point to your database cluster and, underneath the `base/` directory, actually contains the database tables.

If you're not sure where your database is located on disk, but if you can connect to the database, the location of this and other important files on the server is available from the `pg_settings` view. This particular detail is in the `data_directory` setting; here's an example of locating it, and a query showing the locations of other interesting files related to the server:

```
postgres=# show data_directory;
```

```
        data_directory
-------------------------------------
 /home/postgres/data/
postgres=# select name,setting from pg_settings where category='File
Locations';
On a standard Centos 7 installation:
pgbench=# show data_directory ;
     data_directory
------------------------
 /var/lib/pgsql/10/data


pgbench=# select name,setting from pg_settings where category='File
Locations';
        name       |                  setting
-------------------+-----------------------------------------
 config_file       | /var/lib/pgsql/10/data/postgresql.conf
 data_directory    | /var/lib/pgsql/10/data
 external_pid_file |
 hba_file          | /var/lib/pgsql/10/data/pg_hba.conf
 ident_file        | /var/lib/pgsql/10/data/pg_ident.conf
```

Assuming $PGDATA is set to point to data_directory, if you create a table and wanted to look for the associated data file, that would start like this:

```
$ psql
postgres=# CREATE TABLE t (s SERIAL, i INTEGER);
NOTICE:  CREATE TABLE will create implicit sequence "t_s_seq" for serial
column "t.s"
CREATE TABLE
pgbench=#  CREATE TABLE t (s SERIAL, i INTEGER);
CREATE TABLE

$ ls $PGDATA/base
1   11872   11880
bash-4.2$ ls $PGDATA/base/
1   13805   13806   16384
```

These four directories each contain one database:

```
postgres=# select oid,datname from pg_database order by oid;
  oid  |  datname
-------+-----------
     1 | template1
 13805 | template0
 13806 | postgres
 16384 | pgbench
template0, template1, the default database and our pgbench
```

The cryptic numbers are what is called an **object identifier (OID)**. In early PostgreSQL versions, every row in every table received an OID, which was, in some cases, used as a way to uniquely identify that row. To reduce overhead, these are no longer included in the individual rows by default. You can still do so if you want, and many of the system catalog tables are created including them. There is more information about the OID and other hidden system columns at `http://www.postgresql.org/docs/current/static/ddl-system-columns.html`.

 Another handy system column to know about is `ctid`, which can still be used as a way to uniquely identify a row, even in situations where you have multiple rows with the same data in them. This provides a quick way to find a row more than once, and it can be useful for cleaning up duplicate rows from a database too.

To decipher the structure of what's in the `base/` directory, we need the `oid` of the database and the relation `oid` (a table is a type of relation) for the table it just created. You can determine those using the `pg_database` and `pg_class` system views; your exact numbers here will likely be different if you try this yourself:

```
postgres=# SELECT datname,oid FROM pg_database WHERE datname='postgres';
  datname  |  oid
-----------+-------
 postgres  | 11880

postgres=# SELECT relname,oid,relfilenode FROM pg_class WHERE relname='t';
 relname |  oid  | relfilenode |
---------+-------+-------------+
 t       | 16391 |    16391    |

postgres=# SELECT datname,oid FROM pg_database WHERE datname='postgres';
  datname  |  oid
-----------+-------
 postgres  | 13806
pgbench=# SELECT relname,oid,relfilenode FROM pg_class WHERE relname='t';
 relname |  oid  | relfilenode
---------+-------+-------------
 t       | 16399 |    16399
```

Here, the `oid` and the file it's stored in are the same. There are a few things you can do to a table that will change the name of the file used to store it without changing the `oid`. Examples include TRUNCATE, REINDEX, and CLUSTER. To find out where a relation really is, you do need to check the `relfilenode` field in its `pg_class` catalog entry.

If you want to do this sort of investigation from the Command Prompt, the command (another optional module like Centos 7; you can find it in the `postgresql10-contrib.x86_64` package) can provide the same information in cases where the `oid` still matches the filename:

```
$ oid2name
All databases:
    Oid  Database Name  Tablespace
--------------------------------------
  16384          pgbench  pg_default
  13806         postgres  pg_default
  13805        template0  pg_default
      1        template1  pg_default

$ oid2name -d pgbench -t t
From database "pgbench":
  Filenode  Table Name
----------------------
     16399            t


$ oid2name
All databases:
    Oid  Database Name  Tablespace
--------------------------------------
  11880         postgres  pg_default
  11872        template0  pg_default
      1        template1  pg_default
$ oid2name -t t
From database "postgres":
  Filenode  Table Name
----------------------
     16391            t
```

In this example, having not inserted anything into this table yet, you'd expect the file for it to be empty, and for there to be no blocks containing its data in the buffer cache, which is the case as follows:

```
$ ls -l $PGDATA/base/16384/16399
-rw-------. 1 postgres postgres 0 24 feb 16.19 base/16384/16399
pgbench=#  SELECT reldatabase, relfilenode, relblocknumber FROM
pg_buffercache WHERE relfilenode=16399;
 reldatabase | relfilenode | relblocknumber
-------------+-------------+----------------
(o rows)
$ ls -l $PGDATA/base/11880/16391*
-rw------- 1 postgres postgres 0 2010-03-01 20:53 /home/postgres/
```

```
data/base/11880/16391
$ psql
postgres=# SELECT reldatabase,relfilenode,relblocknumber FROM
pg_buffercache WHERE relfilenode=16391;
 reldatabase | relfilenode | relblocknumber
-------------+-------------+----------------
(0 rows)
```

Creating a new block in a database

Once you insert something into this table, a page is allocated in the buffer cache to hold that new information, and a standard 8 KB block is allocated on disk. Now we make an insert on the table t and check if the block is dirty:

```
pgbench=# INSERT into t(i) values (0);
INSERT 0 1
bash-4.2$ ls -l $PGDATA/base/16384/16399
-rw-------. 1 postgres postgres 8192 24 feb 16.48 base/16384/16399
pgbench=# SELECT reldatabase,relfilenode,relblocknumber,isdirty,usagecount
FROM pg_buffercache WHERE relfilenode=16399;
reldatabase | relfilenode | relblocknumber | isdirty | usagecount
-------------+-------------+----------------+---------+------------
16384 |16399 |0 | t|1
```

Now make another insert and then check again if the block is dirty:

```
$ psql -c "INSERT into t(i) values (0)"
INSERT 0 1
$ ls -l $PGDATA/base/11880/16391*
-rw------- 1 postgres postgres 8192 2010-03-01 21:03
/home/postgres/pgwork/data/base/11880/16391
```

and then check:

```
$ psql -c "SELECT reldatabase,relfilenode,relblocknumber,isdirty,usagecount
FROM pg_buffercache WHERE relfilenode=16391;"
reldatabase  | relfilenode | relblocknumber | isdirty | usagecount
-------------+-------------+----------------+---------+------------
   11880     |    16391    |       0        |    t    |    1
```

That means that the version in memory has not been written out to disk yet. Also note that the usagecount for it is 1. This means that one database process has accessed this block since its section of the buffer cache was last considered a candidate for reuse.

Showing the `usagecount` in `pg_buffercache` is only available in PostgreSQL 8.3 and later.

Writing dirty blocks to disk

There are a couple of ways blocks that are dirty can be written to disk. The easiest one to trigger at will is a checkpoint:

```
postgres=# checkpoint;
CHECKPOINT
postgres=# SELECT reldatabase,relfilenode,relblocknumber,isdirty FROM
pg_buffercache WHERE relfilenode=16391;
 reldatabase | relfilenode | relblocknumber | isdirty |
-------------+-------------+----------------+---------+
       11880 |       16391 |              0 | f       |
$ ls -l $PGDATA/base/11880/16391*
-rw------- 1 postgres postgres 8192 2010-03-01 21:05
/home/postgres/pgwork/data/base/11880/16391

pgbench=# SELECT reldatabase,relfilenode,relblocknumber,isdirty,usagecount
FROM pg_buffercache WHERE relfilenode=16399;
 reldatabase | relfilenode | relblocknumber | isdirty | usagecount
-------------+-------------+----------------+---------+-----------
       16384 |       16399 |              0 | f       |          1

$ ls -l $PGDATA/base/16384/16399
-rw-------. 1 postgres postgres 8192 24 feb 16.52 base/16384/16399
```

You can see the block is no longer dirty after the checkpoint, and the last updated time for the file saving its data on disk has moved forward to match this write.

From the perspective of the database, each table is a series of numbered blocks, each 8 KB in size, starting at 0 when you create the first row and moving forward from there. As you further extend the size of the table, the upper limit for individual files is 1 GB. Beyond that size, you'll see multiple files.

There are two other ways that a dirty block can be written out, which are described in the next few sections. To cover the full life cycle of how blocks get in and out of the buffer cache, a diversion into crash recovery and checkpoints is needed to explain some of the activity you'll see going on.

Crash recovery and the buffer cache

If you had to write out every database change to disk immediately after it's made, the database performance would really suffer. This is particularly true on blocks that you change all the time, which would then be written very often. But, you have to be able to recover if the server crashes before things are written out completely too. Periodic database checkpoints take care of that.

Checkpoint processing basics

A checkpoint iterates over every dirty block in the system as of a point in time, writing them out to disk. Then, that information is flushed to permanent storage, via the same mechanisms WAL writes are. Once that's done, if your system crashes, recovery from the crash will start from this new last point where the database was sure that everything on disk was consistent. In this way, the database constantly takes forward the recovery-starting position to the point in time the previous checkpoint started at. Everything that happened to dirty blocks before this is guaranteed to have been written to the database blocks on disk, and therefore the amount of potential information that might be lost in a crash is kept under control.

Write-ahead log and recovery processing

In Chapter 2, *Database Hardware*, the PostgreSQL WAL was introduced as the mechanism used to recover data lost in a crash. Its documentation starts at http://www.postgresql.org/docs/current/static/wal.html.

The WAL is mainly a stream of information about database blocks. When you commit a data block change, if this is the first time since the last checkpoint the block has been changed, the entirety of the original block is written out. That means an 8 KB WAL write even if you're changing only a single byte. This behavior is optional, but necessary if you want safe crash recovery; see the documentation on full_page_writes for more information: http://www.postgresql.org/docs/current/static/runtime-config-wal.html. Once a page has been written out at least once after a checkpoint, just the information about the row that's changed needs to be written.

One side-effect of this structure is that just after a checkpoint, there is a possibility of write I/O to the WAL to spike, because every page that is dirtied is going to get a full page write. Once the more popular blocks, such as high-level index structures have been fully written once, additional WAL updates to those pages will only include the row deltas, and therefore generate less write volume than the first change.

If you ever wondered how the database was able to recover from crashes even if they involved partial writes of blocks to disk, this is the mechanism that makes it happen. After a crash, recovery starts from wherever the last checkpoint ended. If you know exactly what was originally in each block you modify, and what changed in it each time it was modified, replaying those changes will include everything needed to put the disk block back into the same state it would have ended up in had the server not crashed.

Checkpoint timing

Checkpoints are valuable because they reduce the amount of time required to recover from a crash, so you want to perform them as often as you can stand. However, the overhead of both the checkpoint writes and the subsequent full page writes to the WAL is expensive, which means you don't want checkpoints to happen often.

You can adjust how often checkpoints occur by modifying two database tunables that control the two primary ways by which a checkpoint starts:

- Each time a 16 MB WAL segment is filled, and a new WAL segment is allocated, the database counts how many WAL segments have been used since the last checkpoint. When this number reaches the `max_wal_size` tunable, another checkpoint is requested. Checkpoints triggered this way are counted by incrementing the `pgstat_bgwriter.checkpoints_req` statistic.
- When `checkpoint_timeout` of time has passed since the last checkpoint, another one will occur regardless of how many segments have been used. This is accounted for in the `pgstat_bgwriter.checkpoints_timed` statistic.

The server's checkpointer process automatically performs a checkpoint every so often. A checkpoint is begun every `checkpoint_timeout` seconds, or if the `max_wal_size` is about to be exceeded, whichever comes first. The default settings are 5 minutes and 1 GB, respectively. If no WAL has been written since the previous checkpoint, new checkpoints will be skipped even if `checkpoint_timeout` has passed. (If WAL archiving is being used and you want to put a lower limit on how often files are archived in order to bound potential data loss, you should adjust the `archive_timeout` parameter rather than the checkpoint parameters.) It is also possible to force a checkpoint by using the SQL command `CHECKPOINT`.

If you do something that manually triggers a checkpoint, such as executing the `CHECKPOINT` command, these are counted in the `checkpoints_req` category. In addition to monitoring the statistics, you can see what exactly happens during each checkpoint by turning on the `log_checkpoints` parameter.

If your `max_waset` is very low, the default is a tiny 3 resulting in a checkpoint after only 48 MB of WAL writes and you reach a segment driven checkpoint required fast enough, a warning about this tuning error is shown in the database logs.

On PostgreSQL 10 `checkpoint_segments`, it has been replaced with `max_wal_size`. The following formula will give you an approximately equivalent setting:

max_wal_size = (3 * checkpoint_segments) * 16 MB

The `log_checkpoints` and `pgstat_bgwriter` parameters are only available in PostgreSQL 8.3 and later. In earlier versions, the only useful way to determine when a checkpoint happened was to set the `checkpoint_warning` to a very high value, such as its maximum of 3600 seconds—which then forces a harmless warning entry into the database log file every time a checkpoint happens. Unless it coincides with a message about the segments being too low, you won't know for sure whether this checkpoint was triggered for time or segment reasons. Generally, you can make a good guess just by noting when the previous checkpoint was. If it was `checkpoint_timeout` before this one, it's likely a time-driven checkpoint.

Checkpoint tuning based on what's inside the buffer cache and the statistics shown in `pg_stat_bgwriter` is a major subject covered later in this book. The basics of their impact on disk I/O can be explained simply—but it does depend heavily on the version of the database you're running.

Checkpoint spikes

As you might guess, if there's a lot of dirty data in a large shared buffer cache, writing it all out once will really cause I/O on your disks to increase. This is particularly true in PostgreSQL Version 8.2 and earlier, which just write the entire dirty portion of the cache out as fast as possible, regardless of its impact on the rest of the system.

Spread checkpoints

Starting in PostgreSQL 8.3, the spread checkpoint feature, tuned by `checkpoint_completion_target`, aims to reduce the amount of writes in any unit of time by spreading them out over a much longer period of time. For recovery to work, it's only necessary that a checkpoint finish before the next one can start. There's no reason you can't have one checkpoint start almost immediately after the previous one, executing and slowly writing everything that happened while the previous checkpoint was active. This is exactly what the spread checkpoint feature does. It estimates when the next checkpoint is coming based on whether checkpoints seem to be happening because of the timeout being reached or because the checkpoint segment limit was reached, and aims to finish at the completion target percentage of that value.

It is still possible to run even into checkpoint spikes, given the spread checkpoint feature. They are particularly common on filesystems that don't know how to force to disk the changes to a single file at a time. On Linux, ext3 has a particularly bad limitation. Any attempt to sync a single file will write the entire write cache for that device out to accomplish that. This can easily lead to a large checkpoint I/O spike as many files worth of data are all forced out at once. Better filesystems, such as XFS and ext4, don't suffer from that particular problem, but checkpoint spikes are still possible even on them.

Database block life cycle

The normal sequence by which a block makes its way through shared memory and either onto (or back onto) disk works like this:

1. A page to hold the database block needed is requested for allocation in the shared buffer cache. If that block already exists in there, no disk read is needed. Otherwise, ask the OS to read the page into memory. In either case, at this point, the page in memory will have its usage count increased, because presumably it's being requested so that it can be used for something. The `pgstat_bgwriter.buffers_alloc` statistics will be incremented to count this allocation.

2. Changes are made to the block. In the last example, an `INSERT` created a new row in a new block. You might also `UPDATE` or `DELETE` something that changes a block. The block is now dirty.

3. The transaction commits to the WAL. At this point, whether or not the dirty block is written out to the database file on disk in the near future, the information needed to make sure that happens eventually is safe, presuming your hardware doesn't have the sort of problematic write-back cache warned against in the disk hardware section.

4. Statistics about all of the mentioned steps, which show up in places like `pg_stat_user_tables`, are updated.

5. The dirty block is written to disk, and the buffer page is marked clean.

Those last two steps are asynchronous: the statistics update and the write of the dirty block don't happen instantly; at the next appropriate junction they happen at the next appropriate junction.

Dirty block write paths

Once a block has been made dirty in shared memory, there are three possible ways it can be written back to the database, each tracked by a counter in `pg_stat_bgwriter`:

- `buffers_checkpoint`: Clearing all of the dirty blocks included as part of a checkpoint write is accounted for here. This value jumps all at once when the checkpoint finishes, which makes monitoring this an alternative way to figure out when checkpoints are finished in addition to the log files.

- `buffers_backend`: A backend (any process besides the background writer that also handles checkpoints) tried to allocate a buffer, and the one it was given to use was dirty. In that case, the backend must write the dirty block out itself before it can use the buffer page.

- `buffers_clean`: The type of backend write described in the last few steps is making some other process stall for a moment while it writes out dirty data. To keep that from happening as often, the process scans forward looking for blocks that might be allocated in the near future that are dirty and that have a low usage count (alternatively called the **Least Recently Used (LSR)** blocks). When it finds them, it writes some of them out pre-emptively, based on historical allocation rates. Should they get dirty again before they're reallocated to a backend, that effort was wasted. The usage count and dynamically tuned approach used by the background writer make that unlikely.

Generally, the best type of write here is the one done by a checkpoint. In each of the other cases, it's possible this block will get dirty again before the next checkpoint, which makes the earlier write a waste of resources. More on using this `pg_stat_bgwriter` data to tune write performance will appear in later chapters.

Database buffer cache versus operating system cache

Unlike many traditional database products, PostgreSQL does not assume or even prefer that the majority of the memory on the system be allocated for its use. Most reads and writes from the database are done using standard OS calls that allow the OS's cache to work in its usual fashion. In some configurations, WAL writes will bypass the OS cache; that's the main exception.

If you're used to a database where most system RAM is given to the database and the OS cache is bypassed using approaches such as synchronous and direct writes, you don't want to set up PostgreSQL that same way. It will be downright counterproductive in some areas. For example, PostgreSQL's stores commit log information in the `pg_xact` directory. This data is both written to and read from regularly, and it's assumed that the OS will take care of optimizing that access. If you intentionally bypass PostgreSQL's intentions by using mounting tricks to convert writes to synchronous or direct, you may discover some unexpected performance regressions due to this issue, among others.

So why not just give all the RAM to the OS to manage? The main reason that the PostgreSQL shared buffer cache can do better than the OS is the way it keeps a usage count of buffers. This allows buffers to get a popularity score from 0 to 5, and the higher the score the less likely it is those buffers will leave the cache. The way this works, whenever the database is looking for something to evict to make more space for data it needs, it decreases that usage count.

Every increase in usage count makes that block harder to get rid of. The implementation used is called a clock-sweep algorithm.

Typical OS caches will only give any buffer one or two chances before that data is evicted, typically with some form of **least-recently-used** (**LRU**) algorithm. If your database has data in it that accumulates a high usage count, it's likely that data is being served better staying in the database's shared RAM than in the OS's.

There are also some optimizations to the PostgreSQL buffer cache to deal with large queries, such as sequential scans of the entire database, and that allow it to hold on to important data that's likely to be blown out of the OS cache as part of doing that job.

Doubly cached data

One reason for not making the shared buffer cache too large is that the OS cache is also being used for reads and writes, and it's extremely likely that there's going to be some wasted overlap there. For example, if you read a database block from disk that's not been requested before by the server, it's first going to make its way into the OS cache, and then it will be copied into the database buffer cache, what's referred to as double buffering. The OS copy and the database cache copy will both be evicted from their respective caches eventually, but for some period of time, there's going to be duplication there. Keeping `shared_buffers` at only a modest percentage of RAM reduces the amount of such data likely to be duplicated.

Inspecting the OS cache

On some OSes, it's possible to extract information from the OS's cache and combine it with details of the PostgreSQL's cache. If available, this provides a more comprehensive view of the data than looking just at the database side of things. Projects viewing this data are still in the early stages; however, some example implementations include:

- `http://www.kennygorman.com/wordpress/?p=250`: Python script showing PostgreSQL objects in Linux memory.
- `http://pgfoundry.org/projects/pgfincore/:%20pgfincore`: PgFincore provides this data directly inside the database itself, where you might combine it with data from `pg_buffercache`. Currently, this targets Linux and PostgreSQL 8.4.

Checkpoint overhead

If your database buffer cache is large, it's also possible a large quantity of data could be dirty when a checkpoint starts, causing a checkpoint I/O spike. When using a later PostgreSQL version that supports spread checkpoints, you can tune checkpoint frequency to reduce the average size of these spikes, and you'll also have the `pg_stat_bwriter` view to help you with that optimization.

But ultimately, you should realize that every bit of data that's inside the database's shared buffer cache needs to be accounted for at checkpoint time, while the data in the OS cache does not. The flip side to this is that keeping data in `shared_buffers` can reduce total write volume, when you modify the same data block more than once per checkpoint, which is common for index blocks in particular. Sizing to optimize has to consider both sides of this trade-off. You should aim for the most frequently used blocks ending up in database shared memory, with the less popular blocks spending more time in the OS cache.

Starting size guidelines

The lore for sizing `shared_buffers` generally specifies a suggestion in terms of a percentage of system RAM. Some advocate only 10-15%. The thorough academic exploration in the paper *Tuning Database Configuration Parameters with iTuned* at `http://www.cs.duke.edu/~shivnath/papers/ituned.pdf` found 40% optimal on a 1 GB system being tested on a wide range of queries. And occasionally, reports appear where 60% or more of total RAM turns out to be optimal.

Generally, if you have a server where OS overhead is small relative to total memory (any modern system with 1 GB or more of RAM), giving the database 25% of total RAM is a reasonable starting setting for `shared_buffers` in the middle of the effective range. It may not be optimal, but it's unlikely to be so high that double buffering becomes an issue. And it's likely to be far better than the tiny default forced on the database by the low shared memory parameters of typical operating system kernel defaults.

Platform, version, and workload limitations

In addition to systems with small amounts of RAM, there are several situations where even 25% of RAM is too much:

- **Early versions**: Using a large buffer cache was made possible by improvements in PostgreSQL 8.1. Earlier versions were hard pressed to even use 512 MB of RAM effectively. Unless you intend to benchmark to prove larger increases are valuable, a reasonable upper limit for 8.0 or earlier is 32768 pages (256 MB versions this early don't allow the utilization of memory units for their parameters either).

- **Windows**: For reasons not yet fully identified by the PostgreSQL community, the Windows platform does not perform well with large shared memory allocations. Peak performance on Windows' installs is typically with `shared_buffers` in the 64 MB to 512 MB range. Using 256 MB would be an aggressive, but likely still safe, maximum value to use, again unless you can benchmark to prove further increases are useful.

- **Checkpoint spikes**: In versions 8.2 and earlier, PostgreSQL performed its checkpoint writes in what's essentially one big dump. This has an extremely high potential to cause other I/O on the system to pause, often for several seconds, until the checkpoint write finishes. If you have a version of PostgreSQL before 8.3, and you have a write-heavy workload, you are more likely to suffer from checkpoint-spike pauses than you are to benefit from having more shared memory for queries-given that the OS cache will supplement for you there. 128 MB of RAM is a reasonable starting size for write-intensive workloads in earlier versions that do not support spread checkpoints.

- **Shared server**: If this is not a dedicated database server, you need to carefully consider the requirements of other applications before allocating a large portion of memory that is dedicated to the database. Since PostgreSQL will always fall back to sharing the OS cache even if it doesn't have dedicated RAM, smaller values for `shared_buffers` can make it much easier to build a high performance host that's doing both database and application duties.

- **Very large system**: Experiments on systems with large amounts of RAM suggest that, likely due to internal partitioning issues in the buffer cache (which haven't been adjusted since PostgreSQL 8.4), setting it larger than approximately 8 GB can be counterproductive. If you have a system with a very large amount of RAM, there is not much information available on where cache sizing breaks down, but it's likely in the multiple gigabyte range. On servers with 8 GB or more of RAM, you might start with only 2 GB dedicated to the database, and only resize upward if cache inspection suggests it's likely to be productive.

The typical PostgreSQL default install, where `shared_buffers` is 32 MB or less, is unlikely to perform very well except in the least demanding situations. But there are plenty of PostgreSQL systems that achieve good performance with `shared_buffers` increased no further than the 128 MB to 256 MB range. If you're going to follow standard guidelines and use a large amount of RAM, you owe it to yourself to confirm it is being used well.

Analyzing buffer cache contents

You've seen and been told how using a block will increase its usage count. You've also seen and been told how a dirty block might make its way out to disk. This wasn't intended just as an academic exercise. Believe it or not, all of this information is useful for determining how large your shared buffer cache should be!

If you want to do better than following a rule of thumb for how big to set `shared_buffers` relative to the OS cache, you have two options. You can run your own benchmarks with your application and see how the results vary, based on the amount of shared memory dedicated to the database. Just be careful to account for the influence of the larger OS cache when running multiple such tests, or you can use knowledge of how the buffer cache works from inside it to help make that decision.

Inspection of the buffer cache queries

Note that due to multiple changes between PostgreSQL in version 8.3, few of these queries will work without modification on earlier versions. You will have to remove all references to `usagecount` and, in some cases, may need to adjust how values are cast between types.

For the following examples, in terms of output (which is scripted into the code sample named `bufcache.sh` included with the book), `shared_buffers` is set to 256 MB, and `pgbench` is initialized with a scale of `50` (full coverage of `pgbench`, another database `contrib` utility, appears in `Chapter 8`, *Database Benchmarking*):

```
$ pgbench -i -s 50 pgbench
$ psql -x -c "select pg_size_pretty(pg_database_size('pgbench')) as
db_size"
-[ RECORD 1 ]---
db_size | 711 MB
$ pgbench -S -c 8 -t 25000 pgbench

$ pgbench -i -s 50 pgbench
$ psql -x -c "select pg_size_pretty(pg_database_size('pgbench')) as
db_size"
-[ RECORD 1 ]---
db_size | 756 MB

$ pgbench -S -c 8 -t 25000 pgbench
starting vacuum...end.
transaction type: <builtin: select only>
scaling factor: 50
query mode: simple
```

```
number of clients: 8
number of threads: 1
number of transactions per client: 25000
number of transactions actually processed: 200000/200000
latency average = 2.262 ms
tps = 3535.931064 (including connections establishing)
tps = 3536.123259 (excluding connections establishing)
```

This makes for a total database size greater than the shared buffer cache can hold, forcing some prioritization of what is and isn't kept in there, via the usagecount mechanism. After creation, the queries run against the accounts table by pgbench makes sure the cache is being used by some sort of workload worth analyzing: in this case, many clients are doing only reads from the accounts table, the largest in the database.

The pg_buffercache module needs to be installed into the pgbench database before any of these queries are run as well.

 pg_buffercache requires broad locks on parts of the buffer cache when it runs. As such, it's extremely intensive on the server when you run any of these queries. They are not recommended for regular monitoring use. A snapshot on a daily basis or every few hours is usually enough to get a good idea how the server is using its cache, without having the monitoring itself introduce much of a load. These are not queries you want to run every minute.

Top relations in the cache

The following example appears in the documentation as an example for how to use pg_buffercache, and it's quite a good way to start your analysis:

```
SELECT
  c.relname,
  count(*) AS buffers
FROM pg_class c
  INNER JOIN pg_buffercache b
    ON b.relfilenode=c.relfilenode
  INNER JOIN pg_database d
    ON (b.reldatabase=d.oid AND d.datname=current_database())
GROUP BY c.relname
ORDER BY 2 DESC
LIMIT 10;
LIMIT 2;
```

Removing the system tables (which has been done on all the examples shown here) shows that almost all of the cache is being used by the pgbench_accounts table and the index enforcing its primary key, as expected, given those accounts are all we were running SELECT statements against:

```
            relname              | buffers
---------------------------------+---------
 pgbench_accounts                |   21838
 pgbench_accounts_pkey           |   10739

            relname              | buffers
---------------------------------+---------
 pgbench_accounts                |    9061
 pgbench_accounts_pkey           |    7168
```

Summary by usage count

That doesn't give any interesting information about the usage counts of either table though; this query will be shown to them:

```
SELECT
    usagecount, count (*), isdirty
FROM pg_buffercache
GROUP BY isdirty, usagecount
ORDER BY isdirty, usagecount;
```

The results don't prove anything interesting so far, they just suggest there's not very much accumulating a high usage count on a straight percentage basis:

```
 usagecount | count | isdirty
------------+-------+---------
          0 | 10544 | f
          1 | 12096 | f
          2 |  2709 | f
          3 |  2308 | f
          4 |  3119 | f
          5 |  1992 | f
```

```
usagecount | count | isdirty
-----------+-------+--------
         0 |  7177 | f
         1 |  7948 | f
         2 |   923 | f
         3 |   168 | f
         4 |    51 | f
         5 |   117 | f
```

Buffer content summary with percentages

This query is where you probably want to start when analyzing a new database. It lets you quickly see not just how much data is being cached for each table, but how much that represents relative to its total size:

```
SELECT
  c.relname,
  pg_size_pretty(count(*) * 8192) as buffered,
  round(100.0 * count(*) /
    (SELECT setting FROM pg_settings
      WHERE name='shared_buffers')::integer,1)
    AS buffers_percent,
  round(100.0 * count(*) * 8192 /
    pg_relation_size(c.oid),1)
    AS percent_of_relation
FROM pg_class c
  INNER JOIN pg_buffercache b
    ON b.relfilenode = c.relfilenode
  INNER JOIN pg_database d
    ON (b.reldatabase = d.oid AND d.datname = current_database())
GROUP BY c.oid,c.relname
ORDER BY 3 DESC
LIMIT 10;
```

pg_relation_size() does not include data that has been stored in a **The Oversized-Attribute Storage Technique (TOAST)** table associated with this one, and therefore may not be an accurate assessment of your table's size. In PostgreSQL 10.0, you can replace this with the pg_table_size() function added in that version, which does include TOAST information in its sum.

See http://www.postgresql.org/docs/current/interactive/storage-toast.html for an introduction to TOAST, and

http://www.postgresql.org/docs/current/interactive/functions-admin.html for documentation of the system size functions.

One troublesome change in PostgreSQL 8.4 that commonly impacts code like this is that `pg_relation_size()` and `pg_total_relation_size()` were changed to run against a `regclass` type instead of a text name. These examples sidestep that by using a join with `pg_class` that provides an `oid`, but your own queries similar to these may not be able to use that trick.

This query needs to be run with `psql -x` to get results that aren't too wide to fit here, and the interesting lines are as follows:

```
-[ RECORD 1 ]-------+-----------------------------------
relname             | pgbench_accounts
buffered            | 171 MB
buffers_percent     | 66.6
percent_of_relation | 27.5
-[ RECORD 2 ]-------+-----------------------------------
relname             | pgbench_accounts_pkey
buffered            | 84 MB
buffers_percent     | 32.8
percent_of_relation | 97.9


-[ RECORD 1 ]-------+-----------------------
relname             | pgbench_accounts
buffered            | 71 MB
buffers_percent     | 55.2
percent_of_relation | 11.0
-[ RECORD 2 ]-------+-----------------------
relname             | pgbench_accounts_pkey
buffered            | 56 MB
buffers_percent     | 43.6
percent_of_relation | 52.1
```

Now we're seeing something useful. While `pgbench_accounts_key` is only using up `32.8` and `43.6` percent of the cache, it's holding on to nearly `97.9` and `52.1` percent of the data in that index. This tells us that the database believes that keeping that data in memory is really important. A breakdown of the `usagecount` data by relation will give more insight into how that is happening.

Buffer usage count distribution

This query breaks down usage counts by relation and `usagecount`, so you can see exactly how usage count distribution differs between tables:

```
SELECT
  c.relname, count(*) AS buffers,usagecount
FROM pg_class c
  INNER JOIN pg_buffercache b
    ON b.relfilenode = c.relfilenode
  INNER JOIN pg_database d
    ON (b.reldatabase = d.oid AND d.datname = current_database())
GROUP BY c.relname,usagecount
ORDER BY c.relname,usagecount;
```

The results make it really obvious what's happening with the tables:

relname	buffers	usagecount
pgbench_accounts	10032	0
pgbench_accounts	10783	1
pgbench_accounts	953	2
pgbench_accounts	66	3
pgbench_accounts	4	4
pgbench_accounts_pkey	512	0
pgbench_accounts_pkey	1312	1
pgbench_accounts_pkey	1756	2
pgbench_accounts_pkey	2241	3
pgbench_accounts_pkey	3115	4
pgbench_accounts_pkey	1803	5

relname	buffers	usagecount
pgbench_accounts	4447	0
pgbench_accounts	4362	1
pgbench_accounts	134	2
pgbench_accounts	1	3
pgbench_accounts_pkey	2871	0
pgbench_accounts_pkey	3338	1
pgbench_accounts_pkey	712	2
pgbench_accounts_pkey	127	3
pgbench_accounts_pkey	27	4
pgbench_accounts_pkey	52	5

The primary key index here isn't using up those many buffers, but the ones it does have in the cache average a very high usage count. Meanwhile, the regular accounts data takes up much more room, but extremely little of it gets a `usagecount` greater than 1. This explains why the database considers `pgbench_accounts_pkey` a popular relation and should keep a large portion in memory, while `pgbench_accounts` is being treated as more transient data. This is really what you want. The ability to look up data in the accounts table requires having the primary key index, so you'd hope and expect as much of that index to be cached as possible.

Using buffer cache inspection for sizing feedback

The recent examples give you the basic two things to look for when deciding if your `shared_buffers` cache is large enough. First, compare what percentage of the relations you believe are important to your application's performance appear to be cached. If this number is low, you may benefit from a larger buffer cache. A helpful secondary look at this information is available if you combine this with hit rates from views such as `pg_stat_user_tables` which will be covered in `Chapter 11`, *Database Activity and Statistics*.

The balance of popular (high usage count) versus transient (low usage count) pages tells you a lot about whether your cache is sized appropriately. If most of your pages have low usage counts (0,1), but you're still getting good hit rates from the table statistics, you can probably decrease the size of the buffer cache without a performance loss. Even the simplest OS LRU algorithm is capable of making good caching decisions, where there aren't particularly popular pages to prioritize over transient ones.

But if you are accumulating a large number of blocks with a high usage count (4,5), this is strong evidence that your data is being served well while stored in the database-shared buffer cache, and that your application might benefit from it being even larger.

Summary

As database servers have so many different types of workloads they might encounter, it's difficult to give any hard rules for optimal configuration just based on server hardware. Some applications will benefit from having really large amounts of dedicated database memory in the form of `shared_buffers`; others will suffer large checkpoint spike problems if you do that. PostgreSQL versions starting with 8.3 do provide you with tools to help monitor your system in this area though. If you combine that with some investigation of just how the server is using the memory you've allocated for it, and preferably add in some of the monitoring techniques covered in later chapters, you'll be much better informed.

A quick look inside the actual content of the database buffer cache will answer all sorts of questions about how the server is using memory, and be much more accurate for planning purposes than guessing.

PostgreSQL allocates one large shared memory block on server startup to cache reads and writes to database disk blocks.

This cache works in cooperation with, rather than, replacing the operating system cache, and should be sized as 15%-40% of total RAM.

The default shared memory allocation limits on many systems are extremely low, and will need to be increased to allow proper shared memory sizing for the database.

Crash recovery is done by writing full copies of the blocks being modified to the WAL before changing the associated file on the database disk.

How far the back recovery must go in order to repair damage after a crash moves forward as each checkpoint finishes.

Checkpoints need to be tuned carefully to move limit crash recovery time, while not impacting the rest of the system's performance.

The `pg_stat_bgwriter` system view tracks how all buffers get into and out of the buffer cache.

The `pg_buffercache` module can be used to see what's inside the shared buffer cache, and this information can be used to determine if it's sized too large or too small.

Server Configuration Tuning

6

The main tunable settings for PostgreSQL are in a plain text file named `postgresql.conf` that's located at the base of the database directory structure. This will often be where `$PGDATA` is set to on Unix-like systems, making the file `$PGDATA/postgresql.conf` on those platforms. This chapter mirrors the general format of the official documentation's look at these parameters at `http://www.postgresql.org/docs/current/static/runtime-config.html`. However, it is more focused on guidelines for setting the most important values, from the perspective of someone interested in performance tuning, rather than describing the meaning of every parameter. This should be considered a supplement to, rather than a complete replacement for, the extensive material in the manual.

Another live resource related to this subject is the article *Tuning Your PostgreSQL Server* at `http://wiki.postgresql.org/wiki/Tuning_Your_PostgreSQL_Server`, which has some overlap with information covered here. The wiki structure of that article makes it conducive to being kept current, so eventually it may include details about future PostgreSQL versions not released at the point this chapter is being written.

Interacting with the live configuration

There are many ways to change the database's parameters beyond just editing its configuration file and restarting. Understanding these can be critical to reducing server downtime just for routine configuration changes, as well as making sure you're adjusting the parameter you want at the time when you want the change to take effect.

Defaults and reset values

The database has two things that you might refer to as a *default*, depending on your context. The first type of default is what the server will set the value to if you don't ever change it to the setting the server starts with before it has even read the `postgresql.conf` file. Starting in PostgreSQL 8.4, you can check this value using the `pg_settings` view by looking at the `boot_val` column: `http://www.postgresql.org/docs/current/static/view-pg-settings.html`. Once the server has started, and you make changes to parameters, there's also a default value those parameters will return to, if you use the `RESET` command documented at `http://www.postgresql.org/docs/current/static/sql-reset.html` to return them to their starting value. This is labeled as `reset_val` in the `pg_settings` view.

Allowed change context

Every configuration setting has an associated context in which it's allowed to be changed.

The `context` is as follows:

```
pgbench=# select distinct context from pg_settings order by 1;
 context
-------------------
 backend
 internal
 postmaster
 sighup
 superuser
 superuser-backend
 user
```

The best way to determine the allowed change `context` for a setting is to ask the database directly. The following example shows one entry with each `context` type (the actual result if you run this query will include every server parameter):

```
postgres=# select name,context from pg_settings;
           name              |   context
-----------------------------+------------
 archive_command             | sighup
 archive_mode                | postmaster
 block_size                  | internal
 log_connections             | backend
 log_min_duration_statement  | superuser
 search_path                 | user
```

The `context` field isn't documented very well in the official manual. Here are the meanings of the various settings you'll find there, sorted from hardest to easiest to change:

- `internal` : These settings are mainly database internals set at compile time. They're included in the view for your information, but cannot be changed without recompiling the server.
- `postmaster`: This is updated only when a full server restart is done. All shared memory settings fall into this category.
- `sighup`: Sending the server a HUP signal will cause it to reload the `postgresql.conf` and any changes made to this parameter will be immediately active. See the next section for information about how to do this.
- `backend`: These settings are similar to the `sighup` ones, except that the changes made will not impact any already running database `backend` sessions. Only new sessions started after this will respect the change. There are very few parameters with this property; most impact behavior only happens when `backend` sessions start or end. The last example shown, `log_connections`, can't be made retroactive to log a connection that's already been made. Only new connections made after `log_connections` is enabled will be logged.
- `superuser`: This can be modified by any database superuser (usually the person who created the database and commonly `postgres`) at any time, and made active without even requiring a full configuration reload. Most of the settings in this category relate to logging various aspects of statements executed by the server.
- `user`: Individual user sessions can adjust these parameters at any time. Their changes will only impact that session. Most parameters here alter how queries execute, which allows tweaking query execution on a per-session basis.
- `superuser-backend`: These settings can be changed in the `postgresql.conf` file without restarting the PostgreSQL server. These values cannot be changed after starting the session, and only the superuser can change this setting.

As you might imagine from this list, the answer to a seemingly simple question such as "what's the current value of `work_mem` ?" can have a very different answer depending on when you ask and the context involved. It might be initially set to one value in the `postgresql.conf` file, have the default changed to another by a configuration reload, then be changed again by one backend adjusting its individual setting before running a query.

Reloading the configuration file

There are three ways you can get the database to reload its configuration, to update values in the `sighup` category. If you're connected to the database as a superuser, `pg_reload_conf` will do that:

```
postgres=# SELECT pg_reload_conf();
 pg_reload_conf
----------------
 t
```

You can send a HUP signal manually using the Unix command:

```
$ ps -eaf | grep "postgres -D"
postgres 11185     1  0 22:21 pts/0    00:00:00
/home/postgres/inst/bin/postgres -D /home/postgres/data/
$ kill -HUP 11185
```

Finally, you can trigger a signal for the server by using `pg_ctl` :

```
$ pg_ctl reload
server signaled
```

No matter which approach you use, you'll see the following in the database log files afterwards, to confirm that the server received the message:

```
LOG:   received SIGHUP, reloading configuration files
```

You can then confirm that your changes have taken place as expected using commands like SHOW, or looking at `pg_settings`.

Commented out settings

What happens when you had something that was set manually but then you disable it on a running server? It depends on the version you're running. Let's say your `postgresql.conf` file started with the following setting active:

```
work_mem = '4MB'
```

You now edit the file to comment that setting out:

```
#work_mem='4MB'
work_mem = '8MB'
```

And then tell the server to re-read the configuration file:

```
$ pg_ctl reload
```

#work_mem is a context setting. Starting with PostgreSQL 8.3, this change will return the value back to the server default (boot_val). And, as of Version 10.0, you'll also get a note in the log file about that:

```
LOG:  received SIGHUP, reloading configuration files
LOG:  parameter "work_mem" removed from configuration file, reset to
default
```

You can confirm the default setting look using:

```
$ psql -x -c "show work_mem"
-[ RECORD 1 ]-
work_mem | 8MB
```

But, if you are running PostgreSQL 8.2 or earlier, what would have happened instead is that there would be no change: work_mem and would still be 4 MB. Only after the server was completely restarted would the return to the default value of 3 happen.

Because this behavior is both complicated and version-dependent, experienced PostgreSQL administrators will usually double-check parameters they intended to change afterward using the SHOW statement, or by looking at pg_settings ,to make sure the settings match what was expected.

Another complicated area here is that it's possible to include additional configuration files from inside the master postgresql.conf. These effectively work as though you have inserted the text of the file into the spot you included it. You can see the file any setting originated from using pg_settings, in this case, along with what line the active version came from. Also note that if you set a parameter more than once, only the last setting matters in any case.

Server-wide settings

While in some cases these parameters might be adjustable in other contexts, generally the ones in this section are only adjusted in the postgresql.conf before the server is started.

Database connections

There are many configuration parameters that control how people can connect remotely and locally to the database. The complete list is documented at `http://www.postgresql.org/docs/current/static/runtime-config-connection.html`.

listen_addresses

Any installation that requires connecting from a remote system will need to change `listen_addresses` to allow that. The default only allows local connections from users logged in to the same system as the database server. A common approach is to accept incoming connections from anywhere, as far as the primary configuration file is concerned, like this:

```
listen_addresses = '*'
```

And then, you can set up the `pg_hba.conf` file described at `http://www.postgresql.org/docs/current/static/auth-pg-hba-conf.html` to control who can actually connect. There is a potential performance concern to this approach, in that filtering out connections using a more focused setting for `listen_addresses` can be more efficient than letting clients connect. If you let a client connect and then validate them against `pg_hba.conf`, it uses some additional service resources and introduces the possibility for a malicious user to launch a denial-of-service attack via this route.

In practice, few PostgreSQL servers are directly exposed to internet-wide queries anyway. Normally, you'd filter out the default port for PostgreSQL (`5432`) at the firewall-level to handle this level of security, which is the most efficient approach, and a common implementation shared for securing other applications too. If you have a system that's exposed to the world, which is increasingly common for situations such as cloud-hosted databases, make sure to use all three layers of defense. Restrict who can connect at the firewall-level; reduce what addresses you listen on if practical; and lock down who can get access to the database using `pg_hba.conf`.

max_connections

One of the settings that you'll always find set to a value, typically 100, in the `postgresql.conf` generated by `initdb` is `max_connections`. As each connection uses a small amount of shared memory, as described in the previous chapter, `Chapter 5`, *Memory for Database Caching*, it's possible for systems with particularly limited shared-memory defaults to not even allow these many connections. Accordingly, like `shared_buffers`, some investigation is done when the database cluster is created, and then the largest value supported up to 100 is saved into the default configuration. In practice, the amount of non-shared memory each client uses for things like sorting will dwarf this, but the shared component can't be completely ignored.

It is important not to set this parameter to a value much higher than you need it. There are several downsides to larger settings. The first is wasted shared memory, typically the last of the things to be concerned about as the amount per connection is small.

There are other resources a client can use, however, with memory allocations for sorting (controlled via `work_mem`, covered in the following section) normally the largest. If a large number of connections are allowed, to be safely conservative these settings must be made smaller too, so that the potential for excess resource use is limited.

 Windows PostgreSQL servers can be extremely limited in the number of connections they support due to resource allocation issues. It's common for only about 125 connections to be possible before running out of memory in the desktop heap area.

Finally, establishing connections in PostgreSQL should be considered a resource-intensive operation. It is not a goal of the database server for the acts of establishing a database connection, authenticating, and reaching the point where a query can be executed to be lightweight operations. Generally, connection overhead starts to become a bottleneck on general server operation after several hundred connections; the exact threshold varies depending on hardware and configuration. Certainly, if you intend to support thousands of queries at once, you cannot do that by allowing each client to connect to the database directly. Putting connection-pooling software between the application and the database is the common way to handle this scalability limitation, and that topic is covered in `Chapter 13`, *Pooling and Caching*.

Shared memory

The shared memory settings are important to get right because they will always require a full database restart to change the server cannot reallocate shared memory dynamically.

shared_buffers

Setting `shared_buffers` usefully was the topic of most of the last chapter.

Free Space Map settings

Space left behind from deletions or updates of data is placed into a **Free Space Map** (**FSM**) by VACUUM, and then new allocations are done from that free space first, rather than by allocating new disk space for them instead.

Starting in PostgreSQL 8.4, the FSM is stored on disk, and therefore scales in size automatically. In PostgreSQL versions up to 8.3, the FSM was stored in shared memory, which required monitoring how much of it was being used, potentially increasing it in size. Making sure the FSM settings in the configuration file, such as `max_fsm_pages` and `max_fsm_relations`, are sufficient should be part of your regular system maintenance on these versions. This can be run manually or by executing VACUUM VERBOSE to measure its current use in more automatic scripted form. More about this subject appears in Chapter 5, *Memory for Database Caching*, and it's a major focus of Chapter 7, *Routine Maintenance*.

Logging

General logging setup is important, but it is somewhat outside the scope of this book. You may need to set parameters such as `log_destination`, `log_directory`, and `log_filename` to save your log files in a way compatible with the system administrations requirements of your environment. These will all be set to reasonable defaults to get started with on most systems. Chapter 7, *Routine Maintenance* will cover adjustments to these for CSV logging, which can be helpful for analyzing query timing.

On Unix-like systems, it's common for some of the database logging to be set in the script that starts and stops the server, rather than directly in the `postgresql.conf` file. If you instead use the `pg_ctl` command to manually start the server, you may discover that logging ends up on your screen instead. You'll need to look at the script that starts the server normally (commonly `/etc/init.d/postgresql`) to determine what it does, if you want to duplicate that behavior. In most cases, you just need to add `-l logfilename` to the `pg_ctl` command line to redirect its output to the standard location.

log_line_prefix

The default `log_line_prefix` is empty, which is not what you want. A good starting value here is the following:

```
log_line_prefix='%t:%r:%u@%d:[%p]: '
```

This will put the following into every log line:

- `%t`: Timestamp
- `%u`: Database user name
- `%r`: Remote host connection is from
- `%d`: Database connection is to
- `%p`: Process ID of connection

It may not be obvious what you'd want all of these values for initially, particularly the process ID. Once you've tried to chase down a few performance issues, the need for saving these values will be more obvious, and you'll be glad to already have this data logged.

Another approach worth considering is setting `log_line_prefix` such that the resulting logs will be compatible with the pgFouine program, described in `Chapter 7`, *Routine Maintenance*. That is a reasonable, general-purpose logging prefix, and many sites end up needing to do some sort of query analysis eventually.

log_statement

The options for this setting are as follows:

- `none`: Do not log any statement-level information.
- `ddl` : Log only **Data Definition Language** (DDL) statements such as CREATE and DROP. This can normally be left on even in production, and is handy to catch major changes introduced accidentally or intentionally by administrators.
- `mod`: Log any statement that modifies a value, which is essentially everything except for simple SELECT statements. If your workload is mostly SELECT based with relatively few data changes, it may be practical to leave this enabled all the time.
- `all`: Log every statement. This is generally impractical to leave on in production due to the overhead of the logging. However, if your server is powerful enough relative to its workload, it may be practical to keep it on all the time.

Statement logging is a powerful technique for finding performance issues. Analyzing the information saved by `log_statement` and related sources for statement-level detail can reveal the true source for many types of performance issues. You will need to combine this with appropriate analysis tools, which are covered in Chapter 7, *Routine Maintenance*.

log_min_duration_statement

Once you have some idea of how long a typical query statement should take to execute, this setting allows you to log only the ones that exceed some threshold you set. The value is in milliseconds, so you might set:

```
log_min_duration_statement=1000
```

And then, you'll only see statements that take longer than one second to run. This can be extremely handy for finding out the source of *outlier* statements that take much longer than most to execute.

If you are running 8.4 or later, you might instead prefer to use the `auto_explain` module at http://www.postgresql.org/docs/8.4/static/auto-explain.html instead of this feature. This will allow you to actually see why the queries that are running slowly are doing so, by viewing their associated EXPLAIN plans.

News on PostgreSQL 10

In PostgreSQL 10.0, we have some news:

- Functions `pg_ls_logdir()` and `pg_ls_waldir()` can be executed by non-superusers with the proper permissions
- The new function `pg_current_logfile()` reads the logging collector's current `stderr` and CSV log output file names:

```
pgbench=# select pg_current_logfile() ;
   pg_current_logfile
------------------------
 log/postgresql-Sun.log
(1 row)
```

Vacuuming and statistics

PostgreSQL databases require two primary forms of regular maintenance as data is added, updated, and deleted.

VACUUM cleans up after old transactions, including removing information that is no longer visible and returning freed space to where it can be reused. The more often you update and delete information from the database, the more likely you'll need a regular VACUUM cleaning regime. However, even static tables with data that never changes once inserted still need occasional care here. ANALYZE looks at tables in the database and collects statistics about them—information such as estimates of how many rows they have and how many distinct values are in there. Many aspects of query planning depend on this statistics data being accurate. There's more about VACUUM in Chapter 7, *Routine Maintenance*, and the use of statistics is covered as part of Chapter 10, *Query Optimization*.

autovacuum

As both these tasks are critical to database performance over the long term, starting in PostgreSQL 8.1, there is an autovacuum daemon available that will run in the background to handle these tasks for you. Its action is triggered by the number of changes to the database exceeding a threshold it calculates based on the existing table size.

The parameter for autovacuum is turned on by default in PostgreSQL 8.3, and the default settings are generally aggressive enough to work out of the box for smaller database, with little manual tuning. Generally, you just need to be careful that the amount of data in the free space map doesn't exceed max_fsm_pages, and even that requirement is automated away from being a concern as of 8.4.

Enabling autovacuum on older versions

If you have autovacuum available but it's not turned on by default, which will be the case with PostgreSQL 8.1 and 8.2, there are a few related parameters that must also be enabled for it to work, as covered at http://www.postgresql.org/docs/8.1/interactive/maintenance.html or http://www.postgresql.org/docs/8.2/interactive/routine-vacuuming.html.

The normal trio to enable in the file in these versions are:

```
stats_start_collector=true
stats_row_level=true
autovacuum=on
```

Note that as warned in the documentation, it's also wise to consider adjusting `superuser_reserved_connections` to allow for the `autovacuum` processes in these earlier versions.

The `autovacuum` you'll get in 8.1 and 8.2 is not going to be as efficient as what comes in 8.3 and later. You can expect it to take some fine tuning to get the right balance of enough maintenance without too much overhead, and because there's only a single worker it's easier for it to fall behind on a busy server. This topic isn't covered at length here. It's generally a better idea to put time into planning an upgrade to a PostgreSQL version with a newer `autovacuum` than to try and tweak an old one extensively, particularly if there are so many other performance issues that cannot be resolved easily in the older versions too.

maintainance_work_mem

A few operations in the database server need working memory for larger operations than just regular sorting. `VACUUM`, `CREATE INDEX`, and `ALTER TABLE ADD FOREIGN KEY` can all allocate up to `maintainance_work_mem` worth of memory instead. As it's unlikely that many sessions will be doing one of these operations at once, it's possible to set this value much higher than the standard per-client `work_mem` setting. Note that at least `autovacuum_max_workers` (defaulting to 3 starting in version 8.3) will allocate this much memory, so consider those sessions (perhaps along with a session or two doing a `CREATE INDEX`) when setting this value.

Assuming you haven't increased the number of autovacuum workers, a typical high setting for this value on a modern server would be at five percent of the total RAM, so that even five such processes wouldn't exceed a quarter of available memory. This works out to approximately 50 MB of `maintainance_work_mem` per GB of server RAM.

default_statistics_target

PostgreSQL makes its decisions about how queries execute based on statistics collected about each table in your database. This information is collected by analyzing the tables, either with the `ANALYZE` statement or via `autovacuum` doing that step. In either case, the amount of information collected during the analyze step is set by `default_statistics_target`. Increasing this value makes analysis take longer, and as analysis of `autovacuum` happens regularly, this turns into increased background overhead for database maintenance. But, if there aren't enough statistics about a table, you can get bad plans for queries against it.

The default value for this setting used to be very low (that is, 10), but was increased to 100 in PostgreSQL 8.4. Using that larger value was popular in earlier versions, too, for general improved query behavior. Indexes using the `LIKE` operator tended to work much better with values greater than 100 rather than below it, due to a hardcoded change at that threshold.

Note that increasing this value does result in a net slowdown on your system if you're not ever running queries where the additional statistics result in a change to a better query plan. This is one reason why some simple benchmarks show PostgreSQL 8.4 as slightly slower than 8.3 at default parameters for each, and in some cases you might return an 8.4 install to a smaller setting. Extremely large settings for `default_statistics_target` are discouraged due to the large overhead they incur.

If there is a particular column in a table you know that needs better statistics, you can use `ALTER TABLE SET STATISTICS` on that column to adjust this setting, just for it. This works better than increasing the system-wide default and making every table pay for that requirement. Typically, the columns that really require a lot more statistics to work properly will require a setting near the maximum of 1000 (increased to 10,000 in later versions) to get a serious behavior change, which is far higher than you'd want to collect data for on every table in the database.

Checkpoints

The mechanics of how checkpoints worked were covered in the previous chapter, Chapter 5, *Memory for Database Caching*, along with the principle tunables involved. The discussion here will focus mainly on common practice for initially setting these values.

checkpoint_segments – max_wal_size

In PostgreSQL 10, `checkpoint_segments` has been replaced with `max_wal_size`. Each WAL segment takes up 16 MB. As described at http://www.postgresql.org/docs/current/interactive/wal-configuration.html, the maximum number of WAL segments you can expect to be in use at any time is:

```
(2 + checkpoint_completion_target) * checkpoint_segments + 1
```

On PostgreSQL 10, `checkpoint_segments` is approximately equivalent to *max_wal_size/(3 * 16 MB)* as seen in `Chapter 5`, *Memory for Database Caching*.

Note that in PostgreSQL versions before 8.3 that do not have spread checkpoints, you can still use this formula; just substitute the following code snippet for the value you'll be missing:

```
checkpoint_completion_target=0
```

The easiest way to think about the result is in terms of the total size of all the WAL segments that you can expect to see on disk, which has both a disk cost and serves as something that can be used to estimate the time for recovery after a database crash.

The expected peak `pg_wal` size grows as shown in the following table: (remember that on PostgreSQL 10, `checkpoint_segments` is approximately equivalent to *max_wal_size/(3 * 16MB)*)

checkpoint_segments	checkpoint_completion_target=0	target=0.5	target=0.9
3	112 MB	144 MB	160 MB
10	336 MB	416 MB	480 MB
32	1040 MB	1296 MB	1504 MB
64	2064 MB	2576 MB	2992 MB
128	4112 MB	5136 MB	5968 MB
256	8208 MB	10256 MB	11904 MB

The general rule of thumb you can extract here is that for every 32 checkpoint segments, expect at least 1 GB of WAL files to accumulate. As database crash recovery can take quite a while to process even that much data, 32 is as high as you want to make this setting for anything but a serious database server. The default of 3 is very low for most systems though; even a small install should consider an increase to at least 10.

Normally, you'll only want a value greater than 32 on a smaller server when doing bulk-loading, where it can help performance significantly and crash recovery isn't important. Databases that routinely do bulk loads may need a higher setting.

checkpoint_timeout

The default for this setting of 5 minutes is fine for most installations. If your system isn't able to keep up with writes and you've already increased `max_wal_size` to where the timeout is the main thing driving when checkpoints happen, it's reasonable to consider an increase to this value. Aiming for 10 minutes or more between checkpoints isn't dangerous; again it just increases how long database recovery after a crash will take. As this is one component to database server downtime after a crash, that's something you need a healthy respect for.

checkpoint_completion_target

This specifies the target of checkpoint completion as a fraction of total time between checkpoints. The default is `0.5`. The `max_wal_size` is a soft limit for total WAL size, so the database will try not to exceed it, but is allowed to, so keep enough free space on the partition and monitor it; the default value of `max_wal_size` is 1 GB, so the database will start a checkpoint after writing 500 MB of WAL, depending on `checkpoint_completion_target` (the default is `0.5`).

It's reasonable at that point to also increase `checkpoint_competion_target` to its practical maximum of `0.9`. This gives maximum checkpoint spreading, which theoretically means the smoothest I/O, too. In some cases keeping the default of `0.5` will still be better however, as it makes it less likely that one checkpoint's writes will spill into the next one.

It's unlikely that a value below `0.5` will be very effective at spreading checkpoints at all. Moreover, unless you have an extremely large value for the number of segments, the practical difference between small changes in its value are unlikely to matter.

You can try first with `checkpoint_completion_target = 0.5` and then with `checkpoint_completion_target = 0.9` with your application, and see which one gives the smoother disk I/O curve over time, as judged by OS-level monitoring.

You might try setting `checkpoint_completion_target` roughly using this formula:

$$(checkpoint\_timeout - 2min)/checkpoint\_timeout$$

For example, 30 minutes is about 0.93.

WAL settings

The PostgreSQL WAL was described in Chapter 5, *Memory for Database Caching*.

wal_buffers

While the documentation on `wal_buffers` suggests that the default of 64 KB is sufficient as long as no single transaction exceeds that value, in practice, write-heavy benchmarks see optimal performance at higher values than you might expect from that, at least 1 MB or more. With the only downside being the increased use of shared memory, and as there's no case where more than a single WAL segment could need to be buffered, given modern server memory sizes the normal thing to do nowadays is to just set:

```
wal_buffers=16MB
```

Then, forget about it as a potential bottleneck or item to tune further. Only if you're tight on memory should you consider a smaller setting; a good starting point is shown at http://pgtune.leopard.in.ua/.

wal_sync_method

Chapter 2, *Database Hardware*, touched on the importance of setting up your server to avoid volatile write-back caches. One purpose of `wal_sync_method` is to tune such caching behavior.

The default behavior here is somewhat different from most of the options. When the server source code is compiled, a series of possible ways to write are considered. The one believed most efficient then becomes the compiled-in default. This value is not written to the `postgresql.conf` file at `initdb` time though, making it different from other auto-detected, platform-specific values such as `shared_buffers`.

Before adjusting anything, you should check what your platform detected as the fastest safe method using `show`; the following is a Linux example:

```
postgres=# show wal_sync_method;
 wal_sync_method
-----------------
 fdatasync
```

On both Windows and macOS X platforms, there is a special setting to make sure the OS clears any write-back caches. The safe value to use on these platforms that turns on this behavior is as follows:

```
wal_sync_method=fsync_writethrough
```

If you have this setting available to you, you really want to use it! It does exactly the right thing to make database writes safe, while not slowing down other applications the way disabling an entire hard drive write cache will do.

This setting will not work on all platforms, however. Note that you will see a performance drop going from the default to this value, as is always the case when going from unsafe to reliable caching behavior.

On other platforms, tuning `wal_sync_method` can be much more complicated. It's theoretically possible to improve write throughput on any Unix-like system by switching from any write method that uses a `write/fsync` or `write/fdatasync` pair, to using a true synchronous write. On platforms that support safe `DSYNC` write behavior, you may already see this as your default when checking it with:

```
wal_sync_method=open_datasync
```

Even so, you won't see it explicitly listed in the configuration file as such. If this is the case on your platform, there's little optimization beyond this that you can likely perform. `open_datasync` is generally the optimal approach, and when available it can even use direct I/O as well to bypass the OS cache.

The Linux situation is perhaps the most complicated. As shown in the last code, this platform will default to `fdatasync` as the method used. It is possible to switch this to use synchronous writes with:

```
wal_sync_method=open_sync
```

Also, in many cases, you can discover this is faster-sometimes much faster, than the default behavior. However, whether this is safe or not depends on your filesystem. The default filesystem on most Linux systems, ext3, does not handle `O_SYNC` writes safely in many cases, which can result in corruption. See *PANIC caused by open_sync on Linux* at `http://archives.postgresql.org/pgsql-hackers/2007-10/msg01310.php` for an example of how dangerous this setting can be on that platform. There is evidence that this particular area has finally been cleaned up on recent (2.6.32) kernels when using the ext4 filesystem instead, but this has not been tested extensively at the database level yet.

In any case, your own tests of `wal_sync_method` should include the pull the cord test, where you power the server off unexpectedly, to make sure you don't lose any data with the method you've used. Testing at a very high load for a long period of time is also advisable, to find intermittent bugs that might cause a crash.

PITR and WAL replication

The `archive_mode`, `archive_command`, and `archive_timeout` settings are discussed in `Chapter 14`, *Scaling with Replication*.

Per-client settings

While all of the settings in this section can be adjusted per client, you'll still want good starting settings for these parameters in the main configuration file. Individual clients that need values outside the standard can always do so using the `SET` command within their session.

effective_cache_size

As mentioned in the last chapter, PostgreSQL is expected to have both its own dedicated memory (`shared_buffers`) as well as utilize the filesystem cache. In some cases, when making decisions such as whether it is efficient to use an index or not, the database compares sizes it computes against the effective sum of all these caches; that's what it expects to find in `effective_cache_size`.

The same rough rule of thumb that would put `shared_buffers` at 25% of system memory would set `effective_cache_size` to between 50 and 75% of RAM. To get a more accurate estimate, first observe the size of the filesystem cache:

- **Unix-like systems**: Add the free and cached numbers shown by the free or top commands to estimate the filesystem cache size
- **Windows**: Use the Windows Task Manager's **Performance** tab and look at the system cache size

Assuming you have already started the database, you need to then add the `shared_buffers` figure to this value to arrive at a figure for `effective_cache_size`. If the database hasn't been started yet, usually the OS cache will be an accurate enough estimate, when it's not running. Once it is started, most of the database's dedicated memory will usually be allocated to its buffer cache anyway.

`effective_cache_size` does not allocate any memory. It's strictly used as input on how queries are executed, and a rough estimate is sufficient for most purposes. However, if you set this value much too high, actually executing the resulting queries may result in both the database and OS cache being disrupted by reading in the large number of blocks required to satisfy the query believed to fit easily in RAM.

It's rare you'll ever see this parameter tuned on a per-client basis, even though it is possible.

synchronous_commit

In `Chapter 2`, *Database Hardware*, the overhead of waiting for physical disk commits was stressed as a likely bottleneck for committing transactions. If you don't have a battery-backed write cache to accelerate that, but you need better commit speed, what can you do? The standard approach is to disable `synchronous_commit`, which is sometimes alternately referred to as enabling asynchronous commits.

This groups commits into chunks at a frequency determined by the related `wal_writer_delay` parameter. The default settings guarantee a real commit to disk at most 600 milliseconds after the client commit. During that window, which you can reduce in size with a corresponding decrease in speed-up, that data will not be recovered afterward if your server crashes.

Note that it's possible to turn this parameter off for a single client during its session rather than making it a server-wide choice. This provides you with the option of having different physical commit guarantees for different types of data you put into the database. A routine activity monitoring table, one that was frequently inserted into and where a fraction of a second of loss is acceptable, would be a good candidate for an asynchronous commit. An infrequently written table holding real-world monetary transactions should prefer the standard `synchronous_commit`.

The `synchronous_commit` specifies whether a transaction commit will wait for WAL records to be written to disk before the command returns a success indication to the client. The default, and safe, setting is on. When off, there can be a delay between when success is reported to the client and when the transaction is really guaranteed to be safe against a server crash. (The maximum delay is three times `wal_writer_delay`.) Unlike `fsync`, setting this parameter to off does not create any risk of database inconsistency: an OS or database crash might result in some recent allegedly-committed transactions being lost, but the database state will be just the same as if those transactions had been aborted cleanly. So, turning `synchronous_commit` off can be a useful alternative when performance is more important than exact certainty about the durability of a transaction. More documentation can be found at
`https://www.postgresql.org/docs/10/static/runtime-config-wal.html#GUC-SYNCHRONO US-COMMIT`.

work_mem

When a query is running that needs to sort data, the database estimates how much data is involved and then compares it to the `work_mem` parameter. If it's larger (and the default is only 1 MB), rather than sorting in memory it will write all the data out and use a disk-based sort instead. This is much, much slower than a memory based one. Accordingly, if you regularly sort data, and have memory to spare, a large increase in `work_mem` can be one of the most effective ways to speed up your server.

A data warehousing report might on a giant server run with a gigabyte of `work_mem` for its larger reports.

The catch is that you can't necessarily predict the number of sorts any one client will be doing, and `work_mem` is a per-sort parameter rather than a per-client one. This means that memory use via `work_mem` is theoretically unbounded, with a number of clients sorting large enough things to happen concurrently.

In practice, there aren't that many sorts going on in a typical query, usually only one or two. And not every client that's active will be sorting at the same time. The normal guidance for `work_mem` is to consider how much free RAM is around after `shared_buffers` is allocated (the same OS caching size figure needed to compute `effective_cache_size`), divide by `max_connections`, and then take a fraction of that figure; a half of that would be an aggressive `work_mem` value. In that case, only if every client had two sorts active all at the same time would the server be likely to run out of memory, which is an unlikely scenario.

The `work_mem` computation is increasingly used in later PostgreSQL versions for estimating whether hash structures can be built in memory. Its use as a client, memory size threshold is not limited just to sorts. That's simply the easiest way to talk about the type of memory allocation decision it helps to guide.

Like `synchronous_commit`, `work_mem` can also be set per-client. This allows an approach where you keep the default to a moderate value, and only increase sort memory for the clients that you know are running large reports.

random_page_cost

This parameter is common to tune, but explaining what it does requires a lot of background about how queries are planned. That will be covered in `Chapter 10`, *Query Optimization*. Particularly, in earlier PostgreSQL versions, lowering this value from its default, for example, a reduction from 4.0 to 2.0, was a common technique.

It was used for making it more likely that the planner would use indexed queries instead of the alternative of a sequential scan. With the smarter planner in current versions, this is certainly not where you want to start tuning. You should prefer getting better statistics and setting the memory parameters as primary ways to influence the query planner.

constraint_exclusion

If you are using PostgreSQL 8.3 or earlier versions, and you are using the database's table inheritance feature to partition your data, you'll need to turn this parameter on, or on partition. The reasons for that are covered in `Chapter 15`, *Partitioning Data*. Starting in 8.4, `constraint_exclusion` defaults to a new smarter setting named `partition` that will do the right thing in most situations without it ever needing to be adjusted.

On PostgreSQL 10.0, allowed values of `constraint_exclusion` are `on` (examine constraints for all tables), `off` (never examine constraints), and `partition` (examine constraints only for inheritance child tables and `UNION ALL` subqueries). `partition` is the default setting. It is often used with inheritance and partitioned tables to improve performance.

Tunables to avoid

There are a few parameters in the `postgesql.conf` that have gathered up poor guidance in other guides you might come across, and they might already be set badly in a server whose configuration you're now responsible for. Others have names suggesting a use for the parameter that actually doesn't exist. This section warns you about the most common of those to avoid adjusting.

fsync

If you just want to ignore crash recovery altogether, you can do that by turning off the `fsync` parameter. This makes the value for `wal_sync_method` irrelevant, because the server won't be doing any WAL sync calls anymore.

It is important to recognize that if you have any sort of server crash when `fsync` is disabled, it is likely your database will be corrupted and no longer start afterward. Despite this being a terrible situation to be running a database under, the performance speedup of turning crash recovery off is so large that you might come across suggestions you disable `fsync` anyway. You should be equally hesitant to trust any other advice you receive from sources suggesting this, as it is an unambiguously dangerous setting to disable.

One reason this idea gained traction is that in earlier PostgreSQL versions, there was no way to reduce the number of `fsync` calls to a lower number to trade some amount of reliability for performance. Starting in 8.3, in most cases where people used to disable `fsync` it's a better idea to turn off `synchronous_commit` instead.

There is one case where `fsync=off` may still make sense: initial bulk loading. If you're inserting a very large amount of data into the database, and do not have hardware with a battery-backed write cache, you might discover this takes far too long to ever be practical. In this case, turning the parameter off during the load, where all data can easily be recreated if there is a crash causing corruption, maybe the only way to get loading time below your target. Once your server is back up again, you should turn it right back on.

Some systems will also turn off `fsync` on servers with redundant copies of the database, for example, slaves used for reporting purposes. These can always resynchronize against the master if their data gets corrupted.

full_page_writes

Much like `fsync`, turning this parameter off increases the odds of database corruption in return for an increase in performance. You should only consider adjusting this parameter if you're doing extensive researching into your filesystem and hardware, in order to assure partial page writes do not happen.

commit_delay and commit_siblings

Before `synchronous_commit` was implemented, there was an earlier attempt to add the same sort of feature enabled by the `commit_delay` and `commit_siblings` parameters. These are not effective parameters to tune in most cases. It is extremely difficult to show any speedup by adjusting them, and quite easy to slow every transaction down by tweaking them. The only case where they have shown some value is for extremely high I/O rate systems. Increasing the delay to a very small amount can make writes happen in bigger blocks, which sometimes turn out better aligned when combined with larger RAID stripe sizes in, particular.

max_prepared_transactions

Many people see this name and assume that as they use prepared statements, a common technique to avoid SQL injection, they need to increase this value. This is not the case; the two are not related. A prepared transaction is one that uses PREPARE TRANSACTION for a two-phase commit (2PC). If you're not specifically using that command and 2PC, you can leave this value at its default. If you are using these features, only then will you likely need to increase it to match the number of connections.

Querying enable parameters

It's possible to disable many of the query planner's techniques, in hopes of avoiding a known bad type of query. This is sometimes used as a work-around for the fact that PostgreSQL doesn't support direct optimizer hints for how to execute a query.

You might see the following code snippet, suggested as a way to force use of indexes instead of sequential scans, for example:

```
enable_seqscan = off
```

Generally, this is a bad idea, and you should improve the information the query optimizer is working with so it makes the right decisions instead. This topic is covered in Chapter 10, *Query Optimization*.

New server tuning

There are a few ways to combine all of this information into a process for tuning a new server. Which is the best is based on what else you expect the server to be doing, along with what you're looking to adjust yourself versus taking rule-of-thumb estimates for.

Dedicated server guidelines

Initial server tuning can be turned into a fairly mechanical process:

1. Adjust the logging default to be more verbose.
2. Determine how large to set shared_buffers to. Start at 25% of system memory. Consider adjusting upward if you're on a recent PostgreSQL version with spread checkpoints and know your workload benefits from giving memory directory to the buffer cache. If you're on a platform where this parameter is not so useful, limit its value or adjust downward accordingly.
3. Estimate your maximum connections generously, as this is a hard limit; clients will be refused connection once it's reached (without a pool manager).
4. Start the server with these initial parameters. Note how much memory is still available for the OS filesystem cache:

   ```
   $ free -m
    total used free shared buffers cached
   Mem: 3934 1695 2239 11 89 811
   -/+ buffers/cache: 793 3141
   Swap: 4091 0 4091
   $ pg_ctl start
   $ free -m
    total used free shared buffers cached
   Mem: 3934 1705 2229 22 89 822
   -/+ buffers/cache: 793 3141
   Swap: 4091 0 4091
   ```

5. Adjust effective_cache_size based on shared_buffers plus the OS cache.

6. Divide the OS cache size by `max_connections`, then by two. This gives you an idea of a maximum reasonable setting for `work_mem`. If your application is not dependent on sort performance, a much lower value than that would be more appropriate.

7. Set `maintenance_work_mem` to around 50 MB per GB of RAM:

   ```
   Set max_wal_size to 1GB.
   ```

8. Increase `checkpoint_segments` to at least 10. If you have server-class hardware with a battery-backed write cache, a setting of 32 would be a better default. Choose a reasonable `checkpoint_timeout` value and `set max_wal_size` high enough to be rarely reached.

9. If you're using a platform where the default `wal_sync_method` is unsafe, change it to one that is.

10. Increase `wal_buffers` to 16 MB.

11. For PostgreSQL versions before 8.4, consider increases to both `default_statistics_target` (to 100, the modern default) and `max_fsm_pages`, based on what you know about the database workload.

Once you've set up some number of servers running your type of applications, you should have a better idea what kind of starting values make sense to begin with. The values for `max_wal_size` in particular can end up being very different from what's suggested here.

Shared server guidelines

If your database server is sharing hardware with another use, particularly the common situation where a database-driven application is installed on the same system, you cannot be nearly as aggressive in your tuning as described in the last section. An exact procedure is harder to outline. What you should try to do is use tuning values for the memory-related values on the low side of recommended practice:

- Only dedicate 10% of RAM to `shared_buffers` at first, even on platforms where more would normally be advised
- Set `effective_cache_size` to 50% or less of system RAM, perhaps less if you know your application is going to be using a lot of it
- Be very stingy about increases to `work_mem`

The other suggestions in the previous section should still hold; using larger values for `max_wal_size` and considering the appropriate choice of `wal_sync_method`, for example, are no different on a shared system than on a dedicated one.

Then, simulate your application running with a full-sized workload, and then measure available RAM to see if more might be suitable to allocate toward the database. This may be an iterative process, and it certainly should be matched with application-level benchmarking if possible. There's no sense in giving memory to the database on a shared system if the application, or another layer of caching such as at the connection-pooler level, would use it more effectively. That same idea of getting reasonable starting settings and tune iteratively based on monitoring works well for a dedicated server, too.

PgTune

Starting with PostgreSQL 8.4, the PgTune program available from `http://pgfoundry.org/projects/pgtune/` can be used to create an initial `postgresql.conf` file for a new server. It allows you to suggest what the intended type of workload is, ranging from a dedicated data warehouse server down to a developer workstation. Based on that input, and system parameters such as the amount of RAM in the server, it produces a tuned configuration for the major system parameters following similar methods to those described in this chapter. This is not going to be as accurate as following the guidelines for a dedicated server and measuring everything yourself, but it will get you up and running with a configuration that's in the right general size very quickly. Any reasonably sized `postgresql.conf` should easily outperform the default one, as that's optimized only for low shared memory use.

There is a web interface (found at `http://pgtune.leopard.in.ua/`) where `postgresql.conf` settings can be generated by prodding some of the parameters:

Summary

There are almost 200 values you might adjust in a PostgreSQL database's configuration, and getting them all right for your application can be quite a project. The guidelines here should get you into the general area where you should start though, help you avoid the most common pitfalls, and give you an idea what settings are more likely to be valuable when you do run into trouble:

- The default values in the server configuration file are very short on logging information and have extremely small memory settings. Every server should get at least a basic round of tuning to work around the worst of the known issues.
- The memory-based tunables, primarily `shared_buffers` and `work_mem`, need to be adjusted carefully and in unison to make sure your system doesn't run out of memory altogether.
- The query planner needs to know about the memory situation, and have good table statistics in order to make accurate plans.
- The process is also critical to make sure the query planner has the right information to work with, as well as to keep tables maintained properly.
- In many cases, the server does not need to be restarted to make a configuration change, and many parameters can even be adjusted on a per-client basis for really fine-tuning.

7
Routine Maintenance

PostgreSQL aims to be easy to maintain. But like any database, heavy activity can lead to a drop in performance due to overhead. The approach taken to handle concurrent read and write scalability in the database can leave behind significant amounts of data that need to be cleaned up properly. Understanding why that happens is valuable for modeling just how often related maintenance needs to occur. Another aspect of maintaining any database server is monitoring how well the queries it runs execute.

In this chapter, we will look into the following topics:

- Transaction visibility with multiversion concurrency control
- Vacuum
- Autoanalyze
- Index bloat
- Dump and restore
- Vacuuming the database/table
- Cluster
- Reindexing
- Detailed data and index page monitoring
- Monitoring query logs

Transaction visibility with multiversion concurrency control

One design decision any database needs to make is how to handle the situation where multiple clients might be interacting with the same data. PostgreSQL uses a popular approach called **Multi-Version Concurrency Control** (**MVCC**) to handle this job. MVCC is also used in BerkeleyDB, Sybase SQL Anywhere, Oracle, and many other database products; it's a general technique and not something specific to PostgreSQL. The introduction to MVCC in the documentation at
`http://www.postgresql.org/docs/current/static/mvcc-intro.html` makes the concept sound more complicated than it is. It's easier to understand with some simple examples, which we'll go through shortly.

Visibility computation internals

Understanding how visibility computation is implemented in the server is helpful both to help predict how statements will act, and so that you can interpret the diagnostic information available.

As transactions are created in the database, PostgreSQL advances a transaction ID counter, usually just called the XID, to keep track of them. When you insert a row into the database, or update an existing row, the new row created by that operation saves the session's transaction ID into a field named the insertion XID, also referred to as the `xmin`. This is the minimum XID capable of seeing this bit of information, once it's been committed:

```
postgres=# CREATE TABLE foo(bar int);
CREATE TABLE
postgres=# INSERT INTO foo VALUES(1);
INSERT 0 1
postgres=# SELECT xmin,xmax,bar from foo;
   xmin   | xmax | bar
----------+------+-----
 10708401 |    0 |   1
(1 row)
```

When a query or statement starts (tracking at either granularity can happen, depending on what mode you're in-- more on this later), it notes the current transaction ID as a hard line for what it should consider visible. As rows are considered for inclusion in the query results, if they are committed and their insertion `xmin` is less than that number, they show up in the query.

A similar mechanism handles deletion. Each row has a delete XID, also referred to as the xmax, that starts as blank to indicate the row is live. When you delete a row, the current transaction ID becomes its xmax, to say it should no longer be visible after that point in time (or technically that point in transaction history). As queries that are running consider rows for visibility, they note any non-blank xmax and only include the row if the commit of that deletion happened before the query's start XID.

xmin and xmax are essentially the visibility lifetime of the row in transaction ID terms. The row is only visible from the perspective of a query whose transaction number is between those two values. What you might not expect is that you can actually look at most of these internal details to see how they work as you run experiments, including the current transaction ID (txid_current) and the xmin/xmax data for every row you can see.

The computations are actually a bit more complicated than this, because they also consider the transactions that were in progress when the query was started too. You can see exactly what information is saved by a query to do its visibility computations by using the txid_current_snapshot() function.

For example: XE "txid_current_snapshot() function"

Updates

Let's create a simple table with one row in it to get started.

The first two lines in the following code are duplicated from Chapter 5, *Memory for Database Caching*. If you've already created them there, you should DROP TABLE t before this session to clear them out:

```
$ psql -c "CREATE TABLE t (s SERIAL, i INTEGER);"
$ psql -c "INSERT into t(i) values (0)"
INSERT 0 1
$ psql -c "SELECT *,xmin,xmax from t;"
 s | i |  xmin  | xmax
---+---+--------+------
 1 | 0 | 158208 |   0
$ psql -c "SELECT txid_current();
 txid_current
--------------
       158209
```

So there's the new row inserted, with the transaction ID xmin active for the statement that inserted it. There's no maximum yet because nothing has ever updated or deleted this row.

Now run psql, start a transaction with BEGIN, and update the row, but don't commit it yet:

```
$ psql
postgres=# BEGIN;
BEGIN
postgres=# select txid_current();
 txid_current
--------------
       158210
postgres=# UPDATE t SET i=100 WHERE s=1;
UPDATE 1
gsmith=# SELECT *,xmin,xmax from t;
 s |  i  |  xmin  | xmax
---+-----+--------+------
 1 | 100 | 158210 |    0
```

From the perspective of this session, the row has been changed. But since it has not been committed yet, other sessions will not see it. You can prove that by connecting to the database from another client session, and, looking at t; it will still show the original value:

```
$ psql -c "SELECT *,xmin,xmax FROM t"
 s | i |  xmin  |   xmax
---+---+--------+--------
 1 | 0 | 158208 | 158210
```

But it already knows that once transaction 158210 commits, this version of the row is obsolete.

This behavior is the essence of MVCC: each database client session is allowed to make changes to a table, but they don't become visible to other sessions until the transaction commits. And even after that point, sessions that are already open will not normally see that change until they are finished. Similarly, once a session starts a transaction, it's blind to most changes made to the database after that point, and its own changes are kept private until it commits. And even those aren't considered final, even in the session that made the change—if you roll back its transaction, the original values better still be around to return to. In this case, even though the last row here is shown with a lifetime ending with an xmax of 158210, if that transaction rolls back ,it doesn't matter.

As you might guess from studying the example, the server actually makes a second row on disk when you issue an UPDATE. Obviously the original one can't be overwritten given this behavior. It has no choice but to duplicate the original row, apply the update, and then save this new version. The change from old to new version is marked with a transaction identification number, which is what's used to determine which sessions that updated row should be visible to.

The first thing to recognize, then, is that an UPDATE consists of the following steps:

1. Read the original row in
2. Change the fields adjusted by the UPDATE
3. Save the new row into a newly allocated location with a new transaction ID
4. When no one else is using it anymore, VACUUM will delete the original row

Accordingly, anything that you UPDATE will temporarily take up twice as much disk space. It's not just overwriting the original row with the new values; both old and new versions will be available for some period.

Row lock conflicts

There is one tricky part left here. At the point the preceding transaction stopped, the first session has an open transaction trying to update the row WHERE s=1. What happens if we try to do something similar in the second session before that's either been committed or rolled back? Let's try the following:

```
$ psql -c "UPDATE t SET i=i+1 WHERE s=1;"
```

Guess what? This statement will hang! The reason is that we've reached the limit of how many sessions can be isolated from one another safely. Once two sessions are both trying to update the same row, some more complicated rules come into play.

Whenever you try to grab a lock on a specific row, which includes UPDATE, DELETE, and the locks SELECT FOR UPDATE or SELECT FOR DELETE obtain, those have to wait for anyone that already has a lock on that row. Once the original locker completes its work, then some decisions have to be made.

If the transaction holding the lock rolled back, no harm done; the newer one continues the originally planned work. But if the original session committed an update, changing the row the second session intended to modify itself, exactly what happens next depends on the configuration of your session.

PostgreSQL operates in two modes for resolving the order of operations in these situations. In what it calls `Read Committed` mode, the default, having another row get changed underneath a session isn't a disaster. What the server will now do is start over the original work it was planning to do with the new copy of the row. If the old row was selected using a `WHERE` clause, the new one will be checked to see if that condition still applies. If not, the new copy is now ignored, that `WHERE` clause doesn't find it anymore. But if all of the reasons for why that row was being updated still seem to apply, the planned update will then just execute against the *modified* copy.

Returning to the example again for a moment, if the original transaction commits it will be the same as if this order of events happened:

```
UPDATE t SET i=100 WHERE s=1;
UPDATE t SET i=i+1 WHERE s=1;
```

This means that `i=101` at the end. This is even though at the point where the second statement started, the other update wasn't complete or visible yet. It will wait for the update in the middle of completing and then add its own work on top of that. This is because Read Committed gets a new snapshot of database activity it might want to pay attention to at the beginning of every *statement*. In cases where just reads are being done, this will be a consistent view throughout the whole transaction. In the event of changes by other sessions, some of that new data can enter into your open session this way.

Serialization

Now, if the idea that `UPDATE` and `DELETE` statements made by other sessions will leak into your view of the database state even within a transaction horrifies you, what you probably want is the other transaction isolation method: **serializable**.

There are actually two slightly different MVCC modes available in PostgreSQL to help address different requirements here. These reflect two behaviors from the SQL standard, introduced at `http://www.postgresql.org/docs/current/static/transaction-iso.html`. The problems described there, such as non-repeatable and phantom reads, require using the database's more complicated serializable mode to avoid them, instead of the simpler and default Read Committed transaction model. It's worth reading about these problems because they tend to haunt complicated applications that never consider the sort of race conditions among database operations.

Following the same basic example, where an open session has an uncommitted UPDATE when a second tries to touch the same row, Serialization initially works the same way as Read Committed. If an UPDATE, DELETE, or lock for a row that's already locked is needed, the session waits for that to clear. If the transaction rolled back or didn't touch the data in the row, everything proceeds as in the cases already explained. But if the first transaction commits, and it actually modified the row with UPDATE or DELETE instead of just having a lock on it, you're done. You will get this error:

```
ERROR: could not serialize access due to concurrent updates
```

And your application has no choice here but to rollback the entire transaction it was in the middle of and start over again. This level of isolation is normally required if you have a transaction that executes multiple statements that absolutely must operate on an identical view of the database. Read Committed lets the visibility snapshot slip forward for things like updates to commonly touched rows as each statement is processed. A serialized session aims to keep a consistent view for the whole transaction, and if something happens to make that possible it throws an error instead of risking a problem.

Deletions

There's something a little different that happens during DELETE instead. Close out any open sessions you might have with unfinished transactions seen before. Now, let's start another transaction to delete a row:

```
postgres=# BEGIN;
BEGIN
postgres=# DELETE FROM t WHERE s=1;
DELETE 1
postgres=# SELECT * from t;
 s | i
---+---
(0 rows)
```

Once again, if you look at this table from another session, because it's not been committed yet, the row deleted here will still be there, just with an xmax value set:

```
$ psql -c "SELECT *,xmin,xmax FROM t;"
 s |  i  |  xmin  |  xmax
---+-----+--------+--------
 1 | 101 | 158213 | 158214
```

Only in the first session has the row been deleted. This brings us to a second form of visibility that needs to be considered: when a row is deleted, it can't actually go away until any session that might need to see the row has ended. So when you commit a deletion, it doesn't actually change the record itself. Instead, it updates the visibility information around that row to say *this is deleted and may not be visible everywhere*, and then each client who checks it will need to make that decision for itself. These are called dead rows in the database; regular rows are described as live.

Another interesting thing to note here is that the way this row looks is exactly like the one left behind by an update; it's just another row with an xmax set waiting for a commit, after which it can be removed. Because of MVCC, whether you update or delete a row, you get the same form of dead row left over at the end. The only exception here is if you are updating in a situation where the **Heap-Only-Tuples** (**HOT**) technique in the database can be used to speed your update, something that will covered in a while. This may be a bit less expensive.

Advantages of MVCC

Why go through all this trouble? The transaction isolation of sessions from one another has an extremely valuable result: it avoids locking many resources that can block other clients from doing their work. The locks required to run a query and read data do not conflict with the ones that are needed to write to the database. Reading never blocks writing, and writing never blocks reading. This model scales quite well into large client counts without running into lock contentions for either tables or rows. You can still explicitly lock a row or table if needed, by methods including the LOCK statement and the lock upgrades implemented in SELECT FOR SHARE and SELECT FOR UPDATE statements.

Disadvantages of MVCC

The main disadvantage of MVCC is the background work necessary to clean up its visibility data and keep disk space under control, the topic of the next section.

You should also be aware that MVCC cannot make all possible concerns about interactions between sessions and ordering magically go away. In fact, not seeing data another session has been altering until later can introduce its own new class of problem, for applications that are used to traditional locking approaches. You've seen how the UPDATE and DELETE order might happen in an unexpected way with a regular Read Committed MVCC session, and you can't just make these go away with serializable without preparing for some transactions to fail badly too.

Transaction ID wraparound

The implementation of MVCC in PostgreSQL uses a transaction ID that is 32 bits in size. It's impractical to make it any longer because as you've just seen, visibility information is stored in each row by as `xmin` and `xmax` values. Having a larger ID would therefore increase the size of each row by a significant amount. A signed 32-bit number can only handle a range of about two billion transactions before rolling over to zero. When it exceeds its range, transactions that used to appear in the past will now appear to be from the future, which as you might imagine will wreak havoc. If this transaction wraparound ever happens to your database, it will fail to operate sanely, and therefore the database will go far out of its way to keep that from happening.

The way that the 32-bit XID is mapped to handle many billions of transactions is that each table and database has a reference XID, and every other XID is relative to it. This gives an effective range of 2 billion transactions before and after that value. You can see how old these reference XID numbers are relative to current activity, starting with the oldest active entries, such as the following:

```
SELECT relname,age(relfrozenxid) FROM pg_class WHERE relkind='r' ORDER BY
age(relfrozenxid) DESC;
SELECT datname,age(datfrozenxid) FROM pg_database ORDER BY
age(datfrozenxid) DESC;
```

One of the things `VACUUM` does is push forward the frozen value once a threshold of transactions have passed, set by the `vacuum_freeze_max_age` parameter, and `autovacuum` has its own setting as `autovacuum_freeze_max_age`. This maintenance is also critical to cleaning up the commit log information stored in the `pg_xact` directory. Some transactions will *fall off the back* here, if they have a transaction ID so old that it can't be represented relative to the new reference values. Those will have their XID replaced by a special magic value called the `FrozenXID`. Once that happens, those transactions will appear *in the past* relative to all active transactions.

The values for these parameter are set very conservatively by default, to start freezing things after only 200 million transactions, even though wraparound isn't a concern until 2 billion. One reason for that is that is to keep the commit log disk space from growing excessively. At the default value, it should never take up more than 50 MB, while increasing the free age to its maximum (2 billion) will instead use up to 500 MB of space. If you have large tables where that disk usage is trivial, and you don't need to run `VACUUM` regularly in order to reclaim space, increasing the maximum free age parameters can be helpful to keep `autovacuum` from doing more work than it has to freezing your tables.

Adjusting the minimum values for when freezing happens is only really a good idea in one situation: just after a form of bulk loading where there's no way you will be modifying the transactions you just added. The problem using a low `vacuum_freeze_min_age` during normal use is that the freezing process will replace transaction information with the special `FrozenXID`, which loses potentially useful data about when those transactions committed. If you ever end up in the unfortunate position where you have to dig into transaction ordering forensics to track down how a problem happened, discovering that the XID data that would have helped sort that out has been frozen is not good news.

The basic trade-off you need to decide a position on is therefore how much of this detailed transaction number diagnostic information you want to keep around, knowing that if you keep it around too much it will take up more disk space and make `pg_xact` less efficient. And at the same time, deciding to delay VACUUM as long as possible also means that when it does happen, a lot of work has to be done. More frequent vacuum work does mean more regular small disruptions though, so some prefer to just schedule that cleanup instead of risking it popping up at a bad time. It's tricky to provide general advice here that works for everyone.

Starting in PostgreSQL 8.3, you can use the system functions described at `http://www.postgresql.org/docs/current/static/functions-info.html` to determine the latest transaction ID in use on the server. `txid_current()` is the simplest value to inspect, as shown in some of the early examples in this chapter. Watching that number grow over time lets you estimate how many transactions are occurring on your system. In order to compensate for transaction wraparound, the value returned is actually 64 bits wide, with the top 32 bits holding a counter of how many times the XID has crossed back to zero. This makes the value returned by `txid_current()` always move forward, even as the actual XID rolls over its upper limit.

Vacuum

If you surveyed a set of experienced PostgreSQL database administrators and asked what part of database maintenance requires the most work, the word **vacuum** would pop up quite often in those conversations. A combination of complexity and some unfortunate terminology choices makes this particular area of database management quite prone to problems and misunderstandings, relative to how little trouble most parts of PostgreSQL administration are.

The need for vacuum flows from the visibility approach described before. The root problem is that clients executing UPDATE or DELETE operations don't know everything happening on the server. They can't make the decision about whether the original, now dead, row can truly be deleted, which is only possible when there are in fact no clients left who need to see it. And sometimes the new rows are never actually committed, leaving behind a different sort of dead row: a rolled back one that never becomes visible.

Cleaning up after all these situations that produce dead rows (UPDATE, DELETE, and ROLLBACK) is the job for an operation named vacuuming. It inspects what transactions have finished and cleans up rows that cannot be visible to any current or future query. It also handles the transaction ID wraparound quirks of the database.

Vacuum implementation

There are two primary sets of internal structures that serve as input and output from data vacuuming.

On the input side, each database row includes status flags called hint bits that track whether the transaction that updated the xmin or xmax values is know to be committed or aborted yet. The actual commit logs (pg_xact and sometimes pg_subtrans) are consulted to confirm the hint bits transaction state if they are not set yet. VACUUM also writes to these hint bits, part of the row itself, as it confirms the known state has changed.

Besides updating the data pages themselves, the additional output from VACUUM is the updated information in the FSM.

Regular vacuum

Vacuum does a scan of each table and index looking for rows that can no longer be visible. The row hint bits are updated to reflect any information discovered, and newly freed space is inserted into the FSM.

Once the FSM for a table has entries on it, new allocations for this table will reuse that existing space when possible, instead of allocating new space from the OS.

Returning free disk space

Usually, administrators are surprised to find that there is no reduction in disk space from using vacuum. There is only one situation where VACUUM can actually reduce the size of a table. If the last data page of a table is empty, completely free of rows, and it's possible to obtain an exclusive lock on the table, VACUUM executes a special disk release process. It will scan backwards from the end, returning all pages it finds to the operating system as now free space, until it finds a data page that isn't empty.

Accordingly, it's only possible for a regular vacuum to reduce the size of a table if it has a contiguous chunk of free space at the end of the table. One common situation that can produce this pattern of disk usage is when a table includes a fixed time period of data, with new records constantly inserted and older ones periodically deleted. If those deletions are cleaned up properly with vacuum, eventually you can expect that the table size will reach a steady state.

In most other situations, VACUUM will never release disk space. In regular operation, your goal should be for VACUUM to run often enough that there never is a large amount of free space in any table to release. This is sometimes unavoidable, however; a large deletion of historical data is one way to end up with a table with lots of free space at its beginning.

Full vacuum

In versions of PostgreSQL before 9.0, the VACUUM FULL command, which is never executed by autovacuum, takes a more aggressive approach to space reuse. It compacts tables by moving rows to the earliest page they can be placed onto. This makes the one situation where vacuum can release disk space, when it's all at the end of the table, very likely. If you have any dead rows in your table, VACUUM FULL will relocate them one at a time to an earlier part of the table, and then shrink it accordingly once the end is all empty space.

There are two major downsides to doing that. The first is that it's very time and resource intensive. VACUUM FULL is likely to take a very long time if your table is larger, and during that time it will have an exclusive lock on the table. That's a very bad combination. The second issue is index bloat, covered in more detail later, and equally troublesome.

The net impact of this combination is that you want to avoid ever running VACUUM FULL, which means that you should also avoid the situations that lead toward it being the only remedy.

PostgreSQL 9.0 has introduced a rewritten VACUUM FULL command that is modeled on the cluster implementation of earlier versions. It does not have the same issues described in this section. Instead, it does have the limitation that you need enough disk space to hold a fresh copy of the table in order for it to work.

HOT

One of the major performance features added to PostgreSQL 8.3 is HOT. HOT allows reusing space left behind by dead rows resulting from DELETE or UPDATE operations under some common conditions. The specific case that HOT helps with is when you are making changes to a row that does not update any of its indexed columns. When this happens, if the new second copy of the row can be fit onto the same page as the existing one, it's put there without a new index entry being allocated for it. Instead, it's added to a list on that existing data block if there's space, in a structure called an update chain.

And in order to make this case more likely to occur, HOT also does a single-block mini-vacuum as part of its work whenever practical to do so. This combination doing a single block VACUUM and avoiding changes to the index structure allows an update that used to touch both the data (heap) block and an index block to instead only touch the heap; thus the name (Heap-Only).

Note that this doesn't completely eliminate the need for other forms of vacuum, because HOT may not be able to do the single-block vacuum. It may not clean up after all possible cases involving aborted transactions as well.

The normal way to check if you are getting the benefit of HOT updates or not is to monitor pg_stat_user_tables and compare the counts for n_tup_upd (regular updates) versus n_tup_hot_upd.

One of the ways to make HOT more effective on your tables is to use a larger fill factor setting when creating them. Having extra empty space available in blocks gives HOT more room to do the shuffling around it is good at, without having to move data to new disk pages.

Cost-based vacuuming

Running a regular VACUUM command is a pretty intensive operation. It's likely to become the most resource intensive process running on your server, and if autovacuum ran in that fashion it would be unusable in many environments.

Fortunately, there's another approach available. Cost-based vacuuming limits the amount of disk I/O any given VACUUM or autovacuum process is expected to do per unit of time. It works by assigning an estimated cost to every I/O operation, accumulating a total for each operation it performs, then pausing once an upper limit on cost per iteration is exceeded.

The cost estimation presumes three basic operations VACUUM performs, each with their own presumed amount of work to handle:

- **Page hit**: A data page was needed, but found in the shared buffer cache. It merely needs to be scanned for dead rows, with no physical I/O involved. This has a reference cost of one unit using vacuum_cost_page_hit, and you shouldn't ever adjust it.
- **Page miss**: The data page needed isn't already buffered, so it must be read from disk before it can be scanned. This default set using vacuum_cost_page_miss makes this cost 10.
- **Page dirty**: After being scanned, the page needed to be modified; it's now dirty and must be written out to disk. The default vacuum_cost_page_dirty is 20.

The preceding parameters are set globally for all tables in the database, and impact both manual VACUUM and autovacuum (which is described in more detail in the next section). The way these are described, such as saying things are *read from disk*, isn't quite right; they're read from the OS cache, which may even have them in regular memory already. Partly because of that class of problem, it's difficult to adjust these values, and only recommended for very experienced PostgreSQL administrators to attempt. Measuring the real-world costs of these operations is hard, and there's not much evidence yet that doing so will improve significantly over the theoretical model used here. It's much better to start vacuum adjustment for workload by tweaking the higher-level settings, described next, instead of these.

A manual vacuum worker will execute until it has exceeded vacuum_cost_limit of estimated I/O, defaulting to 200 units of work. At that point, it will then sleep for vacuum_cost_delay milliseconds, defaulting to 0, which disables the cost delay feature altogether with manually executed VACUUM statements.

However, autovacuum workers have their own parameters that work the same way. autovacuum_vacuum_cost_limit defaults to -1, which is a shorthand saying to use the same cost limit structure (the ratios between individual costs) as manual vacuum. The main way that autovacuum diverges from a manual one is it defaults to the following cost delay:

```
autovacuum_vacuum_cost_delay = 20ms
```

So, where a regular VACUUM will just keep going each time it accumulates >200 cost units of operations, autovacuum will instead sleep for 20ms each time it reaches that point.

Note that if you want to adjust a manual VACUUM to run with the cost logic, you don't need to adjust the server postgresql.conf file; this is a user setting. You can tweak it before issuing any manual VACUUM and it will effectively limit its impact for just that session:

```
postgres=# SET vacuum_cost_delay='20';
postgres=# show vacuum_cost_delay;
 vacuum_cost_delay
-------------------
 20ms
postgres=# VACUUM;
```

It's extremely difficult to turn all these estimated cost figures into a predicted real-world I/O figure. But if you combine adjusting this value with monitoring both the database and the I/O load at the operating system, it does allow some iterative tuning methods.

autovacuum

With VACUUM being so critical to performance, automating it as much as possible has been one of the most regularly improved aspects of the database during the last few years of development. Major advancements per version include the following:

- **3, 7.4, 8.0**: autovacuum is available as a contrib module (contrib/pg_autovacuum). It requires custom scripting to keep it running all the time.
- **1**: The autovacuum daemon is introduced as a distinct process managed by the server, always running whenever the server is enabled.
- **2**: Last vacuum and last analyze times are saved to pg_stat_all_tables so that you can monitor activity better.
- **3**: autovacuum is turned on by default, and it can run multiple workers at once. Additional log detail is possible via log_autovacuum_min_duration.
- **4**: Disk-based FSM means no max_fsm_pages overflow. Control of per-table behavior is switched to use table storage parameters.

Also note that in versions before 8.3 when it became enabled by default, running autovacuum also required some optional table statistics be collected. The common recipe to make this feature work in 8.2 and earlier is as follows:

```
stats_start_collector = on
```

```
stats_block_level = on
stats_row_level = on
autovacuum = on
```

autovacuum logging

In versions before 8.3, autovacuum mentioned when it was visiting each database in the logs but not much information beyond that. It's possible to watch it more directly by setting:

```
log_min_messages =debug2
```

But, be warned this level of debugging could potentially log a line or more for every statement your server executes, which is both a major performance drag and a source for running out of disk space. It's generally practical to use this much logging to track down an autovacuum problem only when you know the server is nearly idle.

In current versions, you can easily monitor the daemon's activity by setting log_autovacuum_min_duration to a number of milliseconds. It defaults to -1, turning logging off. When set to a value >=0, any autovacuum action taking longer than that amount of time will be logged. Since autovacuum can run quite often doing trivial operations you don't necessarily care about, setting this to a moderate number of milliseconds (for example 1000=1 second) is a good practice to follow.

autovacuum monitoring

As log files can easily get lost, the best way to approach making sure autovacuum is doing what it should is to monitor what tables it's worked on instead:

```
SELECT schemaname,relname,last_autovacuum,last_autoanalyze FROM
pg_stat_all_tables;
```

You can trim down the information here by changing all in the preceding code to name one of the alternate views: pg_stat_sys_tables shows only system tables, while pg_stat_user_tables shows only your user tables.

Autovacuum triggering

If any database is in danger of overflowing the maximum allowed transaction ID, autovacuum will first work on that situation. autovacuum will kick in to work on XID wraparound even if you've disabled it. It looks at the transaction age, a measure of how many transactions have happened since a database was last reset to use a new XID basis.

You can monitor the highest age on any database and see them for individual databases or tables using queries such as the following:

```
SELECT max(age(datfrozenxid)) FROM pg_database;
SELECT datname,age(datfrozenxid) from pg_database ORDER BY
age(datfrozenxid) DESC;
SELECT relname, age(relfrozenxid) FROM pg_class WHERE relkind = 'r' ORDER
BY age(relfrozenxid) DESC;
```

Once that check is passed without requiring any work, `autovacuum` next considers the statistics collected about each table during routine operation. Each table in the database has an estimated live and dead row count, as well as an estimated total number of rows (its tuple count). These are combined to form a threshold for how many rows must change before `autovacuum` processes the table, like the following:

*autovacuum_vacuum_scale_factor * tuples + autovacuum_vacuum_threshold*

As `autovacuum_vacuum_threshold` is small by default (50), once your table is of modest size it will no longer be the main component here. Instead, you'll get `autovacuum` triggering using the scale factor, which defaults to triggering after changes impact 20% of the table. Particularly on large tables, that value can be much too high—20% of a billion row table is quite a bit of dead space to be hanging around without vacuum cleanup.

This query will show you whether each table in your database qualifies for autovacuum processing, and exactly where that line is relative to the total amount of changes in there right now:

```
SELECT *,
  n_dead_tup > av_threshold AS "av_needed",
  CASE WHEN reltuples > 0
    THEN round(100.0 * n_dead_tup / (reltuples))
    ELSE 0
    END
      AS pct_dead
FROM
(SELECT
  N.nspname,
  C.relname,
  pg_stat_get_tuples_inserted(C.oid) AS n_tup_ins,
  pg_stat_get_tuples_updated(C.oid) AS n_tup_upd,
  pg_stat_get_tuples_deleted(C.oid) AS n_tup_del,
  pg_stat_get_live_tuples(C.oid) AS n_live_tup,
  pg_stat_get_dead_tuples(C.oid) AS n_dead_tup,
  C.reltuples AS reltuples,
  round(current_setting('autovacuum_vacuum_threshold')::integer
```

```
        + current_setting('autovacuum_vacuum_scale_factor')::numeric *
C.reltuples)
        AS av_threshold,
    date_trunc('minute',greatest(pg_stat_get_last_vacuum_time(C.oid),
    pg_stat_get_last_autovacuum_time(C.oid))) AS last_vacuum,
    date_trunc('minute',greatest(pg_stat_get_last_analyze_time(C.oid),
    pg_stat_get_last_analyze_time(C.oid))) AS last_analyze
  FROM pg_class C
    LEFT JOIN pg_namespace N ON (N.oid = C.relnamespace)
    WHERE C.relkind IN ('r', 't')
        AND N.nspname NOT IN ('pg_catalog', 'information_schema') AND
        N.nspname !~ '^pg_toast'
) AS av
ORDER BY av_needed DESC,n_dead_tup DESC;
```

This simple query doesn't pay any attention to the fact that you can actually customize `autovacuum` parameters for each table.

Per-table adjustments

Sometimes, individual tables have vacuum requirements that don't match the rest of the database, and it is possible to tweak the `autovacuum` behavior for each table.

> The pgAdmin III GUI interface has a simple interface for this sort of adjustment, using its **Vacuum settings** tab for an individual table you're viewing. This is one area where adjustments with the command line can be hard to get right.

Up until PostgreSQL 8.3, the per-table `autovacuum` parameters were stored in the `pg_autovacuum` system table, documented at
`http://www.postgresql.org/docs/8.3/static/catalog-pg-autovacuum.html`.

A common request is turning `autovacuum` off for just one relation, perhaps because it's being processed by a daily off-hours manual vacuum:

```
INSERT INTO pg_autovacuum (
    vacrelid,enabled,
    vac_base_thresh,vac_scale_factor,
    anl_base_thresh,anl_scale_factor,
    vac_cost_delay,vac_cost_limit,
    freeze_min_age,freeze_max_age)
VALUES
    ('mytable'::regclass,false,-1,-1,-1,-1,-1,-1,-1,-1);
```

Values that you don't want to override, and instead inherit values from the standard `autovacuum` settings, should be set to −1 as used for all of the numeric parameters in this example. You replace any parameter and set it to something new in the appropriate place.

As of version 8.4, per-table `autovacuum` information is stored as standard table storage parameters, similar to things such as the table's fill factor. These are normally set at table creation time: `http://www.postgresql.org/docs/current/static/sql-createtable.html`.

The `psql` utility displays table storage parameters when using its `d+` mode, as shown by the following example that demonstrates disabling `autovacuum` on a table:

```
postgres=# alter table t SET (autovacuum_enabled=false);
ALTER TABLE
postgres=# \d+ t
                                   Table "public.t"
 Column |  Type   |                  Modifiers                      | Storage
| Description
--------+---------+-------------------------------------------------+--------
-+-------------
 s      | integer | not null default nextval('t_s_seq'::regclass) | plain
|
 i      | integer |                                                 | plain
|
Has OIDs: no
Options: autovacuum_enabled=false
```

Common vacuum and autovacuum problems

In many of the situations where VACUUM and related cleanup, such as VACUUM FULL or CLUSTER, need to happen, such as index bloat and excessive dead tuples taking up disk space, the work involved can be so intensive that administrators decide VACUUM is something to be avoided. This is actually the opposite of what should be concluded. In reality, the answer to most vacuum-related problems is to vacuum more often. This reduces the amount of work done by each individual vacuum, and it promotes earlier reuse of space that keeps table sizes from getting so big in the first place. Do not reach the wrong conclusions from a painful vacuum situation—that almost always means you didn't vacuum often enough, not that you should avoid running VACUUM as much as possible in the future.

There are however a few known issues that you can run into with VACUUM and autovacuum that will inhibit attempts to follow recommended vacuum practice, or otherwise seem unexpected.

autovacuum is running even though it was turned off

If your table is approaching transaction ID wraparound, autovacuum will process it regardless of whether it's turned on or off globally or for that table. This is one of the many reasons why running with autovacuum off, instead of tuning it to run smoothly all the time, is dangerous. If you haven't done that tuning, and just turned it off instead, when autovacuum does start anyway to deal with wraparound it will not be adjusted appropriately to avoid interference with activity going on.

autovacuum is constantly running

While autovacuum stays running all the time, it shouldn't be doing active work all the time. If it is, there are two common issues to investigate.

Each time VACUUM runs out of its allocated space for maintenance_work_mem, it needs to start over and make an additional pass over the table. Accordingly, if you have set this tunable too low relative to the size needed to vacuum your tables, VACUUM can run much less efficiently than it should, and therefore autovacuum will be running much more often just to keep up.

Another autovacuum problem is related to having a large number of databases. Autovacuum tries to start one worker on each database every autovacuum_naptime seconds (defaulting to one minute), up the maximum set by autovacuum_max_workers. So if you have 60 databases, a new worker will be started every second with the default parameters. You probably need to increase the nap time value if you have more than a dozen databases in your cluster.

Out of memory errors

If you are too aggressive with setting maintenance_work_mem, you may discover that autovacuum periodically causes out of memory errors on your system. You can typically identify that situation because the amount of memory listed in the logs for the allocation failure attempt will match that database setting.

Don't forget that up to `autovacuum_max_workers` can be active, each using that much memory. When estimating the available RAM on the system, it's better to err on the small side initially with this setting. Ramp it up after you've done enough monitoring to know what the peak memory usage on your server is.

Not keeping up with a busy server

The default value for `autovacuum_vacuum_cost_delay` of 20 ms is a medium one appropriate for a smaller system. If you have a busy server, you can easily discover that autovacuum never quite keeps up with incoming traffic. Particularly if you have a system that's capable of good I/O performance, you can drop this setting significantly in order to give autovacuum more opportunities to keep pace with your server.

Large servers will commonly run with a cost delay in the 1 ms to 5 ms range. Your first response to not having autovacuum run often enough to keep up should be to reduce this parameter until you've reached that range. As OS timers sometimes won't delay for less than 10 ms at a time, at some point you may need to switch to increasing `autovacuum_cost_limit` instead to get additional autovacuum work accomplished. That's the general order in which to tune these two settings: the delay first, down to either 10 ms if that's the best your OS will do or down to 1 ms, and then the cost limit for additional increases in VACUUM activity. Adjusting the rest of the parameters should be considered a last resort, as they are more complicated, more likely to be functional at the default settings, and easier to set badly.

autovacuum is too disruptive

The opposite case to the previous is also possible: autovacuum can easily consume too much I/O capacity on a server without a lot of it to spare. In that case, increases of `autovacuum_vacuum_cost_delay` to as high as 100 ms are common. This is the preferred way to deal with the situation where VACUUM seems to be consuming too many resources. Increasing the cost delay to make autovacuum's actions less disruptive is the way you should be dealing with the situation where it seems you can't run VACUUM during your busy times.

Long running transactions

One problem that can block all vacuum-related activity on a server is a long running transaction. If you have a query running that needs to see very old information, the server can't clean up past that point until it completes. The easiest way to monitor long running transactions is watch for them in `pg_stat_activity`, using a query such as the following:

```
SELECT procpid, current_timestamp - xact_start AS xact_runtime, current_query
FROM pg_stat_activity ORDER BY xact_start;
```

This will show just how long any open transaction has been running for.

FSM exhaustion

One of the major problems in PostgreSQL versions up to 8.3 is that the **Free Space Map (FSM)** is stored in shared memory, and is of a fixed size. If your database has a large number of deletions, updates, and/or rollbacks in between when a manual or automatic VACUUM runs, it's possible for this FSM to run out of room and therefore not be able to track additional free space. This can quickly lead to catastrophic amounts of table and index bloat.

You can track how much of the FSM is being used only through watching the output of manual vacuums. Here is an example showing the information provided by an 8.3 server:

```
postgres=# VACUUM VERBOSE;
INFO:  free space map contains 49 pages in 62 relations
DETAIL:  A total of 992 page slots are in use (including overhead).
992 page slots are required to track all free space.
Current limits are:  204800 page slots, 1000 relations, using 1265 kB.
```

In earlier versions, you'd see the totals, but not the limits for reference. You can always check them using the SHOW command:

```
postgres=# SHOW max_fsm_pages;
 max_fsm_pages
---------------
 204800
```

Now in PostgreSQL, free space is recorded in _fsm relation forks so max_fsm_pages and max_fsm_relations settings have been removed.

In either case, you want to confirm the total page slots used (992 in this example) with the upper limit (204800 here). If those numbers are even close, you should be thinking about increasing `max_fsm_pages` by a significant amount when you can next arrange to restart the server. One common approach is to double it each time you run into this situation, at least until you've reached the millions of slots, then continue increases at a more moderate pace. It's not unusual for a large system to set this parameter to 10 M or more. And if your number of relations is close to that limit, set by `max_fsm_relations`, you similarly need to increase it, albeit not as aggressively in most cases.

If you are analyzing your log files using pgFouine, it has a vacuum logging reader that knows how to look for the output from VACUUM VERBOSE in the logs. If you're using that software and a PostgreSQL version before 8.4, you should consider generating its FSM report regularly to monitor this area.

Recovering from major problems

If you ever find yourself with so much free space you need reclaimed that VACUUM FULL seems the only way out, you should consider a few things.

First, can you use CLUSTER to rebuild the table? It essentially makes a clean second copy of the table and then substitutes it for the original once finished. While this still requires a long lock and some processing time, this is far more efficient in most cases than VACUUM FULL. Note that CLUSTER is only completely safe for this use as of PostgreSQL 8.3. In earlier versions, a common trick was to use ALTER TABLE in a way that would rewrite the entire table with a new version.

Second, how can you adjust your VACUUM and/or autovacuum strategy to keep this large of problem from showing up again? Generally the answer to this is *vacuum more often* instead of less.

If index bloat is the main issue, perhaps aggravated by a past VACUUM FULL run, REINDEX can be useful instead of CLUSTER for recovering from that. REINDEX doesn't require an exclusive lock, but it will block writers to the table while it is executing. There is unfortunately no simple way yet to run a REINDEX in a way similar to CREATE INDEX CONCURRENTLY so that it doesn't block other processes. It's sometimes possible to create a new index and use a pair of index renaming operations to swap it out for the one you want to rebuild, then allowing you to drop the original. This doesn't work for any index that enforces a constraint, which keeps this technique from being useful on UNIQUE and PRIMARY KEY indexes. And you need to be careful that no transactions still using the old index are still executing before the final setup here.

Autoanalyze

While technically a part of the same autovacuum daemon, the autoanalyze logic works a bit differently. The server keeps an internal count of how many tuples (rows) were in each table the last time it was analyzed. It then adds the estimated counts it keeps for live and dead tuples in the database (the ones you can see in `pg_stat_user_tables`) and triggers when these numbers drift too far. While regular autovacuum only cares about rows that are dead because of `UPDATE`, `DELETE`, and `ROLLBACK`, autoanalyze also counts tables that have expanded through simple `INSERT` additions, too.

By the time you've made it through the much more difficult to set up and monitor autovacuum work on your server, the similar but simpler autoanalyze work should be straightforward. While you can't see the internal tuple count to predict exactly when it will kick in, the main two statistics that drive it, the live and dead tuple counts, are shown along with the last time the two types of analysis were done in `pg_stat_user_tables`. They all appear in the more complicated *autovacuum triggering* example seen previously too. Because running analyze on a table is relatively fast and there's no concerns about XID wraparound, it's easier to just lower the parameters that control how often autoanalyze runs to make it happen more frequently or to run it manually on a regular schedule.

Note that there are some known problems with autoanalyze triggering, including that it can be fooled into inactivity by HOT activity not adjusting its counters properly. This logic was improved starting from PostgreSQL 9.0 to make this class of problem less likely to run into. It's still a good idea to manually search out tables that haven't been analyzed for a long time and give them some maintenance attention if they might not have accurate statistics. It's not a hard bit of work to keep up with compared to keeping them free of dead rows via regular vacuum work.

Index bloat

PostgreSQL's default index type is the binary tree (B-tree). While a B-tree gives good index performance under most insertion orders, there are some deletion patterns that can cause large chunks of the index to be filled with empty entries. Indexes in that state are referred to as bloated. Scanning a bloated index takes significantly more memory, disk space, and potentially disk I/O than one that only includes live entries.

There are a few main sources for index bloat to be concerned about. The first involves deletion, and is concisely described by the documentation about routine re-indexing:

> *"Index pages that have become completely empty are reclaimed for re-use. There is still a possibility for inefficient use of space: if all but a few index keys on a page have been deleted, the page remains allocated. So a usage pattern in which all but a few keys in each range are eventually deleted will see poor use of space."*

The second source has been removed as of PostgreSQL 9.0. In earlier versions, VACUUM FULL compacts tables by moving rows in them to earlier portions in the table. The documentation on VACUUM FULL describes how that creates index bloat:

> *"Moving a row requires transiently making duplicate index entries for it (the entry pointing to its new location must be made before the old entry can be removed); so moving a lot of rows this way causes severe index bloat."*

A third source is that any long-running transaction can cause table bloat and index bloat just because it blocks the efforts of any vacuum procedure to properly clean up tables.

Measuring index bloat

When you first create a new table with an index on it and insert data into it, the size of the index will grow almost linearly with the size of the table. When you have bloated indexes, that proportion will be very different. It's not unusual for a bloated index to be significantly larger than the actual data in the table. Accordingly, the first way you can monitor how bloated an index is, is by watching the index size relative to the table size, which is easy to check with the following query:

```
SELECT
    nspname,relname,
    round(100 * pg_relation_size(indexrelid) / pg_relation_size(indrelid))
/ 100
        AS index_ratio,
    pg_size_pretty(pg_relation_size(indexrelid)) AS index_size,
    pg_size_pretty(pg_relation_size(indrelid)) AS table_size
FROM pg_index I
LEFT JOIN pg_class C ON (C.oid = I.indexrelid)
LEFT JOIN pg_namespace N ON (N.oid = C.relnamespace)
WHERE
  nspname NOT IN ('pg_catalog', 'information_schema', 'pg_toast') AND
  C.relkind='i' AND
  pg_relation_size(indrelid) > 0;
```

As an example of what this looks like when run, if you create a `pgbench` database with a scale of 25, the index will be 13% of the size of the table:

```
relname     | accounts_pkey
index_ratio | 0.13
index_size  | 43 MB
table_size  | 310 MB
```

Assuming you have a version of PostgreSQL before 9.0, where VACUUM FULL will bloat indexes, you can easily get this table into the situation where its data pages can be cleaned up but not its indexes. Just sparsely delete some of the rows in the table, so that no index pages can be reclaimed, then issue VACUUM FULL:

```
DELETE FROM pgbench_accounts WHERE aid % 2 = 0;
VACUUM FULL;
```

The table will be named just `accounts` on PostgreSQL versions before 8.4. Now, running the index ratio query shows a very different proportion:

```
relname     | accounts_pkey
index_ratio | 0.27
index_size  | 43 MB
table_size  | 155 MB
```

Now the index is 27% of the size of the table, clearly quite bloated compared with its original, compact representation. While the exact threshold where the ratio is so far off that an index is obviously bloated varies depending on the structure of the table and its index, if you take a periodic snapshot of this data it's possible to see if bloat growth is increasing or not. And if you know what the ratio should be on a fresh copy of the data, perhaps after a REINDEX or CLUSTER, you can guess when bloat is likely to be bad by comparing against that figure.

If you don't have that data available, it's possible to get a rough estimate of how much dead row bloat is in a table or an index by running some computations based on the size of various structures in the table and index. The PostgreSQL monitoring plugin for Nagios, `check_postgres`, includes such an estimate, and some other sources have their own checks that are often derived from that original source. A full list of bloat checking utilities is available at `http://wiki.postgresql.org/wiki/Index_Maintenance`.

Note that for the case given, the `check_postgres` index bloat test (as of version 2.14.3) doesn't estimate the bloat change as significant. You can see exactly what query it estimates that with by running the program in verbose mode, copying the code it executes, translating the \n characters in there to either spaces or carriage returns, and then pasting the result into `psql`:

```
$ ./check_postgres.pl --action bloat -db pgbench -v -v -v
$ psql -d pgbench -x
pgbench=#  SELECT
  current_database(), schemaname, tablename,
  reltuples::bigint, relpages::bigint, otta
...
iname               | accounts_pkey
ituples             | 1250000
ipages              | 5489
iotta               | 16673
ibloat              | 0.3
wastedipages        | 0
wastedibytes        | 0
wastedisize         | 0 bytes
```

In general, so long as you have an unbloated reference point, monitoring the index to table size ratio will give you a more accurate picture of bloat over time than something working with the table statistics, such as check_postgres, can provide.

Detailed data and index page monitoring

If you really want to get deep into just what's happening with the disk space use on your server, there are a few more available PostgreSQL contrib modules that provide additional information:

- pgstattuple: Maybe you don't trust the running estimates for dead rows the database is showing. Or perhaps you just want to see how they are distributed. This information and lots of other tuple-level data is available using the pgstattuple module. The module includes functions to give detailed analysis of both regular row tuple data and index pages, which lets you dig into trivia like exactly how the B-tree indexes on your server were built.

- pg_freespacemap: Lets you look at each page of a relation (table or index) and see what's in the FSM for them. The data provided is a bit different in 8.4, where the FSM was rewritten, than in earlier versions. There is an example of using this utility inside of the Nagios check_postgres utility, a program discussed more in Chapter 11, *Database Activity and Statistics*.

Monitoring query logs

If you want to profile what your server has done, one of the most effective ways is to analyze the logs of what queries it executed. There are many ways you can approach that problem, and several tools available to then analyze the resulting log files.

Basic PostgreSQL log setup

This is what the default settings in the `postgresql.conf` setting look like for the main logging setup parameters:

```
log_destination = 'stderr'
logging_collector = off
log_line_prefix = ''
log_directory = 'pg_log'
log_filename = 'postgresql-%Y-%m-%d_%H%M%S.log'
```

It's important to know what all these lines mean before changing them:

- `log_destination`: Write server log messages to the standard error output of the process starting the server. If you started the server manually, these might appear right on your console. If you sent the server output to another spot, either using the `pg_ctl -l` option or by using command-line redirection, they'll go to the file you specified there instead.
- `logging_collector`: Off means don't collect the information written to standard error to redirect it somewhere else.
- `log_line_prefix`: An empty string means don't add anything to the beginning.
- `log_directory`: When the logging collector is on, create files in the `pg_log` directory underneath of your database directory (typically `$PGDATA`).
- `log_filename`: Name any files the logging collector creates using date and time information.

`log_directory` and `log_filename` can be set to whatever makes sense for your environment. The other parameters have some specific situations where you will want to change them from the defaults, covered in the next few sections.

The server doesn't clean up log files if you turn collection on. You have to manage that yourself, perhaps using standard Unix log rotation utilities.

Log collection

While most server startup scripts will save the log file output that the server writes for you, that's typically going to be into a single file, such as how RedHat systems create a `pg_startup.log` for you.

 The parameter shown in all these examples as `logging_collector` was renamed in PostgreSQL 8.3. Before then, it was known as `redirect_stderr`. The change in name reflects the fact that it's also used to redirect for the `csvlog` format in addition to `stderr` as of that version. The new parameter has the same basic behavior.

If you want to save log files for query analysis, or you just want the log files to be created in batches (per day by default), you'll want to turn the `logging_collector` parameter on. Afterwards, instead of a single file, you'll get one named after whatever `log_filename` pattern has been specified.

log_line_prefix

There are three basic formats of line prefix that will match the standard of sorts introduced by the requirements of pgFouine, a popular log parsing utility covered next. To ensure compatibility with that tool, you should use one of these three in your `postgresql.conf`, if you don't have any specific reason not to:

- `log_line_prefix = '%t [%p]: [%l-1] '`
- `log_line_prefix = '%t [%p]: [%l-1] user=%u,db=%d '`
- `log_line_prefix = '%t [%p]: [%l-1] user=%u,db=%d,remote=%r '`

Note the trailing space in all these examples; that is important to always include in your prefix setting. The first line just logs basic information. The second upgrades that to also include the user and database information for the connection, which allows filtering on those two fields when running `pgFouine` or similar utilities.

The final line also adds the remote host the connection came from, which for some applications is an extremely useful bit of information for analyzing the logs (even though pgFouine won't do anything with that).

Note that if you're using syslog or the CSV format logs, the timestamp and process information will be inserted for you automatically. You don't need to include it into the prefix of the PostgreSQL log output, too.

Multiline queries

Sometimes client tools and psql sessions can execute queries that span more than one line. Here's an example of such, generated using psql:

```
postgres=# show log_line_prefix
postgres-# ;
```

With statement logging enabled, this will show up in the standard text logs like this:

```
2010-03-28 21:23:49 EDT [10669]: [1-1]
user=postgres,db=postgres,remote=[local] LOG:   duration: 0.923 ms
statement: show log_line_prefix
        ;
```

That's two lines of output. The dangling semicolon is the only thing on the second line, with no prefix appearing. Because of that, there's no way to associate that line with the rest of the query, given that log lines are not guaranteed to be grouped together in a more complicated environment; another line might get in between these two in the text format logs.

Log file analysis tools that want to follow every line in a query have no way to sort out what to do here, and the better ones will warn you about this problem when they run if it shows up. There are alternate logging formats besides simple plain text that avoid this issue.

Using syslog for log messages

On Unix-like systems, one approach for database logging that leverages existing operating infrastructure is to redirect log_destination to use the syslog facility.

 On Windows systems, you can use log messages to the Windows Event Log similarly to how syslog is used here.

The main thing to be concerned about when using `syslog` is a warning you'll find in the documentation at
`http://www.postgresql.org/docs/current/static/runtime-config-logging.html`:

"Note: The logging collector is designed to never lose messages. This means that in case of extremely high load, server processes could be blocked due to trying to send additional log messages when the collector has fallen behind. In contrast, syslog prefers to drop messages if it cannot write them, which means it may fail to log some messages in such cases but it will not block the rest of the system."

This means the exact time when you want data the most, when the server is overloaded, is when you are most likely to lose your logs if using `syslog`. That's one reason why it's not a more popular approach. The complexity of setting up `syslog` (or the improved `syslog-ng`) is another reason database administrators tend to avoid this setup.

In addition to allowing use of common `syslog` analysis tools, another advantage of the `syslog` format is that it knows how to handle multiline messages in a way that tools such as pgFouine can use.

CSV logging

Another way to avoid multiline query issues is to use CSV logging, added to PostgreSQL in version 8.3. This logs every statement in a delimited fashion that clearly marks line breaks so that multiline queries can be imported without a problem into tools. You can even import these logs files into the database for analysis; the documentation at
`http://www.postgresql.org/docs/current/static/runtime-config-logging.html` shows a sample table for that purpose in the *Using CSV-Format Log Output* section.

 Note that format of the CSV output fields and therefore the sample table changed in 9.0 (`application_name` was added) compared with 8.3/8.4. Make sure you're using the right table definition for your version, or `COPY` will complain that the column count doesn't match when you try to import.

To turn on this feature, you need to adjust the `log_destination` and make sure the collector is running:

```
log_destination = 'csvlog'
logging_collector = on
```

The server must be completely restarted after this change for it to take effect. After this change, the log files saved into the usual directory structure the collector uses will now end with .csv instead of .log. If you followed the right documentation for your version to create the postgres_log file, you would import it like the following:

```
postgres=# COPY postgres_log FROM '/home/postgres/data
/pg_log/postgresql-2010-03-28_215404.csv' WITH CSV;
```

Having all of the log data in the database allows you to write all sorts of queries to analyze your logs. Here's a simple example that shows the first and last commit among the logs imported:

```
SELECT min(log_time),max(log_time) FROM postgres_log WHERE
command_tag='COMMIT';
```

You might instead ask at what elapsed time since session start each command happened:

```
SELECT log_time,(log_time - session_start_time) AS elapsed FROM
postgres_log WHERE command_tag='COMMIT';
```

Using this particular example against an imported pgbench run will show you that pgbench keeps one session open for all the work each client does.

You can use this log to figure out what statement executes before a given commit too, by looking for entries with the same session_id but with lower session_line_num values. Often when people run into situations where a COMMIT statement is the one that takes a long time, for example when a large queue of CHECK constraints have built up, knowing what happened before the commit is critical and difficult to discover information. The CSV format logs make this easy to determine, because they contain every bit of session information.

The main disadvantage of the CSV log format is that you're writing out a lot of logging information, and that can be too intensive on the exact type of system that needs better logging the most: ones that are overloaded by bad queries.

Logging difficult queries

A straightforward way to generate log files only for the complex, long running queries on your server-cutting out routine logging of small queries and therefore reducing logging overhead—is to set a minimum statement duration to log.

A typical configuration would be as follows:

```
log_min_duration_statement = 1000
log_duration = off
log_statement = 'none'
```

The first line there will log every statement that takes over `1000` ms (one second) without logging anything else. The other two are actually the defaults.

An alternate approach you'll sometimes see instead aims to just capture every query:

```
log_min_duration_statement = -1
log_duration = on
log_statement = 'all'
```

Since setting `log_min_duration_statement` to 0 will also log every statement with a duration, that's an easier way to get this behavior. It only requires tweaking one value, and it's easy to adjust upward so that it's only triggered when appropriate. Because that's easier to manage, you should prefer that approach over increasing the overall statement verbosity.

This area of PostgreSQL continues to expand as advances on the server and on additional external utilities are finished. `http://wiki.postgresql.org/wiki/Logging_Difficult_Queries` tracks the latest work in this area.

auto_explain

One of the great features added in PostgreSQL 8.4 is `auto_explain`, documented at `http://www.postgresql.org/docs/current/static/auto-explain.html`.

This is a `contrib` module not necessarily installed by default. See the discussion of `contrib` modules in Chapter 1, *PostgreSQL Versions*.

To enable the feature, edit your `postgresql.conf` to add parameters such as this:

```
shared_preload_libraries = 'auto_explain'
custom_variable_classes = 'auto_explain'
auto_explain.log_min_duration = '1s'
```

That will trigger `auto_explain` on any query longer than a second. You'll need to completely restart the server after making this change before it goes into effect.

Once that's done, any query that takes longer than this will be logged with a full explain plan for the output. This is what one of the common slow pgbench UPDATE statements looks like:

```
duration: 1955.811 ms plan:
Query Text: UPDATE pgbench_accounts SET abalance = abalance + -3410 WHERE
aid = 9011517;
Update (cost=0.00..10.03 rows=1 width=103)
  ->  Index Scan using pgbench_accounts_pkey on pgbench_accounts
(cost=0.00..10.03 rows=1 width=103)
        Index Cond: (aid = 9011517)",,,,,,,,,""
```

The plans will be spread across multiple lines if in the regular logs, but will be in a single column if loaded into a CSV format log. The syslog logs will also tag the multiple line output appropriately.

As for what you can use this for, a look at the logs shows the delay is happening even when updating the tiny branches table:

```
duration: 1490.680 ms  plan:
Query Text: UPDATE pgbench_branches SET bbalance = bbalance + -2792 WHERE
bid = 4;
Update  (cost=0.00..4.50 rows=1 width=370)
  ->  Seq Scan on pgbench_branches  (cost=0.00..4.50 rows=1 width=370)
        Filter: (bid = 4)",,,,,,,,,""
```

Knowing information like this, that the UPDATE hang is happening even when updating a table extremely likely to be in the buffer cache, is extremely valuable for tracking down the true cause of slow statements.

Log file analysis

Once you have some log files saved, next you'll want to analyze the results. The common information you'll get is a profile of what queries were run, how long each took individually, and sums showing the totals broken down by type of query. There are several tools available for this purpose, with different trade-offs in terms of things like how active their development community is, how fast the tool runs, and how extensive the installation requirements are.

Normalized query fingerprints

To a person, it would be obvious that the following two queries are fundamentally the same:

```
UPDATE pgbench_accounts SET abalance = abalance + 1631 WHERE aid = 5829858;
UPDATE pgbench_accounts SET abalance = abalance + 4172 WHERE aid = 567923;
```

This isn't necessarily obvious to a log file parsing program though. Good database programming practice will often convert these to executing with prepared statements, which offers both a security improvement (resistance to SQL injection) as well as a potential performance gain. The pgbench program used to generate many of the examples in this book can be converted to them internally for executing statements:

```
$ pgbench -c4 -t 60 -M prepared pgbench
```

Using prepared statements makes it obvious that these statements have the same query fingerprint, that the main structure is the same:

```
UPDATE pgbench_accounts SET abalance = abalance + $1 WHERE aid = $2;
```

Some log file analysis programs are capable of doing a process named query normalizing in order to extract a query fingerprint from even unprepared statements. If you don't use prepared statements, that will be a feature you need if you want to group similar queries together for analysis purposes.

pg_stat_statements

While in many cases you might still want to save full logs, the pg_stat_statements feature added in PostgreSQL 8.4 can substitute as a way to analyze queries without needing an intermediate logging facility. The feature is documented at http://www.postgresql.org/docs/current/static/pgstatstatements.html.

This is a contrib module, not necessarily installed by default. See the discussion of contrib modules in Chapter 1, *PostgreSQL Versions*. Like pg_buffercache, it needs to be installed in each database you use it against. Here's an example of installing it on a system with the RedHat Linux directory layout for PostgreSQL:

```
$ psql -d pgbench -f
/usr/share/postgresql/contrib/contrib/pg_stat_statements.sql
```

You enable this using a `postgresql.conf` addition such as the following:

```
shared_preload_libraries = 'pg_stat_statements'
custom_variable_classes = 'pg_stat_statements'
pg_stat_statements.max = 10000
pg_stat_statements.track = all
```

This is followed by fully restarting the server. Once you've run some queries and therefore populated the information in `pg_stat_statements`, you can look at them the same as any other view:

```
pgbench=# SELECT round(total_time*1000)/1000 AS total_time,query FROM
pg_stat_statements ORDER BY total_time DESC;
 total_time | query
     78.104 | UPDATE pgbench_accounts SET abalance = abalance + $1 WHERE
aid = $2;
      1.826 | UPDATE pgbench_branches SET bbalance = bbalance + $1 WHERE
bid = $2;
      0.619 | UPDATE pgbench_tellers SET tbalance = tbalance + $1 WHERE tid
= $2;
      0.188 | INSERT INTO pgbench_history (tid, bid, aid, delta, mtime)
VALUES ($1, $2, $3, $4, CURRENT_TIMESTAMP);
      0.174 | SELECT abalance FROM pgbench_accounts WHERE aid = $1;
      0.026 | vacuum pgbench_branches
      0.015 | vacuum pgbench_tellers
      0.011 | BEGIN;
      0.011 | END;
      0.001 | truncate pgbench_history
```

It's extremely handy to have this facility built into the database, without needing external tools. There are a few limitations. There's no query fingerprint normalization for you if you don't use query parameters; the preceding example required running `pgbench` in its prepared statement mode. The number of saved messages has a hard limit on it. It's easy to lose an interesting statement log as new activity occurs on the server.

And not necessarily every operation you can see in the logs will appear here. For example, note that in the preceding log from a standard `pgbench` test, timings for the UPDATE statements are listed, but the commits from the END statements are not accumulating a lot of time. A very different view of this information shows up if you look at the log file data, as shown in the next section.

PostgreSQL 9.0 adds an additional ability to `pg_stat_statements`: it can now also track the amount of database cache buffers used while processing a statement.

Starting from PostgreSQL 9.0 by `pg_stat_statements` you can also track the amount of database cache buffers used while processing a statement.

pgBadger

pgBadger is a PostgreSQL log analyzer built for speed with fully detailed reports from your PostgreSQL log file. It's a single and small Perl script that outperform any other PostgreSQL log analyzer. It is written in pure Perl language and uses a javascript library (`flotr2`) to draw graphs so that you don't need to install any additional Perl modules or other packages. Furthermore, this library gives us more features such as zooming. pgBadger also uses the Bootstrap javascript library and the Font Awesome web font for better design. Everything is embedded.

A very useful tool to examine PostgreSQL logs and make reports is pgBadger. With the tool it is possible to analyze very simply connected users, most frequently used queries, slow queries, vacuum operations and so on. pgBadger is available at `http://dalibo.github.io/pgbadger/`.

Summary

Properly maintaining every aspect of a database is time-consuming work, but the downside of not doing it can be even worse. This is particularly true when it comes to good vacuuming practice, where routine mistakes can build up over time into extremely expensive operations requiring downtime to fully recover. Similarly, monitoring your query logs to be proactive about finding ones that execute slowly takes regular review, but the downside there can also be downtime if your server falls apart under a heavy load.

MVCC will keep routine read and write conflicts from happening, but you still need to code applications to lock resources when only one session should have access to a row at once.

Any time you UPDATE, DELETE, or ROLLBACK a transaction, it will leave a dead row behind (and potentially a dead index entry) that needs to be cleaned up later by some form of vacuum.

It's better to tune for a steady stream of low intensity vacuum work, preferably using the autovacuum feature of the database, instead of disabling that feature and having to do that cleanup in larger blocks.

Avoid ever using the `VACUUM FULL` command. Instead use `CLUSTER` as the main way to reorganize a badly damaged table, or `REINDEX` to fix bad indexes.

Saving basic query logs to disk with proper prefix lines is vital to catching execution slowdowns before they get too bad.

A variety of log query analyzer programs are available in order to report on where your query time is being spent, each with their own strong and weak points.

8
Database Benchmarking

PostgreSQL ships with a benchmarking program named `pgbench` that can be used for a variety of tests. The default tests included are useful, but it also includes a database benchmarking scripting language that allows for customizing them. You can even use the `pgbench` core—an efficient, scalable multi-client database program to write completely custom tests. There are also some industry-standard tests available that let you compare PostgreSQL with other database products, albeit without officially audited results in most cases.

The topics we will cover in this chapter are as follows:

- PostgreSQL benchmarking tool `pgbench`
- Built-in `pgbench` benchmarks
- Custom benchmark using `pgbench`

pgbench default tests

The original inspiration for the `pgbench` test is the **Transaction Processing Performance Council (TPC)** benchmark named TPC-B: `http://www.tpc.org/tpcb/`.

Originally developed in 1990 (and now considered obsolete from the TPC's perspective), this benchmark models a simple bank application that includes a set of bank branches, each of which has some number of tellers and accounts.

Table definition

The main table definition SQL adds these tables:

- pgbench_branches:

```
CREATE TABLE pgbench_branches(bid int not null, bbalance int,
filler char(88));
ALTER TABLE pgbench_branches add primary key (bid);
```

- pgbench_tellers:

```
CREATE TABLE pgbench_tellers(tid int not null,bid int, tbalance
int,filler char(84));
ALTER TABLE pgbench_tellers add primary key (tid);
```

- pgbench_accounts:

```
CREATE TABLE pgbench_accounts(aid int not null,bid int, abalance
int,filler char(84));
ALTER TABLE pgbench_accounts add primary key (aid);
```

- pgbench_history:

```
CREATE TABLE pgbench_history(tid int,bid int,aid int,delta int,
mtime timestamp,filler char(22));
```

 Before PostgreSQL 8.4, these tables did not have the pgbench_ prefix in their names. This was dangerous because a badly written pgbench run could wipe out a real table named accounts far too easily. Having done that once, I can tell you it can be quite embarrassing to have to explain why all the accounts are now missing from a live database server.

The intention of the various filler fields is to make sure that each row inserted into the database is actually a full 100 bytes wide. This doesn't actually work as intended; the way data is inserted, the filler doesn't take up any space beyond a small amount of column overhead. This problem has never been corrected because doing so would make it no longer possible to compare historical pgbench results with later ones.

What you should realize is that every record type inserted by the standard `pgbench` test is extremely narrow; only a small number of bytes are inserted for each of them. In practice, even the smallest `INSERT` or `UPDATE` will dirty a standard 8K database page and require that large of a write anyway. The fact that only a fraction is actually dirtied after each change does help reduce total WAL write volume, but only once you've written the usual `full_page_writes` copy of each page, which will end up as the bulk of actual WAL throughput anyway.

Scale detection

The number of branches is referred to as the **database scale**, with each branch adding another 10 tellers and 100,000 accounts to the database. This value is input when you initialize the database `pgbench` is told to create tables into. Here's an example that creates a database for `pgbench` and then populates it with the `pgbench` tables:

```
$ createdb pgbench
$ pgbench -i -s 10 pgbench
```

This will initialize (`-i`), the `pgbench` tables using a scale of 10 (`-s 10`) into the database named `pgbench`. You don't have to use that name, but it's a common convention.

When `pgbench` runs in a regular mode (not initialization), it first checks whether you have manually told it the database scale using `-s`; if so, it uses that value. If not, and you're running one of the default tests, it will try to detect the scale using the following query:

```
SELECT count(*) FROM pgbench_branches;
```

If you run a custom query, the scale will never be detected for you, it will always be assumed to be 1. You must be careful when running custom tests to set it yourself in any case where the test script you're running assumes the scale will be set properly. That includes customized variations of the built-in tests you might create, like those distributed with `pgbench-tools`.

Query script definition

Like the preceding table code, the actual queries run by the built-in standard `pgbench` tests are compiled into its source code, making the only way you can see them to refer to documentation such as `http://www.postgresql.org/docs/current/static/pgbench.html`.

The default transaction script, what's called the TPC-B (sort of) transaction when you run the test (and referred to here as the TPC-B-like transaction), issues seven commands per transaction. It looks like this inside the program:

```
\set nbranches :scale
\set ntellers 10 * :scale
\set naccounts 100000 * :scale
\setrandom aid 1 :naccounts
\setrandom bid 1 :nbranches
\setrandom tid 1 :ntellers
\setrandom delta -5000 5000
BEGIN;
UPDATE pgbench_accounts SET abalance = abalance + :delta WHERE aid = :aid;
SELECT abalance FROM pgbench_accounts WHERE aid = :aid;
UPDATE pgbench_tellers SET tbalance = tbalance + :delta WHERE tid = :tid;
UPDATE pgbench_branches SET bbalance = bbalance + :delta WHERE bid = :bid;
INSERT INTO pgbench_history (tid, bid, aid, delta, mtime) VALUES (:tid,
:bid, :aid, :delta, CURRENT_TIMESTAMP);
END;
```

The first three lines compute how many branches, tellers, and accounts this database has based on `scale`, which is a special variable name set to the database scale, determined using the logic described in the last section.

The next four lines create random values to use, simulating a bank transaction where someone went to a specific teller at a specific branch and deposited/withdrew some amount of money from their account.

 The presumption that one is using a regular teller for all transactions rather than a bank's **automated teller machine** (**ATM**) is another clue as to how old the benchmarking being simulated here really is. `pgbench` is not simulating any real-world situation that still exists, and the TPC retired TPC-B as useful some time ago. `pgbench` should be considered a completely synthetic workload at this point, useful for testing some things but not indicative of true real-world database performance at all.

The main core here is five statements wrapped in a transaction block, so they execute either all together not at all. That way the sum of money accounted for in the bank should match from the branch down to account level. Note that the statement will still take up some time and resources on the server even if it is rolled back.

Each of the statements has a very different practical impact:

- UPDATE pgbench_accounts: As the biggest table, this is by far the statement most likely to trigger disk I/O.
- SELECT abalance: Since the previous UPDATE will have left the information needed to answer this query in its cache, it adds very little work in the standard TPC-B-like workload.
- UPDATE pgbench_tellers: With so many less tellers than accounts, this table is small and likely cached in RAM, but not so small it tends to be a source of lock issues either.
- UPDATE pgbench_branches: As an extremely small table, the entire contents of it are likely to be cached already and essentially free to access. However, because it's small, locking might turn into a performance bottleneck here if you use a small database scale and many clients. Accordingly, the general recommendation is always to make sure scale is greater than clients for any test you run. In practice, this problem is not really that important, although you can see it in one of the examples below. Disk I/O on the accounts table and commit rate will be more of a limiter than locking concerns in most cases.
- INSERT INTO pgbench_history: The history table acts as an append-only one that is never updated or queried later, and accordingly it doesn't even have any indexes on it. As such, this insert turns out to be a low volume write, relative to the much more expensive indexed UPDATE statements.

This is the default test. There are two others:

- -N: Same as previously, but skipping the two small UPDATE statements impacting tellers and branches. This reduces the main potential for lock contention, while keeping the primary source of heavy writes.
- -S: Just the SELECT statement on the accounts table, which then doesn't need to be wrapped in a transaction block either.

It's unlikely you'll have any use for the test that skips some of the UPDATE statements, but running just SELECT statements is very useful for examining the cache sizes on your system and for measuring maximum CPU speed.

Configuring the database server for pgbench

All of the queries used for the built-in tests are simple: They are at most using a primary key index to look a row up, but no joins or more complicated query types. But the statements executed will heavily stress writes and the buffer cache's ability to keep up.

Accordingly, parameters you might adjust break down into three major categories:

- **Important to note and possibly tune**: `shared_buffers`, `max_wal_size`, `autovacuum`, `wal_buffers`, and `checkpoint_completion_target`.
- **Impacts test results significantly**: `wal_sync_method`, `synchronous_commit`, and `wal_writer_delay`. Adjust on systems where a change is appropriate to get good and/or safe results.
- **Does not matter**: `effective_cache_size`, `default_statistics_target`, `work_mem`, `random_page_cost`, and most other parameters. The various `bgwriter` settings do have an impact, just usually not a positive one. Unlike some real workloads where it might help, making the background writer more aggressive usually results in a net loss in raw throughput on `pgbench` tests, without improving latency either.

Sample server configuration

Some `pgbench` samples are provided next, from a server with the following specifications:

- Quad-core Intel Q6600
- 8 GB DDR2-800 RAM
- Areca ARC-1210 SATA II PCI-e x8 RAID controller, 256 MB write cache
- Database on 3x160 GB Western Digital SATA disks using Linux software RAID 0 (database)
- WAL on 160 GB Western Digital SATA disk
- Linux Kernel 2.6.22 x86 64
- Untuned ext3 filesystem

The OS was on a different disk from any of the database files.

Here is a basic, minimally tuned `postgresql.conf` capable of running `pgbench` usefully on such a server, with 8 GB of RAM, following the usual guidelines for `shared_buffers` sizing:

- `shared_buffers = 2 GB`
- `max_wal_size = 1GB`
- `checkpoint_completion_target = 0.9`
- `wal_buffers = 16 MB`
- `max_connections = 300`

Running pgbench manually

As a simple example of running a test, you could execute only the SELECT test for a small number of transactions. Here's a quick test from the sample server:

```
$ pgbench -S -c 4 -t 20000 pgbench
starting vacuum...end.
transaction type: SELECT only
scaling factor: 10
query mode: simple
number of clients: 4
number of threads: 1
number of transactions per client: 20000
number of transactions actually processed: 80000/80000
tps = 17070.599733 (including connections establishing)
tps = 17173.602799 (excluding connections establishing)
```

This is simulating the situation where four database clients are all active at the same time and continuously asking for data. Each client runs until it executes the requested number of transactions.

Since this is a Linux system, the `pgbench` driver program itself is known to limit performance here when run as a single thread, described in more detail next. Using more threads (only available in PostgreSQL 9.0 and later) shows a dramatic improvement in speed:

```
$ pgbench -S -c 4 -j 4 -t 20000 pgbench
starting vacuum...end.
transaction type: SELECT only
scaling factor: 10
query mode: simple
number of clients: 4
number of threads: 4
number of transactions per client: 20000
```

```
number of transactions actually processed: 80000/80000
tps = 31222.948242 (including connections establishing)
tps = 31509.876475 (excluding connections establishing)
```

Rather than worrying about the transaction count, a simpler approach available starting in PostgreSQL 8.4 is to specify a runtime instead. The preceding code block took 2.6 seconds; you could run for a full five seconds instead like this:

```
$ pgbench -S -c 4 -j 4 -T 5 pgbench
```

It's possible to get useful test results for a SELECT only test in a few seconds. You will need a much longer test, in the minutes range, to get a TPC-B-like write test result that is meaningful. A 10 minute-long TPC-B-like test, which is usually long enough, could be run like this:

```
$ pgbench -c 4 -j 4 -T 600 pgbench
```

In earlier versions before the timed run was available, estimating how many transactions were needed to get a useful runtime could take a few tries to get right.

Graphing results with pgbench-tools

Running a full, thorough pgbench evaluation of a server takes several days of system runtime. Starting with PostgreSQL 8.3, the pgbench-tools program, available from http://git.postgresql.org/gitweb?p=pgbench-tools.git, allows for automating multiple runs of pgbench, including production of graphs showing the results. Earlier PostgreSQL versions did not save all of the needed information to allow for graphing results over time.

On a system that supports running the git version control software, you can retrieve the source code like this:

```
$ git clone git://git.postgresql.org/git/pgbench-tools.git
$ cd pgbench-tools/
```

If you're on a database server that doesn't support running git, you may need to run the preceding mentioned command on a newer system that does, then use that system to create an archive; here are two examples that produce a .tar and .zip file respectively:

```
$ git archive --prefix=pgbench-tools/ HEAD > pgbench-tools.tar
$ git archive --prefix=pgbench-tools/ --format=zip HEAD > pgbench-tools.zip
```

Configuring pgbench-tools

The README file that comes with pgbench-tools is the definitive documentation about how to use the program. Current recommended practice, that the examples here will follow, is to create two databases for it to use. The primary one should be named pgbench and it will contain the main database being tested. The second, named results by default, will contain a summary of information about each test after it finishes.

Here is a sample session that creates both databases and initializes the results database:

```
$ cd pgbench-tools/
$ createdb pgbench
$ createdb results
$ psql -d results -f init/resultdb.sql
```

This may give you some error messages about the tables that it deletes not existing; these are normal, they are because DROP TABLE IF EXISTS isn't available until PostgreSQL 8.2, and pgbench-tools can in special cases be configured to run against 8.1 databases.

The results database doesn't even need to be on the same server as the one being tested. Making it remote keeps pgbench-tools itself from disturbing the database being tested and the associated OS cache, so this can be a better way to set things up. The default configuration and examples here don't assume you've done that simply because it complicates the configuration and use of the program for limited benefit; the cache disruption is not that large relative to the system RAM nowadays.

Once you know where each database is located, edit the config file at the root of the pgbench-tools directory and update the settings for TEST and RESULT variables set there. You may want to customize the number of worker threads as well; see notes on that in the following section and in the pgbench-tools documentation.

Customizing for 8.3

If you're using PostgreSQL 8.3, you will also need to follow the notes in the config file to swap which set of table names you are using. Some lines in the default one must be commented out, while others must be enabled in their place.

Sample pgbench test results

The sample test results all come from the sample server and configuration described previously, and are the sort of graph that you get from `pgbench-tools` each time it is run. These results were all created using PostgreSQL 9.0 and later, allowing up to four `pgbench` worker threads (one per core).

Select-only test

When running the simple read-only test, results will be very good while the database fits in RAM, then drop off fast after that. Note that the straight line you'll see on all these graphs is always the database size value, which is in units shown by the right axis scale:

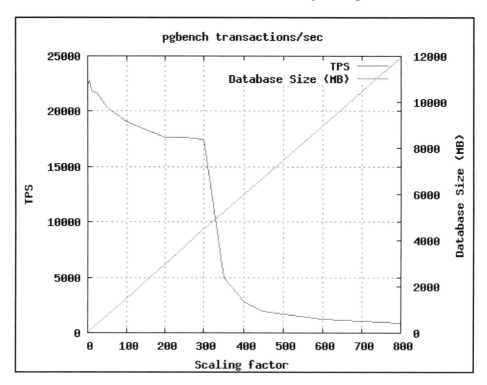

This curve has a similar shape no matter what hardware you have. The only thing that changes is where the two big break points are at, depending on how much RAM is in the server. You're limited by the speed of well cached system RAM on the left side, by disk seek rate on the right, and some mix of the two in between.

TPC-B-like test

The scaling diagram has the same basic curve on the write-heavy test, but with fewer transactions occurring:

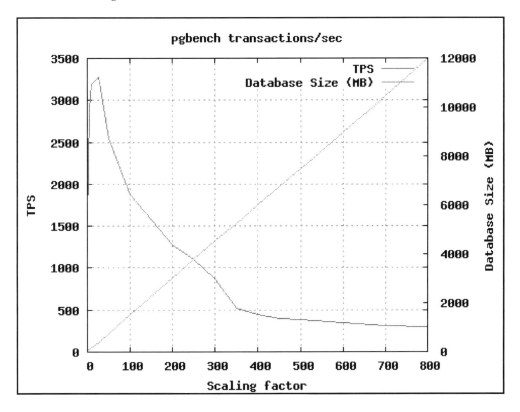

If you look carefully at the left side of this, you can see one of the issues warned about above and in the pgbench documentation: results at a very low database scale are lower than when the database is a bit larger. This is due to lock contention for the small branches table in particular, when running at higher client counts with a tiny scale.

The preceding results are averaged across all the client counts used. The number of clients also impacts results quite a bit:

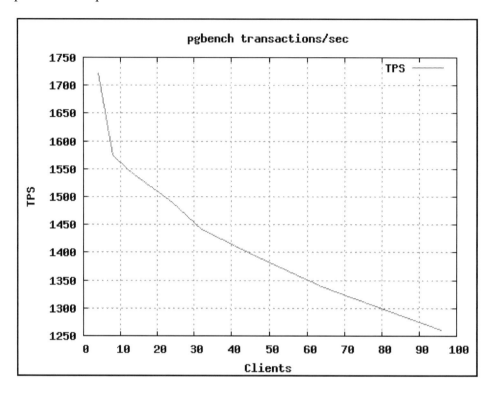

Corresponding, the client results are also averaged out over all the scaling factors. The client scaling for the read-only test looks similar, just with smaller total values.

To get a really clear picture of the system, you should also take a look at the web report produced by `pgbench-tools`. The number of clients and database scale that produced the greatest single TPS value is usually an interesting number to note, the included utility script `fastest.sql` will show you the best results from a run.

Latency analysis

Most of the time, you can think of **latency**—the time taken to process a single transaction—as the number of inverse transactions per second. However, worst-case latency is an extremely important number to note for many applications, and you cannot determine it from any average measurement of TPS.

Another useful measure is to note a point above most, but not all, latency values. You can usefully quantify this with a percentile measurement, which aims at some percentage of the data and says what value is at the top of them. The 90th percentile is a common target, which computes a value so that 90% of the latency times observed were below that time.

Accordingly, `pgbench-tools` always saves the latency data `pgbench` can produce, and it computes average, worst-case, and the 90th percentile of latency results in the HTML results it generates. This data, and the graphs that go along with it, are a major reason to use this toolset instead of running `pgbench` manually. If you're lucky, your results will look like this, a TPS over time graph from one of the fastest TPC-B-like individual runs in the set graphed before:

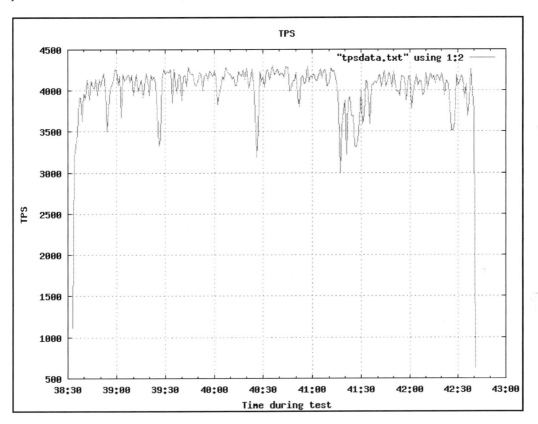

This run averaged 4036 transactions/second, and, aside from early ramp-up and shutdown, the transactions processed on any second were still quite high. The program also shows latency and how long each statement took to run, and graphs that for you. Graphing the latency of individual statements can show you both exactly how bad the worst-case is and what the distribution of those slow statements looks like:

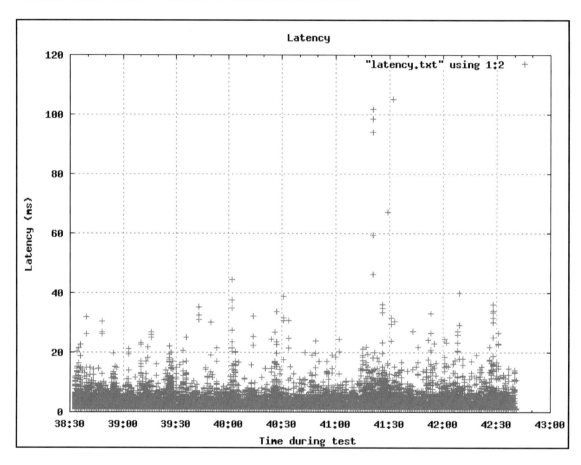

Worst-case latency peaked at just over 100 ms. The way the slow cases are clustered around the same period here is quite common in these results; when the server slows down, it will usually impact all the active clients at that time.

What does a bad result look like? The following example still had a reasonable average throughput of 1082 TPS, given it was running with a much larger database and client size (scale=250, clients=96). That's still an average latency of just under 1 ms. But, in this case, the worst-case latency is a frightening 6348 ms, some clients waited for over 6 seconds to get a response to their request. You can easily see how intermittent the server's responses were by looking at the TPS graph, too:

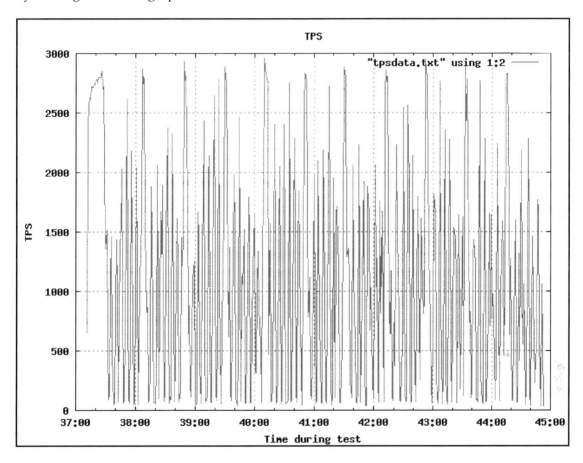

The only reason the average TPS was so high is that when the server was working, it processed results quite quickly. But there were just as many periods it dropped to processing very few transactions in any given second, and sometimes not at all for several seconds.

When using pgbench to tweak write performance on a server, you need to be careful not to optimize for throughput at the expense of worst-case latency. Few applications would prefer an extra few percent throughput if it means a several-second delay. The smoothness of the TPS graph and, correspondingly the worst-case latency results, are just as important (and possibly more so) than the average value.

Unfortunately, long delays are quite common on write-heavy pgbench tests, just due to how it always writes at the maximum possible speed possible from the hardware. The typical cause is simple filling of the write cache on whatever controller is involved. In this example, the 256 MB write cache on the Areca controller used is simply taking a few seconds to clear when it's filled with random I/O that's blocking access to some resource a client needs. Behavior in this situation is commonly bad on Linux, where the kernel developers rarely optimize for latency at the expense of throughput, and it's easy to get backed up like this. More modern benchmarks typically introduce pauses called think times where clients aren't actively pushing work into the system, which allows for scaling their size upwards and seeing useful latency results without being hammered all the time by disk writes queuing. pgbench should not be considered representative of any real-world workload, as most programs don't constantly write.

Sources of bad results and variation

There are many ways to get bad results from pgbench, ones that don't mean anything valid. And there are even more ways to get results that vary so much from one pgbench run to another that they don't mean what you would imagine them to. Normally you should run any pgbench test at least three times and observe the average and variation before presuming that test is valid. Taking the middle of three results is a common median technique for filtering those results into a single one for comparison.

You must let the test run for a while to get useful results. As a general rule of thumb, if you haven't executed a minute's worth of runtime, you're unlikely to have gotten useful results at all. The main exception is the SELECT only test, which can give useful results in a small number of seconds. Generally, if you've seen more than 100,000 transactions, that's enough that you can start to believe the results, and fast hardware can execute that may SELECT statements in a few seconds nowadays. pgbench-tools includes some buffer report scripts aimed to help investigate this area, and the output from one of them is included in the web report results directory.

For write-heavy tests such as the TPC-B-like default one, you need to run long enough for a full checkpoint cycle to have occurred at least a few minutes, sometimes as long as 10 minutes, for the results to be meaningful. If you don't, you'll see the run to run variation will be very large, depending on whether that particular one included an active checkpoint in it or not.

Pay attention to the database size, relative to the amount of RAM and other caches in your system, so that you understand what you're testing, and don't forget to set the database scale manually if executing a custom test yourself. pgbench-tools tries to take care of this detail for you—that is, at least when you're using the standard pgbench tables.

Longer runs of pgbench will eventually end up triggering autovacuum and eventually can even bloat the database. That improved significantly in PostgreSQL 8.3 due to the HOT feature, and the overhead of autovacuum was lowered due to the FSM changes in 8.4. As all of the updates done in the standard pgbench test qualify for the mini-vacuum work that HOT can perform, and the updates to the pgbench_accounts table are the most difficult single statements to execute, it benefits quite a bit from that feature.

Whether or not autovacuum is running really alters how the test performs. You can get useful results with it turned on or off; just make sure you note which when you're testing, be consistent about it, and understand that your test results will be impacted by that choice.

Developer PostgreSQL builds

If you have built PostgreSQL with the full set of development options turned on, your pgbench results will be considerably slowed by that. This is something to watch out for particularly in the alpha and beta builds of the software, where these features may even be turned on in packaged versions, such as the beta RPMs.

The worst performance hit comes from having assertions, checks in the code for unexpected conditions, enabled. The assertion overhead scales upward as you increase shared_buffers, which can result in the unexpected situation where large buffer cache sizes actually decrease performance on the benchmark. Whenever you're starting to use pgbench, it's a good idea to check that you don't have an assertions enabled build like this:

```
postgres=# show debug_assertions;
 debug_assertions
-------------------
 off
```

That will keep you from wasting time running benchmarks that have confusing results.

Worker threads and pgbench program limitations

Always in earlier PostgreSQL versions and still by default, the `pgbench` program itself runs as a single process on the system. It queues up statements for each client to execute, then feeds them new ones as they report they're finished responding to the previous one. In all situations, it is possible to have that process slow if you have a large number of clients active. A common approach to work around that has been to run the `pgbench` program itself on another system, which does unfortunately add its own overhead, too.

The situation is particularly bad on Linux systems running kernel 2.6.23 or later. The **Completely Fair Scheduler** (**CFS**) introduced in that version is not very fair to `pgbench`, when it runs in its standard mode using a socket connection. The end result is that throughput only scales into the low tens of thousands of transactions per second, acting as if only one database core or processor is working right. Note how large of a speedup using multiple threads was on the initial read-only sample shown in the text previously—an increase from 17 K to 31 K TPS certainly shows the single `pgbench` worker was the bottleneck. The worst manifestation of this problem is usually avoided when using `pgbench-tools`, as that always uses the TCP/IP host-based connection scheme instead.

Starting in PostgreSQL 9.0, you can work around these problems by increasing the number of worker threads that `pgbench` runs in parallel to talk to clients with. Each worker is assigned an equal share of clients that it opens and manages, splitting the load of clients up so no single process has to service them all. The number of workers must be a multiple of the client count, so you need to choose that carefully. The program will abort complaints of bad input rather than doing anything if it can't divide the client count requested equally among the number of workers specified; the way the program is written, each worker must have the same number of clients assigned to it.

Generally, you'll want one worker thread per core on your system if you have a version this capability exists in. `pgbench-tools` allows you to set a maximum worker count while aiming to keep the clients properly divisible among workers; see its documentation for details. Using multiple workers is usually good for at least a 15% or greater speedup over using only a single one and, as suggested earlier, increases of over 100% are possible. If you create too many workers, for example making one worker per client when the number of clients far exceeds system cores, you can end up right back to where excessive swapping between processes on the system limits performance again.

pgbench custom tests

While the built-in tests are interesting, you can use pgbench instead as a testing harness to run your own database tests. This gets you multiple clients running at once, executing concurrent queries with a minimum of scripting.

Insert speed test

To give an idea how this might be useful, imagine you want to test how fast your system can write data to disk using insert. You might copy the filler concept from the built-in tables, where you just want to create some strings with a particular length, and therefore size in bytes, without caring about the content (this is included in pgbench-tools as init/insertsize.sql):

```
create table data(filler text);
```

But then create a custom script that actually fills that much space up (also included as insert-size.sql):

```
insert into data (filler) values (repeat('X',:scale));
```

This borrows the concept of scale from the regular tests and uses it to specify the size of the data inserted. You can create your own variables with other names, pass values for them on the command line, and then refer to them in your scripts.

Here's a sample session showing the installation of this test using the sample version included with pgbench-tools, followed by manually running this custom test once with pgbench:

```
$ createdb insert
$ psql -d insert -f init/insertsize.sql
$ pgbench -s 1000 -f tests/insert-size.sql -n -c 4 -t 25000 insert
```

As with most custom tests, you have to manually specify the scale if you want that to be set correctly, and you have to skip the VACUUM step that normally would be done on the standard tables with -n.

This data point isn't all that interesting by itself, but update the end of the `pgbench-tools` config to run this test at a variety of sizes and client loads as follows:

```
SCALES="10 100 1000 10000"
SCRIPT="insert-size.sql"
TOTTRANS=100000
SETTIMES=1
SETCLIENTS="1 2 4 8 16"
SKIPINIT=1
```

Then run that set, and you'll likely see a more interesting pattern emerge. On my test system, the amount of `insert` statements per second doesn't vary much whether you're writing 1 or 10000 bytes into each one. It's primarily bounded by disk commit speed, which is always far less than the rated sequential write speed of the drive.

But, once you've reached a large enough number of clients combined with more bytes written each time, eventually the total completed `insert`/second rate starts to drop off. Find that point, measure actual disk writes using OS monitoring tools, and you'll have determined your database system's burst ability for writing out new data from inside the database itself, under a concurrent workload—something that's not very easy to measure directly.

This is a moderately complicated synthetic database benchmark, with variable client and workload sizes, and writing a client application this complicated from scratch would take a while. By leveraging `pgbench` and `pgbench-tools`, you can easily script something this complicated in only a few lines of code. And you'll end up with a `results` database you can analyze for patterns using standard SQL queries and tools.

Transaction Processing Performance Council benchmarks

The TPC-B benchmark is just one of many created by the TPC. It's the second benchmark from them for what's called an **Online Transaction Processing (OLTP)** workload, which is one heavy on database writes. A more current benchmark in that same style is their TPC-C (http://www.tpc.org/tpcc/) which includes what can be a fairly complicated mix of transaction types that all revolve around order entry and related inventory in a warehouse.

Using genuine TPC benchmarks isn't something practical to do on your own unless you're a major vendor prepared to license them and follow stringent reporting guidelines. However, there are free and open source clones of some of their benchmarks available, which follow the spirit of the benchmark without giving results that you can necessarily compare as directly across different types of systems. The Database Test (dbt) project has produced clones of some of these tests, outlined at `http://osdldbt.sourceforge.net/`, but not necessarily available in the best form from there.

The benchmarking wiki page at `http://wiki.postgresql.org/wiki/Category:Benchmarking` lists a variety of benchmarking programs and resources related to using them with the database. The open source alternative to TPC-C, named `dbt-2`, has its best documentation linked to from there. It targeted PostgreSQL as its original development platform although there are more databases supported now. If you'd like to simulate something that behaves more like a real-world workload than `pgbench`, but would like to keep things very heavy on writes, `dbt-2` is the standard program used in the PostgreSQL community for that purpose. Past tuning of the database itself has relied heavily on validation through improvements in `dbt-2` results.

The latest OLTP benchmark from the TPC is TPC-E, which models a large stock trading brokerage firm. An open version is available as `dbt-5`, but that code is still in active development. It may take a bit of work to get it running on your system.

Another popular test is TPC-H, which aims to model a decision support system running many moderately complicated queries at the same time. The TPC has released all of the code and data necessary to run this particular benchmark, and one of the links on the benchmarking wiki page leads to information about that. However, not all of the types of queries used by TPC-H are handled well by PostgreSQL, mainly because they haven't shown up in enough real-world workloads for anyone to optimize for them. The various commercial database vendors have to make sure they do well on each of these major benchmarks, so there's considerably more work put into making sure those products do well on TPC-C, TPC-E, and TPC-H in particular.

Summary

Benchmarking databases is a very extensive topic, and this chapter just introduces the major concepts. Having the `pgbench` tool bundled with the database is handy for doing smaller tests, but you need to be careful of its limitations before you rely too much on its results for your tuning efforts.

The basis for the built-in `pgbench` tests is outdated, and it's unlikely to match real-world performance. It can still be useful as a synthetic performance test.

You can write your own custom tests, either against the standard `pgbench` tables or new ones, and use the `pgbench` scripting capability to run those tests against multiple clients at once. Only a small number of the general database settings will impact `pgbench` results since its queries are so simple. Using a benchmarking tool chain that graphs transaction rate and latency, such as `pgbench-tools`, is vital to monitor latency in addition to throughput rate.

Getting some modern, serious TPC benchmarking running with PostgreSQL will provide much more useful test results, but they are much harder to get started with too. In the next chapter we will learn how to index our database.

Database Indexing

9

An **index** is simply an organized list of values that appear in one or more columns in a table. The idea is that if you only want a subset of the rows of that table, a query can use the index to determine which rows match, instead of examining every row. Because an index has an order to it, they can also be used to speed up situations where a section of a table has to be sorted in order to return its values.

Indexes help the database cut down on the amount of data it needs to look at in order to execute a query. It's hard to write about indexes without knowing how queries are executed, and it's hard to discuss query execution without knowing what indexes do. This chapter tries to break that explanation deadlock by using simple index examples, where the associated query plans should make some sense even without the query tuning background covered in the next chapter, Chapter 10, *Query Optimization*.

Indexes should not be relied upon to force ordering of a query. If you want a query to be ordered a particular way, use ORDER BY to request it. The existence of an index with that order is more likely to be selected to execute that query, as it will skip a sorting step to do so. But just because a query normally uses an index that happens to have an order in it to return results, that does not mean you'll always receive them ordered this way. Query plans will change over time to best match the underlying data as it changes too.

The main new thing to know to get started here is that if you put EXPLAIN ANALYZE in front of a SELECT statement, the database will show you how much work it expected that query to take, as well as how much it actually did. Reading EXPLAIN output is covered in more detail in the next chapter. You might discover you get more out of this chapter if you return to it again after reading Chapter 10, *Query Optimization*.

The topics we will cover in this chapter are:

- Index creation and maintenance
- Combining indexes
- Discussing different types of indexes and their use

Indexing example walkthrough

Discussion of indexes and query plans can quickly reach an overwhelming level of theory. Instead, this section will lead you through running various queries, with and without useful indexes, and showing how the query execution changes.

Measuring query disk and index block statistics

The best way to really understand how indexes work to save on the number of disk reads is to show how many blocks were actually used to satisfy that query. The following view merges together the two main sources for relevant table statistics, `pg_stat_user_tables` and `pg_statio_user_tables`:

```
CREATE OR REPLACE VIEW table_stats AS
SELECT
 stat.relname AS relname,
 seq_scan, seq_tup_read, idx_scan, idx_tup_fetch,
 heap_blks_read, heap_blks_hit, idx_blks_read, idx_blks_hit
FROM
 pg_stat_user_tables stat
 RIGHT JOIN pg_statio_user_tables statio
 ON stat.relid=statio.relid;
```

For the examples coming up, the following snippet of code is used after each statement (with `t` being the only table they use) to show the buffer usage count statistics that follow the query:

```
SELECT pg_sleep(1);
\pset x on
SELECT * FROM table_stats WHERE relname='t';
SELECT pg_stat_reset();
\pset x off
```

The idea is that if you reset all the database statistics after the previous query, run a new query, and then show the statistics; presuming no other activity is happening, the stats you see will only reflect what that last query did. The reason for the `pg_sleep` there is that statistics are at best only updated a few times per second. If you display them immediately after a query, they may not reflect recent activity. The `pset` commands are toggling on and off the optional query output mode in `psql`, and show each row returned on a separate line, which is much easier to read in the text for this data. This is equivalent to the `\x` that you'll see used sometimes in other sections of this book, except that instead of toggling the value it's explicitly setting it on or off; it works the same as specifying `-x` when running `psql` too.

Starting in PostgreSQL 9.0, it's possible to get a subset of this information—the part you're most likely to want—by using the `EXPLAIN (ANALYZE ON, BUFFERS ON)` syntax. An example is shown at the end of the walkthrough.

Running the example

The complete demo used to generate these examples is included with this book's sample files, and it was transformed into text by running an example like the following:

```
$ psql -e -f indextest.sql > indextest.out
```

You might want to tinker with the source code or set up and try running it yourself in this way. The general technique used to create sample data, execute a query, and gather usage statistics around it is a very common one used for iteratively improving a given query as you tweak either its indexing or database parameters.

To keep complete control over what's going on while running this demo, the `autovacuum` parameter was first turned `off` in the `postgresql.conf` file:

```
$ psql -c "show autovacuum"
autovacuum
------------
off
```

If you have `autovacuum` turned `on`, you'll see slightly different results. It will do the appropriate `ANALYZE` work needed to make things work right automatically, instead of waiting for the manual execution shown here to take care of that.

Sample data setup

To create some sample data to demonstrate how indexes work, let's create a table with a simple key/value structure. Each key can be an incrementing number, while the values vary from 0 to 10. It's simple to use `generate_series` to create data like that:

```
DROP TABLE IF EXISTS t;
CREATE TABLE t(k serial PRIMARY KEY,v integer);
INSERT INTO t(v)
 SELECT trunc(random() * 10)
  FROM generate_series(1,100000);
```

Creating a serial field as a PRIMARY KEY will create a sequence and one index for you, as noted when you run the preceding code:

```
NOTICE:  CREATE TABLE will create implicit sequence "t_k_seq" for serial
column "t.k"
NOTICE:  CREATE TABLE / PRIMARY KEY will create implicit index "t_pkey" for
table "t"
```

The first valuable thing to know is how many pages (blocks of 8 KB each) the table has, and how many tuples (rows) the query planner believes the table to have. As autovacuum is turned off, that information won't have appeared yet:

```
SELECT relname,relpages,reltuples FROM pg_class WHERE relname='t';
relname | relpages | reltuples
---------+----------+----------
t       |        0 |         0
```

This shows why turning autovacuum on, by default in 8.3 was so valuable: in earlier versions it was easy to miss this step, and end up running queries using completely wrong statistical information. A manual ANALYZE step will make sure all the statistics are current, and you can even compute the average number of rows stored per page of data. Here VACUUM ANALYZE is used because it also updates the hint bits related to the table, reducing variation in query runtimes later:

```
VACUUM ANALYZE t;
VACUUM
SELECT relname,relpages,reltuples FROM pg_class WHERE relname='t';
relname | relpages | reltuples
---------+----------+----------
t       |      443 |    100000
SELECT relname,round(reltuples / relpages) AS rows_per_page FROM pg_class
WHERE relname='t';
relname | rows_per_page
---------+--------------
t       |           226
```

At a higher level, 100000 rows of data are taking up 443, 8 K blocks on disk, each one of which holds approximately 226 rows.

Simple index lookups

If you use the primary key on the table, which was built using an index, it's possible to retrieve a row using that index quite quickly. This uses what's unsurprisingly called an `Index Scan`:

```
EXPLAIN ANALYZE SELECT count(*) FROM t WHERE k=1000;
QUERY PLAN
----------
Aggregate  (cost=8.28..8.29 rows=1 width=0) (actual time=0.034..0.036
rows=1 loops=1)
        ->  Index Scan using t_pkey on t   (cost=0.00..8.28 rows=1 width=0)
(actual time=0.020..0.023 rows=1 loops=1)
              Index Cond: (k = 1000)
    Total runtime: 0.104 ms
    seq_scan       | 0
    seq_tup_read   | 0
    idx_scan       | 1
    idx_tup_fetch  | 1
    heap_blks_read | 0
    heap_blks_hit  | 1
    idx_blks_read  | 0
    idx_blks_hit   | 3
```

The second part here demonstrates what comes out of the `pg_stat_reset/table_stats` combination used around each of the statements in the preceding example, as shown and used in the provided source code example.

This demonstrates the first thing to recognize about indexes. Note the counts here for `heap_blks_hit` and `idx_blks_hit`. Even when you can use an index to look up something by its primary key, you cannot return the result without looking at the associated row. Here, there are three index blocks used to navigate down to the block where the row needed was located, then that single heap (row data) block was returned. The reason for this is because PostgreSQL doesn't include visibility information in the indexes yet. The actual row must be consulted to determine if it's visible; it's not enough to confirm the key value `1000` exists in the index and then include it in the count here.

Accordingly, it's quite easy for an indexed scan to use more I/O than one that doesn't use an index. The index must be selective-filter out a significant portion of the rows, before it is worth using.

Full table scans

If you ask for data that does not have a selective index available, such as anything related to the unindexed v column, the query can only occur by running a full sequential scan over all the rows in the table:

```
EXPLAIN ANALYZE SELECT count(*) FROM t WHERE v=1;
QUERY PLAN
----------
Aggregate   (cost=1717.76..1717.77 rows=1 width=0)  (actual
time=74.535..74.537 rows=1 loops=1)
       ->  Seq Scan on t   (cost=0.00..1693.00 rows=9903 width=0)  (actual
time=0.015..56.847 rows=10054 loops=1)
             Filter: (v = 1)
   Total runtime: 74.600 ms
   seq_scan        | 1
   seq_tup_read    | 100000
   idx_scan        | 0
   idx_tup_fetch   | 0
   heap_blks_read  | 0
   heap_blks_hit   | 443
   idx_blks_read   | 0
   idx_blks_hit    | 0
```

You can see that every single one of the 443 blocks in this table were required to satisfy this query.

Another thing to recognize is that just because a query skips a portion of a table, it doesn't automatically mean that an index will be useful to execute it. You have to skip enough of a table for it to be worthwhile to do so. The following compound query for example scans the whole table, even though it's only looking for a part of the key values:

```
EXPLAIN ANALYZE SELECT count(*) FROM t WHERE k>9000 AND v=5;
QUERY PLAN
----------
   Aggregate   (cost=1965.94..1965.95 rows=1 width=0)  (actual
time=94.196..94.197 rows=1 loops=1)
       ->  Seq Scan on t   (cost=0.00..1943.00 rows=9176 width=0)  (actual
time=3.254..78.297 rows=9097 loops=1)
             Filter: ((k > 9000) AND (v = 5))
   Total runtime: 94.266 ms
   seq_scan        | 1
   seq_tup_read    | 100000
   idx_scan        | 0
   idx_tup_fetch   | 0
   heap_blks_read  | 0
```

```
heap_blks_hit  | 443
idx_blks_read  | 0
idx_blks_hit   | 0
```

Generally, any time a query is expected to hit a significant percentage of a table, you can expect a full sequential table scan to happen even if an index is usable there.

Index creation

To try and improve things, let's create an index on the `value` column and look at how large it is:

```
CREATE INDEX i ON t(v);
SELECT relname,reltuples,relpages FROM pg_class WHERE relname='i';
relname | reltuples | relpages
---------+-----------+---------
i       |    100000 |      221
SELECT relname,round(reltuples / relpages) AS rows_per_page FROM pg_class
WHERE relname='i';
relname | rows_per_page
---------+---------------
i       |           452
```

One thing you should notice here is that the index is certainly not tiny compared to the table, which is the case surprisingly often. It's about half the size of the table, at `221` pages. You should always note how large any index created is relative to the table when determining whether it's a worthwhile addition. The disk and maintenance overhead of an index can be considerable, and it needs to be justified by a performance improvement when running queries.

Lookup with an inefficient index

Is this new index worth being created? Consider a simple query that uses it to filter out based on the value:

```
EXPLAIN ANALYZE SELECT count(*) FROM t WHERE v=1;
QUERY PLAN
----------
Aggregate  (cost=756.55..756.56 rows=1 width=0) (actual time=31.962..31.963
rows=1 loops=1)
      ->  Bitmap Heap Scan on t  (cost=165.01..731.79 rows=9903 width=0)
(actual time=1.821..18.010 rows=10054 loops=1)
            Recheck Cond: (v = 1)
```

```
              ->  Bitmap Index Scan on i   (cost=0.00..162.53 rows=9903
  width=0)  (actual time=1.721..1.721 rows=10054 loops=1)
                    Index Cond:  (v = 1)
    Total runtime: 32.019 ms
    relname          | t
    seq_scan         | 1
    seq_tup_read     | 100000
    idx_scan         | 1
    idx_tup_fetch    | 10054
    heap_blks_read   | 0
    heap_blks_hit    | 886
    idx_blks_read    | 25
    idx_blks_hit     | 0
```

We expect 1/10 of the table, or around 10,000 rows, to be returned by the Index Scan, and that's what happens (9903 in this case). It is effectively doing two scans of the whole table to do that though (*443 blocks + 443 blocks=886 blocks*), plus the overhead of the index lookup itself (*25* blocks). This is clearly a step back from just looking at the whole table. This shouldn't really come as any surprise. Given how this table was created, there's likely to be a value where v=1 on every data block, so we can't help but scan them all here. The planner doesn't know this (yet!) though, and it's actually made executing this query worse.

You might wonder why it executes faster than the previous code despite this. No special work was done to isolate out caching effects; most of the data here is already sitting in the database's buffer cache this time. Generally, you need to run any query you're measuring three times if you want to get a feel for caching. If the first is much slower, and the second and third are about the same runtime, it's likely just the case that the data had to be read from disk or the OS cache for the first, while it was found in the database cache for the later ones.

Combining indexes

However, this doesn't mean the v index is useless. If you are running something that is selective based on the k index, the one on v can be combined with that. With the index in place, this earlier example now uses a complicated query plan:

```
EXPLAIN ANALYZE SELECT count(*) FROM t WHERE k>9000 AND v=5;
QUERY PLAN
-------------------------
Aggregate  (cost=787.97..787.98 rows=1 width=0) (actual time=40.545..40.546
rows=1 loops=1)
      ->  Bitmap Heap Scan on t   (cost=170.38..765.03 rows=9176 width=0)
 (actual time=4.107..24.606 rows=9097 loops=1)
```

```
            Recheck Cond: (v = 5)
            Filter: (k > 9000)
            -> Bitmap Index Scan on i   (cost=0.00..168.08 rows=10110
width=0) (actual time=3.255..3.255 rows=9993 loops=1)
                Index Cond: (v = 5)
    Total runtime: 40.638 ms
    seq_scan        | 0
    seq_tup_read    | 0
    idx_scan        | 1
    idx_tup_fetch   | 9993
    heap_blks_read  | 0
    heap_blks_hit   | 443
    idx_blks_read   | 23
    idx_blks_hit    | 1
```

It doesn't turn out to be any more efficient (because all the data blocks were pulled anyway), but the amount of duplication isn't very bad, just a small amount of extra index overhead. It does demonstrate the next useful thing to know about indexes. We provided single column indexes covering k and on v. The query looked for specific ranges or values for both parameters. The query planner can combine those using what it calls a `Bitmap Index Scan`. There was no need to create an index on the two fields together—(k,v) or (v,k) to get this behavior. Two single column indexes were sufficient. This is normally the case with PostgreSQL. You can put an index on each of the columns you want to filter on, and they can be very efficiently combined in most cases. You really need to prove that a compound index covering more than one field is a worthwhile performance improvement before you add one, particularly given they will only provide a useful speedup in queries that use that exact combination. Combining single column indexes is often as fast, and you can use them in any query that references a column that you indexed.

Switching from indexed to sequential scans

Previously, it was pointed out that when the query planner knows much of the table is going to be returned, it will just execute a sequential scan. This still isn't the case even in the very poor plan that is given, if we want all the values from 0 to 3 here:

```
EXPLAIN ANALYZE SELECT COUNT(*) FROM t WHERE v<4;
QUERY PLAN
----------
Aggregate  (cost=1706.53..1706.54 rows=1 width=0) (actual
time=112.030..112.031 rows=1 loops=1)
        -> Bitmap Heap Scan on t  (cost=665.33..1606.83 rows=39880 width=0)
(actual time=5.712..59.564 rows=40144 loops=1)
                Recheck Cond: (v < 4)
```

```
            ->  Bitmap Index Scan on i   (cost=0.00..655.36 rows=39880
  width=0)  (actual time=5.609..5.609 rows=40144 loops=1)
                Index Cond: (v < 4)
```

But, even with the relatively small amount of data we're giving the planner (more on that in a while), if you ask for more than that it realizes a sequential scan will execute better:

```
EXPLAIN ANALYZE SELECT COUNT(*) FROM t WHERE v<5;
QUERY PLAN
----------
Aggregate  (cost=1817.10..1817.11 rows=1 width=0)  (actual
time=149.846..149.848 rows=1 loops=1)
      ->  Seq Scan on t  (cost=0.00..1693.00 rows=49640 width=0)  (actual
time=0.010..82.892 rows=49989 loops=1)
                Filter: (v < 5)
```

Note that this second plan actually executes slower as shown, because it's doing more work: the `Aggregate` step has to process `49989` rows instead of the `40114` handled previously, and when all the data is in RAM you can assemble a `Bitmap Index Scan` of it quite quickly. Against a large table that wasn't cached in memory, where random index scans touching every single block would be quite a bit slower than one sequential one to do the same, this second form of plan could be an order of magnitude or more faster.

Planning for plan changes

This behavior that index scans will flip into sequential ones once they access enough of a table is one of the more surprising ones to many people. Random disk access is so much slower than sequential that it makes sense to do so. But if all your data is cached in RAM (the case on examples shown here), the advantages aren't as obvious. And that may very well always be the case with your data. In that case, you could even consider lowering database query parameters like `random_page_cost` to make the optimizer understand your true situation.

This whole area is one of the things to be wary of when executing your own queries that expect to use indexes. You can test them out using some subset of your data, or perhaps using the initial production set. If you then deploy onto a system with more rows, or the production system expands its data size, these plans will change. What was once an indexed query might turn into an unindexed full sequential scan. What can be even more frustrating for developers is the opposite: a query coded against a trivial subset of the data might always use a sequential scan, just because the table is small and the selectivity of the index low. Run the same query against the production data set, where neither is true anymore, and it could instead run using an index.

Whether an index will be used or not is a combination of both the query and the underlying table it's executing against, determined based on the statistics about the table. This is another topic discussed more in the next chapter, Chapter 10, *Query Optimization*.

Clustering against an index

If you want to lookup things in this data set based on the values in the v column, the fundamental issue here has already been described. Each page of data has about 226 rows in it, which you can expect to have around 22 rows that contain each value present. So there's no way to pick a value that only shows up in a subset of the table data blocks.

If there is a particular value you do want your data to be organized around, it's possible to do so using the CLUSTER command, described in more detail next:

```
CLUSTER t USING i;
ANALYZE t;
```

Since autovacuum is off, this is followed by a manual ANALYZE to make sure the change in structure of the table is noted. In particular, the statistics for the data will now reflect that the structure of the table is highly correlated with the v field.

Now, if you execute a query that only looks at a portion of the table based on the value field, it can be executed efficiently using an Index Scan:

```
EXPLAIN ANALYZE SELECT COUNT(*) FROM t WHERE v<4;
QUERY PLAN
----------
Aggregate  (cost=1339.40..1339.41 rows=1 width=0) (actual
time=140.149..140.151 rows=1 loops=1)
      ->  Index Scan using i on t  (cost=0.00..1239.13 rows=40107 width=0)
(actual time=0.105..76.797 rows=40144 loops=1)
             Index Cond: (v < 4)
    seq_scan      | 0
    seq_tup_read  | 0
    idx_scan      | 1
    idx_tup_fetch | 40144
    heap_blks_read | 0
    heap_blks_hit  | 178
    idx_blks_read  | 90
    idx_blks_hit   | 0
```

Note that the combined I/O here (178 heap blocks, 90 index blocks) is indeed less than scanning the whole table (443) blocks looking for 40% of it. This is only true on an Index Scan that's expected to do sequential transfers; using a scattered 40% of an index would not be so efficient. Again, the measured times here are impacted by caching effects and some random variation, so don't read too much into the fact that actual runtime here (140 ms) is actually slower than how long this took previously (112 ms) before the table was clustered during the individual executions I grabbed snapshots for. Ultimately, on a system where everything doesn't fit in RAM, lowering total blocks fetched is normally a big win.

There's still a threshold here. At some point, getting even more of the table will switch to a sequential scan again:

```
EXPLAIN ANALYZE SELECT COUNT(*) FROM t WHERE v<6;
QUERY PLAN
----------
Aggregate  (cost=1842.53..1842.54 rows=1 width=0) (actual
time=215.587..215.589 rows=1 loops=1)
       -> Seq Scan on t  (cost=0.00..1693.00 rows=59810 width=0) (actual
time=0.019..116.624 rows=59982 loops=1)
             Filter: (v < 6)
  seq_scan       | 1
  seq_tup_read   | 100000
  idx_scan       | 0
  idx_tup_fetch  | 0
  heap_blks_read | 0
  heap_blks_hit  | 443
  idx_blks_read  | 0
  idx_blks_hit   | 0
```

This is because the index will not be considered selective enough to justify the overhead of using it anymore.

Explain with buffer counts

These examples should have proven to you that looking at the counts of blocks hit and read is valuable for determining whether a query plan is really being executed correctly or not. PostgreSQL 9.0 adds a feature to make this easier than before. Instead of looking at the pg_stat* data as done in the previous example, you can request a count of buffers accessed directly when running EXPLAIN:

```
EXPLAIN (ANALYZE ON, BUFFERS ON) SELECT count(*) FROM t WHERE v=5;
QUERY PLAN
----------
```

```
Aggregate  (cost=332.92..332.93 rows=1 width=0) (actual time=39.132..39.134
rows=1 loops=1)
        Buffers: shared hit=46 read=23
        -> Index Scan using i on t  (cost=0.00..308.21 rows=9883 width=0)
(actual time=0.069..21.843 rows=9993 loops=1)
              Index Cond: (v = 5)
              Buffers: shared hit=46 read=23
```

To see how well this works, try running that query again after dropping the index that's selective on v:

```
DROP INDEX i;
EXPLAIN (ANALYZE ON, BUFFERS ON) SELECT count(*) FROM t WHERE v=5;
QUERY PLAN
-----------------------------------
    Aggregate  (cost=1717.71..1717.72 rows=1 width=0) (actual
time=75.539..75.541 rows=1 loops=1)
        Buffers: shared hit=443
        -> Seq Scan on t  (cost=0.00..1693.00 rows=9883 width=0) (actual
time=20.987..58.050 rows=9993 loops=1)
              Filter: (v = 5)
              Buffers: shared hit=443
```

This shows the sequential scan running against the full 443 pages of data this table is known to occupy. You can see that the counter in the second query is bigger than in the first.

Index creation and maintenance

Creating an index is one of the most intensive operations you can do on a database. When populating a database using tools such as pg_restore, the time spent building indexes can be the longest part of the data loading. And you can't necessarily just ignore them afterwards. Index rebuilding can be an expected part of regular database maintenance, particularly in the case where many rows (but not all of them) are being deleted from a section of an index. There's more information about that topic back in Chapter 7, *Routine Maintenance*.

Unique indexes

A unique indexes enforces that you won't have more than one row containing a particular key value. These are quite common in proper database design, both for improving performance—an indexed unique lookup is normally fast as well as data integrity, preventing erroneous duplications of data. Only B-tree indexes can currently be used as unique ones.

There are three ways you can create a unique index, only two of which are recommended. The first you saw at the beginning of the chapter walkthrough: when you mark a field as PRIMARY KEY, a unique index is created to make sure there are no key duplicates.

But a PRIMARY KEY is just a specially marked case of having a unique constraint on a table. The following two statement sets give almost identical results:

```
CREATE TABLE t(k serial PRIMARY KEY,v integer);

CREATE TABLE t(k serial,v integer);
ALTER TABLE t ADD CONSTRAINT k_key UNIQUE (k);
```

However, the PRIMARY KEY case is labeled better in the system catalog (and is therefore preferable from an internal database documentation standpoint). Note that the index created for the purpose of enforcing uniqueness is a perfectly functional index usable for speeding up queries. There's no need in this case to create a regular index on k so that you can look up values by the key faster; the unique index provides that already.

It's also possible to directly create an index using CREATE UNIQUE INDEX. This is considered a bad form and you should avoid doing so. It effectively creates a constraint, without labeling it as such in the list of constraints. If you want values to be unique, add a constraint; don't add the index manually.

One caveat when using unique indexes is that null values are not considered equal to one another. This means that you could have several entries inserted such that each have a null value for their key. To avoid the problems this can introduce, it's recommended to always add NOT NULL to the fields that are going to participate in the index when the table is created. Rejecting null values when they don't make sense in your data is a good habit to adopt beyond this particular issue; most fields in a well designed database will reject null values.

Concurrent index creation

When you build an index normally, it locks the table against writes. This means that reads using SELECT against the table will work fine, but any attempt to insert, update, or delete a row in it will block until the index creation is finished. The statement will pause and wait for the index lock to be released, instead of throwing an error immediately. As index rebuilding on large tables can easily take hours, that's a problem. There's some potential for a deadlock producing error here as well, if the client backend already had some locks on that table before the index build began.

Accordingly, on any production database with significant table sizes, where a user being blocked for a long time is an issue, you usually want to build indexes using CREATE INDEX CONCURRENTLY. This is not the default because the concurrent index build is much less efficient than the standard one that takes a lock. It scans the table once to initially build the index, then makes a second pass to look for things added after the first pass.

There is also a risk to any concurrent index build on indexes that enforce some constraint, such as any UNIQUE index. If an unacceptable row is found during that second pass, such as a uniqueness violation, the concurrent index build fails, having wasted resources without accomplishing anything. The resulting index will be marked INVALID when viewed with the psql utility and will not be usable for queries. But, changes to the table will still update values in it wasted overhead. You can recover from this situation by dropping the index and trying to build it again, presuming you know the same issue won't pop up again (for example, all duplicate values have been erased). You can also use REINDEX to fix it, but that can't be done concurrently; it will take the usual write lock the whole time.

Clustering an index

CLUSTER works by making a whole new copy of the table, sorted by the index you asked to traverse the original in. It's as if you had inserted them in that order in the first place. Once built, the original copy of the data is dropped. CLUSTER requires an exclusive lock on the table and enough disk space to hold the second, reorganized copy-essentially, twice the amount of disk space, temporarily. You should run ANALYZE afterwards in order to update the statistics associated with this table to reflect its new ordering.

Clustering is useful for getting faster results from range-based queries, when selecting a set of values that is between two end points (with the beginning or end being considered an end point in that context). It can generally speed up access to fragmented data that might have been introduced from any number of sources.

Clustering is a one-time act. Future insertion does not respect the clustered order, even though the database does remember what index you last used if you cluster again.

Starting in PostgreSQL 9.0, the way VACUUM FULL is executed uses the same basic logic as CLUSTER: rewrite the whole thing, instead of trying to clean up problem spots inefficiently.

Fill factor

When you create a new index, not every entry in every index block is used. A small amount of free space, specified by the FILLFACTOR parameter, is left empty. The idea is that the first set of changes to that index either updates or insertions can happen on the same index blocks, therefore reducing index fragmentation.

The default FILLFACTOR for B-tree indexes is 90%, leaving 10% free space. One situation where you might want to change this is a table with static data, where the data won't change after index creation. In this case, creating the index to be 100% full is more efficient:

```
CREATE INDEX i ON t(v) WITH (FILLFACTOR=100);
```

On tables that are being populated randomly, or ones that are heavily updated, reducing the fillfactor from its default can reduce index fragmentation, and therefore the amount of random disk access required to use that index once it's more heavily populated.

Reindexing

When indexes become less efficient due to being spread over disk inefficiently, either scattered around too randomly or too bloated with now unused values, the index will benefit from being rebuilt. This is most easily done with the REINDEX command, and that can't be done concurrently. More information about detecting when indexes need to be rebuilt and how to do so is in Chapter 7, *Routine Maintenance*. Remember that the B-tree indices VACUUM and autovacuum always involve a REINDEX operation; this is not true for the other kind of indexes.

Index types

Indexing in PostgreSQL is completely programmable. It's straightforward (albeit not quite easy) to create a totally custom index type, even with customized operators for how to compare values. A few unusual index types are included with the core database.

B-tree

The standard index type is the **B-tree**, where the B stands for balanced. A balanced tree is one where the amount of data on the left and right side of each split is kept even, so that the amount of levels you have to descend to reach any individual row is approximately equal.

The B-tree can be used to find a single value or to scan a range, searching for key values that are greater than, less than, and/or equal to some value. They also work fine on both numeric and text data. Recent versions of PostgreSQL (8.3 and later) can also use an index to find (or avoid) null values in a table.

Text operator classes

It's possible to use an index on a text field to speed finding rows that start with a substring of interest. A query like this that uses LIKE to match the start of a string:

```
SELECT * FROM t WHERE t.s LIKE 'start%';
```

It can use an index on that string field to return answers more quickly. This is not useful if your comparison tries to match the middle or end of the column though. In addition, if your database uses something other than the simple C locale, the default way values are compared in indexes, can't be used for this purpose. You'll need to create the index using a special mode for locale sensitive character by character comparisons, like the following:

```
CREATE INDEX i ON t (s text_pattern_ops);
```

In this example, s would be a text field; there are different operators for varchar and char types. In addition to LIKE, this form of index can also be used for some types of text regular expression matches too.

See the *Operator Classes and Operator Families* section of the PostgreSQL manual for more information on this topic. You can confirm your locale, and decide whether you need to use this approach, by looking at the lc_collate parameter:

```
postgres=# show lc_collate;
lc_collate
-------------
en_US.UTF-8
```

This sample database is not using the C locale, and therefore would need to use the `text_pattern_ops` operator class in order for the LIKE queries to use an index on a text field.

Hash

The hash index type can be useful in cases where you are only doing equality (not range) searching on an index, and you don't allow null values in it. However, it is easy for hash indexes to become corrupt after a database crash, and therefore ineffective for queries until manually rebuilt. The advantages to using a hash index instead of a B-tree are small compared to this risk. You normally shouldn't ever use the hash index type. But, if you are willing to spend a considerable amount of time analyzing its usefulness and ensuring the index will be rebuilt if it becomes corrupt, it is possible you can find a purpose for them.

Starting from PostgreSQL 10.0 hash indexes are WAL based , so now they are crash safe and they can be replicated.

Now, let's populate a table with 5000000 records and let's evaluate the creation time and the size of the hash indexes compared to the B-tree indexes:

```
pgbench=# create table pgtest (id serial not null, field_text text);
CREATE TABLE

pgbench=# insert into pgtest(field_text) select
md5(generate_series(1,50000000)::text);
INSERT 0 50000000
```

Now we have a table with 5000000 records, the time of creation of a btree index on this table is:

```
pgbench=# \timing
pgbench=# create index field_text_bree on pgtest using btree(field_text);
CREATE INDEX
Time: 596544,497 ms (09:56,544)
```

And the time of creation of a hash index on this table is:

```
pgbench=# create index field_text_hash on pgtest using
hash(field_text);CREATE INDEX
Time: 177209,473 ms (02:57,209)
```

As you can see the creation time of a `hash` index is less than the time of creation of a `btree` index, but its dimensions are greater:

```
pgbench=# select relname,pg_size_pretty(relpages::int8*8192) from pg_class
where relname like 'field_te%';
     relname      | pg_size_pretty
------------------+----------------
 field_text_bree  | 2816 MB
 field_text_hash  | 1351 MB
(2 righe)
```

Let's see now some examples of the execution times:

```
pgbench=# explain analyze select * from pgtest where field_text =
md5('1029290');
        QUERY PLAN
----------------------------------------------------------------
 Index Scan using field_text_hash on pgtest   (cost=0.00..8.02 rows=1
width=37) (actual
time=0.395..0.397 rows=1 loops=1)
    Index Cond: (field_text = 'dbafb94acd0f5bb51afb63a64a03bf2f'::text)
 Planning time: 1.048 ms
 Execution time: 0.413 ms
(4 righe)

pgbench=# explain analyze select field_text from pgtest where field_text =
md5('10292');
        QUERY PLAN
----------------------------------------------------------------
 Index Scan using field_text_hash on pgtest   (cost=0.00..8.02 rows=1
width=33) (actual
time=0.010..0.011 rows=1 loops=1)
    Index Cond: (field_text = 'dbafb94acd0f5bb51afb63a64a03bf2f'::text)
 Planning time: 0.061 ms
 Execution time: 0.022 ms
(4 righe)

pgbench=# drop index field_text_hash ;
DROP INDEX

pgbench=# explain analyze select field_text from pgtest where field_text =
md5('10292');
        QUERY PLAN
----------------------------------------------------------------
 Index Only Scan using field_text_bree on pgtest   (cost=0.56..8.58 rows=1
width=33) (ac
tual time=3.979..3.981 rows=1 loops=1)
```

```
    Index Cond: (field_text = 'dbafb94acd0f5bb51afb63a64a03bf2f'::text)
    Heap Fetches: 1
 Planning time: 0.092 ms
 Execution time: 3.995 ms
(5 righe)

pgbench=# explain analyze select * from pgtest where field_text =
md5('12232932');
QUERY PLAN
-----------------------------------------------------------------
 Index Scan using field_text_bree on pgtest   (cost=0.56..8.58 rows=1
width=37) (actual
time=2.976..2.979 rows=1 loops=1)
    Index Cond: (field_text = '00c868ab5c9b0d3ab329009faf8de0e5'::text)
 Planning time: 0.059 ms
 Execution time: 2.994 ms
(4 righe)
```

As you can see, the search by `hash` indexes is faster than the search performed by B-tree indexes even if hash indexes do not support the index-only scan method.

GIN

Regular indexes are optimized for the case where a row has a single key value associated with it, so that the mapping between rows and keys is generally simple. The **Generalized Inverted Index** (**GIN**) is useful for a different sort of organization. GIN stores a list of keys with what's called a posting list of rows, each of which contain that key. A row can appear on the posting list of multiple keys too.

With the right design, GIN allows efficient construction and search of some advanced key/value data structures that wouldn't normally map well to a database structure. It leverages the ability to customize the comparison operator class used for an index, while relying on a regular B-tree structure to actually store the underlying index data.

GIN is useful for indexing array values, which allows operations such as searching for all rows where the array column contains a particular value, or has some elements in common with an array you're matching against. It's also one of the ways to implement full-text search. There are several examples that use GIN that suggest how it can be utilized to build custom data storage among the example PostgreSQL `contrib` modules.

Anytime you're faced with storing data that doesn't match the usual single key to single value sort of structure regular database indexes expect, GIN might be considered as an alternative approach. It's been applied to a wide range of interesting indexing problems.

B-tree GIN versus bitmap indexes

PostgreSQL doesn't have bitmap indexes as Oracle does, but GIN is also very good at handling duplicates. The internal structure of a GIN index is actually quite similar to a bitmap index. Bitmax indexes are used for fields with low cardinality, and GIN indices are used in the same way. Let's now look an example of using the GIN indexes as substitutes for bitmap indexes:

```
pgbench=# create table test_gin (n1 integer,n2 integer);
CREATE TABLE

pgbench=#  insert into test_gin (n1, n2) select n, n % 2 from
generate_series(1, 1000000) n;
INSERT 0 1000000

pgbench=# create extension btree_gin ;
CREATE EXTENSION
pgbench=# create index n2_btree on test_gin using btree(n2);
CREATE INDEX
pgbench=# create index n2_gin on test_gin using gin(n2);
CREATE INDEX

pgbench=# \di+

List of relations
-[ RECORD 1]+----------------------
Schema      | public
Name        | n2_btree
Type        | index
Owner | postgres
Table       | test_gin
Size   | 21 MB
Description |
-[ RECORD 2 ]+----------------------
Schema      | public
Name        | n2_gin
Type        | index
Owner | postgres
Type     | test_gin
Size   | 1088 kB
Description |
```

As you can see, for this type of field, the B-tree-gin indexes are very useful

GiST

A **Generalized Search Tree (GiST)** provide a way to build a balanced tree structure for storing data, such as the built-in B-tree, just by defining how keys are to be treated. This allows using the index to quickly answer questions that go beyond the usual equality and range comparisons handled by a B-tree.

For example, the geometric data types that are included in PostgreSQL include operators to allow an index to sort by the distance between items and whether they intersect.

GiST can also be used for full-text search, and it too has a very rich library of `contrib` modules that use its features. When you need a really customized type of index, with operators that go beyond the normal comparison ones, but the structure is still like a tree, consider using GiST when a standard database table doesn't perform well.

Advanced index use

Many PostgreSQL users will only ever use simple B-tree indexes on a single column. There are of course a few ways to build more complicated ones too though.

Multicolumn indexes

Consider a database table that is storing a category and a subcategory for a series of data. In this case, you don't expect to ever specify a subcategory without also providing a category. This is the sort of situation where a multicolumn index can be useful. B-tree indexes can have to up 32 columns they index, and anytime there's a natural parent/child relationship in your data this form of index might be appropriate.

Create an index for that sort of situation:

```
CREATE INDEX i_category ON t (category,subcategory);
```

The index could be used for queries that look like the following:

```
SELECT * FROM t WHERE category='x' and subcategory='y';
SELECT * FROM t WHERE category='x';
```

But it is unlikely to be useful for the following form:

```
SELECT * FROM t WHERE subcategory='y';
```

Had you instead created two indexes for both category and subcategory, those could satisfy either individual type of search, as well as the combined one (combining with a `Bitmap Index Scan`). However, the result would likely be larger and involve more overhead to update than the multicolumn version, the downside to that flexibility, as well as being a bit less efficient when a query selecting on both columns is run.

Indexes for sorting

B-tree indexes store their entries in ascending order. Starting in PostgreSQL 8.3, the nulls are also stored in them, defaulting to last in the table. You can reverse both of those defaults, such as the following:

```
CREATE INDEX i ON t(v DESC NULLS FIRST);
```

The query planner will use an index that returns rows in sorted order in some cases when `ORDER BY` has been specified. Generally, this only happens when a small number of rows are being returned by the table, which is the opposite of what you might expect. This is because reading the index blocks is optional. You can always derive the data by sorting the data, and the planner considers index reads to be random instead of sequential access. If a large percentage of the table is being read, directly reading the table sequentially and sorting the result will have a lower estimated cost than the redundant disk access of reading both the random index blocks and the data blocks too. Expecting to see an index used for `ORDER BY`, and instead having all the data read in and sorted, is one way you can end up with considerable unexpected disk activity, in the form of temporary sorting files.

If you are using `ORDER BY` and `LIMIT`, an index is much more likely to be used. In that case, an index might immediately return the limited number of rows needed using the index, while a standard query will have to read all the rows and sort just to return any of them.

Partial indexes

Indexes do not have to cover the entirety of a table. You can create smaller, targeted indexes that satisfy a particular `WHERE` clause, and the planner will use those when appropriate. For example, consider the case where you are tracking a set of customer accounts, and want to flag a small number of them for special processing; let's just say they are flagged as interesting with a Boolean of that name. You could then create a partial index:

```
CREATE INDEX accounts_interesting_index ON accounts WHERE interesting IS
true;
```

(That's intentionally more verbose than necessary just to demonstrate the syntax.) You'd expect this index to be very small, relative to one that included every account. And it would return the list of interesting accounts quite quickly, because the index will only contain them not the whole table. As always, this index could also be combined with others using a `Bitmap Index Scan`.

Expression-based indexes

The classic example for an expression-based index is when you typically search based on a name only after converting it to a particular case:

```
CREATE INDEX i_lower_idx ON t (lower(name));
SELECT * FROM t WHERE lower(name) = 'x';
```

This query will run using that expression index, which turns it into a single value indexed lookup in the table. An index based on the username without converting to lowercase first will not be useful in that context.

One non-obvious thing you can implement using partial indexes is forcing uniqueness for an expression, instead of just a combination of fields:

```
CREATE UNIQUE INDEX I ON lower(username);
```

This would only allow one row to exist at any time with that value for the expression. You might want to handle this as a constraint instead though.

Note that every time you insert or update an entry in a table with this sort of index, the function used needs to be called to compute an appropriate value for the index. This makes the insert/update overhead of this sort of index higher than one that just uses a column list. Even more so than regular indexes, the index needs to give you something that's selective against your data for the overhead of building the index to be worthwhile.

Indexing for full-text search

PostgreSQL includes a capable **full-text search** (**FTS**) package, available as a core feature starting in 8.3. Both GIN and GiST indexes can be used to accelerate text searches done that way. The basic idea is that GIN is better suited for relatively static data, while GiST performs better with frequently updated, dynamic text. The trade-offs involved in choosing between those index types are heavily documented in the PostgreSQL manual chapter devoted to full-text search.

That documentation can also be considered a tutorial on the relative strengths and weaknesses of GIN versus GiST, which can be useful when trying to decide which of them to use for other applications. For example, the `hstore` key/value implementation available as a `contrib` module can be handy for efficiently storing that sort of data when it doesn't need to have full SQL semantics, an approach popularized by the NoSQL movement recently. There are both GIN and GiST implementations of `hstore` available, and choosing between the two is complicated. Knowing more about their relative insert versus query performance characteristics, as seen from the context of FTS, provides a useful vantage point to compare the two that you can extrapolate from.

Indexing like or like queries with pg_trgm contrib

The B-tree type indexes can also index this kind of query:

```
select * from table where field like 'aaaa%',
```

To do this, we need to create the index using the OPCLASS `varchar_pattern_ops`:

```
pgbench=#  create table test_like(id serial,field_text text);
CREATE TABLE
pgbench=# insert into test_like(field_text)
values('orange'),('apple'),('tomato'),('potato');
INSERT 0 4
pgbench=# explain select * from test_like where field_text like 'toma%';
        QUERY PLAN
-----------------------------------------------------------
 Seq Scan on test_like   (cost=10000000000.00..10000000025.88 rows=6
width=36)
    Filter: (field_text ~~ 'toma%'::text)
(2 rows)

pgbench=# create index test_like_idx on test_like (field_text
varchar_pattern_ops);
CREATE INDEX
pgbench=# explain select * from test_like where field_text like 'toma%';
 ....  QUERY PLAN
-----------------------------------------------------------
  Index Scan using test_like_idx on test_like  (cost=0.13..8.15 rows=1
width=36)
    Index Cond: ((field_text ~>=~ 'toma'::text) AND (field_text ~<~
'tomb'::text))
    Filter: (field_text ~~ 'toma%'::text)
(3 rows)
```

```
pgbench=# explain select * from test_like where field_text like '%toma%';
                  QUERY PLAN
-----------------------------------------------------------
 Seq Scan on test_like  (cost=10000000000.00..10000000001.05 rows=1
width=36)
    Filter: (field_text ~~ '%toma%'::text)
(2 rows)


pgbench=# explain select * from test_like where field_text like '%toma';
                  QUERY PLAN
-----------------------------------------------------------
 Seq Scan on test_like  (cost=10000000000.00..10000000001.05 rows=1
width=36)
    Filter: (field_text ~~ '%toma'::text)
(2 rows)
```

The btree can not index searches like '%aaaa' or searches like '%aaaa%' , iif you want to use an index for this type of search you have to use the pg_trgm extension, this extension also indexes ilike (insensitive like) searches.:

```
pgbench=# create extension pg_trgm ;
CREATE EXTENSION
pgbench=# create index test_like_gin_idx on test_like using gin (field_text
gin_trgm_ops);
CREATE INDEX
pgbench=# explain select * from test_like where field_text like '%toma';
          QUERY PLAN
-----------------------------------------------------------------------
-------
 Bitmap Heap Scan on test_like  (cost=16.00..20.01 rows=1 width=36)
    Recheck Cond: (field_text ~~ '%toma'::text)
    ->  Bitmap Index Scan on test_like_gin_idx  (cost=0.00..16.00 rows=1
width=0)
          Index Cond: (field_text ~~ '%toma'::text)
(4 rows)
pgbench=# explain select * from test_like where field_text like '%toma%';
...              QUERY PLAN
-----------------------------------------------------------------------
-------
 Bitmap Heap Scan on test_like  (cost=12.00..16.01 rows=1 width=36)
    Recheck Cond: (field_text ~~ '%toma%'::text)
    ->  Bitmap Index Scan on test_like_gin_idx  (cost=0.00..12.00 rows=1
width=0)
          Index Cond: (field_text ~~ '%toma%'::text)
(4 rows)
```

Indexing JSON datatype

Starting from version 9.4 PostgreSQL natively supports the JSON datatype and it is possible to create an index on it. In the following example, we will now see how to perform an indexed search on a JSON type:

```
pgbench=# create table test_json( id serial, field_json jsonb);
CREATE TABLE
pgbench=#  INSERT INTO test_json (field_json)
VALUES
  (
  '{ "customer": "Billy", "items": {"product": "Apple","qty": 2}}'
  ),
  (
  '{ "customer": "Molly", "items": {"product": "Orange","qty": 1}}'
  ),
  (
  '{ "customer": "Billy", "items": {"product": "Orange","qty": 10}}'
  ),
  (
  '{ "customer": "Frank", "items": {"product": "Potato","qty": 2}}'
  );
INSERT 0 3

create index field_json_idx on test_json using gin (field_json jsonb_ops);

pgbench=# select field_json->'items'->>'product' as product from test_json
where field_json @>'{"customer":"Billy"}';
 product
---------
 Apple
 Orange
(2 rows)

pgbench=# explain select field_json->'items'->>'product' as product from
test_json where field_json @>'{"customer":"Billy"}';
        QUERY PLAN
------------------------------------------------------------ Bitmap Heap
Scan on test_json  (cost=12.00..16.02 rows=1 width=32)
   Recheck Cond: (field_json @> '{"customer": "Billy"}'::jsonb)
   ->  Bitmap Index Scan on field_json_idx  (cost=0.00..12.00 rows=1
width=0)
        Index Cond: (field_json @> '{"customer": "Billy"}'::jsonb)
(4 rows)
```

Summary

Choosing what indexes to add to your tables remains one of those areas where creative tuning work can still trump mechanical attempts to measure and react. There are some index tuning wizards available for other databases, but even the best of them just provide suggestions instead of dependable advice. It's important to be systematic about your indexes though. Because adding an index increases overhead every time you add or change rows in a table, each index needs to satisfy enough queries to justify how much it costs to maintain. There is more information about determining whether the indexes on your system are working effectively in Chapter 11, *Database Activity and Statistics*.

Measure actual block reads to determine whether an index is truly effective. Queries cannot be answered using only the data in an index. The data blocks must be consulted for row visibility information in all cases. An index is only useful if it is selective; it can be used to only return a small portion of the rows in a table. Indexes can be quite large relative to their underlying table. If two useful indexes exist to answer a query, they can be combined, and that's preferable in many cases to using a multicolumn index. Building an index can take a long time, and will block activity if not done with the concurrent option enabled.

Indexes can require periodic rebuilding to return them to optimum performance, and clustering the underlying data against the index order can also help improve their speed and usability for queries.

A variety of advanced techniques are available to build customized index structures in PostgreSQL, for situations where the standard B-tree index on simple fields isn't powerful enough.

Next, we will study the query optimization, which involves explaining queries and working with JOIN, Aggregate, and WINDOW functions.

10
Query Optimization

For some database administrators and application developers, query optimization is the most important part of database performance tuning. Earlier chapters have wandered some distance from there, because if your fundamental server setup isn't good, no amount of query tuning will help you. But things like selecting good hardware for a database server are rare. Figuring out why a query is slow and how to improve it is something you can expect to happen all the time. This is particularly true because query plans drift over time, and some aspects of your database will become less efficient. Maintenance to improve the latter problem is covered in the next few chapters. How queries execute and improving that execution is this chapter's topic.

The chapter will cover the following topics:

- Explanation of the EXPLAIN command
- Query plan node structure
- Cost computation
- Processing nodes
- Scans
- Subquery scan and subplan
- CTE scan
- Joins
- Statistics

Sample data sets

To show you queries to optimize, you need data. So far, randomly generated data for a small number of tables has been good enough for that, but that has its limits and they were reached in the previous chapter, Chapter 9, *Database Indexing*.

Obtaining sample data of a significant size for benchmarking purposes is a never-ending struggle, because the pace of hardware progress means yesteryear's massive test database can be today's trivial workload. A listing that's kept up to date with useful new sources for test databases is at http://wiki.postgresql.org/wiki/Sample_Databases and some of these are part of a PostgreSQL sample database project, which has several examples that are worth checking out.

Pagila

The pagila database is a particularly interesting sample because it showcases many advanced PostgreSQL features. It relies heavily on stored procedures and even partitions some of its data. The main reason it's not used for examples here is because it's very small, only a few megabytes in size. The non-free license on the documentation for the original database it's based on (Sakila, a part of MySQL) makes it problematic to quote from here too.

dellstore2

dellstore2 was originally distributed by Dell at http://linux.dell.com/dvdstore/ as part of an effort to create a vendor-neutral comparison test. It includes everything from the database to an e-commerce web application. Its sample store sells DVDs to customers and includes products, orders, inventory, and customer history.

A PostgreSQL port of the database part of the Dell Store application is available from the sample databases project at http://pgfoundry.org/projects/dbsamples/.

While the benchmark can theoretically be targeted to create 3 sizes, only the small (10 MB) version is available for PostgreSQL so far. The data generators for the medium (1 GB) and large (100 GB) stores haven't been implemented for PostgreSQL yet. This makes the dellstore2 a modest test database for examples here, but not a real representative of a serious workload by modern standards.

Obtaining and installing `dellstore2` can be very simple:

```
$ wget
http://pgfoundry.org/frs/download.php/543/dellstore2-normal-1.0.tar.gz
$ tar xvfz dellstore2-normal-1.0.tar.gz
$ cd dellstore2-normal-1.0/
$ createdb dellstore2
$ psql -f dellstore2-normal-1.0.sql -d dellstore2
$ psql -d dellstore2 -c "VACUUM VERBOSE ANALYZE"
```

With indexes and related overhead, the result is actually 21 MB:

```
$ psql -d dellstore2 -c "SELECT
pg_size_pretty(pg_database_size('dellstore2'))"
     pg_size_pretty
    ----------------
      21 MB
```

This means that even the tiny default `shared_buffers` on most systems can hold the whole set of data, but the queries aren't completely trivial. Here are the major tables and indexes:

```
            table          |   size
  -------------------------+---------
  public.customers         | 3808 kB
  public.orderlines        | 2840 kB
  public.cust_hist         | 2368 kB
  public.products          | 808 kB
  public.orders            | 800 kB
  public.inventory         | 400 kB
          index            |   size
  -------------------------+---------
  public.ix_orderlines_orderid   | 1336 kB
  public.ix_cust_hist_customerid | 1080 kB
  public.ix_cust_username        | 544 kB
  public.customers_pkey          | 368 kB
  public.ix_order_custid         | 232 kB
  public.orders_pkey             | 232 kB
  public.ix_prod_special         | 192 kB
  public.ix_prod_category        | 192 kB
  public.products_pkey           | 192 kB
  public.inventory_pkey          | 192 kB
```

The examples in this chapter will be using the `dellstore2` example installed, as shown before, unless otherwise noted.

The structure of this data is easy to understand if you've ever shopped online:

- There are a number of products the store sells, each of which fits into a category
- The store has customers
- Customers place orders
- Each order has a number of lines to it, each of which references the product being purchased
- A customer history is saved listing all the products that customer has ever ordered

EXPLAIN basics

If you have a query that's running slowly, the first thing to try is running it with EXPLAIN before the statement executes. This displays what's called a **query plan**, the list of what's expected to happen when that query is executed. If you instead use EXPLAIN ANALYZE before the statement, you'll get both the estimation describing what the planner expected, along with what actually happened when the query ran. Note that this form will actually execute the statement as if you run it manually. Consider the following statement:

```
EXPLAIN ANALYZE DELETE * FROM t;
```

This is not only going to show you a query plan for deleting those rows, it's going to delete them; that's the only way to know for sure how long actually executing the plan is going to take. It's much harder to get a consistent setup to compare timing of operations that do INSERT, UPDATE, or DELETE using EXPLAIN ANALYZE because the act of collecting the data will change what a subsequent execution of the same statement will do.

Timing overhead

Assume you're executing a simple query to count all the customers in the database, and want to time how long this takes:

```
dellstore2=# \timing
Timing is on.
dellstore2=# SELECT count(*) FROM customers;
 count
-------
 20000
Time: 7.994 ms
```

You may then be curious to know which query plan was used to get this result. The amount of time taken to determine that may shock you:

```
dellstore2=# EXPLAIN ANALYZE SELECT count(*) FROM customers;
QUERY PLAN
----------
Aggregate  (cost=726.00..726.01 rows=1 width=0) (actual time=68.836..68.838
rows=1 loops=1)
        -> Seq Scan on customers  (cost=0.00..676.00 rows=20000 width=0)
(actual time=0.012..33.609 rows=20000 loops=1)
   Total runtime: 68.934 ms
   Time: 69.837 ms
```

This fairly trivial query was picked because it demonstrates something close to a worst-case scenario here, where instrumenting the query causes the result to slow dramatically, to almost 10 times as long. Using EXPLAIN ANALYZE is great for getting real times, but you shouldn't assume the exact proportions or time to be the same when running the query normally.

Hot and cold cache behavior

Returning to the regular version of the query seen previously, it executed in 7.994 milliseconds. This represents **hot** cache behavior, meaning that the data needed for the query was already in either the database or OS caches. It was left behind in the cache from when the data was loaded in the first place. Whether your cache is hot, or cold (not in the cache), is another thing to be very careful of. If you run a query twice with two different approaches, the second will likely be much faster simply because of caching, regardless of whether the plan was better or worse.

You can look at how long a query against the entire table takes as a way to measure the effective transfer rate for that table. In the hot cache case, it gives you an idea how quickly data moves between two sections of memory:

```
SELECT pg_size_pretty(CAST(pg_relation_size('customers') / 7.994 * 1000 as
int8)) AS bytes_per_second;
 bytes_per_second
------------------
 465 MB
```

As this was run on a simple laptop, getting 456 Mbps of rows processed by a query is respectable. In this case, repeatedly running the query takes around the same amount of time each run, which means that the amount cached is staying constant and not impacting results. In this case, it's 100% cached.

Clearing the cache

The exact way to clear all these caches and to get cold cache performance again varies based on the OS. Just stopping the database server isn't enough, because the OS cache can be expected to still have plenty of information cached. On Linux, you can use the `drop_caches` feature to discard everything it has in its page cache. Here's a complete example of cleaning the data out of memory for this database on Linux:

```
$ pg_ctl stop
$ sudo su -
# sync
# echo 3 > /proc/sys/vm/drop_caches
# logout
$ pg_ctl start -l $PGLOG
```

The `sync` here is to try to flush all data to the disk before we just blow away the caches. This `drop_caches` feature on Linux is not intended for regular production server use; it is more of a debugging feature that's potentially dangerous.

Rerunning the same benchmark a shows quite different performance:

```
$ psql -d dellstore2
dellstore2=# \timing
Timing is on.
dellstore2=# SELECT count(*) FROM customers;
 count
-------
 20000
Time: 204.738 ms
dellstore2=# SELECT pg_size_pretty(CAST(pg_relation_size('customers') /
204.738 * 1000 as int8)) AS bytes_per_second;
 bytes_per_second
------------------
 18 MB
```

Now you're seeing hard drive sequential read speeds 18 MB/s from a laptop hard drive, and this data isn't necessarily even contiguous. It's hard to achieve full drive speed on something so small though.

Repeating the query now returns to the original speed we know to expect from a hot cache run:

```
dellstore2=# SELECT count(*) FROM customers;
Time: 8.067 ms
```

Tests against real data sets need to be very careful to recognize whether their data is already in the cache or not. The usual technique is to run each query three times. If the first is much slower than the second and the third, it probably started with a cold cache. If the times are all the same, the cache was likely hot before starting. And if all three vary in some other way, there's probably another variable involved besides just whether the data is in the cache. It may take a larger number of queries to extract the pattern of why speeds vary.

Examples in this chapter are all run with a hot cache, so you're seeing processing time but not disk access time. This makes them slightly unrealistic, but the Dell Store sample available for PostgreSQL is not big enough to be uncached for very long on modern hardware. The larger-scale versions haven't been ported to the database yet.

Query plan node structure

EXPLAIN output is organized into a series of plan nodes. At the lowest level, there are nodes that look at tables, scanning them, or looking things up with an index. Higher-level nodes take the output from the lower-level ones and operate on it. When you run EXPLAIN, each line in the output is a plan node.

Each node has several numeric measurements associated with it as well:

```
# EXPLAIN ANALYZE SELECT * FROM customers;
QUERY PLAN
----------
Seq Scan on customers  (cost=0.00..676.00 rows=20000 width=268) (actual
time=0.011..34.489 rows=20000 loops=1)
Total runtime: 65.804 ms
```

This plan has one node, a Seq Scan node. The first set of numbers reported are the plan estimates, which are the only things you see if you run EXPLAIN without ANALYZE:

- cost=0.00..676.00: The first cost here is the startup cost of the node. That's how much work is estimated before this node produces its first row of output. In this case, that's zero, because a Seq Scan immediately returns rows. A sort operation is an example of something that instead takes a while to return a single row. The second estimated cost is that of running the entire node until it completes. It may not be a node with a limit on it; for example, it may stop long before retrieving all the estimated rows.

- `rows=20000`: The number of rows this node expects to output if it runs to completion.
- `width=268`: The estimated average number of bytes each row output by this node will contain. For this example, `20000` rows of `268` bytes each means this node expects to produce 5,360,000 bytes of output. This is slightly larger than the table itself (3.8 MB) because it includes the overhead of how tuples are stored in memory when executing in a plan.

The actual figures show how well this query really ran:

- `actual time=0.011..34.489`: The actual startup cost wasn't quite zero; it took a small fraction of time to start producing output. Once things started, it took `34.489` seconds to execute this plan node in total.
- `rows=20000`: As expected, the plan output `20000` rows. Differences between the expected rows and the number actually produced by a node are one of the most common sources of query problems, where the optimizer made a bad decision.
- `loops=1`: Some nodes, such as ones doing joins, execute more than once. In that case, the loops value will be larger than one, and the actual time and row values shown will be per loop, not the total. You'll have to multiply by the number of loops to get a true total.

Understanding how decisions are made using this data requires more knowledge about how the estimated costs are computed.

Basic cost computation

The job of the query optimizer is to generate many possible plans that could be used to execute a query, and then pick the one with the lowest cost to actually execute. The cost computations are done using arbitrary units only loosely associated with real-world execution cost:

- `seq_page_cost`: How long it takes to read a single database page from the disk when the expectation is you'll be reading several that are next to one another, a sequential read of a section of disk. The rest of the cost parameters are essentially relative to this value, being the reference cost of 1.0.
- `random_page_cost`: The read cost when the rows involved are expected to be scattered across the disk at random. This defaults to 4.0.

- `cpu_tuple_cost`: How much it costs to process a single row of data. The default is 0.01.
- `cpu_index_tuple_cost`: The cost to process a single index entry during an index scan. The default is 0.005, lower than what it costs to process a row because rows have a lot more header information (such as the visibility `xmin` and `xmax`) than an index entry does.
- `cpu_operator_cost`: The expected cost to process a simple operator or function. If the query needs to add two numbers together, that's an operator cost, and it defaults to the very inexpensive 0.0025.

It's easier to see in a table how these all numerically compare, showing a speed ratio relative to the reference value for `seq_page_cost`:

Parameter	Default value	Relative speed
XE "seq_page_cost parameter"seq_page_cost	1.0	Reference
XE "random_page_cost parameter"random_page_cost	4.0	4 times slower
XE "cpu_tuple_cost parameter"cpu_tuple_cost	0.01	100 times faster
XE "cpu_index_tuple_cost parameter"cpu_index_tuple_cost	0.005	200 times faster
XE "cpu_operator_cost parameter"cpu_operator_cost	0.0025	400 times faster

We can use these numbers to compute the cost shown in the previous example. A sequential scan on `customers` has to read every page in the table and process every resulting row. If you look at the statistics the optimizer uses to estimate the pages in the table and the number of rows, then combine them with its internal cost parameters:

```
SELECT
  relpages,
  current_setting('seq_page_cost') AS seq_page_cost,
  relpages *
    current_setting('seq_page_cost')::decimal AS page_cost,
  reltuples,
  current_setting('cpu_tuple_cost') AS cpu_tuple_cost,
  reltuples *
    current_setting('cpu_tuple_cost')::decimal AS tuple_cost
FROM pg_class WHERE relname='customers';
relpages      | 476
seq_page_cost | 1
```

```
page_cost        | 476
reltuples        | 20000
cpu_tuple_cost   | 0.01
tuple_cost       | 200
```

Add the cost to read the pages (476) to the cost to process the rows (200) and you get 676.00, exactly the cost shown by the EXPLAIN plan for the sequential scan in the previous section. We're not going to show how to compute the costs for every plan shown here, but this example shows you how you can do that yourself for ones you're particularly interested in. Ultimately, every plan node breaks down into these five operations: sequential read, random read, process a row, process an index entry, or execute an operator. Everything else builds more complicated structures based on these basics.

Estimated costs and real-world costs

Now, if you were paying attention to Chapter 3, *Database Hardware Benchmarking*, you may just be wondering why the random reads are only considered four times as expensive as the sequential ones. In reality, that ratio is closer to 50:1. Unfortunately, building a robust query cost model isn't as easy as measuring each of the underlying real-world costs the theoretical units model, then setting the costs based on those. One of the most obvious ways that the planner costs don't reflect reality is that the optimizer doesn't know what pages are in the database or the OS cache. Random page reads often result from index scans. And the data associated with the most used indexes is also the most likely to be in the database and the OS cache. So, even though the actual random page cost is much more expensive than four times a sequential one, the odds of an indexed scan reading a random page from the cache are quite high.

In real-world PostgreSQL deployments, you're not going to find people changing random_page_cost to a higher value that reflects the real random read speed of their drives relative to their sequential speeds. Instead, you'll probably find them decreasing it. On systems with a lot of RAM where much of the database is known to be in memory, dropping the random_page_cost to 2.0 or even lower is a very common optimization.

Explain analysis tools

Explain plans are pretty complicated to read. Figuring out which portion of the plan is causing the main performance issues is not necessarily obvious. A few tools have sprung up to help with analyzing them, making it easier to identify the slow portions.

Visual explain

Complicated query plans can be difficult to read, with only the indentation level suggesting how nodes that fit into one another are connected. One way to help visualize complicated plans is to graph them using visual explain, a feature available in the pgAdmin III tool: `http://www.pgadmin.org/`.

Seeing how the nodes fit together for the more complicated structures like multilevel joins is extremely valuable for learning how they work. One useful bit of trivia for the graphic display used: when you see lines connecting nodes in the plan, their thickness is proportional to how costly that section of the plan is. You can get an idea where the parts taking a while to execute are, just by looking for the wide lines; the thin ones aren't contributing as heavily to the query runtime.

Verbose output

If you're interested in what columns are actually being passed around by your queries, an explain plan using VERBOSE will show them:

```
EXPLAIN VERBOSE SELECT * FROM customers;
QUERY PLAN
----------
Seq Scan on public.customers  (cost=0.00..676.00 rows=20000 width=268)
        Output: customerid, firstname, lastname, address1, address2, city,
state, zip, country, region, email, phone, creditcardtype, creditcard,
creditcardexpiration, username, password, age, income, gender
```

This can be valuable for extremely complicated queries which aren't easy to figure out on your own, or when running queries generated by programs such as an **object-relational mapper** (**ORM**) that sometimes include more information than they necessarily need to.

Machine-readable EXPLAIN output

Starting with PostgreSQL 9.0, there are several new formats you can produce EXPLAIN output in. In addition to the old text format, you can output in XML and JSON, which allows analysis using the rich library of tools found in many programming languages for operating on that sort of data. You can also produce plans in YAML format, which is interesting because it is both machine parsable and arguably easier to read than the standard format. Consider this relatively simple plan:

```
EXPLAIN SELECT * FROM customers WHERE customerid>1000 ORDER BY zip;
QUERY PLAN

----------

Sort   (cost=4449.30..4496.80 rows=19000 width=268)
   Sort Key: zip
   ->  Seq Scan on customers  (cost=0.00..726.00 rows=19000 width=268)
         Filter: (customerid > 1000)
```

The same plan output in YAML format is much larger, but quite easy to read too:

```
EXPLAIN (FORMAT YAML) SELECT * FROM customers WHERE customerid>1000 ORDER
BY zip;
                    QUERY PLAN
----------------------------------------
  - Plan:                              +
      Node Type: Sort                  +
      Startup Cost: 4449.30            +
      Total Cost: 4496.80              +
      Plan Rows: 19000                 +
      Plan Width: 268                  +
      Sort Key:                        +
        - zip                          +
      Plans:                           +
        - Node Type: Seq Scan          +
          Parent Relationship: Outer   +
          Relation Name: customers     +
          Alias: customers             +
          Startup Cost: 0.00           +
          Total Cost: 726.00           +
          Plan Rows: 19000             +
          Plan Width: 268              +
          Filter: (customerid > 1000)
```

Starting from PostgreSQL 9.0, this feature hasn't been utilized heavily yet by developers. The hope is that generating machine-parsable output will also make it far easier to write programs to read EXPLAIN output, and therefore increase the number of tools that assist with query-analysis work.

Plan analysis tools

There are already some tools available on the web that already know how to do the dirty work to analyze the old text format EXPLAIN output. The best of the currently available ones is at http://explain.depesz.com/, where you can submit a plan and get a version highlighting potential problem areas. For example, if the estimated row counts don't match the actual ones, that jumps right out in the color-coded plan output.

Assembling row sets

To understand how to optimize the way a query runs, you have to first understand the options for how it can be executed. Now that you're armed with some basics on how nodes fit together and costs are computed, the next stage to understanding how queries work is to see the options for bottom-level plan nodes that are usually selecting rows.

Tuple ID

Each row in the database has a tuple ID, a number visible as the system column named ctid in each row. You can use these to look up a row:

```
SELECT ctid,customerid FROM customers limit 3;
 ctid  | customerid
-------+------------
 (0,1) |          1
 (0,2) |          2
 (0,3) |          3
    EXPLAIN SELECT customerid FROM customers WHERE ctid='(0,1)';
                       QUERY PLAN
    ------------------------------------------------------------
    Tid Scan on customers  (cost=0.00..4.01 rows=1 width=4)
       TID Cond: (ctid = '(0,1)'::tid)
```

These TID sequences cannot be relied upon as a stable way to access a particular row outside of a transaction, because common operations including UPDATE will change them. If you're referring to a row more than one in the same transaction, perhaps in a procedural programming language, the Tid Scan can be a quick way to operate a second time on a row located earlier. The ctid value can also be used to distinguish between rows that are otherwise identical, for example when trying to eliminate duplicate rows.

Object ID

In earlier versions of PostgreSQL, every database row had a unique **object identification number (OID)** that could be used to identify it. The overhead of storing these OIDs was considered too high, and, as of PostgreSQL 8.1, they now default to off. You can still include them in a table by specifying CREATE TABLE... WITH OIDS, and the system catalog tables include them. Using an OID to find a record works the same as any other indexed scan:

```
SELECT oid,relname FROM pg_class WHERE relname='customers';
   oid  |  relname
--------+-----------
 16736 | customers
EXPLAIN SELECT relname FROM pg_class WHERE oid=16736;
QUERY PLAN
------------------
Index Scan using pg_class_oid_index on pg_class   (cost=0.00..8.27
rows=1 width=64)
      Index Cond: (oid = 16736::oid)
```

There's little reason to use an OID for your own tables when the more portable primary key type can be used instead.

Sequential scan

The previous examples (and many in Chapter 9, *Database Indexing*) have shown you plenty of examples of tables being scanned sequentially. You can expect a Seq Scan when there isn't a useful index, or when such a large portion of the table is expected to be returned so that using an index would just add needless overhead. They'll also be used when there is only a very small amount of data to access; the index overhead is disproportionately large if the table takes up only a few pages on disk.

Note that a Seq Scan must read through all the dead rows in a table, but will not include them in its output. It's therefore possible for their execution to take much longer than would be expected to produce all the required output if the table has been badly maintained and is quite bloated with dead rows.

Index Scan

An `Index Scan` is what you want if your query needs to return a value fast. If an index that is useful to satisfy a selective `WHERE` condition exists, you'll get one in a query plan that looks like the following:

```
EXPLAIN ANALYZE SELECT * FROM customers WHERE customerid=1000;
QUERY PLAN
----------
Index Scan using customers_pkey on customers  (cost=0.00..8.27 rows=1
width=268) (actual time=0.029..0.033 rows=1 loops=1)
       Index Cond: (customerid = 1000)
     Total runtime: 0.102 ms
```

The main component to the cost here are the two random page reads (4.0 each, making a total of 8.0), both the index block and the one the database row is in. If you remember, that the data blocks must always be read in PostgreSQL, even if the `Index Scan` is just being used to determine whether a row exists, because visibility must be checked in the row data. This will, however, turn into random disk seeks against the actual table, the true overhead of which depends on how much of it is already cached.

Regular index scans are the only type that will return rows that are already sorted. This makes them preferred by queries using a `LIMIT`, where the sort cost may otherwise be proportional to the full table size. There are also some upper-node types that need input in sorted order.

Bitmap heap and index scans

As mentioned in the last chapter, `Chapter 9`, *Database Indexing*, PostgreSQL is capable of combining indexes together when two of them are relevant for answering a query. The `customers` table in the Dell Store example has an index on both the `customerid` and the `username`. These are both pretty boring bits of data:

```
SELECT customerid,username from customers limit 3;
 customerid | username
------------+----------
          1 | user1
          2 | user2
          3 | user3
```

The following somewhat contrived query returns only two rows, but it can use both indexes to accelerate that, and, after tweaking the number of values referenced, it's possible to demonstrate that:

```
SELECT customerid,username FROM customers WHERE customerid<10000 AND
username<'user100';
  customerid | username
 ------------+----------
           1 | user1
          10 | user10
EXPLAIN ANALYZE SELECT customerid,username FROM customers WHERE
customerid<10000 AND username<'user100';
QUERY PLAN
----------
Bitmap Heap Scan on customers  (cost=5.71..370.28 rows=95 width=13) (actual
time=0.036..0.043 rows=2 loops=1)
   Recheck Cond: ((username)::text < 'user100'::text)
   Filter: (customerid < 10000)
   ->  Bitmap Index Scan on ix_cust_username  (cost=0.00..5.69 rows=191
width=0) (actual time=0.019..0.019 rows=2 loops=1)
         Index Cond: ((username)::text < 'user100'::text)
      Total runtime: 0.099 ms
```

Here, the query optimizer thought, based on its statistics, that it may have one or two hundred rows returned by each of the two relevant indexes to sort through, so using the index to find them out of the 20,000 possible rows and then using the AND operation to get the two conditions together was considered the faster approach. It had no way of knowing that just searching on username would quickly find the only two matching rows.

Bitmap index scans are executed by reading the index first, populating the bitmap, then reading the table in sequential order. This makes them read sequentially, as the data is expected to be laid out of disk approximately, regardless of what the real underlying row order is. Each block is read, and then the drive is expected to skip forward to the next block. Because this gives output sorted using physical order on disk, the results can easily require sorting afterwards for upper nodes that expect ordered input.

The index bitmaps built by the scans can be combined with standard bit operations, including either AND (return rows that are on both lists) or OR (return rows that are on either list) when appropriate. For non-trivial queries on real world databases, the Bitmap Index Scan is a versatile workhorse you'll find showing up quite often.

Processing nodes

Once you have a set of rows, the next type of node you'll encounter when using a single table are ones that process that set in various ways. These nodes typically take in a row set and output a different row set, of either the same size or smaller (perhaps only a single value).

Sort

Sort nodes can appear when you insert ORDER BY statements into your queries:

```
EXPLAIN ANALYZE SELECT customerid FROM customers ORDER BY zip;
QUERY PLAN
----------
Sort (cost=2104.77..2154.77 rows=20000 width=8) (actual
time=162.796..199.971 rows=20000 loops=1)
    Sort Key: zip
    Sort Method:  external sort  Disk: 352kB
    -> Seq Scan on customers (cost=0.00..676.00 rows=20000 width=8)
(actual time=0.013..46.748 rows=20000 loops=1)
Total runtime: 234.527 ms
```

Sort operations can either execute in memory using the quicksort algorithm, if they're expected to fit, or will be swapped to disk to use what's called an external merge sort—the case in this example. The threshold at which that happens depends on the work_mem setting on the server. This example may be surprising because the memory used (352 KB) appears under the default value for that parameter, as used on this test server:

```
SHOW work_mem;
 work_mem
----------
  1MB
```

There's a good explanation for that: the size needed for an in-memory Sort is bigger than the amount of disk needed for an external one. External disk sorts in PostgreSQL are done by writing a set of sorted files out and then merging the results, and that takes significantly less memory than the quicksort. Watch what happens if the work_mem parameter is increased and the statement is planned again (which you can do using SET for a single query; the server configuration doesn't have to be modified to increase this setting):

```
SET work_mem='2MB';
EXPLAIN ANALYZE SELECT customerid FROM customers ORDER BY zip;
QUERY PLAN
```

```
-----------------------
Sort  (cost=2104.77..2154.77 rows=20000 width=8) (actual
time=69.696..94.626 rows=20000 loops=1)
      Sort Key: zip
      Sort Method:  quicksort  Memory: 1372kB
      -> Seq Scan on customers  (cost=0.00..676.00 rows=20000 width=8)
(actual time=0.009..33.654 rows=20000 loops=1)
    Total runtime: 121.751 ms
```

This shows why the default wasn't sufficient: doing the Sort in memory actually requires 1.3 MB, so it was just rejected at the default value as too big. If you turn on log_temp_files to look for how often disk swap sorts are happening, and notice sorting files that are below work_mem in size, this may be the reason for that behavior.

Using ORDER BY is more important to SQL than many newcomers realize, because there is no row ordering guaranteed when you query, unless you request one. You cannot expect you'll get rows back in the order you inserted them, even though that's often the case. A common counter-example is when the synchronized scan features in PostgreSQL 8.3 and later are used. When that kicks in, a second table scan running against a table you are already executing against will just tag along with the first, starting to return rows from whatever point the original is at. This will get you rows returned offset from a completely random point, only circling back to the beginning once the first scan has finished.

In addition, when you're asking for explicit ordering, it's also possible to see a Sort node in situations where another type of node needs its input sorted to operate. Examples include a unique node, some types of joins and grouping, and some set operations.

Limit

Like everything else, query limits are built on top of existing scans that return a set of rows:

```
EXPLAIN ANALYZE SELECT customerid FROM customers LIMIT 10;
QUERY PLAN
----------
Limit  (cost=0.00..0.34 rows=10 width=4) (actual time=0.016..0.063 rows=10
loops=1)
      -> Seq Scan on customers  (cost=0.00..676.00 rows=20000 width=4)
(actual time=0.013..0.030 rows=10 loops=1)
Total runtime: 0.117 ms
```

Note the actual rows output by the Seq Scan here. This shows one of the aspects of query execution that isn't necessarily obvious. The way queries are carried out, the top node in the query plan is started, and it asks its children nodes for things on demand. It's a top-down execution model; nodes only produce output when said output is required. In this case, the Seq Scan on the customers table could have an output with as many as 20000 rows. But because the limit was reached after only 10 rows, that's all the Seq Scan node was a/sked to produce. The action where an upper node asks for a row from one of its children is referred to as it pulling one from it.

Limit nodes work a little differently than most, because depending on how large the limit is relative to the total number of rows the startup cost of the node can become more important than the total cost. If the optimizer knows that only a few rows need to be produced, it can favor a plan that starts to quickly produce rows over one that is lower in total cost, but has most of that cost in startup. Putting a small limit on a query biases plans that quickly produce output rows, and whether or not that works well is vulnerable to whether the estimates the optimizer is working with are correct.

Offsets

When OFFSET is added to a query, it isn't handled by its own node type. It's handled as a different form of limit. Essentially, the first few rows the underlying scan produces are thrown away. This is easy to see given a variation on the LIMIT query seen previously:

```
EXPLAIN ANALYZE SELECT customerid FROM customers OFFSET 10 LIMIT 10;
QUERY PLAN
----------
Limit  (cost=0.34..0.68 rows=10 width=4)  (actual time=0.052..0.101 rows=10
loops=1)
      -> Seq Scan on customers  (cost=0.00..676.00 rows=20000 width=4)
(actual time=0.012..0.047 rows=20 loops=1)
 Total runtime: 0.157 ms
```

Note how, this time, the Seq Scan node produced 20 rows of output. The first 10 were skipped by the OFFSET, then the next 10 satisfied the LIMIT node, at which point the query was finished.

Aggregate

Aggregate functions take in a series of values and produce a single output. Examples of aggregates are AVG(), COUNT(), EVERY(), MIN(), MAX(), STDDEV(), SUM(), and VARIANCE(). To compute an aggregate, all of the rows are typically read, then fed through the Aggregate node to compute a result:

```
EXPLAIN ANALYZE SELECT max(zip) FROM customers;
QUERY PLAN
----------
Aggregate  (cost=726.00..726.01 rows=1 width=4) (actual time=75.168..75.169
rows=1 loops=1)
    -> Seq Scan on customers  (cost=0.00..676.00 rows=20000 width=4)
(actual time=0.007..32.769 rows=20000 loops=1)
 Total runtime: 75.259 ms
```

This isn't always the case, though, because some values can be computed with indexes instead. Looking for the highest customerid in the customers table, where that's the primary key, doesn't have to look at every row:

```
EXPLAIN ANALYZE SELECT max(customerid) FROM customers;
QUERY PLAN
----------
Result  (cost=0.05..0.06 rows=1 width=0) (actual time=0.047..0.048 rows=1
loops=1)
        InitPlan 1 (returns $0)
          -> Limit  (cost=0.00..0.05 rows=1 width=4) (actual
time=0.038..0.039 rows=1 loops=1)
                -> Index Scan Backward using customers_pkey on customers
(cost=0.00..963.25 rows=20000 width=4) (actual time=0.034..0.034 ro
    ws=1 loops=1)
                    Index Cond: (customerid IS NOT NULL)
Total runtime: 0.089 ms
```

HashAggregate

A versatile node type, the HashAggregate node takes in a set of nodes and outputs a series of derived data in buckets. A major reworking in PostgreSQL 8.4 turned several common types of operations into ones that are implemented using a HashAggregate node. They are now commonly used to compute distinct values, GROUP BY results, and unions. The main value is that hashing this way can avoid needing to sort the values, which is sometimes an expensive step. There are plenty of examples of the HashAggregate node type next in fact. In current PostgreSQL versions, the hardest thing to do is not see it used!

Sometimes, aggregates that are being computed by GROUP BY or even DISTINCT will use a HashAggregate to compute their output. Consider this example that looks at which category each product belongs to:

```
EXPLAIN ANALYZE SELECT category, count(*) FROM products GROUP BY category
ORDER BY category;
QUERY PLAN
----------
    Sort  (cost=251.52..251.56 rows=16 width=4) (actual time=40.834..40.860
rows=16 loops=1)
        Sort Key: category
        Sort Method:  quicksort  Memory: 17kB
        -> HashAggregate  (cost=251.00..251.20 rows=16 width=4) (actual
time=40.738..40.775 rows=16 loops=1)
                -> Seq Scan on products  (cost=0.00..201.00 rows=10000
width=4) (actual time=0.011..17.313 rows=10000 loops=1)
        Total runtime: 40.987 ms
```

In this case, there are only 16 categories involved, easily fitting into a set of hash table buckets. In PostgreSQL 10.0, you can get a bit more detail about exactly what these various hash types are up to in the EXPLAIN plans than on earlier versions.

Unique

A Unique node takes a sorted set of rows as an input and outputs one with all the duplicates removed. It can appear when using DISTINCT and when UNION is eliminating duplicates in its output. The output will be sorted the same as the input.

As of PostgreSQL 8.4, DISTINCT will usually be implementing using a HashAggregate node instead of a Unique one, which on smaller tables can collect the unique values without having to explicitly sort them first:

```
EXPLAIN ANALYZE SELECT DISTINCT(state) FROM customers;
QUERY PLAN
----------
HashAggregate  (cost=726.00..726.51 rows=51 width=3) (actual
time=91.950..92.048 rows=52 loops=1)
    -> Seq Scan on customers  (cost=0.00..676.00 rows=20000 width=3)
(actual time=0.009..49.466 rows=20000 loops=1)
Total runtime: 92.319 ms
```

To see the old implementation in current PostgreSQL versions with something the size of the Dell Store data, it's easiest to just turn that optimization off:

```
SET enable_hashagg=off;
EXPLAIN ANALYZE SELECT DISTINCT(state) FROM customers;
QUERY PLAN
----------
Unique  (cost=2104.77..2204.77 rows=51 width=3) (actual
time=149.003..204.945 rows=52 loops=1)
        -> Sort  (cost=2104.77..2154.77 rows=20000 width=3) (actual
time=148.999..178.338 rows=20000 loops=1)
           Sort Key: state
           Sort Method:  external sort  Disk: 232kB
           -> Seq Scan on customers  (cost=0.00..676.00 rows=20000 width=3)
(actual time=0.012..42.860 rows=20000 loops=1)
      Total runtime: 205.772 ms
```

As this earlier implementation of Unique had the side-effect of sorting its output, this can be an application-breaking change when switching from earlier versions of PostgreSQL to 8.4 or later. This serves as another reminder of why explicit ordering should be requested in your queries, not assumed just because the output you're seeing now seems always to be ordered correctly.

WindowAgg

The SQL windowing functions added this type of aggregation to PostgreSQL 8.4. An example of it is shown as part of the discussion of that new feature at the end of this chapter.

Result

Sometimes, a node just needs to return a result computed by a statement:

```
EXPLAIN ANALYZE SELECT 1;
QUERY PLAN
----------
Result  (cost=0.00..0.01 rows=1 width=0) (actual time=0.003..0.005 rows=1
loops=1)
Total runtime: 0.038 ms
```

`Result` nodes are basically quick pass through nodes when individual values are being operated on, instead of sets of rows. They can be used to collapse and therefore optimize sections of a `WHERE` clause that can be computed once:

```
EXPLAIN ANALYZE SELECT * FROM customers WHERE customerid=(SELECT
min(customerid) FROM customers)+1;
QUERY PLAN
----------
Index Scan using customers_pkey on customers   (cost=0.06..8.33 rows=1
width=268) (actual time=0.085..0.088 rows=1 loops=1)
    Index Cond: (customerid = ($1 + 1))
    InitPlan 2 (returns $1)
        -> Result   (cost=0.05..0.06 rows=1 width=0) (actual
time=0.061..0.062 rows=1 loops=1)
            InitPlan 1 (returns $0)
                -> Limit   (cost=0.00..0.05 rows=1 width=4) (actual
time=0.052..0.054 rows=1 loops=1)
                    -> Index Scan using customers_pkey on customers
(cost=0.00..963.25 rows=20000 width=4) (actual time=0.047..0.047 row
    s=1 loops=1)
                        Index Cond: (customerid IS NOT NULL)
Total runtime: 0.189 ms
```

They can also show up in some spots where they serve as useful intermediaries to match node types that otherwise don't quite fit together. Note how one appears in the `max(customerid)` example in the `Aggregate` samples seen previously.

Append

Like `Unique`, `Append` is another node type that's less popular than it used to be. In earlier PostgreSQL versions, Append nodes were used to produce some types of `UNION` merges. As of PostgreSQL 8.4, most of these are done by the versatile `HashAggregate` instead:

```
EXPLAIN ANALYZE SELECT * FROM customers WHERE state='MA' UNION SELECT *
FROM customers WHERE state='MD';
QUERY PLAN
----------
HashAggregate   (cost=1476.06..1480.07 rows=401 width=268) (actual
time=25.847..27.104 rows=401 loops=1)
        -> Append   (cost=0.00..1456.01 rows=401 width=268) (actual
time=0.031..22.559 rows=401 loops=1)
            -> Seq Scan on customers   (cost=0.00..726.00 rows=214
width=268) (actual time=0.027..10.800 rows=214 loops=1)
                Filter: ((state)::text = 'MA'::text)
            -> Seq Scan on customers   (cost=0.00..726.00 rows=187
```

```
width=268) (actual time=0.063..10.514 rows=187 loops=1)
                    Filter: ((state)::text = 'MD'::text)
Total runtime: 27.956 ms
```

This plan is dramatically easier to read than the earlier behavior, and can be forced by turning off the new optimization:

```
SET enable_hashagg=off;
EXPLAIN ANALYZE SELECT * FROM customers WHERE state='MA' UNION SELECT *
FROM customers WHERE state='MD';
QUERY PLAN
----------
 Unique  (cost=1473.35..1494.40 rows=401 width=268) (actual
time=23.993..26.892 rows=401 loops=1)
        -> Sort  (cost=1473.35..1474.35 rows=401 width=268) (actual
time=23.987..24.619 rows=401 loops=1)
             Sort Key: public.customers.customerid,
public.customers.firstname, public.customers.lastname,
public.customers.address1, public.
    customers.address2, public.customers.city, public.customers.state,
public.customers.zip, public.customers.country, public.customers.region,
public.customers.email, public.customers.phone,
public.customers.creditcardtype, public.customers.creditcard,
public.customers.creditc
     ardexpiration, public.customers.username, public.customers.password,
public.customers.age, public.customers.income, public.customers.gender
             Sort Method:  quicksort  Memory: 121kB
             -> Append  (cost=0.00..1456.01 rows=401 width=268) (actual
time=0.027..22.796 rows=401 loops=1)
                    -> Seq Scan on customers  (cost=0.00..726.00 rows=214
width=268) (actual time=0.025..10.935 rows=214 loops=1)
                          Filter: ((state)::text = 'MA'::text)
                    -> Seq Scan on customers  (cost=0.00..726.00 rows=187
width=268) (actual time=0.062..10.620 rows=187 loops=1)
                          Filter: ((state)::text = 'MD'::text)
Total runtime: 27.750 ms
```

In this case, the external Sort is a small one, but in larger types of UNION operations, the improvement from using the newer implementation can be significant.

Group

Yet another node type left behind by progress, the GROUP node was the way earlier PostgreSQL versions implemented GROUP BY. It required that the input data was sorted by the grouping column set. As of PostgreSQL 7.4, that's commonly done by a HashAggregate instead:

```
EXPLAIN ANALYZE SELECT state,COUNT(*) FROM customers GROUP BY state;
QUERY PLAN
----------
HashAggregate  (cost=776.00..776.64 rows=51 width=3) (actual
time=85.793..85.916 rows=52 loops=1)
        -> Seq Scan on customers  (cost=0.00..676.00 rows=20000 width=3)
(actual time=0.010..33.447 rows=20000 loops=1)
      Total runtime: 86.103 ms
```

You can once again see the old behavior by turning off this optimization:

```
SET enable_hashagg=off;
EXPLAIN ANALYZE SELECT state,count(*) FROM customers GROUP BY state;
QUERY PLAN
----------
GroupAggregate  (cost=2104.77..2255.41 rows=51 width=3) (actual
time=223.696..281.414 rows=52 loops=1)
        -> Sort  (cost=2104.77..2154.77 rows=20000 width=3) (actual
time=223.043..252.766 rows=20000 loops=1)
            Sort Key: state
            Sort Method:  external sort  Disk: 232kB
            -> Seq Scan on customers  (cost=0.00..676.00 rows=20000
width=3) (actual time=0.010..45.713 rows=20000 loops=1)
  Total runtime: 282.295 ms
```

Not having to do the external merge Sort on disk is the main reason the hash style of plan is preferred now, which improves the runtime of this style of query. You can still see the older GroupAggregate execution show up when the input already happens to be ordered, which happens in the Merge Join example shown later.

Subquery scan and subplan

These two types of node are used for shuffling rows around between nodes in some types of UNION and sub-select queries. They have little performance impact and have also become rare in current PostgreSQL versions due to the HashAggregate optimizations.

Subquery conversion and IN lists

A few types of things that you may expect to be executed as subqueries will actually turn into types of joins instead. This happens when using a Subquery to find a list of rows then used for IN:

```
EXPLAIN ANALYZE SELECT * FROM orders WHERE customerid IN (SELECT customerid
FROM customers where state='MD');
QUERY PLAN
----------
Hash Semi Join  (cost=728.34..982.61 rows=249 width=36)  (actual
time=11.521..55.139 rows=120 loops=1)
        Hash Cond: (orders.customerid = customers.customerid)
        -> Seq Scan on orders  (cost=0.00..220.00 rows=12000 width=36)
(actual time=0.009..20.496 rows=12000 loops=1)
        -> Hash  (cost=726.00..726.00 rows=187 width=4)  (actual
time=11.437..11.437 rows=187 loops=1)
                Buckets: 1024  Batches: 1  Memory Usage: 5kB
                -> Seq Scan on customers  (cost=0.00..726.00 rows=187
width=4)  (actual time=0.066..11.003 rows=187 loops=1)
                        Filter: ((state)::text = 'MD'::text)
        Total runtime: 55.429 ms
```

As you can see, this is silently converted into a regular join; the exact type used, a Hash Semi Join, is covered later. There's no Subquery node involved there. Performance of PostgreSQL IN queries can be quite good because this sort of conversion is always done. Then, all the usual join optimization tricks are available to improve the result. This one is stuck doing a Seq Scan on each table simply because there are no indexes useful here. If they were, the rewritten form might execute quite quickly.

Other types of subqueries will be considered for similar rewrites into joins where doing so is logically equivalent, for example the following slightly odd query:

```
EXPLAIN ANALYZE SELECT * FROM orders WHERE customerid IN (SELECT customerid
FROM customers WHERE customerid=1000 OR customerid=2000);
```

It will be rewritten into a Nested Loop join with inner Index Scan in any recent PostgreSQL version.

Set operations

The easiest way to show how a set operation works is to look at a query that uses one:

```
SELECT * FROM customers WHERE state='MD'
INTERSECT
SELECT * FROM customers WHERE zip='21340';
```

This is obviously a trivial example—you could just put both WHERE clauses into a single line and get the same result more easily. But there are more complicated types of queries you can build using INTERSECT, INTERSECT ALL, EXCEPT, and EXCEPT ALL that are the easiest way to write what you're looking for. EXCEPT is shown later for helping determine whether two queries give the same output, for example.

SetOp changed to HashSetOp in PostgreSQL 8.4. Here are the new and old types of plans you can get when executing an INTERSECT or EXCEPT:

```
EXPLAIN ANALYZE SELECT * FROM customers WHERE state='MD' INTERSECT SELECT *
FROM customers WHERE zip='21340';
 QUERY PLAN
 ----------
 HashSetOp Intersect  (cost=0.00..1463.28 rows=1 width=268) (actual
time=28.379..28.381 rows=1 loops=1)
        -> Append  (cost=0.00..1453.88 rows=188 width=268) (actual
time=0.160..27.547 rows=188 loops=1)
             -> Subquery Scan on "*SELECT* 2"  (cost=0.00..726.01 rows=1
width=268) (actual time=0.156..13.618 rows=1 loops=1)
                  -> Seq Scan on customers  (cost=0.00..726.00 rows=1
width=268) (actual time=0.150..13.608 rows=1 loops=1)
                       Filter: (zip = 21340)
             -> Subquery Scan on "*SELECT* 1"  (cost=0.00..727.87 rows=187
width=268) (actual time=0.070..13.213 rows=187 loops=1)
                  -> Seq Scan on customers  (cost=0.00..726.00 rows=187
width=268) (actual time=0.063..12.098 rows=187 loops=1)
                       Filter: ((state)::text = 'MD'::text)
Total runtime: 28.672 ms
```

Let's disable hashagg:

```
SET enable_hashagg=off;
EXPLAIN ANALYZE SELECT * FROM customers WHERE state='MD' INTERSECT SELECT *
FROM customers WHERE zip='21340';
   QUERY PLAN
   ----------
   SetOp Intersect  (cost=1460.98..1470.85 rows=1 width=268) (actual
time=26.539..27.613 rows=1 loops=1)
```

```
         -> Sort  (cost=1460.98..1461.45 rows=188 width=268) (actual
time=26.499..26.785 rows=188 loops=1)
            Sort Key: "*SELECT* 2".customerid, "*SELECT* 2".firstname,
"*SELECT* 2".lastname, "*SELECT* 2".address1, "*SELECT* 2".address2,
   "*SELECT* 2".city, "*SELECT* 2".state, "*SELECT* 2".zip, "*SELECT*
2".country, "*SELECT* 2".region, "*SELECT* 2".email, "*SELECT* 2".phon
   e, "*SELECT* 2".creditcardtype, "*SELECT* 2".creditcard, "*SELECT*
2".creditcardexpiration, "*SELECT* 2".username, "*SELECT* 2".password,
   "*SELECT* 2".age, "*SELECT* 2".income, "*SELECT* 2".gender
            Sort Method:  quicksort  Memory: 66kB
            -> Append  (cost=0.00..1453.88 rows=188 width=268) (actual
time=0.146..25.366 rows=188 loops=1)
               -> Subquery Scan on "*SELECT* 2"  (cost=0.00..726.01
rows=1 width=268) (actual time=0.143..13.409 rows=1 loops=1)
                  -> Seq Scan on customers  (cost=0.00..726.00
rows=1 width=268) (actual time=0.137..13.399 rows=1 loops=1)
                     Filter: (zip = 21340)
               -> Subquery Scan on "*SELECT* 1"  (cost=0.00..727.87
rows=187 width=268) (actual time=0.070..11.384 rows=187 loops=1)
                  -> Seq Scan on customers  (cost=0.00..726.00
rows=187 width=268) (actual time=0.062..10.544 rows=187 loops=1)
                     Filter: ((state)::text = 'MD'::text)
 Total runtime: 27.918 ms
```

All of the standard, older `SetOp` implementations require sorted input to identify identical rows to eliminate or include in the output. In this example, the `HashSetOp` is just barely more efficient than the original `SetOp` implementation, but that's just because so few rows are being returned here.

Materialize

Normally, nodes return their output row when their parent node asks for them. Sometimes when executing a sub-select, or inside part of a join, the planner may consider it more efficient to materialize that node instead. This produces the entire row set at once instead of having each upper-limit row grab them. This is rare enough that it's hard to even show a good example of it.

A much more common use of materialize involves merge joins, and in some cases nested loops, and those are specifically covered in a later section.

CTE scan

Another new PostgreSQL 8.4 feature, **Common Table Expressions** (**CTEs**) add new efficient ways to execute queries that even let you put recursion into SQL. One way they can be used is as a sort of in-line view, which makes for an easy way to demonstrate the feature and the resulting type of plan node:

```
EXPLAIN ANALYZE WITH monthlysales AS
  (SELECT EXTRACT(year FROM orderdate) AS year,
  EXTRACT(month FROM orderdate) AS month,
  sum(netamount) AS sales
  FROM orders GROUP BY year,month)
  SELECT year,SUM(sales) AS sales FROM monthlysales GROUP BY year;
    QUERY PLAN
    ----------
    HashAggregate  (cost=447.34..449.84 rows=200 width=40) (actual
time=122.002..122.004 rows=1 loops=1)
      CTE monthlysales
        -> HashAggregate  (cost=430.00..438.21 rows=365 width=12) (actual
time=121.872..121.893 rows=12 loops=1)
            -> Seq Scan on orders  (cost=0.00..340.00 rows=12000
width=12) (actual time=0.026..56.812 rows=12000 loops=1)
      -> CTE Scan on monthlysales  (cost=0.00..7.30 rows=365 width=40)
(actual time=121.880..121.942 rows=12 loops=1)
      Total runtime: 122.133 ms
```

This starts with sales data summarized by month and year, then uses a CTE to summarize only by year. It's a useless example (you might as well have grouped that way in the first place), but it shows how the query executor uses the CTE node type. Note that, as these queries use EXTRACT, which isn't something PostgreSQL has statistics on, the estimated number of rows for the CTE scan is really off from the 365 expected, 12 actually produced. This example is also expanded in the SQL window section later.

Joins

If all the query planner had to do was decide between index scan types and how to combine them using its wide array of derived nodes, its life would be pretty easy. All the serious complexity in the planner and optimizer relates to joining tables together. Each time another table is added to a list that needs to be joined, the number of possible ways goes up dramatically. If there's, say, three tables to join, you can expect the query plan to consider every possible plan and select the optimal one. But if there are 20 tables to join, there's no possible way it can exhaustively search each join possibility. As there are a variety of techniques available to join each table pair, that further expands the possibilities. The universe of possible plans has to be pruned somehow.

Fundamentally, each way two tables can be joined together gives the same output. The only difference between them is how efficient the result is to execute. All joins consider an outer and inner table. These alternately may be called the left and the right, if considering a query plan as a tree or a graph, and that usage shows up in some of the PostgreSQL internal documentation.

Nested loop

If you need every possible row combination joined together, the Nested Loop is what you want. In most other cases, it's probably not. The classic pseudo code description of a Nested Loop join looks like the following:

```
for each outer row:
  for each inner row:
    if join condition is true:
      output combined row
```

Both the inner and outer loops here could be executing against any of the scan types: sequential, indexed, bitmap, or even the output from another join. As you can see from the code, the amount of time this takes to run is proportional to the number of rows in the outer table multiplied by the rows in the inner. It is considering every possible way to join every row in each table with every other row.

It's rare to see a real `Nested Loop` without an inner index scan, the type covered in the next section. Joining data using merges and hashes is normal for the real world that tends to be indexed or has a clear relationship between tables. You can see one if you just forget to put a `WHERE` condition on a join, though, which then evaluates the cross product and outputs a ton of rows. The following is the one that produces by far the longest runtime of a query in this chapter:

```
EXPLAIN ANALYZE SELECT * FROM products,customers;
QUERY PLAN
----------
Nested Loop  (cost=0.00..2500902.00 rows=200000000 width=319) (actual
time=0.033..893865.340 rows=200000000 loops=1)
        -> Seq Scan on customers  (cost=0.00..676.00 rows=20000 width=268)
(actual time=0.010..57.689 rows=20000 loops=1)
        -> Materialize  (cost=0.00..251.00 rows=10000 width=51) (actual
time=0.006..15.319 rows=10000 loops=20000)
            -> Seq Scan on products  (cost=0.00..201.00 rows=10000
width=51) (actual time=0.004..16.126 rows=10000 loops=1)
      Total runtime: 1146091.431 ms
```

That's a 19-minute runtime, which sounds like a lot until you realize it's producing 200 million output rows. That works out to 175 K of row each second being processed, not really that shabby.

Note that a `Nested Loop` is the only way to execute a `CROSS JOIN`, and it can potentially be the only way to compute complicated conditions that don't map into either a useful merge or a `Hash Join` instead.

Nested loop with inner index scan

The standard situation you'll see a `Nested Loop` in is one where the inner table is only returning back a limited number of rows. If an index exists on one of the two tables involved, the optimizer is going to use it to limit the number of rows substantially, and the result may then make the *inner * outer* rows runtime of the `Nested Loop` acceptable. Consider the case where you're looking for a single order using a field with no index (so every order must be scanned), but then joining with its matching `orderlines`:

```
EXPLAIN ANALYZE SELECT * FROM orders,orderlines WHERE
orders.totalamount=329.78 AND orders.orderid=orderlines.orderid;
QUERY PLAN
----------
Nested Loop  (cost=0.00..265.41 rows=5 width=54) (actual time=0.108..12.886
rows=9 loops=1)
        -> Seq Scan on orders  (cost=0.00..250.00 rows=1 width=36) (actual
```

```
time=0.073..12.787 rows=1 loops=1)
            Filter: (totalamount = 329.78)
        ->  Index Scan using ix_orderlines_orderid on orderlines
(cost=0.00..15.34 rows=5 width=18) (actual time=0.024..0.050 row
    s=9 loops=1)
            Index Cond: (orderlines.orderid = orders.orderid)
Total runtime: 12.999 ms
```

The main way this type of scan can go wrong is if the optimizer's sensitivity guess for the inner relation here is quite wrong. This inner Index Scan was expecting five rows, but nine actually came out, a reasonable error that wouldn't have changed the plan type. It's possible for that guess to be extremely wrong instead. Being off by factor of 1,000 or more is quite possible due to bad table statistics or limitations in the optimizer's cost model. Then the resulting join will be very inefficient, and could have potentially been executed better another way.

Another way this plan may be avoided, even though it's an otherwise good candidate, is because effective_cache_size is too small to cope with the inner Index Scan. See the section on that parameter later for more information.

A Nested Loop can also show up when both the inner and outer scan use an index:

```
EXPLAIN ANALYZE SELECT * FROM orders,orderlines WHERE
orderlines.orderid=1000 AND orders.orderid=orderlines.orderid;
QUERY PLAN
----------
Nested Loop  (cost=0.00..23.66 rows=5 width=54) (actual time=0.052..0.093
rows=6 loops=1)
        ->  Index Scan using orders_pkey on orders  (cost=0.00..8.27 rows=1
width=36)  (actual time=0.029..0.031 rows=1 loops=1)
            Index Cond: (orderid = 1000)
        ->  Index Scan using ix_orderlines_orderid on orderlines
(cost=0.00..15.34 rows=5 width=18) (actual time=0.013..0.028 row
    s=6 loops=1)
            Index Cond: (orderlines.orderid = 1000)
Total runtime: 0.190 ms
```

This form should execute even faster, as in this case. But it is even more dangerous, because a sensitivity mistake on either the inner or outer relation can cause this node to do much more work than expected.

Merge Join

A `Merge Join` requires that both its input sets are sorted. It then scans through the two in that sorted order, generally moving forward one row at a time through both tables as the joined column values change. The inner table can be rescanned more than once if the outer one has duplicate values. That's where the normally-forwards scan on it goes backwards, to consider the additional matching set of rows from the duplication.

You can only see a `Merge Join` when joining on an equality condition, not an inequality or a range. To see one, let's ask for a popular report: how much net business was done by each customer?

```
EXPLAIN ANALYZE SELECT C.customerid,sum(netamount) FROM customers C, orders
O WHERE C.customerid=O.customerid GROUP BY C.customerid;
QUERY PLAN
----------
GroupAggregate  (cost=0.05..2069.49 rows=12000 width=12) (actual
time=0.099..193.668 rows=8996 loops=1)
        ->  Merge Join  (cost=0.05..1859.49 rows=12000 width=12) (actual
time=0.071..146.272 rows=12000 loops=1)
              Merge Cond: (c.customerid = o.customerid)
              ->  Index Scan using customers_pkey on customers c
(cost=0.00..963.25 rows=20000 width=4) (actual time=0.031..37.242
rows=20000 loo
    ps=1)
              ->  Index Scan using ix_order_custid on orders o
(cost=0.00..696.24 rows=12000 width=12) (actual time=0.025..30.722
rows=12000 loop
    s=1)
Total runtime: 206.353 ms
```

That's executed how you'd probably expect it to be: follow the `customerid` indexes on the `customers` and `orders` table to match the two tables up, which gives the output in sorted order. The query executor can then use an efficient `Merge Join` to combine them, and aggregate the now-joined-together result. As the result is still sorted, it's therefore also easy to group using the `GroupAggregate` implementation, instead of using the `HashAggregate` grouping method.

Nested Loop and Merge Join materialization

Sometimes, there can be a substantial amount of the rescanning of inner rows required for a Merge Join. And full inner rescans are the expected case when executing a Nested Loop. In this case, as mentioned previously, a Materialize node can be inserted specifically to cache the output from the inner scan, in the hope that will be faster at the expense of using additional memory. This can be particularly valuable on the common inner Index Scan case, where going backwards could potentially even turn into random I/O under particularly unfortunate caching circumstances. Also, not all operators can be rescanned, making materialization necessary in all cases where they're used.

Starting from PostgreSQL 9.0, a model has been introduced, where rescans have a different cost model than when the rows are initially scanned, to try and accurately estimate when this materialization is a saving. As such, the situations in which you will and won't see Materialize nodes show up in that version are very different than earlier versions.

Hash joins

The primary alternative to a Merge Join, a Hash Join doesn't sort its input. Instead, it creates a hash table from each row of the inner table, scanning for matching ones in the outer. The output will not necessarily be in any useful order.

A query to find all the products that have at one point been ordered by any customer shows a regular Hash Join:

```
EXPLAIN ANALYZE SELECT prod_id,title FROM products p WHERE EXISTS (SELECT 1
FROM orderlines ol WHERE ol.prod_id=p.prod_id);
QUERY PLAN
-------------------
Hash Join  (cost=1328.16..2270.16 rows=9724 width=19) (actual
time=249.783..293.588 rows=9973 loops=1)
       Hash Cond: (p.prod_id = ol.prod_id)
       -> Seq Scan on products p  (cost=0.00..201.00 rows=10000 width=19)
(actual time=0.007..12.781 rows=10000 loops=1)
       ->  Hash  (cost=1206.62..1206.62 rows=9724 width=4) (actual
time=249.739..249.739 rows=9973 loops=1)
             Buckets: 1024  Batches: 1  Memory Usage: 234kB
             -> HashAggregate  (cost=1109.38..1206.62 rows=9724 width=4)
(actual time=219.695..234.154 rows=9973 loops=1)
                   -> Seq Scan on orderlines ol  (cost=0.00..958.50
rows=60350 width=4) (actual time=0.005..91.874 rows=60350 lo
    ops=1)
Total runtime: 306.523 ms
```

Whether a `Hash Join` is better or worse than the other possibilities depends on things such as whether input is already sorted (in which case, a `Merge Join` may be inexpensive) and how much memory is required to execute it. The hash tables built for the inner scan here require enough memory to store all the rows, which can be large.

To keep that under control, larger `Hash Join` executions will split the output into multiple batches. In this example, only one was required, to hold 10 K rows. This type of join is particularly popular when the inner relation is small and building the hash is therefore inexpensive.

Hash semi and anti-joins

One of the hash improvements in PostgreSQL 8.4 is introducing `Hash Semi` and anti-joins. A semi join is used when the optimizer needs to confirm that a key value exists on one side of the join, but doesn't particularly care what that value is beyond that. The opposite, an anti join, looks specifically for entries where the key value doesn't exist. The most common way to see these two types of join is when executing `EXISTS` and `NOT EXISTS`. The inverse of the query in the previous section is finding all the products that have never been ordered by any customer; it executes most efficiently with an anti-join:

```
EXPLAIN ANALYZE SELECT prod_id,title FROM products p WHERE NOT EXISTS
(SELECT 1 FROM orderlines ol WHERE ol.prod_id=p.prod_id);
QUERY PLAN
----------
Hash Anti Join  (cost=1919.88..2536.70 rows=276 width=19) (actual
time=204.570..246.624 rows=27 loops=1)
      Hash Cond: (p.prod_id = ol.prod_id)
      -> Seq Scan on products p  (cost=0.00..201.00 rows=10000 width=19)
(actual time=0.008..15.032 rows=10000 loops=1)
      ->  Hash  (cost=958.50..958.50 rows=60350 width=4) (actual
time=203.107..203.107 rows=60350 loops=1)
            Buckets: 8192  Batches: 2  Memory Usage: 715kB
            ->  Seq Scan on orderlines ol  (cost=0.00..958.50 rows=60350
width=4) (actual time=0.006..98.247 rows=60350 loops=1)
Total runtime: 247.355 ms
```

The main reason to restructure the plan this way is just for efficiency. It can require considerably less index reading to work this way than the earlier approach for executing queries like this, which would do a pair of index scans and combine them with a filter.

This example uses more memory for hashing than the similar query in the last section. Two batches are used to hold 60 K rows. The way batches are processed internally requires keeping some in memory while others are flushed to disk, and the optimizer eventually works through them all.

There is actually an interesting optimization in that section of code, one that happens with all hash joins (not just the semi and anti variations). If the outer relation in the join isn't uniform, if it has some **most common values** (MCVs) that represent a significant portion of the table, the execution will prefer to keep batches containing those in memory to process first. If you suspect a skewed distribution of values in your data set, with many MCVs and this type of join, you may want to check statistics targets and possibly increase them until the optimizer recognizes this fact. This can improve the odds that you'll hit the optimized path available.

As for examples of standard semi joins, there are two elsewhere in this chapter. *Subquery conversion and IN lists* seen previously has a simple one, while *Avoiding plan restructuring with OFFSET* later gives a more complicated one to review.

Join ordering

As the overall query costs go up exponentially and the number of joins increases, controlling that complexity is a major component to both query tuning and to ongoing improvement in the PostgreSQL optimizer. The differences between a sequential scan or using an index on a table will be magnified, as those results are then joined to additional tables.

Forcing join order

Consider this three-way join that takes the `cust_hist` table and joins it to its matching `products` and `customer` keys:

```
SELECT * FROM cust_hist h INNER JOIN products p ON (h.prod_id=p.prod_id)
INNER JOIN customers c ON (h.customerid=c.customerid);
```

This join is identical to an implementation that uses an implicit join and a WHERE clause:

```
SELECT * FROM cust_hist h,products p,customers c  WHERE h.prod_id=p.prod_id
AND h.customerid=c.customerid;
```

In either case, the query optimizer is free to choose plans that execute these joins in several orders. It could join `cust_hist` to `products`, then to `customers`, or it could join to `customers`, then to `products`. The results will be identical, and the cheapest one will be used.

However, this doesn't have to be the case. Doing these searches for optimal plans is time consuming, and it has the potential to make a bad decision. If you are sure of the right way to join the tables efficiently and want to reduce planning time, you can force the optimizer to use the order you specified when doing a series of explicit `JOIN` operations. Reduce the `join_collapse_limit` parameter from its default of eight to do so; typically, the useful value here is to prevent all `JOIN` re-ordering by lowering it to one. So, the following code is going to start with `cust_hist`, join to `products`, then to `customers` in every case:

```
SET join_collapse_limit = 1;
SELECT * FROM cust_hist h INNER JOIN products p ON (h.prod_id=p.prod_id)
INNER JOIN customers c ON (h.customerid=c.customerid);
```

Alternate plans won't be considered. This can be useful in two main contexts. If query planning time is large for a particular complicated join, discovering the usual order that will be executing and making it explicit in the query can save significant planning time. And, in cases where the optimizer selected order was poor, this is one form of hint you can provide to it on what right things to do.

There is a similar parameter named `from_collapse_limit` that controls how much freedom the query optimizer has to merge sub-queries into upper ones. Generally, both these values are set to the same value, so behavior is easier to predict. There may be cases for setting them to different values if you are being quite careful about tweaking for planning time versus query execution time.

Join removal

Starting from PostgreSQL 9.0, a new feature will remove joins in circumstances where they aren't really required. The following `JOIN` would be common to many queries running against this data that wanted to match up a product with its matching inventory data:

```
SELECT * FROM products LEFT JOIN inventory ON
products.prod_id=inventory.prod_id;
```

You could even put this into a view as a shorthand for the combined result, then filter it down from there, so that not everyone has to remember how to do the join. But, some queries using that general form might not even need to use the inventory data, such as this one that only references `products` fields:

```
EXPLAIN ANALYZE SELECT products.title FROM products LEFT JOIN inventory ON
products.prod_id=inventory.prod_id;
QUERY PLAN
----------
Seq Scan on products  (cost=0.00..201.00 rows=10000 width=19) (actual
time=0.014..18.910 rows=10000 loops=1)
Total runtime: 34.266 ms
```

Note that there's no join at all here, it has been optimized away. There are three sensible requirements before this logic can kick in:

- A `LEFT JOIN` is happening
- A unique index exists for the join columns
- None of the information in the candidate table to remove is used anywhere

Because of the current restrictions on this optimization, if it's possible for you to use `LEFT JOIN` instead of `INNER JOIN` when you write a query, that would be preferable if you also suspect removable joins may creep into your execution plans. Removing inner ones may eventually be supported in PostgreSQL, but it doesn't know how to do that yet.

While this particular mistake is obvious here, in complicated database setups where the physical table structure is abstracted away by views and programmatically generated queries, having the optimizer throw out the redundant joins can be a useful improvement.

Genetic query optimizer

Once the number of joins gets large enough, there is really no hope the query optimizer can evaluate all of them exhaustively and still return plans in a reasonable period of time. When this happens, the **Genetic Query Optimizer (GEQO)** is called in to work on the problem instead. It numbers each of the tables to be joined as an integer, starting with 1, so a possible plan for a five-table join would be encoded as 1-2-3-4-5. GEQO starts by creating some number of such plans essentially at random. It then evaluates each of these for fitness, specifically how large the execution cost is for each of them. The best plans are kept, the worst ones dropped, some changes to the plans are made (mutation), and the process repeats for some number of generations.

Be warned that, because there's so much randomization involved in this process, you can't expect the plans that come out of GEQO to be the same every time, even given the same input query and statistics. Starting with PostgreSQL 9.0, it's possible to control that for more consistent plans, by fixing the random seed used to generate them, to always be the same value. See the PostgreSQL documentation for more information.

Whether GEQO comes into play or not depends on `geqo_threshold`, which defaults to 12. As there aren't even that many tables in the sample database used for this chapter, it's certainly not something that can be easily demonstrated. If you have that many tables to join, expect to spend some time learning how GEQO works and about its tunable parameters. There's little information available on doing so available beyond what's included in the PostgreSQL documentation.

Statistics

The least-appreciated part of query optimization is the collection of database statistics. Often, when questions such as "why isn't the optimizer using my index?" are asked, it is poor statistics that are really to blame.

Statistics are collected for each column in every table in a database when `ANALYZE` is executed against the table. If you're running with `autovacuum` turned on, it will usually run often enough to keep accurate statistics available. Unlike a complete vacuum cleanup, which can take quite some time on large tables, analyzing a table should take only a few seconds at any table size. It doesn't take anything other than a read lock while running, either.

Viewing and estimating with statistics

The statistics information collected for each table is easiest to see using the `pg_stats` view. The amount of information it returns is a bit overwhelming though, and not well suited to the standard display format. The following script is named `table-stats.sh` in the book's file set, and it tries to display the statistics information for a particular table (with an optional database too) in a way that makes the information as readable as possible:

```
#!/bin/bash
if [ -z "$1" ]; then
  echo "Usage: table-stats.sh table [db]"
  exit 1
fi
TABLENAME="$1"
```

```
if [ -n "$2" ] ; then
  DB="-d $2"
fi
PSQL="psql $DB -x -c "
$PSQL "
SELECT
  tablename,attname,null_frac,avg_width,n_distinct,correlation,
  most_common_vals,most_common_freqs,histogram_bounds
FROM pg_stats
WHERE tablename='$TABLENAME';
" | grep -v "-[ RECORD "
```

A typical usage would be:

```
./table-stats.sh customers dellstore2
```

Note that the script as currently written doesn't show the inherited information necessary to sort out statistics on tables using inheritance, such as ones that are partitioned. An alternate way to display some of the data displayed horizontally in the preceding query is to use `array_to_string` to break it into rows, such as the following:

```
SELECT attname,inherited,array_to_string(most_common_vals, E'n') AS
most_common_vals FROM pg_stats;
```

Here are some examples of the information about the `customers` table returned by `table-stats.sh` with some of the less interesting pieces (table name and `null_frac`) removed:

```
attname           | customerid
avg_width         | 4
n_distinct        | -1
correlation       | 1
most_common_vals  |
most_common_freqs |
histogram_bounds  | {1,200,400,600,800,1000,... 19600,19800,20000}
```

As this is the primary key on the table, the number of distinct values doesn't have to be estimated by probing the data, thus the -1 for that value. It can be computed based on the running estimate for total row count kept updated as part of the table statistics, instead of relying just on what the last ANALYZE noticed.

The histogram bounds data divides the range of data sampled into buckets of equal frequency. To compute how selective a range query will be, the optimizer figures out where the value selected fits into the histogram. Let's say you were running a query that grabbed the first 300 rows of data here. This would cover all of the first bucket's range (1–200) and half the second bucket's range (200–400). The formula used looks like the following:

```
selectivity = (1 + (value - bucket[2].min)/
      (bucket[2].max - bucket[2].min)) / num_buckets
selectivity = (1 + (300 - 200)/(400 - 200))/(20000 / 200)
selectivity = 0.015
rows = total row count * selectivity
rows = 20000 * 0.02 = 300
```

And that's how the optimizer would correctly guess that this query will return 300 rows:

```
EXPLAIN ANALYZE SELECT * FROM customers WHERE customerid<=300;
QUERY PLAN
----------
Index Scan using customers_pkey on customers  (cost=0.00..20.50 rows=300
width=268) (actual time=0.041..0.670 rows=300 loops
     =1)
Index Cond: (customerid <= 300)
Total runtime: 1.192 ms
```

This computation is probably indecipherable to you on a quick first read. Study this for a bit and try to understand how it works. A basic working knowledge of how histogram buckets help the query optimizer make decisions will put you way ahead of many people who try to optimize queries without understanding how statistics drive the process.

This simulation does depend on collecting enough buckets of information to make sure the histogram tracked the true distribution of the data. If only a small amount of data was sampled, you could end up with a very misleading perspective on how the data was distributed.

PostgreSQL even tries to improve on this estimate to noting the end of indexed values when available, which helps improve estimates when you normally insert data at the start or end of the column's range (a very common situation). If your query needs data from either the first or last bucket, and the corresponding left or right edge can be determined by a quick index lookup, the optimizer will do that to correctly set its edge boundary. The histogram data ANALYZE puts into a statistics bucket may grow out of date, while looking up the edge with an index is guaranteed to give the real minimum or maximum.

For text data, instead of a histogram you get common values and frequencies:

```
attname            | country
avg_width          | 5
n_distinct         | 11
correlation        | -0.613603
most_common_vals   |
{US,Chile,Australia,Russia,Canada,Germany,China,UK,Japan,France,"South
Africa"}
most_common_freqs  |
{0.5,0.05235,0.0517,0.0506,0.0502,0.0502,0.0501,0.0501,0.04945,0.04855,0.04
675}
histogram_bounds   |
```

The most common value and frequency data is paired up taking a matching entry from each. So that translates into the following:

Country	% of data
US	50
Chile	5.235
Australia	5.17
Russia	5.06

It is like this for all 11 of the other countries listed. If there were more distinct countries than the number of saved statistics buckets, only the most popular ones would be saved this way, and the remainder would be estimated more roughly.

The `income` column is an integer. There's not much data in there, so it should also include a complete distribution instead of a histogram in its statistics:

```
attname            | income
avg_width          | 4
n_distinct         | 5
correlation        | 0.198876
most_common_vals   | {20000,80000,40000,60000,100000}
most_common_freqs  | {0.2033,0.2032,0.2027,0.1961,0.1947}
histogram_bounds   |
```

This data gets combined together as additional conditions are added to a WHERE clause, presuming that the individual columns are independent of one another. For example, if you were filtering on country and income, the selectivity would be combined like the following:

```
country = 'US':    50% selectivity
income=80000':   20.32% selective
country = 'US' AND income=80000':   50% * 20.32% = 10.16%
rows = total row count * selectivity
rows = 20000 * 10.16% = 2032
```

And, sure enough, 2,032 is the estimated row count the query planner computes for that query:

```
EXPLAIN ANALYZE SELECT * FROM customers WHERE country='US' AND
income=80000;
    QUERY PLAN
    ----------
    Seq Scan on customers  (cost=0.00..776.00 rows=2032 width=268) (actual
time=0.043..32.947 rows=2039 loops=1)
        Filter: (((country)::text = 'US'::text) AND (income = 80000))
Total runtime: 36.279 ms
```

If the planner has no idea how selective something is because it's missing data on it, the guess is it selects 0.5% of the rows.

Statistics targets

It should be obvious from the previous section that the number of buckets used to hold common values or histogram samples significantly influences how accurate query row estimates will be. The number of them ANALYZE aims to collect is called its target. The postgresql.conf parameter default_statistics_target sets the standard target for tables in each database. The default target was 10 up to PostgreSQL 8.3, increasing to 100 in 8.4. This means that the 8.4 version has significantly more statistics to work with by default, which normally results in better queries. The cost for that is slightly worse query planning time as well as significantly longer ANALYZE processing (that second part not being something most people care very much about).

If you only have simple queries to plan, and query-planning time is large in a later PostgreSQL version where the target starts at 100, it's possible to reduce default_statistics_target back to the older starting value of 10 and re-analyze the whole database. This can give about a few percent performance boost to running trivial queries in newer versions.

Adjusting a column target

The maximum number of target buckets is either 1,000 or 10,000 depending on the version, you can confirm which you have using the following:

```
SELECT name,max_val FROM pg_settings WHERE
name='default_statistics_target';
```

Setting an extremely large value here does incur overhead on every query that is planned, and, as mentioned before, just the increase from 10 to 100 measurably detuned the trivial query runtime in PostgreSQL 8.4. There are however some table columns where it takes substantially larger settings to get sufficient statistics about the data to make accurate estimates. It's not unheard of in a large data warehouse setting to increase the target to 1,000 or more to sample enough of a giant table to represent it. But you don't want to pay that penalty for every query, just the ones that need it.

Luckily, the target is set per column, so you can override the value just on that basis for those that need it instead for every table and query run. The per-column value starts at -1, which means using the system default. You can adjust it like this:

```
ALTER TABLE t ALTER COLUMN k SET STATISTICS 1000;
```

Then you can run a new ANALYZE against that table.

Distinct values

Starting in PostgreSQL 9.0, it's possible to override the estimates ANALYZE makes for the number of distinct values in a table with your own values, in situations where it's not making a good estimate on its own:

```
ALTER TABLE t ALTER COLUMN k SET (n_distinct = 500);
```

In addition to just putting a value in there, you can also set this to a negative value, at which point it's used as a multiplier on the number of rows in the table. That lets you set a distinct estimate that scales along with your data based on current and future expectations about it. There is also a n_distinct_inherited parameter that can be set on a parent that multiple tables inherit from.

Difficult areas to estimate

If no data has ever been collected about a table using ANALYZE, the planner has to make up completely arbitrary estimates. This is the worst sort of statistics issue to have.

Another area where statistics can fail is situations where the query optimizer just doesn't know how to estimate something. You can watch it utterly fail to estimate this simple query correctly:

```
EXPLAIN ANALYZE SELECT * FROM customers WHERE customerid=customerid;
QUERY PLAN
----------
    Seq Scan on customers  (cost=0.00..726.00 rows=100 width=268) (actual
time=0.012..30.012 rows=20000 loops=1)
      Filter: (customerid = customerid)
Total runtime: 55.549 ms
```

It's obvious to a person that all 20,000 rows will be returned. What's happening is that, because it has no idea how selective the test here is, the optimizer has to make a wild guess. The standard estimate it uses in this situation is 0.5% of the rows, which is where the figure of 100 expected rows comes from.

When row counts are underestimated, this can result in an Index Scan instead of the correct Seq Scan, or in running a long Nested Loop instead of a hash or merge join. When row counts are overestimated, you can get a Seq Scan instead of an Index Scan, and a Merge or Hash Join instead of a Nested Loop.

Other query-planning parameters

Now that all of the ways a query executes have been covered, some of the more obscure query-planning parameters can be explained usefully.

effective_cache_size

Defaulting to 128 MB, effective_cache_size is used to represent approximately how much total disk space is available for caching the database. This is normally set to the total of shared_buffers plus the size of the operating system disk buffer cache after the database is started. This turns out to be greater than half of the total system memory on a typical dedicated database server. This setting does not allocate any memory itself; it simply serves as an advisory value for the planner about what should likely be available.

The only thing this is used for is estimating whether an index scan will fit into the memory, with the alternative being a sequential scan. One area that is particularly impacted by this setting is Nested Loop joins that are using an inner Index Scan. As you reduce effective_cache_size, it's less likely that will be considered an effective query execution plan.

While the scope where this parameter comes into play is pretty limited, these use cases do pop up regularly. The penalty for deciding an index can't be processed in memory is getting a sequential scan or a poor join type choice, which can make for a rather expensive mistake. And the default value is this parameter is quite small relative to the amount of RAM in modern servers.

The main thing to be careful about here is that, like work_mem, PostgreSQL isn't tracking client-related memory resources in any way that limits them across the whole database. If you have two clients executing queries that require scanning an extremely large index to work well at the same time, because each thinks it can use half or more of the RAM in the server for that purpose, you may discover your operating system cache is fighting to retain any data but those indexes. This may be fine if it makes the large queries execute much faster, because they're using a selective index, but there is a risk here if you set this value too high. Instead of strictly looking at total system RAM to set this parameter, you may instead do a sanity check by seeing just how large the indexes you may expect to participate in Nested Loop with inner Index Scan queries might be. Then, set effective_cache_size to something large enough to fix them comfortably.

As effective_cache_size is a client-side parameter, another alternative approach here that isn't used very often yet is to treat its sizing more like how work mem is typically managed. You can set a moderate, but not too high value, in the main postgresql.conf. Then, only in queries that really need a high setting to execute, do you increase it. This approach will reduce the odds of the potential problem where multiple really large index scans expected to fit in cache actually turn out to exhaust cache when running simultaneously. But, it will still allow an increase for queries where you know that's the only good way to approach things.

work_mem

If you are sorting data, work_mem determines when those sorts are allowed to execute in memory and when they have to swap to disk instead. Starting in PostgreSQL 8.3, you can turn on log_temp_files and see all the cases where work_mem was not large enough, and the external merge Disk sort is used instead. Note that you may be confused to see such usage appear in the logs even though the value shown is smaller than work_mem. An example and the reason behind why that happens is explained in the *Sort* section seen earlier.

Setting a value for this parameter is tricky. Ideally, you'd like it to be large on a system with plenty of memory, so that sorts happen quickly. But every client can use this much memory for each sort node in a query it's busy executing. Standard sizing will therefore put an upper bound at around the following:

```
work_mem = Total RAM / max_connections / 4
```

This is based on the assumption that half of system memory could be used for other purposes, and that it's unlikely every client will be doing more than two sorts at a time. This is actually a quite aggressive setting; a safer setting would be as follows:

```
work_mem = Total RAM / max_connections / 16
```

A good tuning strategy here is to pick a number in between those two values then monitor total RAM used by PostgreSQL processes, free memory, and sorts that still exceed the setting that are logged as going to disk. If there appears to be plenty of memory unused at peak times and disk sorts are happening, increase work_mem. If memory use looks high, try lowering it instead.

Note that you can set work_mem for a single query before running it, which is the preferred technique for situations like an occasional large report that runs each day. If you know only a small number of clients can be running a query at a time, you can be much more aggressive about how much memory is allocated just for those.

work_mem is also used for some other sizing decisions in the query optimizer, particularly in PostgreSQL 8.4 and later, where it's become an increasingly important parameter. Hash table construction and materialization creation will also use this value as a guide to how much memory they can use. This does increase the concern with newer versions that it's hard to predict how many simultaneous operations using work_mem worth of memory may happen. You can normally estimate the number of sorts in a query just by looking at it or its EXPLAIN plan, but hash and materialization use isn't so obvious from the query itself, and is more subject to shifting around as the table changes. In PostgreSQL 8.4 and particularly 9.0 and 10.0, it's better to err on the size of caution, using a smaller work_mem setting initially. Be careful about using a large value here until you have an idea how aggressively clients are allocating working memory for all of its possible purposes.

constraint_exclusion

If you are using partitioned tables that use constraints, enabling constraint_exclusion allows the planner to ignore partitions that can't have the data being searched for when that can be proven. This parameter originally defaulted to off, meaning that, unless toggled on partitioned tables, it will not work as expected. Starting in PostgreSQL 8.4, this was improved such that a new default value, partition, will do the right thing here in most cases without adding the overhead to the ones it isn't necessary for. It is theoretically possible to see a tiny performance improvement by turning this feature off in newer versions where it defaults to partition, in cases where there are no partitions on your system.

cursor_tuple_fraction

When you start a query using a cursor instead of a regular statement, PostgreSQL doesn't know for sure how many rows you'll then retrieve. To lean towards both the possibility that you will only access a subset of them and the fact that cursor-based programs tend to be sensitive to latency, cursor_tuple_fraction allows you to lower the expected number of rows that cursor originated queries are expected to return. If set to 1.0, cursors will work the same as regular queries. At its default of 0.1, the query optimizer biases toward query plans that quickly return rows, assuming that only 10% of the total rows will be requested. This works similar to when a LIMIT is used on a query.

Executing other statement types

The same basic execution logic is used to handle all four of the basic SQL query types: SELECT, INSERT, UPDATE, and DELETE. For example, when doing an UPDATE, the identified rows to update are found in a familiar way and then fed to an Update node:

```
EXPLAIN ANALYZE UPDATE customers SET state=state WHERE customerid=1;
    QUERY PLAN
    ----------
    Update  (cost=0.00..0.28 rows=1 width=274) (actual time=63.289..63.289
rows=0 loops=1)
        -> Index Scan using customers_pkey on customers   (cost=0.00..0.28
rows=1 width=274) (actual time=0.054..0.063 rows=1 loop
    s=1)
             Index Cond: (customerid = 1)
    Total runtime: 63.415 ms
```

UPDATE and DELETE can execute efficiently by keeping track of the tuple ID uniquely identifying each of the rows they are then called to operate on. Note that the preceding UPDATE doesn't actually do anything; the values it's setting the state field to are what it already contains. PostgreSQL never looks at what you're updating to figure out if the change being made by an UPDATE does something or not; it will always execute it instead. It can be a useful optimization to add a WHERE clause to prevent this. To show this with an example that doesn't make any business sense; let's say every customer were to suddenly be relocated to Maryland. The appropriate query to do that would be:

```
UPDATE customers SET state='MD' WHERE NOT state='MD';
```

This will avoid adding a redundant row for the situation where the state was already set to that value. Avoiding updates this way can save a lot of unnecessary writes and vacuum cleanup in some applications.

Improving queries

Once you understand what a query is doing, getting it to do something better can be a difficult road to walk down. There are some common techniques that mesh with the areas PostgreSQL is known to be good and bad at.

Note that your first steps to improve queries should be to check whether the statistics the optimizer is working with seem reasonable. If it's bad, you may fix the problem by rewriting the query you have today to improve things. But, you can expect that future queries will run into the same class of issue, so fixing that from a statistics standpoint is the preferred way, the one that's more likely to continue reflecting future trends in the data. But improving the statistics about your data only goes so far some days.

Optimizing for fully cached data sets

A basic assumption of the query optimizer is that data is not cached in memory, and therefore all access to an index or table might require some disk activity to retrieve. The planner parameters seq_page_cost and random_page_cost being very high relative to cpu_index_tuple_cost reflects this pessimism.

If in fact the data you are reading is expected to be fully cached in memory, it can be appropriate to dramatically lower these parameters in recognition of that fact. In some cases, it may be appropriate to go so far to make index and table lookups appear no more expensive than the CPU cost of looking at a single row:

```
SHOW cpu_index_tuple_cost;
 cpu_index_tuple_cost
---------------------
     0.005
SET seq_page_cost=0.005;
SET random_page_cost=0.005;
```

It's unlikely you want to set values this low in your postgresql.conf for every query, unless your entire database has proven to be quite small compared to system RAM. As you can adjust these parameters at session time before executing a query, you can tweak them down for the queries that benefit from knowing the completely cached nature of the data they are operating on.

Testing for query equivalence

In one of the Hash Join examples, a complicated query using EXISTS was used to determine whether each product had ever been ordered. There's theoretically another way to figure that out: the inventory information for each product includes a sales count. If those are complete—every product is included in that inventory, even if it's never been sold—then a query looking for zero sales of an item should give the same results:

```
SELECT prod_id FROM inventory WHERE sales=0;
```

This looks like the same list, but it's long enough that comparing every entry would be tedious. You can easily compare the output from two queries to see whether they produce the same rows using the `EXCEPT` construct:

```
SELECT prod_id FROM products p WHERE NOT EXISTS (SELECT 1 FROM orderlines
ol WHERE ol.prod_id=p.prod_id)
    EXCEPT
    SELECT prod_id FROM inventory WHERE sales=0;
```

This is particularly useful to know when working on optimizing queries by rewriting them. It's easy to break a query when doing that such that it doesn't quite produce the same output anymore. When you have a rewritten query that appears to give the same results as an earlier one, but runs faster, constructing a regression test showing that no rows come out of an `EXCEPT` construct including the two versions is a handy way to prove that.

Disabling optimizer features

Sometimes the optimizer doesn't do what you want, and you may want some tools to either force it to change its mind or to see what alternatives it's considering but rejecting. Consider this simple query that searches for one order and joins with its matching customer record:

```
EXPLAIN ANALYZE SELECT C.customerid,O.orderid FROM customers C,orders O
WHERE c.customerid=o.customerid AND o.orderid=10000;
    QUERY PLAN
    ----------
    Nested Loop  (cost=0.00..16.55 rows=1 width=8) (actual
time=0.038..0.049 rows=1 loops=1)
        -> Index Scan using orders_pkey on orders o  (cost=0.00..8.27
rows=1 width=8) (actual time=0.018..0.020 rows=1 loops=1)
            Index Cond: (orderid = 10000)
        -> Index Scan using customers_pkey on customers c  (cost=0.00..8.27
rows=1 width=4) (actual time=0.011..0.014 rows=1 loops=1)
            Index Cond: (c.customerid = o.customerid)
Total runtime: 0.140 ms
```

This is a nice efficient query. But the type of join used is very sensitive to just how many rows are expected to be returned from the `orders` table, ones that is done then they have to be matched against customers. This style of query continues to be preferred all the way up to one that selects 195 customers:

```
EXPLAIN ANALYZE SELECT C.customerid,O.orderid FROM customers C,orders O
WHERE c.customerid=o.customerid AND o.orderid BETWEEN 11805 AND 12000;
    QUERY PLAN
    -----------------------------
```

```
      Nested Loop  (cost=0.00..900.11 rows=195 width=8)  (actual
time=0.048..4.042 rows=196 loops=1)
        -> Index Scan using orders_pkey on orders o  (cost=0.00..13.15
rows=195 width=8)  (actual time=0.028..0.450 rows=196 loops=1)
            Index Cond: ((orderid >= 11805) AND (orderid <= 12000))
        -> Index Scan using customers_pkey on customers c  (cost=0.00..4.54
rows=1 width=4)  (actual time=0.009..0.011 rows=1 loops=196)
            Index Cond: (c.customerid = o.customerid)
Total runtime: 4.447 ms
```

Make the query just a bit less selective, so one more row is considered, and the join type changes completely. When there are a fairly large number of matches expected, the planner uses a Hash Join with an inner Index Scan for the order key, while matching against the entire customers table. It builds a hash table holding the relevant information from all 20,000 rows of it instead of using a Nested Loop:

```
    EXPLAIN ANALYZE SELECT C.customerid,O.orderid FROM customers C,orders O
WHERE c.customerid=o.customerid AND o.orderid BETWEEN 11804 AND 12000;
    QUERY PLAN
    ----------
    Hash Join  (cost=15.62..893.58 rows=196 width=8)  (actual
time=1.390..72.653 rows=197 loops=1)
        Hash Cond: (c.customerid = o.customerid)
        -> Seq Scan on customers c  (cost=0.00..676.00 rows=20000 width=4)
(actual time=0.007..33.279 rows=20000 loops=1)
        -> Hash  (cost=13.17..13.17 rows=196 width=8)  (actual
time=0.955..0.955 rows=197 loops=1)
            Buckets: 1024  Batches: 1  Memory Usage: 6kB
            -> Index Scan using orders_pkey on orders o
(cost=0.00..13.17 rows=196 width=8)  (actual time=0.029..0.541 rows=197
loops=1)
                    Index Cond: ((orderid >= 11804) AND (orderid <= 12000))
    Total runtime: 73.077 ms
```

That's exactly where the threshold is on this particular copy of the Dell Store database: 195 records expected gets a Nested Loop join, 196 gets a Hash. This gives you an idea just how fast a query plan can completely change on you in production. If the execution time on the Hash Join version of this was really terrible, that one extra record that showed up would kill the performance of your server. And, unless you were logging query plan EXPLAIN data, it's unlikely you'd have any idea what hit you.

What if the whole table is being scanned? That's even less selective, and the Hash Join is still preferred:

```
    EXPLAIN ANALYZE SELECT C.customerid,O.orderid FROM customers C,orders O
WHERE c.customerid=o.customerid AND o.orderid BETWEEN 1 AND 12000;
```

```
QUERY PLAN
----------
    Hash Join   (cost=926.00..1506.00 rows=12000 width=8)  (actual
time=89.580..153.567 rows=12000 loops=1)
        Hash Cond: (o.customerid = c.customerid)
        ->  Seq Scan on orders o   (cost=0.00..280.00 rows=12000 width=8)
(actual time=0.012..21.598 rows=12000 loops=1)
            Filter: ((orderid >= 1) AND (orderid <= 12000))
        ->  Hash   (cost=676.00..676.00 rows=20000 width=4)  (actual
time=89.536..89.536 rows=20000 loops=1)
            Buckets: 2048   Batches: 1   Memory Usage: 469kB
            ->  Seq Scan on customers c   (cost=0.00..676.00 rows=20000
width=4)  (actual time=0.005..42.196 rows=20000 loops=1)
    Total runtime: 170.234 ms
```

Because query plan changes can be so disastrous to a production server, some database administrators like to provide what are called optimizer hints to the server. These are strong suggestions to the optimizer that it execute a query a particular way. PostgreSQL doesn't explicitly support hints, based on two observations. First, it makes users better motivated to provide feedback to the database developers on what the optimizer does badly at, to continue improving it. Second, many plan changes are actually the right thing to do. The original hint could have been based on statistics that are now far out of date compared to what's actually in the table now.

There is a way to simulate something like an optimizer hint, though. PostgreSQL allows individual queries to turn off particular optimizer features. If you disable the type of plan you'd prefer not to see, that's effectively hinting toward the plan you want. The list of features you can toggle off as of PostgreSQL 10.0 are:

- enable_bitmapscan
- enable_gathermerge
- enable_hashagg
- enable_hashjoin
- enable_indexscan
- enable_indexonlyscan
- enable_material
- enable_mergejoin
- enable_nestloop
- enable_seqscan
- enable_sort
- enable_tidscan

Note that turning these off doesn't actually disable the feature; it just increases its estimate cost so it's much less likely to be executed. There are some queries that it's only possible to execute with a `Nested Loop` for example, so even if you turn off `enable_nestloop` you'll still get one. And, if you have no index on something, you can turn off `enable_seqscan` but a `Seq Scan` will nonetheless happen.

Let's see what happens if hash joins are disabled on this query:

```
SET enable_hashjoin=off;
EXPLAIN ANALYZE SELECT C.customerid,O.orderid FROM customers C,orders O
WHERE c.customerid=o.customerid AND o.orderid BETWEEN 1 AND 12000;
QUERY PLAN
----------
Merge Join  (cost=0.05..1919.49 rows=12000 width=8) (actual
time=0.080..150.624 rows=12000 loops=1)
    Merge Cond: (c.customerid = o.customerid)
    ->  Index Scan using customers_pkey on customers c
(cost=0.00..963.25 rows=20000 width=4) (actual time=0.031..37.928
rows=20000 loops=1)
    ->  Index Scan using ix_order_custid on orders o  (cost=0.00..756.24
rows=12000 width=8) (actual time=0.032..36.635 rows=12000 loops=1)
            Filter: ((o.orderid >= 1) AND (o.orderid <= 12000))
    Total runtime: 167.991 ms
```

Now we get a `Merge Join` between the two tables, which turns out to be as or more efficient in practice (even though the cost is slightly higher). What about if neither Hash nor `Merge Joins` are allowed?

```
SET enable_hashjoin=off;
SET enable_mergejoin=off;
EXPLAIN ANALYZE SELECT C.customerid,O.orderid FROM customers C,orders O
WHERE c.customerid=o.customerid AND o.orderid BETWEEN 1 AND 12000;
QUERY PLAN
----------
Nested Loop  (cost=0.00..5750.08 rows=12000 width=8) (actual
time=0.038..184.266 rows=12000 loops=1)
    ->  Seq Scan on orders o  (cost=0.00..280.00 rows=12000 width=8)
(actual time=0.012..23.524 rows=12000 loops=1)
            Filter: ((orderid >= 1) AND (orderid <= 12000))
    ->  Index Scan using customers_pkey on customers c  (cost=0.00..0.44
rows=1 width=4) (actual time=0.006..0.007 rows=1 loops=12000)
            Index Cond: (c.customerid = o.customerid)
    Total runtime: 200.741 ms
```

Now the old `Nested Loop` shows up, with a plan the optimizer considers much more expensive than either of the other two. Because this is using the inner `Index Scan` variation, the actual runtime isn't that much worse on this small data set, but on a seriously large query this could be a disastrous plan.

Here's another example you can try that will show the various ways another pair of tables can be joined as you disable optimizer options, presuming you start with a fresh session with the default settings (not just after the previous example, where some of these were already disabled):

```
EXPLAIN ANALYZE SELECT * FROM inventory,products WHERE
inventory.prod_id=products.prod_id;
SET enable_hashjoin = off;
EXPLAIN ANALYZE SELECT * FROM inventory,products WHERE
inventory.prod_id=products.prod_id;
SET enable_mergejoin = off;
EXPLAIN ANALYZE SELECT * FROM inventory,products WHERE
inventory.prod_id=products.prod_id;
SET enable_bitmapscan = off;
EXPLAIN ANALYZE SELECT * FROM inventory,products WHERE
inventory.prod_id=products.prod_id;
```

I find it particularly amusing to watch how creative the optimizer gets at using increasingly less efficient index scans once the better join types go away. The last join in particular will be extraordinarily slower than the other ones once all access to the indexes is made impractical; here are some sample runtimes:

Join type	Execution time (milliseconds)
Hash Join	119
Merge Join	126
Nested Loop **with inner** Index Scan	171
Nested Loop **with inner** Bitmap Index Scan	219
Nested Loop **with inner** Seq Scan	292,491

Playing with these optimizer options to work around a query problem is tempting, because it can feel like an easy fix to a bad plan issue. It's dangerous though, because the plan that makes sense today can be totally wrong when either the amount or distribution of your data changes in the future. The reason good tutorials about database queries try to explain how queries execute, including details such as how statistics and costs fit together, is because understanding that theory is what can give you the background to make difficult decisions in this area.

Working around optimizer bugs

Only if you can't get the statistics or cost data to work as expected should you then take drastic measures such as disabling optimizer features. But bear in mind that flags such as enable_hashjoin and enable_seqscan can be valuable for another reason altogether. Sometimes, bad optimizer behavior can result from a database bug or limitation. If you know or suspect that, toggling optimizer features off can help you determine which code path may be involved in your issue. Also, there's nothing wrong with temporarily working around a bad plan by putting one of these optimizer hacks into place as a triage measure, to buy yourself time to figure out what's really wrong. Resist doing that in the server configuration through these sorts of changes belong in the code that executes the individual problem queries, not server-wide.

Avoiding plan restructuring with OFFSET

Another technique that shows up sometimes to work around bad plan issues is using OFFSET 0 strategically in a query. Having no offset from when results return doesn't change the query result, but it is considered a volatile change that prevents some types of plan node changes—sometimes in a good way, despite what the planner predicts.

A good example of how this can work comes from a potential performance regression from certain types of joins that was introduced in PostgreSQL 8.4, and also still exists in 9.0 and 10.0. It's an interesting case study in how progress in improving the PostgreSQL optimizer tends to happen. The problem is described by Andres Freund using a test case and associated query plans at http://archives.postgresql.org/pgsql-hackers/2010-05/msg00889.php but not with actual data. It's possible to recreate the basic setup using the Dell Store data. Let's say you have a small set of orderline data you're searching for. You want to confirm the existence of matching customer and order rows that go along with this fairly small set of orderlines. That doesn't have a strong real-world meaning, given the existence of those rows is guaranteed by foreign key constraints. But a query doing that and showing the problem behavior looks like this:

```
EXPLAIN ANALYZE
SELECT
  l.prod_id
FROM
    orderlines l
WHERE
    EXISTS (
        SELECT *
        FROM customers
                JOIN orders USING (customerid)
        WHERE orders.orderid = l.orderid
        )
    AND l.orderdate='2004-12-01';
QUERY PLAN
----------
Hash Semi Join  (cost=1596.00..2708.47 rows=155 width=4) (actual
time=192.570..194.552 rows=183 loops=1)
      Hash Cond: (l.orderid = orders.orderid)
   ->  Seq Scan on orderlines l  (cost=0.00..1109.38 rows=155 width=8)
(actual time=27.980..29.440 rows=183 loops=1)
            Filter: (orderdate = '2004-12-01'::date)
   ->  Hash  (cost=1446.00..1446.00 rows=12000 width=4) (actual
time=164.545..164.545 rows=12000 loops=1)
          Buckets: 2048  Batches: 1  Memory Usage: 282kB
          ->  Hash Join  (cost=926.00..1446.00 rows=12000 width=4)
(actual time=89.383..145.439 rows=12000 loops=1)
                Hash Cond: (orders.customerid = customers.customerid)
                ->  Seq Scan on orders  (cost=0.00..220.00 rows=12000
width=8) (actual time=0.008..16.105 rows=12000 loops=1)
                ->  Hash  (cost=676.00..676.00 rows=20000 width=4)
(actual time=89.347..89.347 rows=20000 loops=1)
                      Buckets: 2048  Batches: 1  Memory Usage: 469kB
                      ->  Seq Scan on customers  (cost=0.00..676.00
rows=20000 width=4) (actual time=0.007..42.141 rows=20000 loops=1)
     Total runtime: 195.460 ms
```

What the database is doing here is constructing a hash table that includes every customer and order entry, on the assumption it can then efficiently join against the matching orderlines that meet the criteria. It is even guessing right about how many order lines will come out here—there are 183 rows returned; it expected 155. But the setup time to build this whole hash structure is high just to join against such a small number of rows. The optimization that tries to do that with a semi join instead was introduced in 8.4. A semi join is one where the optimizer only outputs outer rows that join to at least one inner row, and only once each.

This particular type of setup—start with a selective query against a low-level table, then search for the existence of matching records in ones that join to it—is not an uncommon one. I have run into this issue on a live customer system and I have seen this sort of plan give a dramatic slowdown compared to earlier PostgreSQL versions.

What can you do about it? If the existence checks include a volatile bit of data, the planner can't assume it can transform around; it can't do this optimization. One such change you can easily use is OFFSET 0, a volatile change which the planner thinks changes queries results in a way it can't predict, but it really doesn't. Watch what happens when that is judiciously inserted into the preceding query:

```
EXPLAIN ANALYZE
SELECT
    l.prod_id
FROM
    orderlines l
WHERE
    EXISTS (
        SELECT *
        FROM customers
            JOIN orders USING (customerid)
        WHERE orders.orderid = l.orderid
        OFFSET 0
    )
    AND l.orderdate='2004-12-01';
QUERY PLAN
--------------------------------
    Seq Scan on orderlines l  (cost=0.00..999932.05 rows=78 width=4)
(actual time=33.946..43.271 rows=183 loops=1)
        Filter: ((orderdate = '2004-12-01'::date) AND (SubPlan 1))
        SubPlan 1
          -> Limit  (cost=0.00..16.55 rows=1 width=300)  (actual
time=0.033..0.033 rows=1 loops=183)
                -> Nested Loop  (cost=0.00..16.55 rows=1 width=300)  (actual
time=0.028..0.028 rows=1 loops=183)
                    -> Index Scan using orders_pkey on orders
(cost=0.00..8.27 rows=1 width=36)  (actual time=0.010..0.010 rows=1
loops=183)
                            Index Cond: (orderid = $0)
                    -> Index Scan using customers_pkey on customers
(cost=0.00..8.27 rows=1 width=268)  (actual time=0.009..0.009 rows=1
loops=183)
                            Index Cond: (customers.customerid =
orders.customerid)
        Total runtime: 43.774 ms
```

Now, instead of joining against the big hash structure, the planner just finds the 183 orderlines it's interested in and executes an index lookup for each of them, probing into the orders and customers table. (Note the rare SubPlan node type making an appearance as part of that). This was what PostgreSQL 8.3 and earlier versions always did, and by defeating the ability to use the newer optimization that behavior is back again. Note how the cost for this is believed to be dramatically higher, when in fact the actual runtime is much faster.

While there is the occasional unfortunate regression such as in this one, for the most part the PostgreSQL query optimizer gets better with every version. Now that the type of query that executes badly here is well understood, and reproducible test cases have appeared, the performance regression seen by this type of join issue is on the roadmap for improvement in PostgreSQL 9.1.

Much like faking optimizer hinting by turning off features, the need to use tricks, such as `OFFSET 0` to prevent bad planner behavior should continue to be less necessary in the future. But it is a handy trick to have in the toolbox when trying to force a query structure you know is better than the one the optimizer prefers. And seeing what happens to plans when you limit the optimizer's ability to restructure them like this is educational too.

External trouble spots

It's also possible to have a query run slowly for reasons that have nothing to do with the query plan itself.

One such situation is where you have triggers running against a table being referenced, particularly in cases where it's an `UPDATE` or `INSERT` running instead of just a regular query. The overhead of triggers can be high, particularly if there aren't any indexes on the underlying foreign keys.

Another issue you can run into is that dead rows can clog a query from executing as fast as expected. This is particularly true if you are frequently updating a popular set of rows without running `VACUUM` often enough. Doing anything with those rows can then require large amounts of wasted time, reading the non-visible data, even when doing an `Index Scan`.

Parallel queries

Starting from version 9.6 to even more on 10, PostgreSQL supports parallel queries. As written in the official documentation: *"Many queries cannot benefit from parallel query, either due to limitations of the current implementation or because there is no imaginable query plan which is any faster than the serial query plan. However, for queries that can benefit, the speedup from parallel query is often very significant. Many queries can run more than twice as fast when using parallel query, and some queries can run four times faster or even more. Queries that touch a large amount of data but return only a few rows to the user will typically benefit most."*

The planner decides when to use this feature and decides it by evaluating these parameters:

- `dynamic_shared_memory_type`: Must be set to a value other than **none**. Parallel query requires dynamic shared memory in order to pass data between cooperating processes, typically Posix on Linux systems.
- `parallel_setup_cost`: Sets the planner's estimate of the cost of launching parallel worker processes.
- `parallel_tuple_cost`: Sets the planner's estimate of the cost of transferring one tuple from a parallel worker process to another process.
- `min_parallel_table_scan_size`: Sets the minimum amount of table data that must be scanned for a parallel scan to be considered. The default is 8 megabytes (8 MB).
- `min_parallel_index_scan_size`: Sets the minimum amount of index data that must be scanned for a parallel scan to be considered. The default is 512 kilobytes (512 KB).

Other parameters that are used are:

- `max_worker_processes`: Sets the maximum number of background processes that the system can support.
- `max_parallel_workers_per_gather`: Sets the maximum number of workers that can be started by a single `Gather` or `Gather Merge` node. Parallel workers are taken from the pool of processes established by `max_worker_processes`, limited by `max_parallel_workers`.

When PostgreSQL decides to use a parallel query plan, the operations that can benefit from it are:

- Parallel sequential scans
- Parallell bitmap heap scan
- Parallel index scan or parallel index-only scan
- Parallel joins
- Parallel aggregation

Here are some examples:

First, we create a table with some data:

```
pgbench=# create table test_parallel as select generate_series(1,10000000)
as field1,generate_series(1,10000000)%2 as field2;
```

And then, we try to make a parallel hash aggregate and a parallel seq_scan on this table:

```
pgbench=# explain analyze select field2,count(*) from test_parallel group
by 1;
        QUERY PLAN
--------------------------------------------------------------- Finalize
GroupAggregate  (cost=107748.76..107748.81 rows=2 width=12) (actual
time=1567.570..1567.571 rows=2 loops=1)
   Group Key: field2
   ->  Sort  (cost=107748.76..107748.77 rows=4 width=12) (actual
time=1567.566..1567.566 rows=6 loops=1)
        Sort Key: field2
        Sort Method: quicksort  Memory: 25kB
        ->  Gather  (cost=107748.30..107748.72 rows=4 width=12) (actual
time=1567.541..1567.554 rows=6 loops=1)
              Workers Planned: 2
              Workers Launched: 2
              ->  Partial HashAggregate  (cost=106748.30..106748.32 rows=2
width=12) (actual time=1557.561..1557.562 rows=2 loops=3)
                    Group Key: field2
                    ->  Parallel Seq Scan on test_parallel
(cost=0.00..85914.87 rows=4166687 width=4) (actual time=0.067..716.097
rows=3333333 loops=3)
 Planning time: 0.145 ms
 Execution time: 1567.772 ms
```

Now, after creating the `test_parallel_field2_idx` index on `field2`, we execute the same query again, and we can see a parallel index-only scan:

```
QUERY PLAN
-----------------------------------------
 Finalize GroupAggregate  (cost=1000.46..367652.69 rows=2 width=12) (actual
time=1935.836..1935.839 rows=2 loops=1)
   Group Key: field2
   ->  Gather Merge  (cost=1000.46..367652.65 rows=4 width=12) (actual
time=1028.072..1935.830 rows=6 loops=1)
         Workers Planned: 2
         Workers Launched: 2
         ->  Partial GroupAggregate  (cost=0.43..366652.16 rows=2 width=12)
(actual time=1018.001..1921.309 rows=2 loops=3)
               Group Key: field2
               ->  Parallel Index Only Scan using test_parallel_field2_idx
on test_parallel  (cost=0.43..345818.81 rows=4166667 width=4) (actual
time=0.565..1516.123 rows=33333
33 loops=3)
                     Heap Fetches: 2764912
 Planning time: 0.248 ms
 Execution time: 1937.871 ms
```

or if we set the index_only_scan parameter to off we can see a parallel index scan:

```
pgbench=# explain analyze select field2,count(*) from test_parallel group
by 1;
 QUERY PLAN
-----------------------------------------
 Finalize GroupAggregate  (cost=1000.46..367652.69 rowsCourier 10 Pitch=2
width=12) (actual time=1875.246..1875.249 rows=2 loops=1)
   Group Key: field2
   ->  Gather Merge  (cost=1000.46..367652.65 rows=4 width=12) (actual
time=964.793..1875.239 rows=6 loops=1)
         Workers Planned: 2
         Workers Launched: 2
         ->  Partial GroupAggregate  (cost=0.43..366652.16 rows=2 width=12)
(actual time=952.390..1855.327 rows=2 loops=3)
               Group Key: field2
               ->  Parallel Index Scan using test_parallel_field2_idx on
test_parallel  (cost=0.43..345818.81 rows=4166667 width=4) (actual
time=0.089..1458.768 rows=3333333 lo
ops=3)
 Planning time: 0.235 ms
 Execution time: 1875.394 ms
```

You can find more details at
`https://www.postgresql.org/docs/10/static/parallel-query.html`.

SQL limitations

SQL is good at a number of things. There are some things it's known to be quite bad at, most of which result from returned rows having no knowledge of one another.

Numbering rows in SQL

Let's say you wanted to know who your top five customers are. That's an easy enough query to write:

```
SELECT customerid,sum(netamount) as sales FROM orders GROUP BY customerid
ORDER BY sales DESC LIMIT 5;
    customerid |  sales
   ------------+---------
         15483 | 1533.76
          9315 | 1419.19
         15463 | 1274.29
         10899 | 1243.14
          3929 | 1196.87
```

Here's a challenge for you: how would you write this query to also include that sales ranking for each customer, from 1 to 5, as part of this list? It's not a simple problem.

One of the subtle things about SQL queries is that each row is its own independent piece. It doesn't have any notion of how many other rows exist in the result set, where it stands in relation to the others; it's just a row of data. There are a couple of ways to solve this problem by using temporary tables, joining the output from `generate_series` against a primary key when one exists, and processing in a stored procedure. There's even a portable SQL way to do this using something like the following downright twisted subquery, which joins each entry in the table with itself and counts how many entries are higher than it to get a rank:

```
SELECT
      (SELECT COUNT(*) FROM
          (SELECT
              sum(netamount) as sales
           FROM orders GROUP BY customerid
```

```
      ) AS orderers WHERE orderers.sales>=leaders.sales
    ) AS rank,
    leaders.*
FROM
  (SELECT
      customerid, sum(netamount) as sales
    FROM orders GROUP BY customerid ORDER BY sales DESC LIMIT 5
  ) AS leaders;
 rank | customerid |  sales
------+------------+---------
    1 |      15483 | 1533.76
    2 |       9315 | 1419.19
    3 |      15463 | 1274.29
    4 |      10899 | 1243.14
    5 |       3929 | 1196.87
```

Not only is this terribly complex, while it looks fine on this subset, it falls apart the minute two customers with matching order balances show up. It's possible to improve that using DISTINCT to note when that happens and add a tie-breaker, but then you'd be looking at an even crazier query.

This example shows the sort of fundamental limitations you can run into with how SQL works. You can't know where rows are in relation to one another. You can't reference what data is in the row before or after the one you're currently referencing either. Another fun query to try and write would be to ask for just what the difference in sales volume between each of these top five customers. That requires a similarly painful self-join or dropping into a procedural language.

Using Window functions for numbering

PostgreSQL 8.4 introduces support to handle this sort of problem using features added to newer SQL standards. These add the concept of a window over which you can get additional data. For example, you can make your window in this type of query to line up with each customer, then use the row_number() function to find out the ranking:

```
SELECT row_number() OVER (ORDER BY sum(netamount) DESC) AS
rank, customerid, sum(netamount) as sales FROM orders GROUP BY customerid
ORDER BY sales DESC LIMIT 5;
 rank | customerid |  sales
------+------------+---------
    1 |      15483 | 1533.76
    2 |       9315 | 1419.19
    3 |      15463 | 1274.29
    4 |      10899 | 1243.14
```

```
    5 |          3929 | 1196.87
```

That's not only a whole lot cleaner, it's way more efficient too.

Using Window functions for cumulatives

As a second example, consider the case where you're computing sales for each month orders were placed:

```
SELECT EXTRACT(year FROM orderdate) AS year, EXTRACT(month FROM
orderdate) AS month,sum(netamount) as sales FROM orders GROUP BY year,month
ORDER BY year,month;
 year | month |    sales
------+-------+------------
 2004 |     1 | 199444.50
 2004 |     2 | 200269.86
 2004 |     3 | 194516.68
 2004 |     4 | 200131.18
 2004 |     5 | 197131.77
 2004 |     6 | 199919.21
 2004 |     7 | 190953.70
 2004 |     8 | 194102.55
 2004 |     9 | 196798.83
 2004 |    10 | 195798.80
 2004 |    11 | 199882.86
 2004 |    12 | 202769.80
```

What if you wanted a cumulative total at each point during the year? As that problem also requires referencing things that are in other rows, it's again not something you can do in the standard SQL model easily. Try it out; it's another fun challenge. Possible solutions include building a complicated query that joins the preceding output with itself, or bypassing SQL limitations altogether by using a function.

But you can easily wrap that with a window function instead too:

```
SELECT *,SUM(sales) OVER (ORDER BY year,month) as cumulative FROM
(SELECT EXTRACT(year FROM orderdate) AS year, EXTRACT(month FROM orderdate)
AS month,sum(netamount) as sales FROM orders GROUP BY year,month ORDER BY
year,month) as m ORDER BY year,month;
 year | month |    sales   | cumulative
------+-------+------------+------------
 2004 |     1 | 199444.50 |  199444.50
 2004 |     2 | 200269.86 |  399714.36
 2004 |     3 | 194516.68 |  594231.04
 2004 |     4 | 200131.18 |  794362.22
```

```
2004  |      5  | 197131.77 |   991493.99
2004  |      6  | 199919.21 |  1191413.20
2004  |      7  | 190953.70 |  1382366.90
2004  |      8  | 194102.55 |  1576469.45
2004  |      9  | 196798.83 |  1773268.28
2004  |     10  | 195798.80 |  1969067.08
2004  |     11  | 199882.86 |  2168949.94
2004  |     12  | 202769.80 |  2371719.74
```

That's not only simpler code to maintain, it's going to be much faster than either of the other solutions too. The plan for it looks like this:

```
QUERY PLAN
----------
    WindowAgg  (cost=453.75..464.70 rows=365 width=48) (actual
time=110.635..110.749 rows=12 loops=1)
        -> Sort  (cost=453.75..454.66 rows=365 width=12) (actual
time=110.592..110.610 rows=12 loops=1)
            Sort Key: (date_part('year'::text,
(orders.orderdate)::timestamp without time zone)),
(date_part('month'::text, (orders.orderdat
    e)::timestamp without time zone))
            Sort Method:  quicksort  Memory: 17kB
            -> HashAggregate  (cost=430.00..438.21 rows=365 width=12)
(actual time=110.503..110.530 rows=12 loops=1)
                -> Seq Scan on orders  (cost=0.00..340.00 rows=12000
width=12) (actual time=0.026..57.025 rows=12000 loops=1)
    Total runtime: 110.902 ms
```

This section has just scratched the surface of what it's possible to do with window queries. If you're using PostgreSQL 8.4 or later, and you find yourself with queries or procedural code that seems to be working to compute things, such as row numbers or cumulative values, you should consider whether those can be rewritten to use SQL Windows instead. The techniques it allows are extremely powerful and efficient.

Summary

A major goal of this chapter was not only to show you how a variety of queries execute, but to demonstrate through many examples how to set up a query testing playground for exploring that yourself.

You shouldn't just read this chapter. You should load the `dellstore2` data into your system and experiment with the queries yourself. It is possible that sometimes the results you get using the explain analyze statement are different; this may depend on the version of PostgreSQL you have, or on the indexes that have been created on the database, or it may depend on whether the system tables are updated (`Analyze`, `Autoanalyze` and `Create Index` are the processes that update the system tables). For example if you are on PostgreSQL >= 9.2 and you have a table with an index in the field `test_field` and execute something such as `SELECT field1 from table where test_field= 1`, you could have an **index only scan type** as explain result; this means that PostgreSQL takes the result directly from the index; if you want to disable this feature you have to execute `set enable_indexonlyscan=off`.

Try to understand how the queries are actually executed in each of these cases, based on the statistics available. Adjust the statistics collected and see whether anything changes. Write new queries and see whether the plans you get match what you expected. Watch how the optimizer degrades as you take away its advanced features. That sort of practice is the only way to really become an expert at query optimization. Once you see how to read query plans and understand how each of the underlying node types work on this relatively simple database, then you should be able to wrestle the queries on a production database.

Queries are executed as a series of nodes that each do a small task, such as a form of table access, aggregation, or joining.

For table access:

- Sequential scans give immediate results, and are the fastest way to scan small tables or large ones where a significant portion of the table will be returned.
- Index scans involve random disk access and still have to read the underlying data blocks for visibility checks. But the output can be quite selective and ordered usefully.
- Bitmap index scans use sequential disk reads but still allow index selectivity on multiple indexes. There is both time and memory overhead involved in building the hash structure before returning any rows, though.

For joins:

- `Nested Loop` joins are generally avoided due to their expense. But when their inner query is small because it uses an index, their ability to quickly output small numbers of rows can make them optimal.
- Merge joins require ordered inputs, making them slow to produce any output unless all inputs are already sorted and even index scans require some random access. They're often preferred for larger data sets where hashing would take too much memory and a `Nested Loop` would be inefficient.
- Hash Joins scan their inner table to produce a hash table to join against, which also has a lot of overhead to produce the first row of output.

Parallel Queries: How does PostgreSQL 10 processes queries in a parallel way?

The following are the troubleshooting query issues:

- Variation between estimated and actual rows can cause major planning issues. Looking into the underlying statistics is one way to determine why that's happening; at a minimum, make sure you have recent statistics from an `ANALYZE`.
- Consider portions of the query that actually had the longest execution time, and see whether they had an appropriate matching cost. If not, this may also suggest a statistics problem.
- Be systematic about looking for all the common causes for query issues to see whether they apply to your case.
- Make sure that optimizer parameters such as `effective_cache_size` and `work_mem` are sized appropriately for the system.
- If nothing else works, consider forcing alternate plans by disabling optimizer features that result in poorly executed plans.
- SQL `WINDOW` queries can be extremely efficient in situations where knowing more about a row's context and data in surrounding rows simplifies the logic.

11
Database Activity and Statistics

PostgreSQL includes a subsystem named the statistics collector which allows the monitoring of various aspects of the database internals. Each of the processes in the server send statistics messages to the collector, which then totals the results and periodically publishes the results to where you can see them. By default (the interval is a compile-time option), statistics updates are published every half second. Each of the statistics values is available using a set of functions that return the current value, all documented at `http://www.postgresql.org/docs/current/static/monitoring-stats.html`.

Topics we will cover in this chapter are:

- PostgreSQL statistics views
- Table and Index statistics
- Database level statistics
- Locks
- Background writer statistic

Statistics views

In practice, a series of views that organize this data are how most people access the statistics collector's output. Reading the SQL source code to these views is quite informative for learning how they can be used. If you have a PostgreSQL source code tree, the file that creates these views is `src/backend/catalog/system_views.sql`; in an installed database binary tree, you'll find them at `share/system_views.sql`; and alternately you can download the source code at `http://anoncvs.postgresql.org/cvsweb.cgi/pgsql/src/backend/catalog/system_views.sql`.

A simple view from there that shows how these are commonly constructed is the `pg_stat_bgwriter` view introduced in version 8.3:

```
CREATE VIEW pg_stat_bgwriter AS
    SELECT
        pg_stat_get_bgwriter_timed_checkpoints() AS checkpoints_timed,
        pg_stat_get_bgwriter_requested_checkpoints() AS
checkpoints_req,
        pg_stat_get_bgwriter_buf_written_checkpoints() AS
buffers_checkpoint,
        pg_stat_get_bgwriter_buf_written_clean() AS buffers_clean,
        pg_stat_get_bgwriter_maxwritten_clean() AS maxwritten_clean,
        pg_stat_get_buf_written_backend() AS buffers_backend,
        pg_stat_get_buf_alloc() AS buffers_alloc;
```

As you can see, this view is just a thin wrapper around the set of functions that each return the individual statistics counters in this area. The rest of the statistics views are similarly constructed. In these systems, views are a useful way to learn how to build queries that execute against the system catalogs to dig information out of them. The exact way the statistics work is valuable to understand because sometimes the view doesn't provide exactly the information you'd like to see, and you may have to go directly to the counters to get what you really want. This was the case in the *Autovacuum triggering* example given in `Chapter 7`, *Routine Maintenance*. It was impractical to use the `pg_stat_user_tables` view because it didn't quite have all the information needed, and the view itself abstracted away critical information needed to join against the other system catalogs needed.

You can find out all the available catalog views using the following query:

```
SELECT
    n.nspname as "Schema",
    c.relname as "Name",
    CASE c.relkind WHEN 'r' THEN 'table' WHEN 'v' THEN 'view' WHEN 'i'
THEN 'index' WHEN 'S' THEN 'sequence' WHEN 's' THEN 'special' END as
"Type",
    r.rolname as "Owner"
FROM pg_catalog.pg_class c
    JOIN pg_catalog.pg_roles r ON r.oid = c.relowner
    LEFT JOIN pg_catalog.pg_namespace n ON n.oid = c.relnamespace
WHERE c.relkind IN ('v','')
    AND n.nspname = 'pg_catalog'
    AND n.nspname !~ '^pg_toast'
    AND pg_catalog.pg_table_is_visible(c.oid)
ORDER BY 1,2;
```

This is exactly the same query `psql` uses to show you view information when executing `\dv` (you can see that by running `psql -E`), except that where that version excludes `pg_catalog` entries, this version only shows views belonging to that schema.

You can actually get the same data out of a much simpler query:

```
SELECT schemaname,viewname FROM pg_views WHERE schemaname='pg_catalog'
ORDER BY viewname;
```

But that's a less useful and educational base to build more complicated catalog queries on.

Cumulative and live views

There are two types of information you can monitor from the database. The main statistics are stored into counters. These counters start at 0 when you create a new database cluster, increasing with all activity related to that statistic. Counters in this category include `pg_stat_database`, `pg_stat_bgwriter`, and all of the other views whose names start with `pg_stat`.

The exact way that you reset these counters back to 0 again varies quite a bit based on your PostgreSQL version:

- **8.1**: `pg_stat_reset()` resets all statistics. Enabling `stats_reset_on_server_start` in the `postgresql.conf` file will reset everything each time the server is started.
- **8.2**: `pg_stat_reset()` resets just block and row level statistics. Enabling `stats_reset_on_server_start` allows resetting all statistics, including the database and cluster wide ones, each time the server is started.
- **8.3, 8.4**: `pg_stat_reset()` resets all statistics just for the current database. There is no way to reset cluster wide statistics such as with `pg_stat_bgwriter`.
- **9.0 and 10.0**: `pg_stat_reset()` resets all statistics just for the current database. `pg_stat_reset_shared('bgwriter')` can be used to reset `pg_stat_bgwriter`. `pg_stat_reset_single_table_counters()` and `pg_stat_reset_single_function_counters()` can be used to reset individual table, index, or function statistics.

It's important to note which fields in a statistics view are cumulative and which are fixed with information like the table name. In order to make sense of the cumulative ones, you should capture that data regularly, with a timestamp, and note how much the values have changed during that time period. An example of how to do this manually for the `pg_stat_bgwriter` data is given at the end of this chapter. Recommended practice here is to track this information with a monitoring/trending tool that knows how to work with cumulative counters, which is covered in the next chapter, Chapter 12, *Monitoring and Trending*.

In addition to the straight statistics counters, there are some live views of database activity that give a snapshot of what's happening right now. These views give transitory information, and while you can compute statistics from them that isn't their primary purpose. Views in this category include `pg_stat_activity`, `pg_locks`, and `pg_prepared_xacts`. Note that prepared transactions, the thing monitoring by `pg_prepared_xacts`, are used for two-phase commit; there is no relation to the much more common use of prepared statements in database applications. Monitoring prepared transactions isn't covered here, but you can find basic documentation about it at `http://www.postgresql.org/docs/current/static/view-pg-prepared-xacts.html` if you are using `PREPARE TRANSACTION` in your application.

Table statistics

Basic statistics about each table in your database are available in the `pg_stat_all_tables` view. Since you probably don't want that cluttered by the many system catalog tables, the data in there is split into two additional views: `pg_stat_sys_tables`, which only shows the system tables, and `pg_stat_user_tables`, which as you might expect only shows your tables. In most cases, `pg_stat_user_tables` is the one you'll want to look at.

The first useful thing you can use this data for is monitoring how well vacuum is working on your database. You get estimated live and dead tuple counts and timestamps for when `VACUUM` and `autovacuum` last processed the table (these are not all available before version 8.3). Information about how to monitor that data is covered in Chapter 7, *Routine Maintenance*.

You can use this view to determine whether tables are being accessed by sequential or index scans:

```
pgbench=# SELECT schemaname,relname,seq_scan,idx_scan,cast(idx_scan AS
numeric) / (idx_scan + seq_scan) AS idx_scan_pct FROM pg_stat_user_tables
```

```
WHERE (idx_scan + seq_scan)>0 ORDER BY idx_scan_pct;
   schemaname |      relname      | seq_scan | idx_scan |idx_scan_pct
  ------------+-------------------+----------+----------+------------
   public     | pgbench_branches  |        3 |        0 | 0.00000
   public     | pgbench_tellers   |        2 |        0 | 0.00000
   public     | pgbench_accounts  |        4 |   144345 | 0.99997
```

In this tiny pgbench database, access to pgbench_branches and pgbench_tellers is being done by sequential scan because all of the data fits into a single data page. The pgbench_accounts table is large enough that SELECT statements on it are using an index to look up values.

What is likely more interesting is exactly how many tuples/rows were actually processed by these scans. This example omits the schema name to make it easier to fit here, and note that it and the previous code have been rounded for better display; they will show more numeric precision when you run these queries:

```
pgbench=# SELECT relname,seq_tup_read,idx_tup_fetch,cast(idx_tup_fetch
AS numeric) / (idx_tup_fetch + seq_tup_read) AS idx_tup_pct FROM
pg_stat_user_tables WHERE (idx_tup_fetch + seq_tup_read)>0 ORDER BY
idx_tup_pct;
      relname      | seq_tup_read | idx_tup_fetch | idx_tup_pct
  -----------------+--------------+---------------+------------
   pgbench_branches |            3 |             0 | 0.00000
   pgbench_tellers  |           20 |             0 | 0.00000
   pgbench_accounts |       400000 |        144345 | 0.26517
```

Here, you can see that each of the four sequential scans shown in the preceding example likely accessed 100,000 tuples each to reach this total. They could easily have had more of an impact on the database than the 144345 index scans, even though there were only four of them. Both the number of scans and how many total tuples each fetched are interesting numbers to monitor, as they suggest both how many queries run and the total volume executed by them.

A similar query worth monitoring is how often HOT is being used to update rows, instead of a less efficient regular update:

```
pgbench=# SELECT relname,n_tup_upd,n_tup_hot_upd,cast(n_tup_hot_upd AS
numeric) / n_tup_upd AS hot_pct FROM pg_stat_user_tables WHERE n_tup_upd>0
ORDER BY hot_pct;
      relname      | n_tup_upd | n_tup_hot_upd | hot_pct
  -----------------+-----------+---------------+--------
   pgbench_accounts |     28142 |         26499 | 0.94161
   pgbench_branches |     28142 |         28142 | 1.00000
   pgbench_tellers  |     28142 |         28142 | 1.00000
```

These numbers are a bit different in that n_tup_upd is already a total that n_tup_hot_upd is a subset of; you don't need to add them together. In this example, almost all of the updates being done are using HOT, which is what you'd like to see for best UPDATE performance. This percentage is particularly valuable to monitor when doing initial testing of your database, to confirm whether or not you are satisfying the conditions HOT kicks in for.

A final useful derived view is to consider the INSERT/UPDATE/DELETE characteristics of your tables:

```
pgbench=# SELECT relname,cast(n_tup_ins AS numeric) / (n_tup_ins +
n_tup_upd + n_tup_del) AS ins_pct,cast(n_tup_upd AS numeric) / (n_tup_ins +
n_tup_upd + n_tup_del) AS upd_pct, cast(n_tup_del AS numeric) / (n_tup_ins
+ n_tup_upd + n_tup_del) AS del_pct FROM pg_stat_user_tables ORDER BY
relname;
      relname      | ins_pct | upd_pct | del_pct
-------------------+---------+---------+--------
 pgbench_accounts  | 0.78038 | 0.21961 | 0.00000
 pgbench_branches  | 0.00003 | 0.99996 | 0.00000
 pgbench_history   | 1.00000 | 0.00000 | 0.00000
 pgbench_tellers   | 0.00035 | 0.99964 | 0.00000
```

This confirms that pgbench_history is what's sometimes called an append-only table —one that is inserted into but never updated or deleted from. It also suggests that pgbench_branches and pgbench_tellers are being heavily thrashed around with updates relative to insertions, which can be valuable for determining what tables are likely to need periodic REINDEX operations. You can use the deletion percentage figure for a similar purpose, finding tables that are likely to have large number of sparse data or index blocks that you might need an operation like CLUSTER to fully clean up after.

Table I/O

In addition to the operation statistic counts, there are also a set of counters in the database that concentrate on physical I/O in pg_statio_user_tables (with all/system variations, too). The first pair of fields monitor use of the shared_buffers structure that caches table data, which is called the heap in this context. When a read happens, the database distinguishes between whether that read could be satisfied using a block already in the database buffer cache (a heap block hit), or whether it required an OS read to satisfy:

```
pgbench=# SELECT relname,cast(heap_blks_hit as numeric) /
(heap_blks_hit + heap_blks_read) AS hit_pct,heap_blks_hit,heap_blks_read
FROM pg_statio_user_tables WHERE (heap_blks_hit + heap_blks_read)>0 ORDER
```

```
BY hit_pct;
        relname     | hit_pct | heap_blks_hit | heap_blks_read
-----------------+---------+---------------+---------------
  pgbench_accounts | 0.98708 |        245298 |           3210
  pgbench_history  | 0.99362 |         28499 |            183
  pgbench_tellers  | 0.99983 |         61091 |             10
  pgbench_branches | 0.99987 |         80176 |             10
```

This is a well cached database; almost none of the reads require actual disk I/O.

 Not all heap block reads actually turn into physical disk I/O; they might instead read the data from the OS cache. Currently the database doesn't have any idea which read happens. But it is possible to monitor this using the DTrace on OS that supports it using the probes available in PostgreSQL.

A similar query shows all of the disk I/O for every index in this table:

```
pgbench=# SELECT relname,cast(idx_blks_hit as numeric) / (idx_blks_hit
+ idx_blks_read) AS hit_pct,idx_blks_hit,idx_blks_read FROM
pg_statio_user_tables WHERE (idx_blks_hit + idx_blks_read)>0 ORDER BY
hit_pct;
        relname     | hit_pct | idx_blks_hit | idx_blks_read
-----------------+---------+--------------+--------------
  pgbench_branches | 0.33333 |            1 |             2
  pgbench_tellers  | 0.33333 |            1 |             2
  pgbench_accounts | 0.99945 |       405206 |           221
```

You don't see `pgbench_history` in the preceding example because it has no indexes.

The table I/O statistics also include counters for I/O related to oversized data stored using the database's TOAST scheme. If your system includes toasted data, you need to account for those reads and writes when computing the total read load associated with a table and its indexes. The three main components to reading blocks in the table (as opposed to the index) in this situation the table blocks, the TOAST blocks, and the TOAST index blocks should be aggregated together into a total:

```
SELECT *,
    (heap_blks_read + toast_blks_read + tidx_blks_read) AS
total_blks_read,
    (heap_blks_hit + toast_blks_hit + tidx_blks_hit) AS total_blks_hit
    FROM pg_statio_user_tables;
```

The hit ratio for that total should be the figure you follow. Since that approach works fine for non-TOAST tables, the TOAST parts will just be zero—always including the TOAST figures is a good habit to adopt.

 PostgreSQL does not allow a single tuple to span around multiple pages (by default 8K). That's mean its impossible to add tuple with very large column data. To overcome this PostgreSQL divide the tuple into multiple physical rows. This is called TOAST tables (**The Oversized-Attribute Storage Technique**). The complete detail can be found at official documentation at `https://www.postgresql.org/docs/current/static/storage-toast.html`.

Index statistics

There are a parallel set of statistics to the table ones that break down activity for each individual index. `pg_stat_user_indexes` also has system/all versions available, and it gives information about how many index scans were done and the rows returned by them.

The naming of the fields in this view are more complicated to distinguish between though. Two fields that look similar are subtly different:

- `idx_tup_read`: Number of index entries returned by index scans.
- `idx_tup_fetch`: Number of live table rows fetched by simple index scans using that index. This number will often be a bit smaller than the `idx_tup_read` value because it won't include dead or not yet committed rows in its count. In addition, the use of *simple* here means that the index access was not a bitmap index scan. When those execute, there are at least two indexes involved. That makes it impossible to properly account for what index was responsible for a particular row being fetched. The server therefore doesn't include it in this total for any index, instead only incrementing the index tuple fetch figure for the table as a whole instead.

Because there are so many situations where `idx_tup_fetch` isn't incremented, if you want to track how heavily an index is being used from the system loading performance, `idx_tup_read` provides the better statistic.

One interesting figure you can derive from this data is how many rows this index scan returns on average, given how the index is being used:

```
pgbench=# SELECT indexrelname,cast(idx_tup_read AS numeric) / idx_scan
AS avg_tuples,idx_scan,idx_tup_read FROM pg_stat_user_indexes WHERE
idx_scan > 0;
         indexrelname     | avg_tuples | idx_scan | idx_tup_read
--------------------------+------------+----------+--------------
 pgbench_accounts_pkey |   1.01016  |  200629  |      202668
```

This shows that pgbench is only grabbing a single row most of the time, which is unsurprising for a primary key. The small amount avg_tuples here is greater than 1.0; this reflects the occasional time a dead row was scanned. This average can give you an idea of how often larger index range scans are being used.

The main thing that the counts in pg_stat_user_indexes are useful for is determining which indexes are actually being used by your application. Since indexes add overhead to the system, ones that aren't actually being used to satisfy queries should be removed from the design. The easiest way to find such indexes is to look for low values for idx_scan, which will appear at the top of this query:

```
SELECT
  schemaname,
  relname,
  indexrelname,
  idx_scan,
  pg_size_pretty(pg_relation_size(i.indexrelid)) AS index_size
FROM
  pg_stat_user_indexes i
  JOIN pg_index USING (indexrelid)
WHERE
  indisunique IS false
ORDER BY idx_scan,relname;
```

This specifically excludes indexes that are enforcing a unique constraint, which you likely can't drop even if they are minimally used.

Index I/O

The same basic I/O statistics available for indexes are also available broken down for each index:

```
pgbench=# SELECT indexrelname,cast(idx_blks_hit as numeric) /
(idx_blks_hit + idx_blks_read) AS hit_pct,idx_blks_hit,idx_blks_read FROM
```

```
pg_statio_user_indexes WHERE (idx_blks_hit + idx_blks_read)>0 ORDER BY
hit_pct;        indexrelname        | hit_pct | idx_blks_hit | idx_blks_read
            ---------------------+---------+--------------+--------------
       pgbench_branches_pkey | 0.33333 |            1 |            2
       pgbench_tellers_pkey  | 0.33333 |            1 |            2
       pgbench_accounts_pkey | 0.99945 |       405206 |          221
```

Indexes tend to be better cached than their underlying tables. If they're not, that's another hint that you might not be indexing your data properly.

Database-wide totals

Many of the same pieces of data available at the table level are also summarized per database. You can get the following information out of `pg_stat_database` and use it in similar ways to `pg_stat_user_tables` and `pg_statio_user_tables`:

```
SELECT datname,blks_read,blks_hit,tup_returned,tup_fetched,tup_inserted
,tup_updated,tup_deleted FROM pg_stat_database;
```

In addition, there are some useful transaction commit statistics available, as well as a count of the total active client backend connections active for each database:

```
SELECT datname,numbackends,xact_commit,xact_rollback from
pg_stat_database;
```

Connections and activity

`pg_stat_activity` provides a way to get a snapshot of what every client on the server is currently doing. Because it includes a process ID, on UNIX-like systems `pg_stat_activity` is also useful to line up with information collected at the OS level by utilities such as `top` or `ps`.

The simplest thing to do with this view is to count how many client backends are currently active:

```
pgbench=# SELECT count(*) FROM pg_stat_activity WHERE NOT
procpid=pg_backend_pid();
  count
-------
    4
```

As the query itself will normally appear in the results, that's filtered out by looking up its process ID and excluding it. This is a good practice to get into queries against this view. This total gives you an idea how close you are to reaching the server's `max_connections` at any time, and monitoring a high-water mark for its value is a good practice to let you know when you're likely to exceed it.

You can use `pg_stat_activity` to see how long a backend has been running and whether it's waiting for anything right now:

```
pgbench=# SELECT procpid,waiting,current_timestamp -
least(query_start,xact_start) AS runtime,substr(current_query,1,25) AS
current_query FROM pg_stat_activity WHERE NOT procpid=pg_backend_pid();
 procpid | waiting |      runtime      |       current_query
---------+---------+------------------+---------------------------
   30302 | f       | 00:00:00.006102  | SELECT abalance FROM pgbe
   30303 | f       | 00:00:00.000928  | <IDLE>
   30304 | f       | -00:00:00.000376 | <IDLE>
   30305 | f       | 00:00:00.000144  | SELECT abalance FROM pgbe
```

This shows a couple of common tricks to get output from `pg_stat_activity` down to a manageable set. In addition to blocking the query itself, the very large query text is cut down to a reasonable size to fit on the screen.

This example also demonstrates two issues that you can run into that aren't so easy to fix. One is that when a backend client has stopped doing work, it will appear as either `<IDLE>` or `<IDLE> in transaction`. In either case, you cannot tell what that client was doing just before becoming idle, so once it's reached an idle state you have limited ability to figure out how it got there.

The second issue you're much less likely to run into is the negative `runtime` shown in one of the rows in the preceding example. The PostgreSQL system time functions that `current_timestamp` belongs to return the time of the current transaction for the client asking for the information. If someone else starts a session after yours, but before you run the query against `pg_stat_activity`, they can have a transaction or query start after what your client believes to be the current time. It's possible to get the true system time instead using the `timeofday()` function. Given that this returns a string instead of a true timestamp that you can further manipulate, it normally isn't worth the effort to avoid this rare situation. In most cases, you should be more interested in long-running transactions instead of just started ones anyway.

PostgreSQL 10 introduces a new feature that allows you to monitor waiting events by the `wait_event_type` field of the `pg_stat_activity` system view.

As we can see in the official documentation, possible values are as follows:

- `LWLocks`: The backend is waiting for a lightweight lock. Each such lock protects a particular data structure in shared memory. `wait_event` will contain a name identifying the purpose of the lightweight lock. (Some locks have specific names; others are part of a group of locks each with a similar purpose.)
- `Lock`: The backend is waiting for a heavyweight lock. Heavyweight locks, also known as manager locks or simply locks, primarily protect SQL-visible objects such as tables. However, they are also used to ensure mutual exclusion for certain internal operations such as relation extension. `wait_event` will identify the type of lock awaited.
- `BufferPin`: The server process is waiting to access a data buffer during a period when no other process can be examining that buffer. Buffer pin waits can be protracted if another process holds an open cursor which last read data from the buffer in question.
- `Activity`: The server process is idle. This is used by system processes waiting for activity in their main processing loop. `wait_event` will identify the specific wait point.
- `Extension`: The server process is waiting for activity in an extension module. This category is useful for modules to track custom waiting points.
- `Client`: The server process is waiting for some activity on a socket from user applications, and the server expects something to happen that is independent from its internal processes. `wait_event` will identify the specific wait point.
- `IPC`: The server process is waiting for some activity from another process in the server. `wait_event` will identify the specific wait point.
- `Timeout`: The server process is waiting for a timeout to expire. `wait_event` will identify the specific wait point.
- `IO`: The server process is waiting for a IO to complete. `wait_event` will identify the specific wait point.

Here is an example:

```
Trasaction 1:

pgbench=# BEGIN;
pgbench=# update test_like set field_text = '';
UPDATE 4

Trasaction 2:
pgbench=# BEGIN
```

```
pgbench=# update test_like set field_text = '';
```

```
pgbench=# SELECT query, wait_event_type, wait_event
    FROM pg_stat_activity WHERE wait_event is NOT NULL;
```

Query	wait_event_type	wait_event
update test_like set field_text = '';	Lock	transactionid
update test_like set field_text = '';	Client	ClientRead

Locks

The MVCC model used in PostgreSQL makes locks less of an issue than in some other databases. However, high performance applications still need to be careful to minimize how often they take stronger locks, and performance tuning work will regularly require looking for situations where locking behavior is a bottleneck.

The details of how locking works in the database is described extensively at
`http://www.postgresql.org/docs/current/static/explicit-locking.html`.

The other useful manual section is the description of the `pg_locks` view that lets you see all the active locks in the database, refer
to `http://www.postgresql.org/docs/current/static/view-pg-locks.html`.

As there are far too many details involved in locking to cover all of them in this chapter, consider those sections of the documentation required reading in addition to what's here. This section will mainly present how to work with `pg_locks` and examples of what sort of information you'll actually see in there. All of these are locks generated by running the standard and select-only `pgbench` tests.

Virtual transactions

One bit that isn't really clear from the documentation is how the database internally handles assignment of transaction identification numbers, called **transaction IDs** or simply XIDs. And you can't easily decode the `pg_locks` information without knowing some trivia here.

Every statement in PostgreSQL executes within a transaction, either explicit or implied. If you want a transaction to span multiple statements, you put it into a transaction block using the BEGIN statement. Giving something an XID in PostgreSQL has some overhead. For example, each one of them is assigned its own space in the database commit logs, stored in the pg_xact directory.

As that involves several types of work including an eventual disk write; this is somewhat expensive. And simple read-only statements, like many SELECT statements, don't really need a transaction ID anyway. Starting in PostgreSQL 8.3, an optimization was added to avoid this overhead when it's not needed, using what's referred to inside the code as *lazy XID allocation*. Transactions are now assigned a real transaction ID, what the pg_locks documentation calls a *permanent ID*, only when they modify a database row. Read-only transactions are never given one.

However, the transaction ID number is what's used to implement transactions waiting on one another for a lock, the information shown in pg_locks. In order to allow this, the lazy allocation scheme also introduced the concept of a virtual transaction ID. These are allocated using a less permanent naming scheme, one that doesn't involve writing the transaction information to disk.

As many applications have far more read-only SELECT statements than ones that modify rows, in addition to reducing disk writes, this optimization significantly reduces the rate at which real transaction IDs are used up within the database. The database has to do some extensive transaction ID wrap around cleanup periodically, as described in Chapter 7, *Routine Maintenance*. Reducing the burn rate of transaction IDs using lazy allocation, preferring virtual XIDs if you can avoid allocating a real one, lowers how often that happens too.

With that background, this somewhat brief statement from the documentation is worth highlighting:

> *"Every transaction holds an exclusive lock on its virtual transaction ID for its entire duration. If a permanent ID is assigned to the transaction (which normally happens only if the transaction changes the state of the database), it also holds an exclusive lock on its permanent transaction ID until it ends. When one transaction finds it necessary to wait specifically for another transaction, it does so by attempting to acquire share lock on the other transaction ID (either virtual or permanent ID depending on the situation). That will succeed only when the other transaction terminates and releases its locks."*

Understanding the way this mechanism for waiting on another transaction ID, either permanent or virtual, works is critical to finding and resolving locking issues in an application. And the way transactions wait for other transactions isn't always just a simple pairing, even though it's displayed as such by the locks display. You can actually end up with more of a tree structure instead, where transaction A is waiting for B, while B is waiting for C.

Decoding lock information

The information provided by `pg_locks` is very basic. In order to understand what it means in more real-world terms, you would want to match its data against several system catalog tables, as well as the activity information for the query. Here's an example showing how to relate this view against the most popular ones to join it against:

```
SELECT
  locktype,
  virtualtransaction,
  transactionid,
  nspname,
  relname,
  mode,
  granted,
  cast(date_trunc('second',query_start) AS timestamp) AS query_start,
  substr(current_query,1,25) AS query
FROM
  pg_locks
    LEFT OUTER JOIN pg_class ON (pg_locks.relation = pg_class.oid)
    LEFT OUTER JOIN pg_namespace ON (pg_namespace.oid =
pg_class.relnamespace),
    pg_stat_activity
  WHERE
    NOT pg_locks.pid=pg_backend_pid() AND
    pg_locks.pid=pg_stat_activity.procpid;
```

Note that the way this query discovers table relation names will only produce results for tables in the currently connected database; they will be blank for locks held against tables in other databases.

You might want to turn the query or transaction start time into a time interval relative to now, similarly to how `runtime` is computed in the `pg_stat_activity` example in the previous section.

There are two extremely common entries you'll see in `pg_locks`. Queries that are accessing a table will obtain a shared lock on that relation, which prevents anyone else from obtaining an exclusive lock on it:

```
locktype            | relation
virtualtransaction  | 2/2478876
transactionid       |
nspname             | public
relname             | pgbench_accounts
mode                | AccessShareLock
granted             | t
query_start         | 2010-04-11 22:44:47
query               | SELECT abalance FROM pgbe
```

And queries will lock their own virtual transaction IDs, which is what queries that haven't needed to get a real transaction ID yet are assigned:

```
locktype            | virtualxid
virtualtransaction  | 2/2478876
transactionid       |
nspname             |
relname             |
mode                | ExclusiveLock
granted             | t
query_start         | 2010-04-11 22:44:47
query               | SELECT abalance FROM pgbe
```

When you run a more complicated query that needs a real transaction ID, such as an UPDATE, it will be assigned one that it then acquires an exclusive lock on (as the owner of that transaction ID), like the following:

```
locktype            | transactionid
virtualtransaction  | 2/2528843
    transactionid       | 328491
    nspname             |
    relname             |
    mode                | ExclusiveLock
    granted             | t
    query_start         | 2010-04-11 22:47:19
    query               | UPDATE pgbench_branches S
```

If another query has to wait for that transaction to end, it would do so by requesting a shared lock on it; one that was then granted after the transaction finished looks like the following:

```
locktype            | transactionid
virtualtransaction  | 1/1165014
transactionid       | 371417
nspname             |
relname             |
mode                | ShareLock
granted             | t
query_start         | 2010-04-11 22:49:09
query               | UPDATE pgbench_branches S
```

In order to actually change a row, statements such as UPDATE acquire an exclusive lock on the row they are changing:

```
locktype            | relation
virtualtransaction  | 1/1165014
transactionid       |
nspname             | public
relname             | pgbench_tellers
mode                | RowExclusiveLock
granted             | t
query_start         | 2010-04-11 22:49:09
query               | UPDATE pgbench_branches S
```

And then a lock will be acquired on the tuple (the actual data in the row); the following is what that looks like before the lock is acquired, showing an example of an ungranted lock that an application is waiting for:

```
locktype            | tuple
virtualtransaction  | 4/2526095
transactionid       |
nspname             | public
relname             | pgbench_branches
mode                | ExclusiveLock
granted             | f
query_start         | 2010-04-11 22:47:19
query               | UPDATE pgbench_branches S
```

Monitoring your application to see what type of locks it acquires, what it acquires them on, and what it ends up waiting on is a great way to get a feel for how the locking mechanism described in the PostgreSQL manual ends up working out in practice.

Transaction lock waits

Locking performance issues will often be evident by an excess of clients that are waiting for a lock to be granted. If you join two `pg_locks` entries together with a matching pair of `pg_stat_activity` ones, it's possible to find out various information about both the locker process that currently holds the lock, and the locked one stuck waiting for it:

```
SELECT
  locked.pid AS locked_pid,
  locker.pid AS locker_pid,
  locked_act.usename AS locked_user,
  locker_act.usename AS locker_user,
  locked.virtualtransaction,
  locked.transactionid,
  locked.locktype
FROM
  pg_locks locked,
  pg_locks locker,
  pg_stat_activity locked_act,
  pg_stat_activity locker_act
WHERE
  locker.granted=true AND
  locked.granted=false AND
  locked.pid=locked_act.procpid AND
  locker.pid=locker_act.procpid AND
(locked.virtualtransaction=locker.virtualtransaction OR
locked.transactionid=locker.transactionid);
```

This variation looks for and provides additional information about `transactionid` lock waits such as the following:

```
locked_pid          | 11578
locker_pid          | 11578
locked_user         | postgres
locker_user         | postgres
virtualtransaction  | 2/2580206
transactionid       | 534343
locktype            | transactionid
```

These will also show up for virtual transactions, as mentioned before:

```
locked_pid         | 11580
locker_pid         | 11580
locked_user        | postgres
locker_user        | postgres
virtualtransaction | 4/2562729
transactionid      |
locktype           | tuple
```

The preceding examples aren't necessarily representative of common situations; note that the `pid` is actually the same in each case, and this lock sequence is due to how the `pgbench` transactions execute. You will likely want to display more of the information available when analyzing locks like this, such as showing enough of the query text for each activity row to see what is happening.

Table lock waits

Clients waiting to acquire a lock on an entire table is something you should aim to avoid. The following will show you when this is happening:

```
SELECT
  locked.pid AS locked_pid,
  locker.pid AS locker_pid,
  locked_act.usename AS locked_user,
  locker_act.usename AS locker_user,
  locked.virtualtransaction,
  locked.transactionid,
  relname
FROM
  pg_locks locked
    LEFT OUTER JOIN pg_class ON (locked.relation = pg_class.oid),
  pg_locks locker,
  pg_stat_activity locked_act,
  pg_stat_activity locker_act
WHERE
  locker.granted=true AND
  locked.granted=false AND
  locked.pid=locked_act.procpid AND
  locker.pid=locker_act.procpid AND
  locked.relation=locker.relation;
```

Output from this query looks similar to the previous `transactionid` examples:

```
locked_pid         | 12474
```

```
locker_pid           | 12247
locked_user          | postgres
locker_user          | postgres
virtualtransaction   | 2/2588881
transactionid        |
relname              | pgbench_accounts
```

You really shouldn't see this form of lock pop up under normal circumstances; this one was generated by doing an explicit lock on a table and then trying to query against it in another session.

Logging lock information

At this point, you'd probably like a more automatic way to log locking problems than to just watch `pg_locks` all day. There are a pair of database parameters that allow doing that, as a by-product of sorts of how the database defends itself against deadlock problems.

Deadlocks

Consider the following sequence:

1. Process 1 acquires a lock on object A.
2. Process 2 acquires a lock on object B.
3. Process 2 tries to acquire a lock on object A. It's now waiting for process 1 to finish.
4. Process 1 tries to acquire a lock on object B.

At this point, the two processes are now in what's called **deadlock**; each is trying to obtain a lock on something owned by the other. They both will wait on each other forever if left in this state. One of them has to give up and release the locks they already have.

To search for this situation and resolve it, PostgreSQL doesn't wait forever for a lock. Instead, it only waits an amount of time determined by the `deadlock_timeout` parameter. After waiting that long, any process trying to acquire a lock will run the deadlock detector algorithm. This logic inside the database looks for deadlock in the form of locks that lead in a circle, either a simple pair or a more complicated chain. If one is found, the process running the deadlock detector, the one waiting for the lock (not the one who already has it), aborts. If it turns out there is no deadlock, and it's just taking a long time to acquire the lock, the process then goes back to sleep and starts over.

When deadlock occurs, this is always logged. If you turn on the `log_lock_waits` parameter in the database, each time the deadlock detector runs and determines there's no deadlock, information about what it's waiting for is also written to the database. You can use this to figure out which locks are taking a long time to acquire in your application.

The default lock wait time here in the form of `deadlock_timeout` is 1 second. This default is reasonable for deadlock detection. If you want to find and log lock waits, you may want to reduce that timeout, so that you can find smaller ones. There is some additional overhead from that change, in that you'll be running the deadlock detector code more frequently, too. This is why the lock timeout doesn't default to something smaller.

Disk usage

The amount of disk space used by tables and indexes in the database is informative in two major ways. As many database operations have execution times proportional to the size of the table, tracking size over time can help you predict how query time is going to increase in the future. And as described in the database maintenance chapter, tables or indexes whose size change in unexpected ways can indicate a problem with the vacuum strategy being employed.

The basic way to find out how much disk space is used by a table or index is to run `pg_relation_size()` on it. This is often combined with `pg_size_pretty()`, which will provide a human-readable version of the size.

 Other useful size queries include `pg_column_size()` and `pg_database_size()`.

A quick example of how to query this information across all the tables in the current database is as follows:

```
SELECT
  nspname,
  relname,
  pg_size_pretty(pg_relation_size(C.oid)) AS "size"
FROM pg_class C
LEFT JOIN pg_namespace N ON (N.oid = C.relnamespace)
WHERE nspname NOT IN ('pg_catalog', 'information_schema')
ORDER BY pg_relation_size(C.oid) DESC
LIMIT 20;
```

On a `pgbench` database with a lot of work done on it, and thus a large history table, output from this might look like the following:

```
  nspname  |        relname         |  size
-----------+------------------------+--------
  public   | pgbench_accounts       | 13 MB
  public   | pgbench_history        | 12 MB
  public   | pgbench_accounts_pkey  | 1768 kB
  public   | pgbench_branches       | 224 kB
  pg_toast | pg_toast_2618          | 208 kB
  public   | pgbench_tellers        | 32 kB
```

This shows the main issue with this simple query: wide columns that have been moved out of the main table into a TOAST relation are broken out as their own entries. There is a `pg_total_relation_size()` function available too, but it also includes indexes.

As of PostgreSQL 9.0, there is a function named `pg_table_size()` that includes all of the TOAST information in its total, but not the indexes. And `pg_indexes_size()` gives a total size for all the indexes of this table. The actual components break down like the following:

```
pg_total_relation_size = pg_table_size + pg_indexes_size
pg_table_size = pg_relation_size + toast table + toast indexes + FSM
```

Starting with PostgreSQL 8.4 the FSM is stored in a separate *relation fork* that takes up some amount of disk space; in earlier versions that isn't a component to the size you need to worry about. There is a way to ask `pg_relation_size()` for the FSM size, but this is ignored in the examples here, as something not particularly useful to track.

This query uses the new functions to display the TOAST and index sizes:

```sql
SELECT
  nspname,
  relname,
  relkind as "type",
  pg_size_pretty(pg_table_size(C.oid)) AS size,
  pg_size_pretty(pg_indexes_size(C.oid)) AS idxsize,
  pg_size_pretty(pg_total_relation_size(C.oid)) as "total"
FROM pg_class C
LEFT JOIN pg_namespace N ON (N.oid = C.relnamespace)
WHERE nspname NOT IN ('pg_catalog', 'information_schema') AND
  nspname !~ '^pg_toast' AND
  relkind IN ('r','i')
ORDER BY pg_total_relation_size(C.oid) DESC
LIMIT 20;
```

In earlier versions, you can compute the TOAST total or the index total manually:

```
SELECT
  nspname,
  C.relname,
  C.relkind as "type",
  pg_size_pretty(pg_relation_size(C.oid)) AS size,
  pg_size_pretty(
    CASE when C.reltoastrelid > 0 THEN
pg_relation_size(C.reltoastrelid) ELSE 0 END +
    CASE when T.reltoastidxid > 0 THEN
pg_relation_size(T.reltoastidxid) ELSE 0 END
      ) AS toast,
  pg_size_pretty(cast(
    (SELECT sum(pg_relation_size(I.indexrelid))
     FROM pg_index I WHERE I.indrelid = C.oid)
     AS int8)) AS idxsize,
  pg_size_pretty(pg_total_relation_size(C.oid)) as "total"
    FROM pg_class C
LEFT JOIN pg_namespace N ON (N.oid = C.relnamespace)
LEFT OUTER JOIN pg_class T ON (C.reltoastrelid=T.oid)
WHERE nspname NOT IN ('pg_catalog', 'information_schema') AND
  nspname !~ '^pg_toast' AND
  C.relkind IN ('r','i')
ORDER BY pg_total_relation_size(C.oid) DESC
LIMIT 20;
```

As this gives the same results as the 9.0 specific version, if you have to support older versions too this is the preferred way to compute disk space use.

Buffer, background writer, and checkpoint activity

Monitoring gross activity in the database buffer cache was very difficult until PostgreSQL 8.3, where the `pg_stat_bgwriter` view was introduced. This allows tracking the general flow of every data page buffer that goes into or out of the cache, along with statistics about the related checkpoint process responsible for much of that. Some questions you can answer with this data include the following:

- What percentage of the time are checkpoints being requested based on activity instead of time passing?

- How much data does the average checkpoint write?
- What percentage of the data being written out happens from checkpoints and backends, respectively?

It's possible to compute these numbers easily enough right from the view. The only additional piece needed is the block size needed to hold a single buffer, available as one of the internal settings exposed in pg_settings or current_setting as the block_size parameter:

```
pgbench=#
SELECT
  (100 * checkpoints_req) / (checkpoints_timed + checkpoints_req)
    AS checkpoints_req_pct,
  pg_size_pretty(buffers_checkpoint * block_size / (checkpoints_timed +
checkpoints_req))
    AS avg_checkpoint_write,
  pg_size_pretty(block_size * (buffers_checkpoint + buffers_clean +
buffers_backend)) AS total_written,
  100 * buffers_checkpoint / (buffers_checkpoint + buffers_clean +
buffers_backend) AS checkpoint_write_pct,
  100 * buffers_backend / (buffers_checkpoint + buffers_clean +
buffers_backend) AS backend_write_pct,
  *
  FROM pg_stat_bgwriter, (SELECT cast(current_setting('block_size') AS
integer) AS block_size) AS bs;
  -[ RECORD 1 ]--------+--------
  checkpoints_req_pct  | 8
  avg_checkpoint_write | 2829 kB
  total_written        | 24 GB
  checkpoint_write_pct | 11
  backend_write_pct    | 88
  checkpoints_timed    | 965
  checkpoints_req      | 87
  buffers_checkpoint   | 371986
  buffers_clean        | 2138
  maxwritten_clean     | 6
  buffers_backend      | 2750221
  buffers_alloc        | 582924
  block_size           | 8192
```

You can see that only 8% of the checkpoints executed are required ones, which suggests the system has not been active enough to run out of WAL segments before hitting the `checkpoint_timeout` value. The average checkpoint write is 2.8 MB, a fairly small amount. A full 88% of the buffers written out were handled by backend writes, which suggests this system isn't configured very well—more should go out using checkpoints. It's like this because `shared_buffers` is tiny on this system.

A look at the total amount written shows you where these cumulative totals start to break down. `24 GB` sounds like a lot, but without a time period to reference it over you can't draw any conclusions about it. Is that `24 GB` per hour? Per month? There's no way to tell.

Saving pg_stat_bgwriter snapshots

In order for this data to really be interesting, you need to save periodic snapshots of it with an associated timestamp. It's easy to create a table for that purpose and put a first snapshot into it:

```
pgbench=# CREATE TABLE pg_stat_bgwriter_snapshot AS SELECT
current_timestamp,* FROM pg_stat_bgwriter;
    SELECT 1
    pgbench=# INSERT INTO pg_stat_bgwriter_snapshot (SELECT
current_timestamp,* FROM pg_stat_bgwriter);
```

Now you can wait until some time has passed, with a representative chunk of activity; at least an hour is recommended, preferably a day. Insert a second snapshot into that table:

```
pgbench=# INSERT INTO pg_stat_bgwriter_snapshot (SELECT
current_timestamp,* FROM pg_stat_bgwriter);
```

And now it's possible to get a difference both in values and in elapsed time between these two. You might even add the previously mentioned `INSERT` to a query scheduling regime using tools such as `cron` or `pgAgent`. Having two snapshots lets you compute averages in units like bytes/second over time. The following giant query shows a full range of interesting statistics you can derive:

```
SELECT
    cast(date_trunc('minute',start) AS timestamp) AS start,
    date_trunc('second',elapsed) AS elapsed,
    date_trunc('second',elapsed / (checkpoints_timed + checkpoints_req))
AS avg_checkpoint_interval,
    (100 * checkpoints_req) / (checkpoints_timed + checkpoints_req)
      AS checkpoints_req_pct,
    100 * buffers_checkpoint / (buffers_checkpoint + buffers_clean +
```

```
buffers_backend) AS checkpoint_write_pct,
    100 * buffers_backend / (buffers_checkpoint + buffers_clean +
buffers_backend) AS backend_write_pct,
    pg_size_pretty(buffers_checkpoint * block_size / (checkpoints_timed +
checkpoints_req))
        AS avg_checkpoint_write,
    pg_size_pretty(cast(block_size * (buffers_checkpoint + buffers_clean
+ buffers_backend) / extract(epoch FROM elapsed) AS int8)) AS
written_per_sec,
    pg_size_pretty(cast(block_size * (buffers_alloc) / extract(epoch FROM
elapsed) AS int8)) AS alloc_per_sec
FROM
(
SELECT
  one.now AS start,
  two.now - one.now AS elapsed,
  two.checkpoints_timed - one.checkpoints_timed AS checkpoints_timed,
  two.checkpoints_req - one.checkpoints_req AS checkpoints_req,
  two.buffers_checkpoint - one.buffers_checkpoint AS
buffers_checkpoint,
  two.buffers_clean - one.buffers_clean AS buffers_clean,
  two.maxwritten_clean - one.maxwritten_clean AS maxwritten_clean,
  two.buffers_backend - one.buffers_backend AS buffers_backend,
  two.buffers_alloc - one.buffers_alloc AS buffers_alloc,
  (SELECT cast(current_setting('block_size') AS integer)) AS block_size
FROM pg_stat_bgwriter_snapshot one
  INNER JOIN pg_stat_bgwriter_snapshot two
    ON two.now > one.now
) bgwriter_diff
WHERE (checkpoints_timed + checkpoints_req) > 0;
```

The following is what the output from the preceding code would look like during a relatively busy period. This is from a laptop that was running the standard pgbench test for a bit during the period monitored:

```
start                  | 2010-04-09 19:52:00
elapsed                | 00:17:54
avg_checkpoint_interval | 00:03:34
checkpoints_req_pct    | 80
checkpoint_write_pct   | 85
backend_write_pct      | 14
avg_checkpoint_write   | 17 MB
written_per_sec        | 94 kB
alloc_per_sec          | 13 kB
```

Here, 80% of the checkpoints were required because the system ran out of WAL segments, and that matches an average time between checkpoints of around 3.5 minutes—pretty frequent. Luckily, most buffers are written out; 85% were written by checkpoints, which is good because a checkpoint write is the most efficient type to have. Each checkpoint average is 17 MB written out. But if you sum all of the write activity, it's only streaming an average of 94 Kbps out to disk, which is still a pretty low amount. On the read side, 13 Kbps of buffers were allocated to satisfy queries. This balance suggests that, for the most part, the majority of buffer churn was things persistently saved in cache, being repeatedly written out to disk, with little corresponding reading going on. That's typical for the standard pgbench test used to generate the load here because it's always dirtying the same blocks in the tellers and branches tables in particular.

A snapshot for the 46 minutes following this, which didn't have any test running, shows what a mostly idle period looks like:

```
start                   | 2010-04-09 20:10:00
elapsed                 | 00:46:26
avg_checkpoint_interval | 00:05:09
checkpoints_req_pct     | 0
checkpoint_write_pct    | 100
backend_write_pct       | 0
avg_checkpoint_write    | 910 bytes
written_per_sec         | 3 bytes
alloc_per_sec           | 0 bytes
```

Note how the checkpoint interval matches the default checkpoint_timeout of 5 minutes, with none of the checkpoints being required; they're all time-based ones. And the average read and allocation rates are slowed to almost nothing.

The alloc_per_second rate is not exactly the same as the read rate from the OS buffer cache, but it is an interesting number suggesting how often internal buffers are being reused, you can combine a look at actual OS reads with. The written_per_sec number is a complete average for writes to the database tables and indexes on disk. This should very closely match averages computed with OS level tools. You do need to recall that other sources for database writes include the WAL, the transaction commit logs, and temporary files used for sorting. This lets you quantify one component of that mixed write set accurately.

Tuning using background writer statistics

Tuning database parameters related to buffering and checkpoints in PostgreSQL is often considered more magic than science. With regular snapshots of the background writer statistics, it's possible to bring a more formal iterative method to tuning adjustments:

1. Start collecting regular `pg_stat_bgwriter` snapshots so you have a performance baseline. Every time you make a change, make sure to generate a new snapshot point after starting the server with the new values.

2. Increase `checkpoint_segments` until most checkpoints are time-driven, instead of requested because the segment threshold has been crossed. Eventually, 90% or more should be time-based, and the `avg_checkpoint_interval` figure should be close to 5 minutes (or whatever you've set `checkpoint_timeout` to).

3. Increase `shared_buffers` by a large amount, 25% or more. If your current value is less than 1/6th of the total RAM in a dedicated server, try a value of at least that amount. Compare a snapshot after that change with the one from before.

4. When your system is using the larger buffer space usefully, the percentage of buffers written at checkpoint time (rather than by backends or the background writer) should increase, and the total I/O `written_per_sec` figure should drop. If the last increase in `shared_buffers` helped by those standards, return to *step 3*, continuing to iterate with size increases until improvements level off.

5. If the values didn't change significantly, your original `shared_buffers` value was already big enough for this workload. You can either keep the new configuration or revert to the older one; in either case you're done with increasing its size.

6. You should now have `checkpoint_segments` and `shared_buffers` set to useful sizes. If a large percentage of writes are coming from `buffers_checkpoint`, and the average I/O figure shown in `written_per_sec` seems high (or the system is obviously slow with excess writes), consider increasing `checkpoint_timeout` to further spread the checkpoints out. If you do that, start over again; you probably have to revisit `checkpoint_segments` again

 Remember that on PostgreSQL 10 `checkpoint_segments` it has been replaced with `max_wal_size`, the following formula will give you an approximately equivalent setting: *max_wal_size = (3 * checkpoint_segments) * 16 MB*

The key to this method is to recognize that any change that shifts your system towards doing more writes as a part of a widely spread checkpoint is an improvement over writing the same data from a backend or the background writer. Your buffer cache should be filled with data that stays around because it's used regularly, accumulating a high usage count. You might even observe that pg_buffercache is used although that's not essential to this tuning technique. The ideal situation is one where anything that's modified regularly is only written out once per checkpoint, not each time it's dirtied. That's the most efficient approach, and improvements in that direction should correspondingly lower total writes, too.

There is one main downside to getting too aggressive about increasing shared_buffers and checkpoint parameters. When checkpoints end, they have to force all the writes done during the checkpoint out to disk. In current PostgreSQL versions, this is done as a fairly tight operation. If the OS didn't actually write those buffers out in advance, you can cause a checkpoint I/O spike proportional to how much data the OS has cached when the checkpoint ends. That is known to be a problem on Linux systems with large amounts of memory; they can get stuck having gigabytes to synchronize to disk.

If you run into this problem, you may have to tune in the opposite direction, less checkpoint writes and more backend and background writer ones, in order to reduce these spikes and the application side latency they introduce. I have some improvements to this area planned for PostgreSQL 9.1, initially aimed at helping Linux systems using the XFS and ext4 filesystems sync write out more smoothly. It's impossible to do a good job here with ext3 because of the limitations in how that filesystem handles cache synchronization, since it will just write out the whole filesystem cache once the first sync request arrives.

If you're going to try and tune your system as described in this section, make sure you turn on log_checkpoints and monitor what that's writing to the database logs, too. If you see the sync time listed at the end of the checkpoint rise, you may be running into this problem. If so, reduce the buffer cache and/or make checkpoints more frequent to reduce its impact, even if that makes the buffer cache statistics worse.

Summary

It seems fitting that a database filled with data can also produce its own set of data by monitoring its internal activity and statistics. While in many cases it's more appropriate to set up monitoring using prebuilt external tools, as covered in the next chapter, Chapter 12, *Monitoring and Trending*, knowing how to directly query and derive interesting values from the database's activity and statistics collector can prove valuable. And when it comes to troubleshooting system performance issues, monitoring activity and locking data yourself is a must.

The database statistics are exposed using views you can either use all of, or reinterpret by joining with additional system catalog and activity data. Most statistics are cumulative values. You'll either need to track how they change over time with an external tool or regularly reset the totals.

Particularly valuable statistics to monitor include table/index caching and query index usage statistics.

Live activity snapshots can be used on their own, or combined with other process-based monitoring, to correlate what's happening inside the database with the rest of the system.

The locking data provided by the database is extensive but very low-level. You'll need to write your own queries to make sense of what's provided, to search for locking issues in database applications.

Tracking the disk space used is valuable for noting how tables change over time, both for finding disk usage problems and for trending predictions.

The statistics provided by the background writer can be used to tune critical checkpoint and buffer cache parameters in a systematic way.

12
Monitoring and Trending

The performance of your database server is directly tied to how well the underlying operating system is working, and where the performance is driven by the hardware you are using. To fit all of these pieces together hardware performance, operating system performance, and database performance, you need a good monitoring system. Once you're capturing all the right data, software that graphs that is vital to tracking general trends in your server's performance. This can help you predict when you're reaching the limits of your systems capacity and see whether the changes made are effective improvements or not.

Topics we will cover in this chapter are as follows:

- Unix monitoring tools
- Monitoring tools compatible with PostgreSQL

UNIX monitoring tools

The simple performance tools on a Unix-derived system are straightforward to use, and it's easy to show examples of good and bad behavior—the best way to teach how those tools are useful for monitoring. Note that the general background here, and the examples of what to look for, are still relevant even on a Windows system. The underlying hardware, the way the operating systems work, and the resulting performance concepts are no different. There's a table in a later section of this chapter that shows how to translate between the Unix and Windows monitoring terminology.

Sample setup

The server used here is the same one described in the pgbench chapter. For these examples, initially a small pgbench database was created with a scale of 100 (one that easily fits into RAM), and the standard mixed test was run:

```
$ pgbench -i -s 100 pgbench
$ pgbench -j 4 -c 8 -T 300 pgbench
```

This gave approximately 2000 transactions/second. Larger tests with lower TPS values will appear later as well.

If you're using a PostgreSQL earlier than 9.0, you'll have to leave out the -j 4 part of the preceding code to try this yourself, and with the pgbench examples shown later. Versions before 8.4 won't handle -T 300 either, and you'll have to find a number of substitute transactions to pass using -t in order to make the test last for a while.

The sample server has the following as its disk layout for the database directories:

- pg_wal: /dev/sdf1.
- Data: /dev/md0. Linux software RAID 0; individual drives are sdc1, sdd1, and sde1.

You'll need this disk layout background to follow the iostat examples shown in the next section.

vmstat

If you post a question to the psql-performance mailing list, that suggests your system might be overloaded the first thing you'll be asked for is a snapshot of vmstat data. It's the most valuable quick summary of what your system is doing. Because it displays a full system snapshot per line, it's even possible to extract short-term trends from staring at a screen full of data.

Since the output from vmstat is a bit too wide to fit on the page at once, it's broken up into a left and right side for now; later examples will include just the interesting columns. Here's the left side showing a few seconds of heavy memory-limited pgbench work:

```
$ vmstat 1
procs -----------memory------------- ---swap--
 r  b   swpd   free    buff   cache   si   so
```

```
8  0       0 2542248 386604 3999148    0    0
3  0       0 2517448 386668 4023252    0    0
1  0       0 2494880 386732 4043064    0    0
7  1       0 2476404 386792 4060776    0    0
```

The explanations for these columns in the manual for `vmstat` are as follows:

- `r`: The number of processes waiting for run time
- `b`: The number of processes in uninterruptible sleep
- `swpd`: The amount of virtual memory used
- `free`: The amount of idle memory
- `buff`: The amount of memory used as buffers
- `cache`: The amount of memory used as cache
- `si`: Amount of memory swapped in from disk (per second)
- `so`: Amount of memory swapped to disk (per second)

Next, you'll see some examples of how to interpret the `procs` data, and what it looks like when the server runs low on RAM. One thing not shown here is what happens when the server starts using swap. On a database server, if you're using swap at all, you've probably made a configuration error, and should reduce memory usage. Therefore, the main thing when monitor the swap figure is that any value other than zero for `si` or `so` is a likely problem. On Linux, the swappiness setting (covered in the `Chapter 4`, *Disk Setup*) can have a major impact on how this works.

The part of the `vmstat` data that's much more interesting for database performance is there on the right side; this is the other half of the four lines seen previously:

```
$ vmstat 1
----io---- --system--- -----cpu------
bi    bo    in    cs us sy id wa st
24 38024  7975 73394 40 18 34  7  0
48 57652 11701 93110 43 16 34  6  0
36 75932 11936 86932 44 15 34  7  0
 4 96628 12423 77317 39 17 37  6  0
```

Here's what the manual page has to say about the preceding code:

- `bi`: Blocks received from a block device (blocks per second)
- `bo`: Blocks sent to a block device (blocks per second)
- `in`: The number of interrupts per second, including the clock

- `cs`: The number of context switches per second
- `us`: CPU Time spent running non-kernel code (user time, including nice time)
- `sy`: CPU Time spent running kernel code (system time)
- `id`: CPU Time spent idle
- `wa`: CPU Time spent waiting for IO
- `st`: CPU Time stolen from a virtual machine

The various *CPU Time* figures are all given in percentages. By default, the Linux `vmstat` being used here is counting blocks in units of 1,024 bytes, which means that the numbers given are in Kbps. Therefore, the first `bo` figure, `38024` means approximately 38 Mbps of disk writes happened during that time. This may not be true on non-Linux systems; see the `iostat` section in a while for more background about block sizes.

All of the `vmstat` examples here are produced using a one second time interval, the parameter passed on the command line in the preceding examples. All of the counts in its data (as opposed to the percentages) are averages per second over the given time period, so the interpretation isn't impacted by the collection period. It just changes the resolution of the data you see.

The other thing to note about `vmstat` and `iostat` is that, when you run them, the first line they output is a long term one summarizing all activity since the server was started. The snapshots of a small unit of time start on the second line printed. If you're writing scripts to collect this data and process it, typically you need to be careful to always throw away the first line.

As a first example of what bad data looks like, here's the data from the preceding `pgbench` run showing a period where the system became less responsive for about two seconds:

```
procs ----io---- --system--- -----cpu------
 r  b   bi    bo    in    cs us sy id wa st
 2  2    4 93448 11747 84051 44 19 32  5  0
 0  3    0 54156  8888 47518 23 10 53 14  0
 0  2    0  6944  1259  1322  1  0 72 27  0
 0  2    0 12168  2025  2422  0  0 65 35  0
 8  0    0 26916  5090 41152 23  9 47 21  0
 2  0    4 57960  9802 54723 31 12 46 11  0
```

Note the dramatic drop in context switches (cs) for the middle two entries there. Since most completed work executed by the server and the pgbench client itself involves a context switch, those low entries represent a period where almost nothing happened. Instead of tens of thousands of things happening during that second, there were only a few thousand. Also note how that corresponds with a jump in the waiting for I/O (wa) category, and the CPUs becoming less active. All these things are characteristic of what a bad performing section of time looks like, when the system is at a bottleneck waiting for the disk drive(s).

iostat

The data vmstat gives is a total across all devices on the system. If you want totals per disk device instead, you need to use iostat for that.

On Linux, iostat defaults to slightly different behavior than vmstat. When it uses *block*, it means a 512 byte chunk of data, not the 1,024 bytes chunk vmstat uses. You can switch iostat to use kilobytes instead of using iostat -k, or you can just divide all the figures by two in order to get them on the same scale. Here's an example of the same data shown both ways:

```
$ iostat
Device         tps Blk_read/s  Blk_wrtn/s  Blk_read  Blk_wrtn
sda1          0.07       3.29        0.24   1579784    115560
$ iostat -k
Device         tps  kB_read/s   kB_wrtn/s   kB_read   kB_wrtn
sda1          0.07       1.64        0.12    789892     57780
```

Since not all Unix versions will have the kilobyte option available, the examples here all use the default 512-byte blocks, and accordingly halve the block figures to interpret using kilobyte units.

You'll likely find that you need to average iostat data over a slightly longer period of time than vmstat data. A single second of vmstat data is a summary of all the disks on the system. A PostgreSQL database goes through several common phases:

- **Just after a checkpoint**: Heavy full-page writes to WAL, fewer writes to database disks because there are fewer dirty buffer evictions.
- **Between checkpoints**: The previous one finished and the most commonly used buffers have had full pages written. Most are an even mix of WAL and database writes.

- **Checkpoint in progress**: Small to moderate WAL writes; increasingly heavy database writes as checkpoint data is written and starts flowing to disk.
- **Checkpoint sync phase**: Minimal WAL writes because fewer full page writes are likely happening; heavy writes to database disks as all data is flushed out of the OS cache.

If you are looking at the vmstat data, or if you don't have the pg_wal WAL data broken out onto a separate disk, you can't see the balance of the data versus WAL writes change; you just see a total. But if you're grabbing really short iostat snapshots, you're likely to see writes bounce between the WAL and database disks, with the exact pattern depending on where in the checkpoint cycle you're at. You need to combine a few seconds of data (5 seconds is used for these examples) in order to have both types of writes usefully averaged out:

```
$ iostat 5
avg-cpu:   %user   %nice %system %iowait   %steal   %idle
           42.69    0.00   18.07    6.69     0.30    32.25
Device     tps Blk_read/s  Blk_wrtn/s  Blk_read  Blk_wrtn
sda        0.00    0.00       0.00         0         0
sda1       0.00    0.00       0.00         0         0
sdc       80.80    0.00    1286.40         0      6432
sdc1      80.80    0.00    1286.40         0      6432
sdd       77.80    0.00    1251.20         0      6256
sdd1      77.80    0.00    1251.20         0      6256
sde       69.40    0.00    1086.40         0      5432
sde1      69.40    0.00    1086.40         0      5432
sdf     2348.20    0.00   88262.40         0    441312
sdf1    2348.20    0.00   88262.40         0    441312
md0      311.40    0.00    2491.20         0     12456
```

You can see that much of the valuable information from vmstat, such as the CPU statistics, also appears here. But with so much more data here, it's much harder to track trends on the console with this tool than with vmstat.

Since all of the activity relates to the single partition on these disks, there's a lot of redundant data in here. You should also note that many of the statistics for the software RAID volume used here are not very interesting—you have to look at the underlying physical disk devices instead. If you're using hardware RAID, that particular problem will go away, but you won't have any easy way to get actual disk performance information out of that abstraction layer either; you'll just see the summary for the whole logical RAID device. The following examples eliminate all the redundant lines and place the md0 array device between its individual components and the device the WAL is on (sdf1), for easier readability.

iotop for Linux

It's also possible on Linux to get per process I/O statistics, so you can see exactly who is reading and writing heavily, using a program named `iotop`. This data isn't available in mainstream Linux until kernel 2.6.20, and the `iotop` program requires Python 2.5, too. RedHat RHEL 5 doesn't meet either requirement. RedHat has been working on getting the I/O statistics back ported to their mainstream 2.6.18 kernel and working through the Python issues too. By RHEL 5.7, it may be fully available; refer to `https://bugzilla.redhat.com/show_bug.cgi?id=557062` to track their progress.

If you're running on a system with a more recent kernel, as may be the case for Debian or Ubuntu users, make sure to try `iotop` out once you've seen heavy I/O wait on a system. It's extremely useful at determining where the reads and writes causing that are coming from.

It's possible to collect similar statistics from older kernels, a topic introduced at `http://www.xaprb.com/blog/2009/08/23/how-to-find-per-process-io-statistics-on-linux/`, and the `blktrace` utility can be used to profile disk I/O as well. Both of these are more complicated tools to use than the simple `iotop` program.

Examples of good performance

When busy but not overloaded, `iostat` data for this system looks like the following:

```
$ iostat 5
avg-cpu:   %user    %nice %system %iowait   %steal    %idle
           18.54     0.00    9.45   23.49     0.15    48.38
Device      tps Blk_read/s  Blk_wrtn/s  Blk_read  Blk_wrtn
sdc1    1068.80      0.00    15740.80          0     78704
sdd1    1041.80      0.00    15459.20          0     77296
sde1    1028.00      0.00    15377.60          0     76888
md0     5969.20      0.00    47753.60          0    238768
sdf1     989.00      0.00    40449.60          0    202248
```

The `%iowait` figure of 23% is high enough to know the disks are busy, but not completely saturated yet. This is showing 20 Mbps (40449.6 512-byte blocks per second) being written to the WAL and 24 Mbps to the entire database disk array, the latter of which is evenly split as almost 8 Mbps to each of the three drives.

Linux also features an extended `iostat` mode. This produces a large number of derived statistics from the underlying data. Since that's too wide to display here, the first example showing all of the data here has been transposed to swap the row for columns and vice versa:

```
$ iostat -x 5
               sdc1      sdd1      sde1       md0     sdf1
rrqm/s            0         0         0         0        0
wrqm/s        411.8     404.6     396.2         0   3975.4
r/s               0         0         0         0        0
w/s           438.6       442     444.2    2461.4   1229.8
rsec/s            0         0         0         0        0
wsec/s       6956.8    6966.4    6915.2   19691.2  41643.2
avgrq-sz      15.86     15.76     15.57         8    33.86
avgqu-sz      67.36     67.09     62.93         0     0.65
await        158.18    158.85    148.39         0     0.55
svctm           1.2       1.2      1.19         0     0.51
%util          52.8     52.88     53.04         0    63.04
```

All of the values here with a *q* in them (most of what's listed on the following bulleted line) represent figures related to the read or write queues on these devices. Since the queue size doesn't correspond with any real-world figure you can benchmark the device against, it's hard to do anything with that data. The number of read and write requests is similarly useless in a database context. The following fields of `iostat -x` data are therefore not that useful here:

- `rrqm/s`
- `wrqm/s`
- `r/s`
- `w/s`
- `avgrq-sz`
- `avgqu-sz`

It won't be discussed in detail. Trimming some of those out also lets the samples fit onto the horizontal space available.

 Solaris has a similar extended mode available using `iostat -xc`.

This next example is similar to the `iostat` one given previously:

```
$ iostat -x 5
avg-cpu:   %user    %nice %system %iowait   %steal    %idle
           21.51     0.00   11.08   23.75     0.10    43.56
Device rsec/s    wsec/s avgrq-sz avgqu-sz    await   svctm   %util
sdc1     0.00   6956.80    15.86    67.36   158.18    1.20   52.80
sdd1     0.00   6966.40    15.76    67.09   158.85    1.20   52.88
sde1     0.00   6915.20    15.57    62.93   148.39    1.19   53.04
md0      0.00  19691.20     8.00     0.00     0.00    0.00    0.00
sdf      0.00  41643.20    33.86     0.65     0.55    0.51   63.04
```

That's 21 Mbps written to the WAL and 20 Mbps to the database disks, about 7 Mbps to each one. However, recall that the total disk read or write throughput available depends heavily on how random the workload is, which is normally a hard thing to estimate. The `%util` figure, which is by far the most valuable of the derived figures shown here, gives you a rough idea of that by noting how congested the device is to achieve that throughput. In this next example, there's minimal database I/O and heavy WAL I/O, typical of the period just after a checkpoint:

```
$ iostat -x 5
avg-cpu:   %user    %nice %system %iowait   %steal    %idle
           49.35     0.00   22.00    3.80     0.25    24.60
Device rsec/s     wsec/s avgrq-sz avgqu-sz    await   svctm   %util
sdc1     0.00    2649.10    15.01     0.76     4.31    0.06    1.04
sdd1     0.00    2895.01    14.95     0.90     4.64    0.06    1.12
sde1     0.00    2728.94    15.06     0.82     4.51    0.06    1.04
md0      0.00    8273.05     8.00     0.00     0.00    0.00    0.00
sdf1     0.00  103760.48    38.11     0.23     0.09    0.09   23.47
```

This is happily getting >50 Mbps out of the WAL volume but it's still only busy 23.5% of the time. This suggests writes to it are being cached by the disk controller and written quite efficiently. One of the reasons to break out the WAL onto its own disk is because it makes it so easy to monitor this balance between WAL and database writes, and to determine if the WAL volume (which only gets sequential writes normally) is keeping up. Since there are techniques to accelerate the WAL writes at the expense of something else, such as switching to an unjournaled filesystem, the `%util` figure can help you determine when the WAL is the system bottleneck and therefore necessary to accelerate that way.

A final example of good performance involves the database disks. There are some operations in PostgreSQL that can bypass writing to the WAL. For example, if you start a transaction that creates a new table and does a COPY into it, as long as you don't have PITR archiving turned on, that data is not put through the WAL before being written to disk. The idea is that if the server crashes, the whole transaction will be rolled back anyway, which includes deleting the table data; therefore, whether it's consistent or not at the block level doesn't matter.

Here is what the database disks are capable of when running such a COPY, which essentially turns into sequential write I/O directly to the database:

```
$ iostat -x 5
avg-cpu:   %user    %nice %system %iowait   %steal   %idle
           16.39     0.00    6.85   12.84     0.00   63.92
Device rsec/s    wsec/s avgrq-sz avgqu-sz   await  svctm  %util
sdc1     25.60 58710.40   249.09    27.22  115.43   1.19  28.08
sdd1     24.00 58716.80   249.11    27.76  117.71   1.20  28.24
sde1      1.60 58667.20   250.51    28.31  120.87   1.14  26.80
md0      51.20 176094.40    8.00     0.00    0.00   0.00   0.00
sdf1      0.00     0.00     0.00     0.00    0.00   0.00   0.00
```

This is over 29 Mbps being written to each database disk, for a total of 88 Mbps to the RAID 0 array, and even that isn't fully utilizing the disks, as shown by the %util at about 28%. Given that this is a four-core server and COPY is the only process running, a %user of 16 means that about 64% of a single CPU is busy here. The CPU and disks are likely waiting for each other a bit in this situation, and you might have to improve both to significantly speed this up. This example is from a server with a battery-backed RAID controller; without one, it's much easier to run into one of the disk bottlenecks here before the CPU ones.

A final iostat hint: on some versions you can switch the output to use megabytes/second as its units, which is often the easiest to read. The following syntax, for example, usually makes for a good summary on Linux systems:

```
$ iostat -x -m 5
```

Overloaded system samples

To get a more realistic workload, the next few samples use a much larger scale of bench database (1000) and more clients (64):

```
$ pgbench -i -s 1000 pgbench
$ pgbench -j 4 -c 64 -T 300 pgbench
```

This gives about 400 TPS on this server. The following snapshot shows one type of problem you can discover from the vmstat data:

```
$ vmstat 1
procs ----io---- --system--- -----cpu------
 r  b   bi    bo    in    cs us sy id wa st
 3 62 4916 34296 11504 23871  8  6  0 85  0
 2 64 7132 35828 13247 32406 11  8  0 81  0
 4 63 6120 40756 11313 29722 35  7  0 58  0
 0 48 3896 13712  6953 19544 28  3  2 66  1
 0 12  400 25564  2222  3417  0  1 25 73  0
 0  5   44  3700   818  1020  0  0 39 61  0
 1 12   64  8364  1388  1773  6  0 44 50  0
 1 45  704  7204  2133  3883 23  1  3 73  0
 5 60 2912 26148  8677 15774 17  3  1 79  0
 0 62 2376 15900  5648 12084  3  2  0 95  0
```

As mentioned, the spots where the cs figures drop dramatically (while the system was under heavy load) represent a drop in total system throughput. This example is a bit different because the wa actually drops, too; the system is so overloaded that it isn't even generating a full-sized write load. This is typical of when the server is so overloaded that it even stops servicing client work, typically because of lock contention. You can see that from how all the user time has disappeared, too. Also, when in a functional state, you can see most of the 64 clients (as well as some other database and system processes) in either the running or sleeping category. During the worst cs entry here, a mere five of those client processes (the b column) got any run time on the server during the one second interval. This profile is common when the cache on a disk controller has completely filled up, and clients are all stuck waiting for WAL data to flush to disk.

Sometimes the slowdown is purely I/O though, as in the following example:

```
$ iostat -x 5
avg-cpu:  %user   %nice %system %iowait  %steal   %idle
           5.21    0.00    2.80   91.74    0.25    0.00
Device  rsec/s    wsec/s avgrq-sz avgqu-sz   await  svctm %util
sdc1   2625.60   2057.60    14.67    38.79  101.47   3.14 100.08
sdd1   2614.40   2000.00    14.90    57.96  162.95   3.23 100.08
sde1   2736.00   1963.20    14.64    48.50  135.26   3.12 100.00
md0    7916.80   7206.40    10.60     0.00    0.00   0.00   0.00
sdf1      0.00  22190.40    50.20     0.84    1.79   1.34  59.20
```

The first thing to notice here is that the `%util` figure is rounded badly so it looks like over 100% in spots. That's a result of some sloppy accounting and computation, and not anything to be worried about. Next, note that the WAL is only getting 11 Mbps of writes to it. Meanwhile, the database disks are 100% utilized, but are actually processing under 8 Mbps in total (an even mix of reads and writes). This is what it looks like when the database has heavy random I/O. These underlying disks are only capable of about 2 Mbps of true random I/O, and sure enough they aren't doing much better than that even with a caching controller sitting in the middle to buffer and sort. This is typical of the checkpoint sync phase, where a large amount of random I/O has been pushed into the write cache and is now being forced out to disk.

To show some really unpleasant performance, now let's crank the scale up to 4,000:

```
$ pgbench -i -s 4000 pgbench
$ pgbench -j 4 -c 64 -T 300 pgbench
```

This managed 250 TPS, but with very intermittent processing. A particularly bad period looks like the following:

```
$ vmstat 1
procs ----io---- --system--- -----cpu-------
 r  b   bi    bo    in    cs us sy id  wa st
 1 63 5444  9864  8576 18268  4  3  0  92  0
 0 42 4784 13916  7969 16716  4  2  3  90  0
 0 59  464  4704  1279  1695  0  0 25  75  0
 0 54  304  4736  1396  2147  0  0 25  74  0
 0 42  264  5000  1391  1796  0  0 10  90  0
 0 42  296  4756  1444  1996  1  0 10  89  0
 0 29  248  5112  1331  1720  0  0 25  75  0
 0 47  368  4696  1359  2113  0  0 23  76  0
 1 48  344  5352  1287  1875  0  0  0 100  0
 0 64 2692 12084  5604  9474  8  2  0  90  0
 1 63 5376  9944  8346 18003  4  3 20  74  0
 0 64 5404 10128  8890 18847  4  3 25  67  0
```

That's an 8-second-long period of seriously degraded performance. Note the low `cs` counts. The total `procs` figures drop below the number of clients, and that shows there's no user time. These should be the familiar characteristics of all the clients getting stuck waiting for something by now. Here, the cause is pretty obvious; `wa` is high the whole time and even hits a full 100%, showing the server just can't keep up with the disk I/O load here.

You might wonder what that disk load looks like through the extended `iostat` data; here's a similar period:

```
$ iostat -x 5
avg-cpu:  %user   %nice %system %iowait  %steal   %idle
           2.35    0.00    1.85   85.49    0.15   10.16
Device rsec/s   wsec/s avgrq-sz avgqu-sz   await  svctm  %util
sdc1   2310.40  1169.60    14.63    39.85  147.59   4.21 100.00
sdd1   2326.40  1216.00    14.53    71.41  264.60   4.10 100.00
sde1   2438.40  1230.40    14.77    47.88  157.12   4.01  99.60
md0    7044.80  4820.80    11.12     0.00    0.00   0.00   0.00
sdf1      0.00 19040.00    70.31     4.20   15.31   2.10  56.88
```

Note how low the read/write rates are, while still having 100% utilization. This shows another I/O load heavy on random reads and writes. Even without the Linux specific `iostat -x` data, you could also tell that from the combination of extremely high %iowait with low throughput:

```
$ iostat 5
avg-cpu:  %user   %nice %system %iowait  %steal   %idle
           1.35    0.00    0.55   88.99    0.10    9.02
Device      tps Blk_read/s  Blk_wrtn/s  Blk_read  Blk_wrtn
sdc1     252.80   1236.80     2550.40      6184     12752
sdd1     268.80   1377.60     2611.20      6888     13056
sde1     264.40   1312.00     2622.40      6560     13112
md0     1234.20   3924.80     7784.00     19624     38920
sdf1     118.00      0.00     6380.80         0     31904
```

We know that on sequential I/O these disks are capable of much higher throughputs than this. So, when the server is at a %iowait of 89% but only managing to write less than 4 Mbps to the database disks, it's sensible to conclude they are coping with a mix of random read and write requests instead.

top

If you want a snapshot of what your server is actually doing right now, from the operating system's perspective, `top` is the easy tool to run. By default, it will sort the active processes by their CPU usage, and it's easy to sort other ways as well.

When looking at the memory accounting of `top` (which is similar to what `ps` uses as well), you'll find three memory totals given. Both the VIRT and SHR figures include shared memory, and accordingly the total memory percentage shown for PostgreSQL processes is probably inflated by some amount. Basically, any memory touched by the client backend from shared memory will get added to its total. The RES figure is the more useful one to monitor for regular client processes.

The most useful `top` trick to know is the fact that PostgreSQL processes update their process information based on what they're doing, essentially modifying what command line they appear to have been started with. Whether this happens or not depends on the `update_process_title` configuration parameter in the database. Both `top` and `ps` are capable of displaying that information. On Linux, you can see it by hitting the C key while top is running, or by running `top -c`. On FreeBSD, `top -a` does the same thing.

It's also possible to run top in a batch mode, where it writes data for every single process on the system out at some interval rather than just showing a screen full of them. Returning to our example with a `pgbench` scale of 4,000 and 64 clients, here's how you might capture 10 seconds worth of top data at one second intervals to a file, find all the postgres backends, and then pick out the first word of what they're doing:

```
$ top -c -b -d 1 -n 10 | tee topdata
$ cat topdata | grep "postgres: postgres" | cut -f 25 -d " "
$ cat topdata | grep "postgres: postgres" | cut -f 25 -d " " | wc -l
    640
```

The second line there (output not shown) gets you COMMIT, UPDATE, or idle for each line. There's no SELECT in here just because those happen so fast it's hard to catch any of them, which won't be the case for most other workloads.

With 64 clients and 10 snapshots, the expected number of 640 lines are there. You can then count by type:

```
$ cat topdata | grep "postgres: postgres" | cut -f 25 -d " " | grep
"COMMIT" | wc -l
    179
$ cat topdata | grep "postgres: postgres" | cut -f 25 -d " " | grep
"UPDATE" | wc -l
    459
$ cat topdata | grep "postgres: postgres" | cut -f 25 -d " " | grep "idle"
| wc -l
    2
$ cat topdata | grep "postgres: postgres" | cut -f 25 -d " " | grep
"SELECT" | wc -l
    0
```

Now, we've learned something interesting just by using `top` that didn't require any database level investigation: at any particular point in time, this sample snapshot of workload had 28% `COMMIT` and 72% `UPDATE` statements executing. This isn't a substitute for a full query profiler, but when you combine it with the fact that you get process-level CPU and memory information, it's a valuable alternative source of information.

Solaris top replacements

Solaris doesn't ship with `top` or with a version of `ps` that shows updated process titles in the default `PATH`. You can use `/usr/ucb/ps` and `/usr/ucb/top` to get versions that are more likely to display this information. In general, getting the process titles to show under Solaris is more difficult, and there are some restrictions on when it happens. There are some additional notes on this subject in the *Standard Unix Tools* section of `http://www.postgresql.org/docs/current/interactive/monitoring.html`.

The standard Solaris monitoring tool recommended instead of `top` is `prstat`. This utility is fine for monitoring overall system activity, but without being able to display the process title updates it's much less useful than a fully functional `top` for monitoring PostgreSQL.

htop for Linux

One entry in the *build a better top* category is a program named `htop` (another is `atop`). It's usually available as a package on modern Linux systems. In addition to niceties like color, two of its features make it a compelling improvement over regular top for some users. The first is that it shows CPU usage broken down by individual CPU. This makes it much easier to distinguish the situation where a single process is using all of a CPU from when many processes are using a portion of one. `htop` also displays processes in a hierarchy tree format, based on which they spawned. This is a particularly useful way to display PostgreSQL processes.

sysstat and sar

After looking at how useful `vmstat` and `iostat` data is, you might be wondering how you can capture it all the time. The standard Unix system package for this purpose is named `sysstat`, and it's not installed or activated on many systems by default. On some systems, you have to install this package just to get `iostat`. The easiest way to test out if you have `sysstat` installed and working is to run its user interface, the `sar` program, and see if anything comes back. If not, you will either have to install `sysstat` (if `sar` isn't even there) or enable it (if it's there but has no data).

Once it's running and collecting data, `sysstat` collects up data quite regularly, and gives you a broad perspective of average server performance during each day. The following comes from the period when all of the benchmark examples described in this chapter were run:

```
$ sar
01:20:02 PM CPU %user %nice %system %iowait %steal  %idle
01:20:02 PM all  0.02  0.00   0.03    0.11   0.01  99.84
01:30:01 PM all 12.18  0.00   5.36   10.74   0.07  71.64
01:40:01 PM all 13.39  0.00   5.71    9.59   0.09  71.22
01:50:01 PM all  1.29  0.00   0.59    0.30   0.01  97.82
02:00:02 PM all 11.22  0.00   5.36   13.68   0.01  69.72
02:10:01 PM all  2.44  0.09   1.59   47.16   0.09  48.62
02:20:01 PM all  5.89  0.00   2.61    4.16   0.01  87.32
02:30:01 PM all 16.09  0.00   6.85   16.58   0.01  60.46
02:40:02 PM all 13.10  0.00   4.52   10.78   0.01  71.58
02:50:02 PM all 11.75  0.00   4.39    9.57   0.01  74.28
03:00:02 PM all  3.48  0.00   6.42   16.63   0.02  73.46
03:10:01 PM all  0.59  0.09   1.19   18.78   0.02  79.34
03:20:01 PM all  1.16  0.00   0.74   40.23   0.08  57.79
03:30:01 PM all  1.92  0.00   1.28   61.33   0.11  35.37
03:40:01 PM all  0.46  0.00   0.38   18.71   0.03  80.41
03:50:01 PM all  0.01  0.00   0.00    0.00   0.01  99.97
```

You can easily see that the disk subsystem was getting hammered around 3:30 PM, with an average `%iowait` of 61%. When averaged over a full 10 minutes, having an average that high means the server was seriously busy. This period corresponded with the tests on the `pgbench` database with a scale of 4,000, and the time just before that includes building the database and its indexes.

One thing `sar` is quite well suited for is monitoring the memory usage on your server. Here's a sample of its memory report, showing just the left side of the result-the right side shows swap use, which in this case was zero:

```
$ sar -r
01:40:01 PM kbmemfree kbmemused  %memused kbbuffers   kbcached
01:40:01 PM   1726444   6077460     77.88    390696    4831784
01:50:01 PM    420440   7383464     94.61    394620    6093328
02:00:02 PM     14948   7788956     99.81      6388    6971368
02:10:01 PM    375372   7428532     95.19     22916    6603856
02:20:01 PM     16512   7787392     99.79      6788    6989596
02:30:01 PM     14060   7789844     99.82      6972    6999284
02:40:02 PM     15140   7788764     99.81      6604    6980028
02:50:02 PM     16008   7787896     99.79      9960    6982620
03:00:02 PM     15380   7788524     99.80      6176    6997812
03:10:01 PM     14172   7789732     99.82     64312    6866432
03:20:01 PM    352876   7451028     95.48     68824    6646456
03:30:01 PM     27452   7776452     99.65     72428    6600724
03:40:01 PM    356212   7447692     95.44     74944    6552036
```

This shows you clearly that the 8 GB of RAM on the server was under serious memory pressure starting after 1:40 PM. The total RAM free shown by `kbmemfree` went from 1.7 GB to 15 MB in 20 minutes. One of the things Linux does in this situation is shred its buffer cache, which you can certainly see as it shrinks `kbbuffers` from 394 MB to 6 MB in 10 minutes. This also captures one of the known Linux oddities, that is once the buffer cache has been reduced, it's sometimes slow to recover afterwards. Eventually, it reallocates to bring that cache back to the 70 MB range, but growth there is gradual. Even after 12 hours, the cache on this system was still at only 119 MB.

Enabling sysstat and its optional features

It's also possible to get disk I/O data out of `sar`, but this is even less likely to be turned on by default due to concerns about collection overhead (specifically disk space used to save the data). The following is the common error you run into:

```
$ sar -d
Requested activities not available in file
```

sar works by collecting data through `cron`. On RHEL/CentOS Linux, the configuration file that does so is at `/etc/cron.d/sysstat`; it defaults to collection every 10 minutes, but you can make that more or less often by tuning it. This calls the `sa1` shell script, which then runs the `sadc` (system activity data collector). `sadc` is the utility that you pass a flag to in order to have it collect disk activity. So, to enable disk collection, edit the sysstat `cron` job file on your system and make it look something like the following:

```
*/10 * * * * root /usr/lib64/sa/sa1 -d 1 1
```

Here, the `-d` turns on disk data collection. Once `cron` has made its next pass over your system, you'll have the same sort of disk activity saved by `iostat` available in the history.

On Debian/Ubuntu Linux systems, installing `sysstat` doesn't start collection. You'll have to edit `/etc/default/sysstat` to change the `ENABLED` entry and then restart the service before data will be collected:

```
$ /etc/init.d/sysstat restart
```

Graphing with kSar

`sar` is a very powerful tool, and you can get monitoring data out in all sorts of ways. A popular add-on is the `kSar` Java application at `http://sourceforge.net/projects/ksar/` that allows graphing the data `sar` saves. Note that `kSar` can require some local adjustments to work. The outline at

`http://arsenicks.wordpress.com/2010/01/28/testing-sar-and-ksar/` adjusts the way the data is collected to be compatible with it, and that's the most straightforward way to handle its requirements. It's also possible to convert the files after collection if you can't adjust the server settings, by running it on a new summary file generated with the right locate—something like the following:

```
export LC_ALL=C
sar -A -f /var/log/sysstat/sa15 > sardata.txt
```

This will output the `sar` data with the right locale for `kSar` to then read it in.

 Note that it's pretty easy to find `sar` data that `kSar` just won't parse right. Normally, the entries it doesn't like will come from the very first line of data collected during a day. Sometimes, those need to be manually trimmed away with an editor before `kSar` will import the file.

Windows monitoring tools

The monitoring tools available on Windows have a slightly different balance of strengths and weaknesses compared to the traditional Unix ones. You can't easily run them directly from the command line, and there are some additional steps required before any data can be saved. On the upside, the graphing capabilities are fully integrated.

Task Manager

The simplest way to monitor what's happening live on a Windows server is to use the Task Manager, available by right-clicking on the Start bar or by hitting *Ctrl + Shift + Esc*. This provides a similar view to the Unix `top` utility.

Sysinternals tools

Another more powerful option is to download the Process Explorer and Process Monitor programs from the `Sysinternals` toolkit; refer to `http://technet.microsoft.com/en-us/sysinternals/`. Process Explorer in particular lets you monitor the system viewing the process title information and is considered a must-have utility for Windows PostgreSQL servers accordingly.

Windows system monitor

Windows also has a set of tools that provide similar capabilities to the Unix `vmstat` and `iostat` utilities, through the Windows system monitor, originally called the Performance Monitor, and the command line to run it is still named `perfmon`. This utility lets you see live views of system activity that includes functional replacements for all of the OS-level monitoring tools described previously.

 It's possible to disable the performance counters that track disk activity on a Windows server, and they were defaulted to off in the earlier versions than is common now. To check that they're turned on, run the `diskperf` command. You can enable them by running `diskperf -y`.

Here is a translation table that suggests the Windows counters that correspond to the UNIX ones discussed previously:

Windows counter	UNIX equivalent
`Processor\% processor time`	`100% - vmstat %idle`
`Processor\% idle time`	`vmstat %idle`
`Processor\% privileged time`	`vmstat %system`
`Processor\% user time`	`vmstat %user`
`Memory\Pages input/sec`	`vmstat si`
`Memory\Pages output/sec`	`vmstat so`
`Memory\Pages/sec`	`vmstat si+so`
`Memory\Available bytes`	`vmstat free`
`Memory\Cache Bytes`	`vmstat cached`
`Paging File(_Total)\% usage`	`vmstat swpd`
`System\Context switches/sec`	`vmstat cs`
`PhysicalDisk\% disk time`	`iostat -x %util`
`PhysicalDisk\Avg. disk Bytes/Read`	`iostat Blk_read/s`
`PhysicalDisk\Avg. disk Bytes/Write`	`iostat Blk_read/s`

If you are using software RAID or similar abstractions over your disk hardware, you might prefer to watch the `LogicalDisk` figures rather than the `PhysicalDisk` ones listed.

As you can see, the same data is available, with similar names in many cases. Since the database works the same basic way in terms of how it uses the CPU and disk, you can look for the same general patterns in things like context switching and disk throughput as they were shown in the problematic examples section on Windows, too. The main concept that doesn't quite translate is how UNIX computes a specific `%iowait` percentage. Windows administrators usually use the average disk queue figures, like `PhysicalDisk/Average Disk Queue Length`, instead. However, the total disk utilization percentages are often a better figure to monitor for database workloads on this platform, too.

Another useful figure to monitor is `PhysicalDisk/disk\avg sec / read or write`. Measuring how long an individual write took on an average is helpful in determining whether commits to the WAL are happening at a good pace, for estimating if database writes are likely executing with a lot of random I/O, and guessing whether a controller write cache might be completely full.

One thing that is certainly easier to do on Windows is account for performance on a per-process basis. The `Process` and `Job Object` counter have some counters that can be used to track processor and I/O statistics per process, using the `Select instances from list` section when adding a counter. This is particularly useful for separating out database activity from that of other processes on the system.

Saving Windows system monitor data

To replace what's done with `sar` on Unix systems, you can enable logging for the counters System monitor tracks. It's then possible to see historical data for the logs, not just the live charts. The exact procedure varies based on version; Microsoft's guides are at the following:

- **Windows 2000, XP, Server 2003**: `http://support.microsoft.com/kb/248345`
- **Vista**: `http://technet.microsoft.com/en-us/library/cc722173(WS.10).aspx`
- **Windows 7, Windows Server 2008 R2**: `http://technet.microsoft.com/en-us/library/dd744567(WS.10).aspx`

Another useful trick to know is that once you've set up logging on a server, you can save that setup and even move it onto another system. Just right-click on the trace data and select **Save Settings As**. The result will be an HTML file with a list of all the counters you're logging, along with the server name embedded in it. If you edit that file to refer to a different server, or just remove all the `\\servername` references altogether (the default is the local host), you can now load that counter onto another server.

Trending software

It's important to know how all these low-level tools work in order to use the more complicated ones, and, when your system is in trouble, there's no substitute for the really detailed, second-by-second information that tools like `vmstat` and `top` deliver. But most of the time, what people prefer is something more like what `sar` provides a basic summary every few minutes, but with graphs, and if you can integrate in the database statistics too, so that everything is visible on a unified timeline, then you're really in a good position to note trends in your server's use.

Types of monitoring and trending software

One of the things that make this area of software complicated to sort through is that there are several different things people lump under the category of *monitoring*. The major requirements are as follows:

- **Monitoring for service interruptions**: Make sure that all the hosts on the network are working, the databases are up, and the applications are running. This category includes monitoring for things like the database disks filling up.
- **Recording performance data**: Track CPU and disk statistics on the server. Take snapshots of database statistics. Here you might also monitor things like the number of connections to the database server.
- **Alert when problems occur**: You might email out warnings, page administrators, or update some sort of operations dashboard. Alerts might be based on either service issues or performance thresholds being exceeded.
- **Graphing trends**: View the historical and current performance data recorded by the monitoring system.

Each of the monitoring and/or trending solutions you evaluate will provide a different quality of implementation for each of these four major areas. Which software makes sense really depends on how you prioritize each component, and it's common for companies that need the best breed of products in multiple categories here to end up combining two monitoring/trending systems to meet their needs.

Storing historical trend data

One of the implementation details that is useful to understand is how the storage of performance data has progressed. Similar to how `pg_stat_bgwriter` was analyzed in the last chapter's examples, many of the interesting performance counters you'll want to monitor and then produce trend graphs of constant increase over time. The data that comes out of such a counter can be thought of as a series of (timestamp, count) samples. Two important questions to answer are where to store this series of points, and how to query them usefully.

The first generation of trend monitoring software was used to chart network performance data, typically collected using the **Simple Network Management Protocol** (**SNMP**) protocol that better routers and switches published their information using. You might ask SNMP for the number of bytes transferred over a port on a router, then store the resulting time/count data somewhere for later analysis.

A program named **Multi Router Traffic Grapher** (**MRTG**) became the popular open-source solution to graphing this data. MRTG is a straightforward Perl script that can be configured to store the resulting data in simple plain text log files, and you might even push the results into a database instead. Problems with this approach include how to clean up old files, and how to handle a situation where the graphing time scales of the original collected data are not exactly the same. These are not problems that are easy to solve in standard databases that use query interfaces, like SQL. If you tried, you'd discover a constant need to worry about things like sample rate conversion and concerns about how to deal with missing data points.

After fighting with that class of problems for a while, the author of MRTG built a second-generation data storage mechanism named the **Round Robin Database tool** (**RRDtool**). The "round robin" part describes the way storage overflow is managed. Each database is designed to store some amount of history and, once filled, the oldest points are replaced with the newest ones, treading the storage as a circular ring. The implementation also provides a good theoretical model to deal with interpolating over missing data and re-sampling to higher time scales. Many of the current second generation of open source trending tools are built using RRDtool.

Nagios

The most commonly mentioned monitoring/trending software compatible with PostgreSQL is Nagios, which is itself a popular open source project active for more than 10 years now. You can monitor just about everything -OS, network, database, and applications- with either the base Nagios or using one of its many plugins.

Nagios is primarily a monitoring system that looks for common problems and then issues alerts when they happen. You can use it to detect when network hosts have gone down, when the database is doing something unexpected, and e-mail out alerts when those conditions are met. If your requirements include things like "page people when the database disk is running out of space based on this on-call support schedule," Nagios is the first tool you should consider using for that purpose.

The simultaneous strength and weakness of Nagios is that the core of the program doesn't really know how to monitor or graph anything. It relies on a vast set of plugins to provide everything beyond the core. This is really flexible, but hard to get started with.

Nagios calls counter recording *Performance Data*. The data comes in using a plugin and it's written to either flat files or a database like PostgreSQL/MySQL. And then some other tool, originally MRTG, is hooked into Nagios as a plugin to draw trend data. Popular graphing plug-ins include Nagios Grapher and PHP4Nagios.

The main limitations of Nagios compared to the other tools is how much work is needed to set up everything if what you want it for higher-level trending work. You'll be editing a lot of unforgiving plain text configuration files, along with selecting and configuring plug-ins for monitoring, data storage, and graphing so they all work together. It's even possible to configure Nagios so it's more like a second-generation tool, storing its data into RRDtool and integrating with the sort of tools it's easier to build on that infrastructure.

If your goal is a single integrated solution and you need the strong alerting features of Nagios, that might all be worthwhile. Most of the alternatives to Nagios lean more towards trending rather than alerting, and accordingly they are usually easier to set up for that purpose, as well as being more powerful in their base installs. You can do just about anything in Nagios, as long as you're willing to go through the trouble of installing and configuring all of the necessary plug-ins required.

Nagios and PostgreSQL

There are a few projects that monitor a PostgreSQL database and output the results in a way that is compatible with Nagios. The best of these tools in terms of active development and the feature set is `check_postgres` available from `http://bucardo.org/wiki/Check_postgres`.

In addition to the usual database statistics, highlights of what you can watch using this program that aren't necessarily obvious how to monitor directly include the following:

- How close the database is to running out of transaction IDs, suggesting a vacuum problem
- Whether tables and indexes appear bloated from poor cleanup of dead rows
- If any particularly long queries or idle transactions are running
- Checking whether checkpoints are occurring regularly and archived files are being shipped properly to a standby server

Note that `check_postgres` can be run from the command line too, so it's not just limited to use with Nagios. If you find the monitoring report data it generates useful, but don't want to use all of Nagios, you could script actions by running it directly and acting on the results. That would save quite a bit of time instead of starting from scratch to develop a similarly high quality of monitoring points for the database, and reading the `check_postgres` source code can be quite educational for learning how to write your own customized monitoring queries.

Nagios and Windows

While you can't install Nagios itself on Windows, if you do have a Unix-like system it will run on that; you can use it to collect data from a Windows server. You simply install a Windows data collection agent that reports back to the main Nagios system, such as NSClient++ or NC_Net. Setting up these agents is covered in the Nagios installation guide.

Cacti

The second most popular application you'll see used to monitor PostgreSQL servers is Cacti. Cacti relies heavily on web application technology and RRDTool to do its work. This approach, heavily leveraging external libraries but including more features in the core, gives working with Cacti a slightly different feel than using Nagios, from installation to usage.

Cacti is primarily a trending system, and it doesn't do alerting. It generally has a nicer UI and is more powerful for analysis purposes than Nagios. But its scope is limited. Where Nagios aims to satisfy all sorts of purposes moderately well, Cacti focuses on the monitoring portions that require trend analysis (the strength of its RRDTool core), trying to do a superior job in that area.

Cacti and PostgreSQL

Currently the support for PostgreSQL-specific monitoring using Cacti is still too rough and under development to properly document here. See `http://wiki.postgresql.org/wiki/Cacti` for a live document covering what's available.

Cacti and Windows

Unlike Nagios, it's possible (albeit complicated) to get Cacti running directly on a Windows host. It requires setting up a web server, PHP, a MySQL database server, and various Cacti components. Reports about the quality of the result are generally positive.

Munin

Munin is a smaller and more recent tool than either Nagios or Cacti. It uses the same RRDTool data analysis structure as Cacti, with an emphasis on making it easy to create new visualization plug-ins. It can integrate into the Nagios alerting structure. The http://www.postgresql.org/ site uses it in that way, combining a Nagios based alerting system with the more powerful graphing capabilities of Munin. There is a PostgreSQL plugin for Munin that supports the basic server monitoring tasks, but not the sort of complicated derived views that check_postgres supports.

Munin is also one of the easiest monitoring projects to get started with and develop additions to. If you set up Munin to monitor hosts and just turn on all of the recommended host checks (CPUs, memory, and disks), the data it will collect and the graphs it creates will include almost everything needed for basic performance analysis. The same is true of its PostgreSQL monitoring plugin. Set it up, point it as your database, and the default set of data collected will be great.

From the perspective of getting high quality graphs that combine operating system and PostgreSQL statistics into one usable set with the minimum of setup work, Munin delivers the best bang for its buck of the open source packages around, and it's easy to combine with Nagios for alerting purposes helps too.

Other trending packages

There are several other alternates for PostgreSQL monitoring and trending with various benefits and drawbacks.

pgstatspack

A slightly different spin on database monitoring than the rest of the packages listed here, pgstatspack does exactly what last chapter's pg_stat_bgwriter example did: it just saves periodic snapshots of the PostgreSQL statistics into tables for later analysis. The design was influenced by the very popular statspack utilities for Oracle.

The main problem with this approach from my personal perspective fall into three categories:

- Database statistics alone are not sufficient to solve complicated performance issues. You have to collect operating system-level information, too.
- Aggregating snapshots stored in this fashion into different time scales is a harder problem to solve than it appears at first. The reason why programs like RRDTool exist is because they solve that particular problem well.
- Graphing data over time is the easiest way to find trends. pgStatspack provides a SQL interface to the data.

I suspect that many people who start with pgStatspack will eventually end up needing to add more powerful trending and monitoring tools to the database anyway, which makes me question the value of this intermediate step. But it's my perspective; it's not shared by everyone.

If you're the type of DBA who is focused on the database and wants to use primary tools hosted within it, pgStatspack may be an appropriate tool for you. Similarly, if you're used to using similar Oracle tools, having this available may make the PostgreSQL environment easier to get used to.

Zenoss

Zenoss is a hybrid license product that is a bit slicker to setup and use than most of the tools mentioned here. The Zenoss Core is an open source monitoring solution, and the company also has a commercial enterprise version as well. While not particularly popular for PostgreSQL use yet, it is supported and the rest of the integrated infrastructure around Zenoss can be valuable for some environments. Extensions to Zenoss come bundled into a module called a ZenPack. A recently released PostgreSQL ZenPack is available at `http://community.zenoss.org/docs/DOC-3389`.

Hyperic HQ

Another commercial product with integrated PostgreSQL monitoring is Hyperic HQ; see `http://www.hyperic.com/products/postgresql-monitoring`.

One advantage of using Hyperic's products is that they monitor a whole lot of other types of software as well. If you want to monitor your database and application server using the same technology, it may be easier to do so with Hyperic than some of the more OS or PostgreSQL focused tools mentioned here. Similarly, there are even Hyperic plugins aimed at monitoring connection poolers like `pgpool`. Its real strength is letting you see how these various levels of your application fit together from a performance perspective. On the flip side, PostgreSQL support in Hyperic HQ is not always kept current. As this is being written, they haven't even added support for PostgreSQL 8.4 yet.

Reconnoiter

After struggling with none of the other tools listed here quite fitting their needs, internet application and support company OmniTI built a solution optimized for their needs named Reconnoiter and released the results to the world recently.

Compared to Nagios, it's less complicated to set up, it is optimized to use less resources, and has built-in trending capabilities. It uses a standard PostgreSQL database to store its data, which provides some synergy if you're already using it for other purposes, and instead use the RRDtool approach where storage is reused aggressively, Reconnoiter considers using large amounts of disk space for logging historical data at a fine time scale a feature rather than a problem.

As shown in the problem examples before, there are often performance situations that really matter to your application that you can only see if you drill down into second-level data, ones that disappear when averaged out over a longer time period. RRDtool, as commonly used in tools like Cacti, stores limited data at any sort of fine time scale. Instead, the assumption is that, if you're going back months instead of hours, you'll be satisfied with minute or hourly level data. Monitoring with Reconnoiter instead would allow finding a similar period in the past and potentially drilling down into all the sub-minute data it still has stored. For applications sensitive to latency, being able to track down performance issues to this resolution scale after the fact can be quite valuable.

Staplr

Staplr was developed by heavy PostgreSQL website for their own trending statistics analysis. Staplr has proven capable of helping to scale up one of the biggest sites using the database around. It's not in heavy use outside of the company yet and the documentation is minimal. So far, it still feels like an internal tool rather than a larger community project. It is worth looking at when evaluating PostgreSQL-centric trending systems.

SNMP tools

Many larger companies rely upon SNMP for their enterprise-wide system monitoring. There is a very basic PostgreSQL SNMP MIB, but it hasn't been updated for several years as of this writing.

Summary

Attempts to improve database and operating system performance are best done using careful observation, not speculation, in order to determine where the system bottlenecks are. You need to start that before you have a performance problem, to record baseline information. Most production database servers should consider basic monitoring and trending setup a requirement of their early deployment.

However, it is helpful to know the low-level tools too because the longer-term views provided by most monitoring and trending tools will miss brief problems. With today's breed of database applications, even a pause lasting a few seconds could be a major response time failure, and it's one that you wouldn't even be able to see in data collected on a minute scale. Both short-term and long-term data collection has considerable value, and knowing when to switch the detail level focused to match the problem at hand is a valuable skill to hone.

Use `vmstat` on a very short timeframe to get a feel for general hardware and operating system performance. If left running on a slightly longer scale, it can work as a simple screen sized trend analyzer too. Running `iostat` allows you to see the balance of reads and writes to the various disks you've split your database and application over.

Watching the total percentage of time a disk is being utilized is more useful than any queue or transfer total figures for determining how close it is to maximum capacity. It even allows you to estimate the random versus sequential balance of the workload that disk is running. Periods with bad database response times will usually have a high waiting for I/O percentage, a drop in context switches and/or a decrease in the number of processes running. Exactly what pattern appears gives you a clue as to where the most likely performance bottleneck is at.

The `top` utility is both a useful source for performance snapshots and something you can use to save simple performance logs for analysis in special cases. If you're on a Linux system where the `htop` or `iotop` utilities are available to you, these provide even more detail that's quite useful for finding real-time performance issues as they happen.

Historical data can be collected and reported on with the `sar` utility, albeit at a rough time scale that will average out some performance spikes into invisibility. Windows has functional replacements for all these UNIX utilities, particularly if you install a small number of useful monitoring tools.

Nagios is primarily a monitoring and alerting system, but it can be used for basic trending as well. A variety of true trending graph analysis packages are available with various degrees of PostgreSQL monitoring support, with Cacti and Munin as the most popular trending focused ones available.

13
Pooling and Caching

One of the unfortunate limitations of any database software, one that's particularly apparent in PostgreSQL, is that there is a lot of overhead you're paying for, even when executing really simple queries. If you have a complicated join happening, you should be happy to pay the expense of query optimization. But if you're just reading a simple table, the overheads for opening a database connection and waiting for that query to execute can be higher than you'd like.

There are two common approaches for reducing that overhead, pooling and caching, and both are introduced in this chapter. This sort of software is external to the database, is relatively complicated to set up, and its use is very application dependent. Accordingly, the focus here is on general theory rather than trying to show a working example. It's unlikely any one example would translate into your environment very well anyway.

We will be covering the following topics in this chapter:

- A connection pooling technique using different tools, such as **pgBouncer** and **pgpoolII**
- Database caching using **memcached** and **pgmemcache**

Connection pooling

PostgreSQL does not highly prioritize making the act of connecting to the database one that happens quickly. Each connection requires starting a new process to talk to the client, a fairly expensive operation, and things such as the `pg_hba.conf` authentication implementation are optimized for security and flexibility even if this comes at the expense of speed. The presumption is that users will run things for a long time relative to how long it takes to connect.

When this isn't true, which can be the case for web applications in particular, connection pooling is one approach to reduce this overhead. The connection pool sits between your application and the database. It makes a fixed number of connections to the database, typically under 100, and keeps them open all the time. As incoming requests come in, those connections in the pool are re-used. The DISCARD ALL command can be used in a PostgreSQL session to make it *fresh* for a new connection. When clients disconnect, the pooler resets the session without dropping the database connection, leaving it ready for a new connection to use.

Pooling connection counts

The fundamental idea behind sizing a connection pool is that you should have enough connections to use all of the available resources, but not significantly more than that. The right size to saturate the server in most cases depends on the number of CPU cores, how much of the database is cached in memory, and the speed of the underlying disks. Once you've moved beyond the point where the server is busy all the time, adding more connections only serves to reduce efficiency, forcing the server to swap among multiple tasks when it would be better served with a smaller number.

It's hard to predict how many pooled connections to the database are necessary to keep it fully loaded without overloading it. Many users report optimal pooling counts to be between two and three times the number of cores on the system, perhaps more on a system with a large number of drives. A standard iterative technique is to start with 100 connections and then tune the number down from there if the server load seems too high. Prepare to be surprised at how low the optimal count really is; it's probably lower than you'd expect. Even though you might think that your server needs lots of connections to service a heavy load, in reality, once you've saturated all of the CPUs on the server, trying to execute more things at once just decreases efficiency. Almost all of the time, you'll be better off queuing the connections, so that they wait without causing contention and then execute on a lightly loaded server.

There are a few rules of thumb for how many connections constitute too many. On typical UNIX derived operating systems such as Linux, the point at which adding additional connections becomes really ineffective is generally between 500 and 1000 active ones. If many of your connections spend a good chunk of their time IDLE (as shown by pg_stat_activity), you can discount their average overhead to some extent.

Generally, having fewer connections than that is optimal, but you don't necessarily want to add the overhead of maintaining a pool until the server is really swamped. If your connections count is well into the thousands of active sessions, you definitely want to use a pool rather than direct connections.

Windows systems don't scale to as many connections in general, and there's a hard limit you'll run into in most cases too. If you are running the PostgreSQL server as a service, rather than directly from the command line, it will typically be assigned 512 KB of desktop heap space to work with. Since each connection takes approximately 3.2 KB of space, expect your server to run out of space in the heap and therefore stop accepting new connections after approximately 125 of them. It's possible to increase the heap size, but there's a potential that your system will not boot if you set it too high. See the "*I cannot run with more than about 125 connections at once, despite having capable hardware*" entry at `http://wiki.postgresql.org/wiki/Running_%26_Installing_PostgreSQL_On_Native_Win dows` for more information about this limitation and possible workarounds. Generally, the best workaround is to use a connection pooler that limits the number of connections to below this threshold, as this will improve server efficiency too.

From a monitoring perspective, connection pooling is likely to help if you have hundreds or more of connections and you see that most of your system's processors are being fully utilized. Connection overheads will show up as a mix of user and system/kernel time, so expect both to reduce with a pooler in front of the database. If your system spends most of its time waiting for disk I/O instead, it's unlikely a pooler will help you out. Caching might, however.

pgpool-II

The oldest of the PostgreSQL compatible packages used for connection pooling that's still in development, pgpool-II, improves on the original pgpool in a variety of ways.

Its primary purpose is not just connection pooling, it also provides load balancing and replication related capabilities. It even supports some parallel query setups, where queries can be broken into pieces and spread across nodes where each has a copy of the information being asked about. The *pool* in pgpool is primarily to handle multiple servers, with the program serving as a proxy server between the clients and a number of databases.

There are a few limitations to pgpool-II setup to serve as a connection pooler. One is that each connection is set up as its own process, similar to the database, only re-used. The memory overhead of that approach, with each process using a chunk of system RAM, can be significant. pgpool-II is not known for having powerful monitoring tools either, but the main drawback of the program is its queuing model. Once you've gone beyond the number of connections that it handles, additional ones are queued up at the OS level, with each connection waiting for its network connection to be accepted. This can result in timeouts that depend on the network configuration, which is never a good position to be in. It's a good idea to proactively monitor the *waiting for connection* time in your application and look for situations where it's grown very large, to let you correlate that with any timeouts that your program might run into.

pgpool-II load balancing for replication scaling

Because of its replication and load balancing related features, for some purposes, pgpool-II is the right approach even though it's not necessarily as optimal as just a connection pool. pgpool-II supports what it calls master/slave mode, for situations where you have a master database that handles both reads and writes, as well as a number of replicated slaves that are only available for reading.

The default replication software it assumes you're using, and the only one available in older versions of the software, requires you have a set of databases all kept in sync using the Slony-I replication software. A common setup is to have a pgpool-II proxy in front of all your nodes, to spread the query load across them. This lets you scale up a read-only load in a way that's transparent to the application, presuming every node is qualified to answer every query.

Starting in pgpool-II 3.0, you can use this feature with the PostgreSQL streaming replication and Hot Standby capabilities too. The read-only slaves will still be subject to the limitations of Hot Standby described in Chapter 14, *Scaling with Replication*. But within those, pgpool-II will handle the job of figuring out which statements must execute on the master and which can run against slaves instead.

As with the Slony case, it does that by actually parsing the statement that's executing to figure out how to route it. The way it makes that decision is covered in the pgpool-II documentation. This is one of the reasons pgpool-II is slower than pgBouncer; it's actually interpreting the SQL that is executing. But as it enables intelligent routing capability too, this may be worth doing.

pgBouncer

The PostgreSQL connection pooler with the highest proven performance in the field is pgBouncer, a project originating as part of the database scaling work done by Skype: http://pgfoundry.org/projects/pgbouncer/.

Designed to be nothing but a high-performance connection pooler, it excels at solving that particular problem. pgBouncer runs as a single process, not spawning a process per connection. The underlying architecture, which relies on a low-level UNIX library named libevent, was already proven for this purpose in the field; the memcached program uses the same approach. The internal queue management for waiting connections is configurable, so it's easy to avoid timeouts.

And when the time comes to monitor the pool itself, it displays its internal information through a database interface you can even send commands to, serving to both provide information and provide a control console. Simply connect to the pgbouncer database on the port where pgBouncer is running, using the standard psql tool, and you can use the SHOW command to get a variety of information about the internal state of the pool. The console interface accepts commands, such as PAUSE and RESUME, to control the operation of the pool.

Another neat feature of pgBouncer is that it can connect to multiple underlying database servers. You can have databases on different hosts look like different databases on the single host the pool is running. This allows a form of partitioning for scaling upward if your system's load is split among many databases. Simply move each database to its own host and merge them together using pgBouncer as the intermediary, and your application won't even need to be changed.

If you have hundreds or thousands of connections and are out of CPU time, pgBouncer should be your first consideration as a way to reduce the amount of processor time being used. The main situations where pgpool-II works better at this point are ones where its load balancing features mesh well with the replication approach being used.

Application server pooling

Depending on the application you're running, you may not need to use a database-level connection pooler. Some programming models include what's referred to as an application server, an idea popularized by Java. Popular application servers for Java include Tomcat, JBoss, and others. The Java database access library, **Java Database Connectivity** (JDBC), includes support for connection pooling. Put those together, and you might get efficient database connection pooling without adding any more software to the mix. Tomcat calls this its **database connection pool** (DBCP). A longer list of open source pooling software is available at `http://java-source.net/open-source/connection-pools` and commercial vendors selling application servers might include their own pooler.

There are also application poolers available for some other programs, too. It's not an idea unique to Java application servers. If you have such an application level pooling solution available, you should prefer it for two main reasons, beyond just reducing complexity. First, it's probably going to be faster than passing through an additional layer of software just for pooling purposes. Second, monitoring of the pool is integrated into the application server already. You'll still need to monitor the database underneath the pool.

Database caching

The fastest type of database query is the one that doesn't happen at all. There are ways to avoid actually passing queries through to the database that can seem like a silver bullet for scaling at first, even if they're only effective at reducing certain types of load. You need to understand the limitations of the underlying technology to make sure that the non-database semantics introduced by that change don't cause your application any issues.

memcached

Memcached starts up with a block of memory it's allowed to use for caching, one that it manages quite efficiently. Like pgBouncer, incoming connections are handled using the `libevent` library, so that any number can be serviced without timeout issues. The interface to the program lets you define key/value pairs of information that are then stored. Keys can only be up to 250 characters long, and values are limited to 1 MB. The program's popularity comes from how easily it can be used to cache content in a website. Returning to the idea that the best database query is the one that doesn't have to happen, the fastest way to return a database-driven web page a second time is to send a cached copy of it. This avoids both the database query and page rendering.

If you can figure out how to map your incoming requests into keys without spaces in them (which is easy for most website URLs), and how to save the result into the amount of space the cache can hold, memcached will do all the dirty work of keeping the cache optimally filled with useful data, and key generation doesn't have to be hard, either. The robust way to generate this is to use a hash code generation scheme, such as the PostgreSQL `hashtext` implementation discussed in `Chapter 15`, *Partitioning Data*; MD5 and SHA are other popular hashing approaches. This will let you arbitrarily turn long strings into smaller ones with minimal chance of a collision in the generated keys.

While not directly a database technique, using memcached to cache higher-level content can avoid page rendering that would have otherwise required a database lookup. You just need to make sure you have a way to invalidate those pages when the underlying content changes. That's the main non-obvious complexity you'll run into with any non-trivial memcached deployment.

pgmemcache

If you can resolve the page invalidation problem in a more general way, it's possible to use memcached as an intermediary for database queries too. When a user on a website is grabbing their own data over and over, but not modifying it, you should be able to figure out how to cache database lookups related to their data usefully. Then you just need to be careful to throw those pages out if the data is modified.

The way to do that in PostgreSQL is quite straightforward: simply add a pair of triggers for `AFTER UPDATE ON` and `AFTER DELETE ON` for any table you are storing in the cache. If you take care of that, you can use the pgmemcache program from `http://pgfoundry.org/projects/pgmemcache/` in order to handle the routine chores of setting up memcached for storing database information.

 There is a second program with the confusingly similar name of pgmemcached that was a development effort related to PostgreSQL/memcached integration. This project was completed and abandoned in 2008. pgmemcache is now recommended as the program to use here even by the original author of pgmemcached.

This technique is particularly well suited to serving key/value data from a PostgreSQL database efficiently, simply by allocating some memory for pgmemcache to cache the most popular parts. This combination gives the fast response times of a cache for read operations and the integrity and complicated query capabilities of a database, with the downside of a small window for write race conditions while the update/delete trigger is modifying the value in the cache.

Recent releases of pgmemcache have broken compatibility with PostgreSQL versions before 8.4. This is covered in the README.pgmemcache file distributed with the program, and a presentation noting that and other useful trivia about the program is available at http://projects.2ndquadrant.com/char10.

One feature PostgreSQL is currently missing is materialized views, a technique that lets you run an expensive query and save its output for use by later clients who want the same data. You can implement a simple version of that technique using pgmemcache. Consider the case of an expensive daily report. You might run that and update the value in the cache manually each day. Then clients can just ask for that cached result, knowing they'll always get the current day's data with low server impact.

Summary

Large deployments of PostgreSQL systems go through several common phases as the number of database clients increases. You're likely to run into disk bottlenecks initially. These can sometimes be bypassed by reorganizing the system so more of the active data is in RAM. Once that's accomplished, and the system is sized properly so the database is mainly returning information that's in fast memory, it's quite easy to move onto a new bottleneck. One possibility is that you might then be limited by the relatively high overhead of creating a database connection and asking it for data.

When reaching that point, there are two major approaches to consider. You can reuse database connections with pooling, or try and cache database activity outside of the database. The best part is that these two approaches both stack on top of one another. You can, for example, use pgmemcache to reduce database reads while also using pgBouncer to reduce the connection overhead for the reads that still happen. Separately or as part of that, you might also scale upwards by replicating the database or partitioning your data set across multiple systems; these subjects will be covered in more detail over the next two chapters.

Opening a new PostgreSQL connection is a fairly expensive operation in terms of CPU used. Connection poolers keep some of those connections open all the time to reduce that overhead. The connection pool should be sized to just use all of the system's resources, typically less than 100 connections.

Systems with more than 500 clients are very likely to benefit from a pool. Windows systems will rarely go above 125 clients before running into resource limits, making pooling an even higher priority.

pgpool-II can be used for connection pooling, but needs to be carefully monitored for network timeout issues. pgpool-II allows load balancing connections among multiple replicated slaves to scale read-only traffic usefully, when combined with Slony-I or the PostgreSQL streaming replication.

pgBouncer is the preferred PostgreSQL connection pooler if you just need pooling. Monitoring pgBouncer is done by connecting to an internal pseudo-database.

Page and/or database caching can limit the amount of work that the database needs to do.

memcached can be used to cache anything you can represent as a key/value pair, most popularly web pages. pgmemcache combined with database triggers allows caching database lookups with little loss in transactional behavior.

14
Scaling with Replication

Sometimes, when trying to improve database performance, the most practical approach is to add more copies of the data and spread the load out over them all. There are a variety of PostgreSQL projects that replicate data across multiple nodes that you might be able to use for that purpose. Also, high-performance systems tend to come with high availability requirements, plus their respective overheads, too. Learning how to co-exist with your replication software may impact your performance tuning work, even if the copies are not being used actively for load distribution.

Note that none of the mature tools mentioned in this chapter usefully support scaling up for high write volume. The best explored solution in that category is using PL/Proxy, as described in `Chapter 15`, *Partitioning Data*. Write volume scaling is also a goal of Postgres-XC. In general, when we're talking about scaling a database upwards by adding nodes, this is allowing more reads to happen against the same data, but without an improvement in the write speed.

The topics that we will look at in this chapter are:

- Hot Standby
- Streaming and synchronous replication
- Replication queue managers
- Different replication tools

Hot Standby

PostgreSQL has shipped with an integrated standby feature since its 8.2 version. This allows creating a master/standby pair of nodes, where the standby regularly receives a log of database updates from the master. With the currently common warm standby configuration, introduced in PostgreSQL 8.2, this allows a high availability setup where, if the master is lost, the slave can be brought up quickly to replace it.

Starting with PostgreSQL 9.0, it's possible to run queries against the standby server or servers as well. This Hot Standby feature lets you scale up read workload by using a pool of multiple read-only servers. You just need to architect your application so that all writes go to the master node.

Terminology

There are several terms that you need to know in order to follow any discussion of warm or Hot Standby setups:

- **Write-ahead log (WAL)**: PostgreSQL writes information to a series of WAL files, in segments of 16 MB in size, before making corresponding changes to the database itself. If you start with an identical pair of databases, and apply the same WAL files to them, the resulting pair will also be identical since the WAL contains all changed data.
- **Basebackup**: A backup made of the database in a way that includes everything needed for the copy to go through crash recovery and be intact, even if files were changed during the time the backup was being made. This requires using the `pg_start_backup` and `pg_stop_backup` commands, as well as making backup copies of both the entire database and the WAL files archived during the period between when those commands were executed.
- **Point-in-time recovery (PITR)**: If you have a base database and a series of WAL files, you can apply just some of them and then stop recovering information from those WAL files; this allows the PITR feature. This even allows complicated recovery situations, such as alternate timelines, where a rebuilt database diverges from its original history, perhaps multiple times, in search of the best place to recover to before the server is started.
- **File-based log shipping**: If you make a base backup of a server and then ship all of the new WAL files, it archives to another server; that new server can be kept in sync with the original.
- **Standby**: A system with a complete base backup and a stream of file-based logs shipped to it can be a standby—a server with exactly the same data as the original. A standby is kept up to date as new transactions appear (or time passes) and WAL files are shipped to it. A warm standby continuously applies new WAL files as they appear.

- **Failover**: Taking the standby out of recovery mode and turning it into an active server, using what's called a trigger file. In intentional failover situations, you can stop the primary first and make sure all its data has been flushed. In a true failure of the primary situation, this will not be possible. Some recent transactions (the ones not yet shipped to the standby) committed on the primary may not be available on the standby that's now promoted to being a primary.

The important thing to realize here is that the WAL is a stream of block-level changes to the database. You can't filter the results by database or any other mechanism; you can only make a perfect copy of an entire PostgreSQL cluster. The transport mechanism used doesn't know anything about the transactions involved, it just knows how that turned into changes to the database on disk.

Setting up WAL shipping

The exact way you set up replication using WAL shipping varies based on the PostgreSQL version, and a fair amount of additional scripting is required. There are several software packages available that fill in the gaps by providing the components required, including a working `archive_command` implementation, base backup, and node management:

- **2warm**: `http://projects.2ndquadrant.com/`
- **walmgr**: Part of SkyTools, `http://pgfoundry.org/projects/skytools/`
- **OmniPITR**: `https://labs.omniti.com/trac/pgtreats/wiki`

As a primary author of the first of these, I'm not an unbiased commentator on which of these is the best solution to this problem. Getting all of the details right here takes more work than is obvious on the surface, and using one of these packages should be preferred to trying to write something from scratch.

The main tunable parameter to note with basic WAL shipping is `archive_timeout`. This determines how long a WAL file can sit on the master before it gets shipped to the standby, regardless of whether it's full or not. If you want to reduce the window of potential data loss, you might reduce this value to a much lower value. But be careful: this can significantly increase the overhead of processing, network use, and disk use from WAL shipping. The 16 MB WAL files pile up surprisingly quickly if you try to do something such as minimize lost transactions by setting the archive timeout to only a few seconds; that really doesn't work.

PostgreSQL 9.1 expects to remove the need for any of this additional software, by instead integrating things such as the base backup into the streaming replication protocol.

Streaming replication

Starting from PostgreSQL 9.0 streaming replication is possible on PostgreSQL. Once the standby server is synchronized with the master, this new feature will asynchronously send new WAL data over the network shortly after it's committed, in something close to real time if things go well. This replication style is sometimes referred to as semi-synchronous replication. It's not fully synchronous, but the delay between commit and replication will be quite short in most cases; it's typically under a second, something impossible to accomplish with earlier versions. Expanding the database feature set to include fully synchronous replication instead when desired is in progress right now, and is expected to be included in the future PostgreSQL 9.1.

Tuning Hot Standby

Imagine the case where the standby is replaying the block changes resulting from a `DROP TABLE` on the master. If you're using Hot Standby to run queries on the standby, it's possible there's one using that table already running when these changes arrive. The server has two choices at this point, it can either apply the changes, or it can continue to let the query run; it can't do both.

While getting rid of a table is a rare situation, this is just the easiest to understand example from a class of problems where Hot Standby cannot replay some blocks without cancelling queries that expect them to be there. One of the most common sources for such changes happens when you vacuum the master database.

What the server should do when this happens really depends on the priorities of your standby server. There are three fundamental things that you might want to do with your standby server:

- **Prioritize keeping the standby current**: Your goal is to have a seamless, quick failover if the master goes down.
- **Prioritize being able to run long queries on the slave**: One popular use for this form of standby is to offload large batch reports, such as end of day or month summaries, to run on the standby. This should reduce the load on the master.
- **Prioritize minimizing the impact of the standby server on the master**: Ideally, the standby would be completely decoupled from the master, but doing that introduces some potential issues.

The nature of the problems here are such that you can only do two of these three things at a time. The good news is that you can pick which two. There are a few tunable parameters and some techniques available that let you decide exactly how to skew your implementation in regards to these three goals. The parameters are as follows:

- `max_standby_archive_delay` and `max_standby_streaming_delay`: Controls how long a block change from the two possible sources here (a shipped archive file and streaming replication) that will interrupt a query, will be allowed to wait before it causes that query to be cancelled. Increasing these values prioritizes running longer queries, at the expense of keeping the standby current.
- `vacuum_defer_cleanup_age`: Increase this parameter on the master in order to delay vacuuming for this number of transactions. This prioritizes running long queries without cancellation, but there will be higher overhead on the master because vacuum will lag behind its normal activity level. While this only improves the situation with cancellation from vacuum activity, since that is the most common source for conflicts in most normal database use (where tables aren't being modified, only the data in them is), it helps quite a bit.

The expected evolution of the Hot Standby design in future versions of PostgreSQL will let the standby export information about what queries are running to the master. This approach lets the master work similarly to how MVCC prevents this sort of problem from happening on a single server: the system will keep old versions of any row that might still be needed for a running query from being cleaned up. It's possible to do this with the current versions of PostgreSQL, starting from PostgreSQL 9.0, by opening a connection from the standby to the master and starting a transaction before running a long query, perhaps using the `dblink` contrib module. The best way of doing that is still a topic of research at the time of writing.

One way to work around the fact that standby servers can't be tuned universally is to simply add more than one of them. There's nothing to prevent you from having two standby systems, one optimized for high availability with low standby delay parameters, while a second is optimized for long reports.

Replication queue managers

At the other end of the spectrum, some replication software does statement-based replication. Rather than sending blocks over, the list of transactions made to each table are extracted from the database, typically with triggers. Then those statements can be saved to a queue, shipped to a number of slave nodes, and then executed there. This introduces some non-trivial overhead on the master server because the overhead of the triggers, queue management, and statement shipping is moderate.

However, the resulting copies are then completely independent of the master server and, unlike WAL shipping approaches, you can pick and choose exactly which tables do and don't get shipped to the standby. In addition, since high-level statements are being shipped, the servers don't even need to match perfectly. This form of replication is therefore useful for doing PostgreSQL version upgrades. You can bring a server running a newer version of the database software up, add it as a replica, and let it stream the data from the master with whatever speed you want until it catches up. Once it's current, a standard fail-over to that new node will allow you to bring the database up, running that newer version.

It's not unusual for developers to think that they can just ship statements between database servers themselves, rather than use one of these packages. One hidden complexity in doing statement level replication is coping with non-deterministic statements, where the exact result will vary if you execute the same thing on a different server. Three sources for such data are calls to generate random numbers, sequence generation, and statements that incorporate a server timestamp. You can expect the latter in particular to haunt the poor developer who decides to reinvent this particular wheel, as such statements are very common in database applications. Getting statement orders to match exactly is another extremely tricky problem. It's unlikely that you'll do a better job in the end than these mature solutions already available. There are good reasons that all these replication packages end up being more complicated than you might think is required for this sort of work; they can't be any simpler and still work correctly.

Synchronous replication

In PostgreSQL 10 it is possible to make synchronous or asynchronous replications. PostgreSQL streaming replication is asynchronous by default. If the primary server crashes then some transactions that were committed may not have been replicated to the standby server, causing data loss. The amount of data loss is proportional to the replication delay at the time of failover.

Synchronous replication offers the ability to confirm that all changes made by a transaction have been transferred to one or more synchronous standby servers; in a synchronous replica, every time a transaction is committed, PostgreSQL will wait until the commit operation to be written both on the primary WAL and on the stand-by WAL; synchronous replication provides greater data protection in case of disaster, but it can slow down write operations. Here are some parameters to reach this goal:

- `synchronous_standby_names` must be set to a non-empty value; `synchronous_standby_names` specifies a list of standby servers that can support synchronous replication. There will be one or more active synchronous standbys; transactions waiting for commit will be allowed to proceed after these standby servers confirm receipt of their data. The synchronous standbys will be those whose names appear in this list and which are both currently connected and streaming data in real time (as shown by a state of streaming in the `pg_stat_replication` view). Specifying more than one synchronous standby can allow for very high availability and protection against data loss.
- `synchronous_commit = on` (default).

You can find more information at the following link `https://www.postgresql.org/docs/10/static/runtime-config-replication.html`.

Logical replication

One of the new features of PostgreSQL 10 is logical replication.

Logical replication is a method of replicating data objects and their changes, based upon their replication identity (usually a primary key). We use the term *logical* in contrast to physical replication, which uses exact block addresses and byte-by-byte replication. PostgreSQL supports both mechanisms concurrently.

Logical replication uses a publish and subscribe model with one or more subscribers subscribing to one or more publications on a publisher node. Subscribers pull data from the publications they subscribe to and may subsequently re-publish data to allow cascading replication or more complex configurations.

The concept is quite simple, a publication is created on the database master and a subscription is created on the slaves.

On the master (Node 1), we have to perform the following steps:

1. Set `wal_level` to `logical` on `postgresql.conf`
2. Create the role `REPLICATION`
3. Give the right permissions to the tables that we want to be replicated
4. Modify the `pg_hba.conf`
5. Create the publication

On the slave (Node 2), we have to perform the following steps:

1. Modify the `pg_hba.conf`
2. Create the structure of the table we want to replicate
3. Create the subscription

Now let's try an example:

```
Node1:

file pg_hba.conf

host        all            replicator   node2/32    md5

db1=# show wal_level;
 wal_level
 -----------
 logical

db1# create ROLE replicator REPLICATION LOGIN PASSWORD 'linux';
CREATE ROLE

db1=# create table mynames (id int not null primary key, name text);
CREATE TABLE

db1=# grant ALL ON mynames to replicator;
GRANT

db1=# create publication mynames_pub for table mynames;
CREATE PUBLICATION


Node 2
db2=# create table mynames (id int not null primary key, name text);
CREATE TABLE

db2=# create subscription mynames_sub CONNECTION 'dbname=db1 host=node1
```

```
user=replicator password=password' PUBLICATION mynames_pub;
CREATE SUBSCRIPTION


Now now enter some data on node1

db1=# insert into mynames values(1,'micky mouse');
INSERT 0 1


..and we see the same data on node2:

db2=# select * from mynames ;
 id |    name
----+-------------
  1 | micky mouse
```

And that's it.

Another thing we can do is change data locally on the slave without affecting the master; here is an example on Node 2:

```
db2=# insert into mynames values(2,'minni');
INSERT 0 1
db2=# select * from mynames ;
 id |    name
----+-------------
  1 | micky mouse
  2 | minni

and on  Node 1 we still have old data:

db1=# select * from mynames ;
 id |    name
----+-------------
  1 | micky mouse
```

If we want to resynchronize the slave with the master, we have to recreate the table and refresh the SUBSCRIPTION:

```
db2=# drop table mynames ;
DROP TABLE

db2=# create table mynames (id int not null primary key, name text);
CREATE TABLE

db2=# alter subscription mynames_sub refresh publication;
ALTER SUBSCRIPTION
```

```
db2=# select * from mynames ;
 id |     name
----+-------------
  1 | micky mouse
```

Logical replication currently has the following restrictions or missing functionality. These might be addressed in future releases:

- The database schema and DDL commands are not replicated
- Sequence data is not replicated
- TRUNCATE commands are not replicated
- Large objects are not replicated
- Replication is only possible from base tables to base tables

That is, the tables on the publication and on the subscription side must be normal tables, not views, materialized views, partition root tables, or foreign tables. In the case of partitions, you can therefore replicate a partition hierarchy one-to-one, but you cannot currently replicate to a differently partitioned setup. Attempts to replicate tables other than base tables will result in an error.

Slony

One of the oldest and most mature PostgreSQL replication solutions, Slony is both a complex and feature-rich replication program; refer to `http://slony.info/`.

It's written in C and is highly optimized for the form of replication it does. Much of the development work on Slony is done by Afilias, which uses Slony for both redundancy and load scaling for a significant portion of the internet **Domain Name Service (DNS)**. It aims at that reliability level.

Slony is a complicated program, which is reflected everywhere from initial setup complexity to extensive monitoring requirements. Expect to devote a significant amount of study to any Slony deployment. The return on that time investment is quite a powerful replication solution with many years worth of thought put into its feature set.

One of the limitations of Slony to be aware of is that every table it replicates needs to have a primary or similar key field for it to operate over.

Londiste

Londiste is a more recent queue-based replication software driven by triggers and that's part of the SkyTools project set: `http://pgfoundry.org/projects/skytools/`.

It's one of the database applications written to support scaling up database operations at Skype. Relative to Slony, Londiste has two highly visible advantages. The first is that it targets a smaller feature set and is therefore less complicated to set up. It also has abstracted away the concept of transporting changes from the master to the slaves a bit more cleanly. The Londiste design is based on a generic queue library that is less coupled to the underlying data transport mechanism used in Slony.

Another advantage for Londiste is that it requires minimal locking in order to replicate. Slony has a few situations that you might run into where the exclusive table locks are required. An example is moving a replication set from one node to another.

Given the way open source software works, where it's expected that you might end up needing to read and perhaps change the source code to add-on software you use, Londiste can also be easier to work with. If you need to get familiar with its internals or make changes to Londiste, it's simpler to do so than it is to gain similar competence with the Slony source code.

Read scaling with replication queue software

When using Slony, Londiste, or similar statement-based replication software, or even streaming replication plus Hot Standby, each of your slaves is going to lag a bit behind the master. If your application can support running queries against that slightly out-of-date information, it's straightforward to put a load balancing program such as pgpool-II in front of the master and a set of slave nodes in order to scale up reads.

This replication approach is also very good for maintaining autonomous remote servers. You might put servers in multiple cities and the application reads against the closest copy of the data, as a way to decrease the load on any one server.

More information about how pgpool-II works for this purpose was covered in the previous chapter, `Chapter 13`, *Pooling and Caching*.

Special application requirements

All of the solutions covered so far are master/slave solutions that, while asynchronous, expect fairly tight contact between all the database nodes. For example, the master in a Hot Standby deployment will eventually run out of disk space and crash if it can't ship WAL files to the slaves it's feeding.

Bucardo

One of the things most PostgreSQL replication solutions have in common is that they have a single master node. Bucardo is instead a multi-master replication solution, also implemented with triggers; refer to `http://bucardo.org/`.

Anytime you have more than one master, this introduces a new form of replication problems. What do you do if more than one node modifies the same record? Solving that is called conflict resolution in replication terminology. Bucardo provides a hook for your application to figure out what to do in that case, after it does the heavy lifting work on the main replication chore.

Bucardo is also very asynchronous. Instead of expecting that nodes are in constant contact with one another as most database replication software does, Bucardo allows a disconnected master to execute an arbitrary amount of work and then resynchronize when connected to the rest of the network again. This makes it particularly well suited to scenarios such as databases hosted on a mobile system. A laptop might run the database server, synchronize before leaving for a trip, and then update in both directions with all the changes made when it returns to the office.

Bucardo probably isn't the right solution for scaling upwards using load balancing, and it's not a replication solution appropriate for most high availability failover requirements. But it can be appropriate for splitting the load among servers in multiple locations, particularly if the links between them are unreliable, a situation that warm standby and Slony/Londiste don't handle particularly well.

pgpool-II

The replication features of pgpool and pgpool-II work quite differently than the rest of the programs covered here. They are implementations of statement-based middleware. This means that they serve as an intermediate proxy server between your application and the database, translating the statements executed into the appropriate ones for each of the destinations. It can provide synchronous replication as just one of its benefits.

pgpool-II works in one of several modes that include connection pooling, replication, master/slave, and parallel query, some of which can be combined to be active at the same time. It provides a useful toolkit of database scaling features, while suffering a bit in complexity from its lack of focus. Other replication solutions that have a more targeted feature set tend to be easier to set up and work with than pgpool-II.

Other interesting replication projects

There is a wide perception that since PostgreSQL hasn't ever shipped with a complete replication solution (even the streaming replication in 9.0 requires some external code support), its replication options are therefore weak. The opposite is true; because the development community isn't focused on a single replication solution. There are actually so many viable options that just describing them all is a chore. The programs listed in this section don't have the general developer mindshare that the ones already covered do. But most of them have a very specific type of replication problem than they solve better than any of the other alternatives:

- **Mammoth Replicator**: Rather than derive statement changes from triggers, Mammoth instead modifies the PostgreSQL source code to generate them. The need for a customized PostgreSQL makes it inappropriate for some uses. If you need statement replication, but can't afford the overhead and complexity of needing triggers to derive them, Mammoth is a mature solution to that problem.
- **PgCluster**: This is a synchronous master/master replication solution developed using customized PostgreSQL code. Applications that need true synchronous transactions, where commits either happen on both nodes or not at all, might find PgCluster appropriate for that need. PgCluster requires modifications to the PostgreSQL source code. It's available in both commercial and open source releases. Usually their open source version lags behind the release schedule of the main PostgreSQL project.

- **Postgres-XC**: Most replication solutions fail to address scaling up write performance. It's rarely as important as scaling up reads and is a much harder problem to deal with. Postgres-XC attacks that problem head-on by building a fully distributed cluster of nodes that provides near-linear write scaling. The software is both very complicated and still fairly new, and, at the time of writing, it isn't a complete feature nor considered stable for generic workloads yet; it only handles relatively simple work; refer to
  `http://sourceforge.net/projects/postgres-xc/`.

- **Rubyrep**: Similar to Bucardo, it's an asynchronous replication solution that can handle multiple masters. As a fairly new piece of software, it still has a fairly simple learning curve and is being actively developed, but isn't yet very mature outside of its originally targeted application types; refer to
  `http://www.rubyrep.org`.

- **Golconde**: A queue-based data distribution system, Golconde aims to scale upward database workloads by handling the chores normally done by replication software at the application level instead. Rather than derive transactions from what's in the database itself, it aims to be a database aware transaction passing mechanism, using one of the many generic message queue solutions available; refer to `http://code.google.com/p/golconde/`.

The number of external projects is expected to shrink following the release of PostgreSQL 9.0 due to its internal streaming replication with associated Hot Standby query taking over, as the obvious built-in way to handle some types of replication. This will be increasingly true after a future version, likely 9.1, integrates synchronous replication features. This feature just missed being included in 9.0.

Replication solution comparison

Replication is very much an area where there is no *one-size fits all* solution. You need to match the solution chosen to what your specific problems and prioritization are. The main replication options break down based on what method they use to replicate and whether that replication is synchronous or not:

Program	Replication method	Synchronization
WAL shipping	Master/slave	Asynchronous
Logical replication	Master/slave	Asynchronous
Slony	Master/slave	Asynchronous

Londiste	Master/slave	Asynchronous
Mammoth	Master/slave	Asynchronous
Bucardo	Master/slave or Master/master	Asynchronous
Rubyrep	Master/slave or Master/master	Asynchronous
PgCluster	Master/master	Synchronous
Postgres-XC	Master/master	Synchronous
pgpool-II	Statement-based middleware	Synchronous

The main difference between the various master/slave solutions is how the database changes are derived.

Hot Standby starting from PostgreSQL 9.0 allows running queries against the type of standby databases used in early versions, only for high availability failover.

The WAL used for creating standby databases logs block changes, and can only be used to make a complete copy of a database cluster, not a subset. Using log shipping replication will result in some archiving lag between the standby and the master, which can be minimized (but not completely avoided) starting from PostgreSQL 9.0 by using the streaming replication feature.

A Hot Standby system can only be tuned for quick failover, long running queries, or minimal impact on the master. But you can only prioritize any two of those three at a time. Replicating database statements instead is more flexible and allows features such as version upgrades, but some statements don't replicate easily and this approach has higher overhead than WAL shipping.

Slony and Londiste are both mature solutions for extracting statement updates using triggers and shipping the results to some number of additional live database systems. pgpool-II can be used to do load balancing across multiple read-only slaves, as well as some forms of synchronous replication. Bucardo supports adding multiple database masters whether or not the systems are connected all the time.

There are many additional replication tools for PostgreSQL available that target specific feature sets that are not covered by the more popular packages.

Summary

Hot Standby allows us to run queries against the type of standby databases used in early versions only for high availability failover. The WAL used for creating standby databases logs block changes, and can only be used to make a complete copy of a database cluster, not a subset. Using log-shipping replication will result in some archiving lag between the standby and the master, but this is resolved in synchronous replication. Replicating database statements instead is more flexible and allows features such as version upgrades, but some statements don't replicate easily and this approach has higher overhead than write-ahead log shipping. Slony, Londiste, and Bucardo are mature solutions for replications. pgpool-II can be used to do load balancing across multiple read-only slaves, as well as some forms of synchronous replication. There are many additional replication tools available for PostgreSQL that target specific feature sets not covered by the more popular packages.

The next chapter will cover the partitioning concepts in PostgreSQL. If a table becomes huge, it becomes necessary to divide it into smaller tables. PostgreSQL provides the portioning concept where, without changing the application, the table can be divided into smaller tables.

15
Partitioning Data

As databases grow, it's common to have a table or two become unmanageably large. If the table itself is much larger than the physical memory, and even its indexes stop fitting comfortably, query execution time will escalate. One way to deal with large tables is to partition them, which breaks the table into a series of smaller, related tables instead. You don't have to change your application, just keep querying the same table. But when the query can be answered by just using a subset of the data, rather than scanning the whole thing, this optimization can occur.

In this chapter we will be covering these topics:

- Table range partitioning
- Declarative partitioning
- Horizontal partitioning with PL/Proxy

Table range partitioning

Returning to the `dellstore2` example database used in `Chapter 10`, *Query Optimization*, consider the structure of the `orders` table:

```
dellstore2=# \d orders;
Table "public.orders"
    Column    |     Type      | Modifiers
--------------+---------------+----------------------------------
    orderid     | integer       | not null default
nextval('orders_orderid_seq'::regclass)
    orderdate   | date          | not null
    customerid  | integer       |
    netamount   | numeric(12,2) | not null
    tax         | numeric(12,2) | not null
    totalamount | numeric(12,2) | not null
Indexes:
    "orders_pkey" PRIMARY KEY, btree (orderid)
```

```
    "ix_order_custid" btree (customerid)
Foreign-key constraints:
    "fk_customerid" FOREIGN KEY (customerid) REFERENCES
customers(customerid) ON DELETE SET NULL
Referenced by:
    TABLE "orderlines" CONSTRAINT "fk_orderid" FOREIGN KEY (orderid)
REFERENCES orders(orderid) ON DELETE CASCADE
```

Imagine that after many years of operation, the store has received so many orders that queries against this table are unwieldy. The usual rule of thumb thresholds for considering table partitioning are when an individual table is larger than the total amount of memory in the server, or when it's reached 100 million rows.

Determining a key field to partition over

There are two potential ways that you could split this data into smaller pieces. The first would be to partition the table into sections based on the orderid field. This is probably what a real-world deployment would need to do here because if the orders table is too large, the orderlines table would be even larger. Both tables could be usefully partitioned by orderid.

However, imagine that orders are only kept for a period of time, perhaps a couple of years. Older orders could therefore be deleted in that situation. The problem with mass deletion in PostgreSQL is that it leaves a lot to be cleaned up after. First, you'll need to vacuum the table to mark the deleted rows as dead. This might return space to the OS, but it's quite possible that it will not. You can also end up with bloated indexes from this usage pattern if data from various time periods is mixed together in the same data block.

If the orders table were partitioned by the orderdate field, there's another way to deal with removing old orders. You can just drop the partitions containing the old data instead. Because this particular pattern is so common timestamp ordered data where the old sections are dropped to keep access times reasonable on newer ones—the example we'll walk through here will partition by the date the orders were placed.

Another important part of partitioned design is that, in order to benefit from splitting the table into pieces, queries need to run against a useful subset of the data. You should consider what fields are being used in the WHERE clauses for queries against the table as part of deciding which field is the right one to split it over.

Sizing the partitions

A useful initial step to breaking a table into partitions is to figure out the range of data it contains, relative to the candidate field, and how large it is:

```
SELECT min(orderdate),max(orderdate) FROM orders;
    min     |    max
------------+------------
 2004-01-01 | 2004-12-31
SELECT relname,relpages FROM pg_class WHERE relname LIKE 'orders%' ORDER BY
relname;
       relname      | relpages
--------------------+----------
 orders             |      100
 orders_orderid_seq |        1
 orders_pkey        |       29
```

This is obviously too small to be worth partitioning but, for a demonstration sample, it's large enough to demonstrate how splitting the table would look. Since there's a year of data here, breaking that into month-sized pieces would be appropriate.

List partitioning

The example here, and the pattern you're most likely to deploy, uses range partitioning. This is where you provide a non-overlapping range of values that each partition uniquely includes. It's also possible to partition based on an explicit list of values that direct which partition a value goes into. For example, if you had queries against the customer's table that were routinely targeted at specific states, you might partition based on that:

```
CHECK ( state IN ( 'AK', 'AL', 'AR','AZ' ))
CHECK ( state = 'CA' )
```

So, that populous states like California (CA) have their own partition.

Note that whether a partition is a range or a list is a choice of descriptive terminology. There's no syntax difference between the two, and to the query planner they're all just constraints that a value is or isn't inside of.

Creating the partitions

Partitioning in PostgreSQL is based on the database's table inheritance feature. This allows a table to have children that inherit all of its columns. For this sample, a partition is needed for each month that inherits from the main orders table:

```
CREATE TABLE orders_2004_01 (
    CHECK ( orderdate >= DATE '2004-01-01' and orderdate < DATE
'2004-02-01')
) INHERITS (orders);
. . .
CREATE TABLE orders_2004_12 (
    CHECK ( orderdate >= DATE '2004-12-01' and orderdate < DATE '2005-01-01')
) INHERITS (orders);
```

But only the column structure is inherited. You'll need to add indexes, constraints, and adjust permissions on each individual partition to match the master table. The output from `psql \d` for the table, as shown for the preceding orders table, can be a helpful guide as to what all of this is.

Each partition needs the same `PRIMARY KEY`:

```
ALTER TABLE ONLY orders_2004_01
    ADD CONSTRAINT orders_2004_01_pkey PRIMARY KEY (orderid);
. . .
ALTER TABLE ONLY orders_2004_12
    ADD CONSTRAINT orders_2004_12_pkey PRIMARY KEY (orderid);
```

This will create an index by `orderid` as well. A manual index on `customerid` is also needed:

```
CREATE INDEX ix_orders_2004_01_custid ON orders_2004_01 USING btree
(customerid);
. . .
CREATE INDEX ix_orders_2004_12_custid ON orders_2004_12 USING btree
(customerid);
```

Each order also contains a `FOREIGN KEY` constraint to ensure that the customer referenced is valid. These need to be applied to each partition:

```
ALTER TABLE ONLY orders_2004_01
    ADD CONSTRAINT fk_2004_01_customerid FOREIGN KEY (customerid) REFERENCES
customers(customerid) ON DELETE SET NULL;
. . .
ALTER TABLE ONLY orders_2004_12
    ADD CONSTRAINT fk_2004_12_customerid FOREIGN KEY (customerid) REFERENCES
customers(customerid) ON DELETE SET NULL;
```

The other constraint involved here is actually against the `orderliness` table, confirming that each order exists. So long as we're careful to never remove an order while working on the partitioning, that constraint can stay in place without modifications. If the table was being dumped and reloaded, you'd have to drop that constraint while that was going on, lest the constraint be violated and cause a problem.

Redirecting INSERT statements to the partitions

Now that the structure is present, the next step is to make rows inserted into the parent table, go into the appropriate partition. The recommended way to do this is with a `TRIGGER` function:

```
CREATE OR REPLACE FUNCTION orders_insert_trigger()
RETURNS TRIGGER AS $$
BEGIN
    IF    ( NEW.orderdate >= DATE '2004-12-01' AND
          NEW.orderdate < DATE '2005-01-01' ) THEN
        INSERT INTO orders_2004_12 VALUES (NEW.*);
    ELSIF ( NEW.orderdate >= DATE '2004-11-01' AND
          NEW.orderdate < DATE '2004-12-01' ) THEN
        INSERT INTO orders_2004_11 VALUES (NEW.*);
    . . .
    ELSIF ( NEW.orderdate >= DATE '2004-01-01' AND
           NEW.orderdate < DATE '2004-02-01' ) THEN
        INSERT INTO orders_2004_01 VALUES (NEW.*);
    ELSE
        RAISE EXCEPTION 'Error in orders_insert_trigger():  date out of
range';
    END IF;
    RETURN NULL;
END;
$$
LANGUAGE plpgsql;
```

Note how the function starts with rows at the end of the range (December). Starting with the latest defined partition is a recommended practice because, in most business scenarios with a split by date, that's the partition you are most likely to be inserting new data into.

Once the function is created, it needs to be called each time a row is inserted:

```
CREATE TRIGGER insert_orders_trigger
    BEFORE INSERT ON orders
    FOR EACH ROW EXECUTE PROCEDURE orders_insert_trigger();
```

You will probably end up needing to update the actual function here to reflect new partitions at some point, but that doesn't require creating the trigger again. It will use the new function automatically once it's replaced.

Dynamic trigger functions

The `orders_insert_trigger()` function shown previously is static; the statements it executes are the same every time. As you might expect from reading the code, the actual execution time will vary based on which partition you are inserting into, and maintaining that trigger code is both monotonous and error prone. It's possible to remove the maintenance chore by just directly computing the partition required:

```
CREATE OR REPLACE FUNCTION orders_insert_trigger()
RETURNS TRIGGER AS $$
DECLARE
    ins_sql TEXT;
BEGIN
    ins_sql :=
        'INSERT INTO orders_'|| to_char(NEW.orderdate, 'YYYY_MM') ||
        '(orderid,orderdate,customerid,net_amount,tax,totalamount)
         VALUES ' ||
        '('|| NEW.orderid || ',' || quote_literal(NEW.orderdate) || ','
           || NEW.customerid ||','||
        NEW.netamount ||','|| NEW.tax || ',' || NEW.totalamount || ')'
        ;
    EXECUTE ins_sql;
    RETURN NULL;
END
$$;
```

The execution time of this version is constant and predictable, whereas the static version's runtime will depend on how many comparisons happen before it finds the right partition to insert into. In return for that and getting rid of needing to keep the more verbose static version up to date, there are a few downsides to this approach though. You have to be careful to handle quoting and NULL values here. Because of how the statement is constructed and then executed as text, this will be slower than the static version, at least when the static one has the active partition as the beginning of its comparison list.

A more subtle downside is that dynamically generating these statements will then accept bad data pointing towards partitions that don't exist, without the clear error message the static version gives in that case. Before using this approach on a production system, you should rewrite this example procedure to catch insertion errors because rows inserted into partitions that don't exist are still going to fail.

Partition rules

There is actually another way to implement the partition redirection being done in the trigger here. PostgreSQL has a feature called rules that allows substituting an alternate command for one you want to change. Here is an example:

```
CREATE RULE orders_2004_01_insert AS
ON INSERT TO orders WHERE
    ( orderdate >= DATE '2004-01-01' AND orderdate < DATE '2004-02-01' )
DO INSTEAD
    INSERT INTO orders_2004_01 VALUES (NEW.*);
```

Using a rule has the potential upside that bulk inserts can be processed more efficiently than using a trigger. As such, benchmarks that focus on that particular measurement might suggest it's the faster approach. But the rule approach has higher overhead for an individual insert, which is what you're probably going to do more over the lifetime of the database. And since the number of rules, and therefore the rules overhead, is proportional to the number of partitions, with no dynamic approach available, the performance of a rules-based partitioning implementation can become quite high once you have many partitions.

A final blow against using rules is that COPY doesn't follow them. If you're using INSERT triggers instead, this work fine. There's very little to recommend rules about partitions and there are several reasons you might want to avoid them. The main reason I bring them up at all is to point out their issues, and to suggest you be skeptical of any recommendation in favor of using them in PostgreSQL.

Empty partition query plans

At this point, the partitions are all in place, but the data is still in the parent table. Since these are new tables, the optimizer doesn't have any statistics on them until ANALYZE is run. Let's do that and see what a query against the orders table looks like now:

```
ANALYZE;
EXPLAIN ANALYZE SELECT * FROM orders;
```

```
QUERY PLAN
----------
 Result  (cost=0.00..456.40 rows=23640 width=45)  (actual time=0.064..99.059
rows=12000 loops=1)
    ->  Append  (cost=0.00..456.40 rows=23640 width=45)  (actual
time=0.059..58.873 rows=12000 loops=1)
        ->  Seq Scan on orders  (cost=0.00..220.00 rows=12000 width=36)
(actual time=0.056..22.522 rows=12000 loops=1)
        ->  Seq Scan on orders_2004_01 orders  (cost=0.00..19.70 rows=970
width=54)  (actual time=0.001..0.001 rows=0 loops=1)
        ->  Seq Scan on orders_2004_02 orders  (cost=0.00..19.70 rows=970
width=54)  (actual time=0.001..0.001 rows=0 loops=1)
...
        ->  Seq Scan on orders_2004_12 orders  (cost=0.00..19.70 rows=970
width=54)  (actual time=0.002..0.002 rows=0 loops=1)
```

Queries are still running against the entirety of the original orders table, and they're also running against each of the partitions. Note that since there are no rows in them, the database doesn't actually have useful row estimates for the partitions. It's guessing that there are 970 rows in each; so, until some data shows up in them, this will throw off plans against the table.

Date change update trigger

One of the optional things usually left out of PostgreSQL partitioning examples is an update trigger. Consider the case where you update a row and change the date; this could require relocating it to another partition. If you want to allow for this case, you need to install a TRIGGER into each partition:

```
CREATE OR REPLACE FUNCTION orders_2004_01_update_trigger()
RETURNS TRIGGER AS $$
BEGIN
   IF ( NEW.orderdate != OLD.orderdate ) THEN
      DELETE FROM orders_2004_01
         WHERE OLD.orderid=orderid;
      INSERT INTO orders values(NEW.*);
   END IF;
   RETURN NULL;
END;
$$
LANGUAGE plpgsql;
CREATE TRIGGER update_orders_2004_01
      BEFORE UPDATE ON orders_2004_01
      FOR EACH ROW
      EXECUTE PROCEDURE orders_2004_01_update_trigger();
```

As in the INSERT trigger case, you could instead write a dynamic version of both the DELETE and INSERT statement. Then you can attach the same function to every partition. This has the same potential benefits and concerns as in the dynamic INSERT trigger shown earlier.

 Starting in PostgreSQL 9.0, it's possible to write UPDATE triggers that are tied to a specific column changing. This technique could be used to slim down and speed up this example, by writing something that only executes when orderdate is modified.

When showing the rest of the examples, it's assumed that you did not install this optional form of trigger. Few applications update data that impacts their primary key afterwards as it's dangerous, and you can always direct data to a specific partition yourself if you need to make such a change manually.

Live migration of a partitioned table

If you executed the creation of partition, index, and TRIGGER functions in this chapter against a live dellstore2 installation, you've now got all of the actual data in the parent orders table, with a number of empty partitions. This is typically how a live migration to partitions would prefer to happen too. The other option is to dump the table, create the partition structure, and then load the data back in again, which involves some downtime.

There is another way though. Consider the UPDATE trigger again. What if you installed one of those against the parent table? You could then migrate to the partitioned structure just by updating every row. Here's what the code looks like for that:

```
CREATE OR REPLACE FUNCTION orders_update_trigger()
RETURNS TRIGGER AS $$
BEGIN
   DELETE FROM orders WHERE OLD.orderid=orderid;
    INSERT INTO orders values(NEW.*);
    RETURN NULL;
END;
$$
LANGUAGE plpgsql;
CREATE TRIGGER update_orders
    BEFORE UPDATE ON orders
    FOR EACH ROW
    EXECUTE PROCEDURE orders_update_trigger();
```

When doing this, the paranoid approach is to wrap all of the changes into a transaction block with BEGIN/COMMIT. That way, if there's a problem you can execute ROLLBACK and make all the changes revert. You'll either migrate all the data successfully or not do anything. This approach was used to debug the preceding code; each early attempt that didn't result in something that looked like sane data was just rolled back. Here's a sample session that succeeds:

```
dellstore2=# BEGIN;
BEGIN
dellstore2=# SELECT count(*) FROM orders;
 count
-------
 12000
dellstore2=# SELECT count(*) FROM orders_2004_01;
 count
-------
     0
dellstore2=# SELECT count(*) FROM orders_2004_12;
 count
-------
     0
dellstore2=# UPDATE orders SET orderid=orderid;
UPDATE 0
dellstore2=# SELECT count(*) FROM orders_2004_01;
 count
-------
  1000
dellstore2=# SELECT count(*) FROM orders_2004_12;
 count
-------
  1000
dellstore2=# SELECT count(*) FROM orders;
  count
-------
  12000
dellstore2=# COMMIT;
COMMIT
```

Counting the number of rows is a good way to confirm that all of the data was migrated over as expected. You can see that the stating configuration had 12000 rows in the parent table and none in the partitions, while the ending one has 1000 rows in each of the 12 partitions. One small quirk to be aware of here, the form of UPDATE trigger being used here doesn't actually report that it did anything. Note how it shows 0 rows processed, even though it obviously executed against all of them.

After the commit is done and any active sessions from before then have ended, you'll want to remove all the dead rows related to the original data. VACUUM isn't enough to clean this up because all it will do is mark those rows as free space. This doesn't help you if you don't ever expect to add more rows to this parent table ever again. One easy way to fully clean the old parent is with CLUSTER, which should produce a new, tiny table from any data that's left behind (zero in this case), and then drop the original version with all the dead rows. And once this conversion is done and the data verified, this trigger is redundant and mainly apt to introduce confusion. It's better to drop it than to keep it around once it's not needed anymore:

```
CLUSTER orders;
DROP TRIGGER update_orders ON orders;
DROP FUNCTION orders_update_trigger();
```

PostgreSQL 10 – declarative partitioning – the built-in partitioning

Starting from PostgreSQL 10, PostgreSQL introduced the declarative partitioning syntax. With this syntax the necessity to define additional triggers or rules disappear, but functionality and performances remain unchanged.

It's possible to use declarative partitioning for list partitioning and/or for range partitioning; first of all, we have to define a master table containing the partition method (list or RANGE). For example, if we want to partition by a list method:

```
create table orders_state
    (orderid integer not null,
    orderdate date not null,
    customerid integer not null,
    tax numeric(12,2) not null ,
    state char(2))
partition by list (state);
```

Next, we have to create the child table, for example, for all US orders:

```
CREATE TABLE ORDERS_US PARTITION OF ORDERS_state FOR VALUES IN ('US');
```

And we create tables for all south Europe orders:

```
CREATE TABLE ORDERS_state_EU PARTITION OF ORDERS_state FOR VALUES IN
('IT','FR','ES','GR','PT');
```

Next, if we insert some data, we can see that all data will be partitioned:

```
insert into orders_state values(1,now()::date,1,10,'IT');
insert into orders_state values(2,now()::date,1,10,'FR');
insert into orders_state values(4,now()::date,1,10,'US');

pgbench=# select * from orders_state;
 orderid |  orderdate  | customerid |  tax  | state
---------+-------------+------------+-------+-------
       4 | 2018-03-29 |          1 | 10.00 | US
       2 | 2018-03-29 |          1 | 10.00 | FR
       1 | 2018-03-29 |          1 | 10.00 | IT

pgbench=# select * from  only orders_state;
 orderid | orderdate | customerid | tax | state
                        ^

pgbench=# select * from only orders_state_EU;
 orderid |  orderdate  | customerid |  tax  | state
---------+-------------+------------+-------+-------
       2 | 2018-03-29 |          1 | 10.00 | FR
       1 | 2018-03-29 |          1 | 10.00 | IT

pgbench=# select * from only orders_state_US;
 orderid |  orderdate  | customerid |  tax  | state
---------+-------------+------------+-------+-------
       4 | 2018-03-29 |          1 | 10.00 | US
```

Range partitioning

Now let's see how to make a RANGE partitioning using the same table structure; we'll try to partition the table by date into four quarters. First, define a master table containing the partition method, RANGE:

```
drop table if exists orders_state;

create table orders_state
        (orderid integer not null,
         orderdate date not null,
         customerid integer not null,
         tax numeric(12,2) not null ,
         state char(2))
partition by  RANGE (orderdate);
```

Next, we have to create the child tables:

```
CREATE TABLE orders_state_q1 PARTITION OF orders_state FOR VALUES FROM
('2018-01-01') TO ('2018-03-01');
CREATE TABLE orders_state_q2 PARTITION OF orders_state FOR VALUES FROM
('2018-03-01') TO ('2018-06-01');
CREATE TABLE orders_state_q3 PARTITION OF orders_state FOR VALUES FROM
('2018-06-01') TO ('2018-09-01');
CREATE TABLE orders_state_q4 PARTITION OF orders_state FOR VALUES FROM
('2018-09-01') TO ('2019-01-01');
```

Now if we insert some data, we can see that all data will be partitioned:

```
insert into orders_state values(1,'2018-01-15'::date,1,10,'IT');
insert into orders_state values(1,'2018-04-15'::date,1,10,'US');
insert into orders_state values(1,'2018-07-15'::date,1,10,'FR');
insert into orders_state values(1,'2018-10-15'::date,1,10,'ES');

pgbench=# select * from orders_state;
 orderid |  orderdate  | customerid |  tax  | state
---------+-------------+------------+-------+-------
       1 | 2018-01-15 |          1 | 10.00 | IT
       1 | 2018-04-15 |          1 | 10.00 | US
       1 | 2018-07-15 |          1 | 10.00 | FR
       1 | 2018-10-15 |          1 | 10.00 | ES

pgbench=# select * from orders_state_q1;
 orderid |  orderdate  | customerid |  tax  | state
---------+-------------+------------+-------+-------
       1 | 2018-01-15 |          1 | 10.00 | IT

pgbench=# select * from orders_state_q2;
 orderid |  orderdate  | customerid |  tax  | state
---------+-------------+------------+-------+-------
       1 | 2018-04-15 |          1 | 10.00 | US

pgbench=# select * from orders_state_q3;
 orderid |  orderdate  | customerid |  tax  | state
---------+-------------+------------+-------+-------
       1 | 2018-07-15 |          1 | 10.00 | FR

pgbench=# select * from orders_state_q4;
 orderid |  orderdate  | customerid |  tax  | state
---------+-------------+------------+-------+-------
       1 | 2018-10-15 |          1 | 10.00 | ES
```

Partition maintenance

Now we will see how to remove old partitions of data and periodically add new partitions for new data.

If we want to detach a partition, we have to execute the following:

```
pgbench=# alter table orders_state detach partition orders_state_q4;
ALTER TABLE
pgbench=# select * from orders_state;
 orderid |  orderdate  | customerid |  tax   | state
---------+-------------+------------+--------+-------
       1 | 2018-01-15 |          1 | 10.00  | IT
       1 | 2018-04-15 |          1 | 10.00  | US
       1 | 2018-07-15 |          1 | 10.00  | FR
```

If we want to create and add a new partition, we use the following:

```
CREATE TABLE orders_state_q5 PARTITION OF orders_state FOR VALUES FROM
('2019-01-01') TO ('2019-03-01');
```

If we want to attach an existing table, we use the following:

```
alter table orders_state attach partition orders_state_q4 FOR VALUES FROM (
'2018-09-01') TO ('2019-01-01');
```

Caveats

As written in the official documentation:

Indexes must be added to each partition with separate commands. This also means that there is no way to create a primary key, unique constraint, or exclusion constraint spanning all partitions; it is only possible to constrain each leaf partition individually.

Since primary keys are not supported on partitioned tables, foreign keys referencing partitioned tables are not supported, nor are foreign key references from a partitioned table to some other table.

Using the ON CONFLICT clause with partitioned tables will cause an error because unique or exclusion constraints can only be created on individual partitions. There is no support for enforcing uniqueness (or an exclusion constraint) across an entire partitioning hierarchy.

An UPDATE trigger that causes a row to move from one partition to another fails because the new value of the row fails to satisfy the implicit partition constraint of the original partition.

Row triggers, if necessary, must be defined on individual partitions, not the partitioned table.

Partitioned queries

Now that the data is in the partitions, it's a good idea to update statistics. It's also important to confirm that the constraint_exclusion feature is active:

```
ANALYZE;
SHOW constraint_exclusion;
 constraint_exclusion
----------------------
 partition
```

constraint_exclusion allows the query planner to avoid including partitions in a query when it can prove they can't provide useful rows to satisfy it. In PostgreSQL 8.4 and later, the default value of partition turns this on, when partitioned tables are referenced, and off otherwise. In earlier versions, it defaults to off. You will have to turn the parameter on once you start using partitions in earlier versions if you expect them to work properly.

Queries against the whole table execute the same as before the rows were relocated, except now the statistics are good for everything except the parent table:

```
EXPLAIN ANALYZE SELECT * FROM orders;
QUERY PLAN
----------
 Result  (cost=0.00..1292.00 rows=12001 width=36) (actual
time=4.453..102.062 rows=12000 loops=1)
        -> Append  (cost=0.00..1292.00 rows=12001 width=36) (actual
time=4.445..62.258 rows=12000 loops=1)
              -> Seq Scan on orders  (cost=0.00..400.00 rows=1 width=36)
(actual time=4.153..4.153 rows=0 loops=1)
              -> Seq Scan on orders_2004_01 orders  (cost=0.00..77.00
rows=1000 width=36) (actual time=0.287..1.971 rows=1000 loops=1)
              -> Seq Scan on orders_2004_02 orders  (cost=0.00..77.00
rows=1000 width=36) (actual time=0.267..2.045 rows=1000 loops=1)
    ...
              -> Seq Scan on orders_2004_12 orders  (cost=0.00..69.00
rows=1000 width=36) (actual time=0.160..1.474 rows=1000 loops=1)
```

Now for an example that shows the value of partitions. Consider a query that only looks for orders on a particular day:

```
EXPLAIN ANALYZE SELECT * FROM orders WHERE orderdate='2004-11-16';
QUERY PLAN
----------
 Result  (cost=0.00..471.50 rows=36 width=36) (actual time=1.437..2.141
rows=35 loops=1)
     -> Append  (cost=0.00..471.50 rows=36 width=36) (actual
time=1.432..2.017 rows=35 loops=1)
          -> Seq Scan on orders  (cost=0.00..400.00 rows=1 width=36)
(actual time=1.189..1.189 rows=0 loops=1)
               Filter: (orderdate = '2004-11-16'::date)
          -> Seq Scan on orders_2004_11 orders  (cost=0.00..71.50 rows=35
width=36) (actual time=0.238..0.718 rows=35 loops=1)
               Filter: (orderdate = '2004-11-16'::date)
     Total runtime: 2.276 ms
```

Instead of executing against every order, as this query would have done before, now it only has to consider the ones in the 2004-11 partition and a brief scan of the empty parent table. The optimizer can prove that none of the others contain rows with this value by considering their respective CHECK constraints.

In this dataset, much like many real-world ones, the orderid key is highly correlated with the creation date. Watch how the following orderid range scan is executed:

```
dellstore2=# EXPLAIN ANALYZE SELECT * FROM orders WHERE orderid<2000;
QUERY PLAN
----------
  Result  (cost=4.26..249.95 rows=2011 width=36) (actual
time=1.113..19.802 rows=1999 loops=1)
     -> Append  (cost=4.26..249.95 rows=2011 width=36) (actual
time=1.107..11.878 rows=1999 loops=1)
          -> Bitmap Heap Scan on orders  (cost=4.26..8.27 rows=1
width=36) (actual time=0.821..0.821 rows=0 loops=1)
               Recheck Cond: (orderid < 2000)
               -> Bitmap Index Scan on orders_pkey  (cost=0.00..4.26
rows=1 width=0) (actual time=0.648..0.648 rows=1999 loops=1)
                    Index Cond: (orderid < 2000)
          -> Seq Scan on orders_2004_01 orders  (cost=0.00..79.50
rows=1000 width=36) (actual time=0.281..2.298 rows=1000 loops=1)
               Filter: (orderid < 2000)
          -> Seq Scan on orders_2004_02 orders  (cost=0.00..79.50
rows=1000 width=36) (actual time=0.276..2.487 rows=999 loops=1)
               Filter: (orderid < 2000)
          -> Index Scan using orders_2004_03_pkey on orders_2004_03
orders  (cost=0.00..8.27 rows=1 width=36) (actual time=0.015..0.015 rows=0
```

```
loops=1)
                        Index Cond: (orderid < 2000)
            ->  Index Scan using orders_2004_04_pkey on orders_2004_04
orders  (cost=0.00..8.27 rows=1 width=36) (actual time=0.007..0.007 rows=0
loops=1)
                        Index Cond: (orderid < 2000)

    . . .

            ->  Index Scan using orders_2004_12_pkey on orders_2004_12
orders  (cost=0.00..8.27 rows=1 width=36) (actual time=0.006..0.006 rows=0
loops=1)
                        Index Cond: (orderid < 2000)
        Total runtime: 23.293 ms
```

The optimizer isn't smart enough to prove that no rows matching the `orderid` value appear in the higher numbered partitions. It does estimate that only one row might match from these though, which is enough to have it do an `Index Scan` on those partitions, to quickly exclude them from the output. Meanwhile, the partitions that do have useful data are sequentially scanned.

In the original un-partitioned table, the optimizer would have needed to choose between a sequential or index scan for the entire dataset. Neither would have produced a very good plan, given this query returns about 16% of the data. You might recall from `Chapter 10`, *Query Optimization*, that the transition point between the two types of scans is around 20%, which means a query returning 16% is going to be expensive to execute relative to the number of rows produced with either option. This is a common improvement when partitioning data; it lets the portions of the dataset reduce in size enough that a sequential scan becomes a more viable and efficient means to query subsets of the data.

Creating new partitions

When you have live data coming in, you can expect that you'll one day need to add new partitions. The example here is only good for 2004 data. Once 2005 starts, inserts into the orders table with an `orderdate` from that year are going to fail.

You need to consider two things when the active partition is about to move forward into the next value. The first is whether your `TRIGGER` function will support it. In cases where that's a static block of code, with a series of hard-coded comparisons, you may need to update it. The second thing is that the partition needs to be created and all its attributes properly set.

Scheduled creation

The simplest way to deal with creating the new partitions is to write a program that adds them, then make sure you're always at least one partition ahead of what's needed. On Unix derived systems this is typically scripted into a `cron` job that executes more frequently than the partition changes, for example, runs weekly given a monthly partitioning scheme. The Windows Task Scheduler could be used similarly.

Dynamic creation

At that point, you might be thinking that there's no need for scheduling partition creation. Why not just create them dynamically as needed? Indeed, that is an option. But there are a few bits of not necessarily obvious complexity to be wary of.

When two sessions both notice a partition is missing at the same time, it's extremely easy to end up with a race condition in the code, where both try to create it, and transaction deadlock is a common side effect of problems in this area.

Sometimes bad data will come into your table. It might come from far in the past or the future relative to right now. You might not want to create a partition for all of those situations.

There are many pieces to get right for partitioning to work. In addition to creating the partition, you need to add the right indexes, constraints, and permissions to the table. Allowing simple users who are inserting data enough power to set up all these things introduces a class of security concerns better avoided, too.

Partitioning advantages

There are quite a few performance-related improvements that partitioning this way provides. The average number of index blocks you'll have to navigate in order to find a row goes down because the first level split there is pushed towards being the query planner's job instead. And, as mentioned already, having smaller blocks of your data might alter when the database can consider a sequential scan of a range a useful technique.

There are some maintenance advantages, too. You can DROP an individual partition to erase all of the data from that range. This is a common technique for pruning historical data out of a partitioned table, one that avoids the VACUUM cleanup work that DELETE leaves behind. If you have monthly data, and you only keep a certain number of months at a time, once a new month starts you just DROP the oldest partition.

Another advantage is that REINDEX operations will happen in a fraction of the time it would take for a single giant index to build. If you only have limited time windows where a REINDEX is practical, you might be able to squeeze in rebuilding an index or two during each of them, and eventually make your way through all of them. If you're finding that a maintenance window big enough to REINDEX your whole table just isn't available anymore, partitioning might get you back to where you can do it again, a subset at a time.

Common partitioning mistakes

There are enough partitioning problems that people run into repeatedly that it's worth mentioning, and the most common are as follows:

- Not turning on constraint_exclusion and therefore always including every partition.
- Failing to add all the same indexes or constraints to each partition that existed in the parent.
- Forgetting to assign the same permissions to each child table as the parent.
- Writing queries that don't filter on the partitioned key field. The WHERE clause needs to filter on constants. A parameterized query will therefore not work right at all, and functions that can change their value such as CURRENT_DATE will also optimize poorly. In general, keep the WHERE clauses as simple as possible, to improve the odds the optimizer will construct the exclusion proof you're looking for.
- Query overhead for partitioning is proportional to the number of partitions. It's barely noticeable with only 10 or 20 partitions, but if you have hundreds you can expect it to be significant. Keep the number of partitions to the two digit range for best performance.
- When you manually VACUUM/ANALYZE, these will not cascade from the parent. You need to specifically target each partition with those operations.
- Fail to account for out of range dates in the INSERT trigger. Expect that bad data will show up one day with a timestamp either far in the past or the future, relative to what you have partitioned right now. Instead of throwing an error, some prefer to redirect inserted rows from outside of the partitioned range into a holding pen partition dedicated to suspicious data.

Another thing worth mentioning is that some people with big database backgrounds tend to partition whether or not they need to, just because that's the mindset their previous database work left them in. You have to put a fair amount of work into a partitioned PostgreSQL deployment. Make sure that there's a true need for the partitions and a useful expected payback for the work, to justify spending time on it first.

Horizontal partitioning with PL/Proxy

If splitting data among several sub-tables on a single server improves performance, then surely splitting it similarly among multiple servers would be even better, right? That's the theory behind PL/Proxy, a procedural language specifically designed to make that easier. Check out the following link for more information: `http://pgfoundry.org/projects/plproxy/`.

PL/Proxy was designed to fit the database scaling needs of Skype, which includes a target of serving a billion users at once. When you have that kind of user base, you just can't fit everyone on a single server.

The basic premise of PL/Proxy is that you first insulate access to the database behind the database functions (also known as stored procedures). Let's say you want to grab a username field that uniquely identifies a user. Rather than selecting it from a table, instead you'd call a function that returns a username. This style of database design is popular for other reasons, too, because it allows refactoring the design of a database with minimal application impact. So long as the function call API remains stable, what it maps to in the database can be changed more easily.

The next thing to do is determine a way to break your workload up into pieces, similar to how that decision is made for a single server partitioning. The main difference is that you just need to identify a key field in most cases, and not figure out how to map that to the underlying partitions; there is a standard, generic approach that will likely work for you there.

Getting PL/Proxy up and running requires a few software installation steps that are outside of PostgreSQL itself, and this chapter doesn't try and provide a complete walkthrough of those. The goal here is more to provide you with sufficient background about how the program works, to know when it could be considered useful to your scaling efforts, not to detail exactly how to set it up.

Hash generation

The standard practice for most PL/Proxy implementations is to partition based on the `hashtext` of the field you're splitting on, which allows splitting among a number of nodes fairly without knowing the distribution of the dataset in advance. `hashtext` is a PostgreSQL-provided internal function that takes in any text input and generates an integer as output with a hash code. If you AND the result at the bit level, to only take the lowest few bits, this turns out to be a very quick and fair way to distribute load among multiple systems. For this to work, the number of partitions needs to be a power of 2 (2, 4, 8, 16, and so on) and then you bitwise AND against one less than that number. So for two partitions that's & 1, for four partitions it's & 3, and so on. Here's what the output from it looks like for the first 10 integers hashed into four partitions:

```
SELECT s,hashtext(s::text) & 3 AS hash FROM generate_series(1,10) AS s;
  s | hash
----+------
  1 |    1
  2 |    2
  3 |    0
  4 |    0
  5 |    2
  6 |    0
  7 |    1
  8 |    0
  9 |    0
 10 |    3
```

This shows you that there's a fairly equal distribution among the four possible partition values (0, 1, 2, 3) available in this subset. Look at the following count of the various hash values for a larger subset:

```
SELECT hash,count(*) FROM (SELECT s,hashtext(s::text) & 3 AS hash FROM
generate_series(1,10000) AS s) AS q GROUP BY hash ORDER BY hash;
 hash | count
------+-------
    0 |  2550
    1 |  2411
    2 |  2531
    3 |  2508
```

This shows you how using a few bits from the `hashtext` can provide a very equal split among partitions without any specific knowledge of your data.

The values returned by the `hashtext` function have changed between PostgreSQL 8.3 and 8.4. If you're running an earlier version than 8.4, you'll see a different output than the preceding one. Upgrading such a system to a newer PostgreSQL version also needs to respect that change—the resulting partition layout will be different by default.

The only reason that this approach isn't more popular for splitting up key ranges in single node PostgreSQL partitioning, is that the planner doesn't know how to do constraint exclusion based on the `hashtext` function.

Scaling with PL/Proxy

Given that hash-based distribution allows splitting among an arbitrary power of two number of partitions, with relatively even load, PL/Proxy makes it straightforward to split large independent tables among multiple nodes in a way that allows almost unbounded scalability.

The key word there is independent. If, in fact, your queries commonly cross partition boundaries, the query optimizer will not be able to help you generate good plans for those. PL/Proxy calls can be configured to run on any available node or on every node. If you need data from all of them, that's going to turn into a number of independent queries that need to be assembled with UNION ALL in order to get the full result. This may not execute as efficiently as if all the data was on a single node, with a unified set of statistics.

If your application is such that it can be split in distinct, independent datasets, one of the unique aspects of PL/Proxy scaling is that it works on both read and write workloads. Many database scaling techniques only improve read scalability. The fact that PL/Proxy-based scaling has worked for database expansion at heavy PostgreSQL users, Skype and myYearbook, shows how powerful a scaling technique it can allow. If you believe your application may become large enough to need this sort of approach, the main thing you need to get started on early is to practice insulating database access through functions. Once you use that technique, whether the result is then executed on a single server, or multiple ones using PL/Proxy, it will be mostly transparent to your application.

Sharding

Sharding is a form of horizontal partitioning and it can be implemented in PostgreSQL using PL/Proxy. Its main distinction is that sharding emphasizes placing shared data structures on every node, so that each of them can operate independently of one another. Typically, the data you'd want on every system is what's normally referred to as dimension, lookup, or fact tables for your application—the pieces that are common to every set of data. The idea is that you should approach a shared-nothing architecture, where each sharded partition is self-sufficient for answering queries related to the data it contains.

The complexity of a sharding style design includes things such as how to co-ordinate an update to those shared structures. The approach that makes sense there is very application-specific. Using a standard replication approach to keep all the copies up to date is a common design choice. The component in Skype's scaling stack to handle that is their Londiste replication program. Like any asynchronous replication solution and like most sharded database deployments, this introduces an element of database inconsistency where data is present in one database but not the rest. It's easy to introduce a race condition into such a design if you're not careful. Also, if an individual client moves between two copies of the database, they can run into a disconcerting situation where they are moving forward and backward in time, relative to changes made to the shared structures. You may need to code something in your application to prefer a particular database's copy of the shared data, once you've used it once in a session.

Sharding style database scaling is a useful refinement on standard horizontal partitioning, but any time you have independent nodes sharing data there's additional complexity and the potential for application bugs. The sort of eventual consistency guarantees you get are very different from the transactional ones a database normally provides.

Scaling with GridSQL

Another way you might be able to approach hash-based distribution among nodes is using GridSQL.

Instead of putting the logic for what node to execute against directly into the database, GridSQL provides a client that speaks to a node coordinator process that handles that job. This process is all relatively transparent to you. The main catch is that not all PostgreSQL features are available, and you need a client driver compatible with GridSQL.

GridSQL uses its own parser, planner, and optimizer, accepting **American National Standard Institute** (**ANSI**) standard SQL, but not all of PostgreSQL's syntax. The driver interface for your applications to talk to the database can look like a standard PostgreSQL one, but not everything a full PostgreSQL application expects will be supported. In stark contrast to PL/Proxy style scaling, instead of relying heavily on the database functions, GridSQL doesn't support running them at all!

Right now the primary driver available is a Java **Java Database Connectivity** (**JDBC**) level one. If you have a Java application you want to scale across multiple nodes, GridSQL allows parallel query against multiple servers, or even against multiple database instances on a single server with many cores. Getting such a deployment working will be relatively little work, compared to building something similarly complicated using most other solutions for this problem. This architecture is also well suited for a sharded configuration, where dimension tables are replicated across nodes to make it easy for a single node to fully answer common queries.

This parallel query feature makes GridSQL most appropriate for building data warehouse style database applications, where long query time is the main performance issue. It's not aimed to accelerate write-heavy transactional loads.

If you have a straightforward Java application and don't need database functions, GridSQL can provide a useful way to scale data warehouse style loads onto multiple cores or nodes. But if you're using other client programming languages, or doing sophisticated database-side programming, it would be much harder to convert your application to using its approach.

Summary

Every form of partitioning in PostgreSQL currently requires a moderate amount of manual setup. Accordingly, it's not something you want to do by default. There needs to be sufficient justification in terms of expected improvement in scalability before partitioning your tables will make sense. When it is effective, partitioning can dramatically speed up some types of queries against the database, improving overall system efficiency.

Partitioning large tables normally makes sense when they or the active portion of a database as a whole exceeds the total amount of memory in the server. Choosing what key field to partition over needs to carefully review all queries made against the table, to make sure they are selective against that field. Individual partitions need to be created manually, along with having any constraints, indexes, or permissions against the parent applied to them as well.

TRIGGER functions are the easiest way to redirect INSERT, UPDATE, or DELETE statements to move the resulting row to the correct partition. It's possible to do a live migration of data from an existing unpartitioned table to a partitioned one, albeit with a temporary doubling of the disk space used by the table.

The query, constraint_exclusion, needs to be turned on for partitioning to work. Queries need to use simple WHERE clauses that compare against the key field in order for constraint exclusion to work. Partitioning improves queries by reducing the number of rows considered, lowering index sizes, and allowing sequential scans where only an index scan would have been appropriate before.

Some database maintenance operations might be improved by partitioning. You'll get quicker individual REINDEX times and the ability to DROP old partitions to remove them almost instantly, instead of using DELETE against all of the old rows. You need to be vigilant in creating partitions before they are used. This is normally a scheduled operation because trying to create the partitions at insert time is tough to do correctly.

The upper limit on the number of partitions you can use effectively is tens of them. Anything using significantly more than 100 partitions can expect to suffer from the overhead of needing to evaluate so many partition constraints whenever a query executes.

Starting from PostgreSQL 10, it's possible to use the declarative partition feature. PL/Proxy can be used to split data among multiple nodes effectively, for nearly infinite expansion possibilities. It can be used to build applications using the sharding approach popular for shared-nothing deployments too.

GridSQL can also split data among multiple nodes, and it includes enough database components to handle accelerating queries to execute in parallel on multiple nodes. But the program only has good support for Java applications, and both functions and PostgreSQL-specific features may not be available.

16
Avoiding Common Problems

Beyond the expected day-to-day setup and design issues, there are some recurring issues PostgreSQL administrators and developers run into regularly that don't have really obvious answers. PostgreSQL has *Frequently Asked Questions* lists available at http://wiki.postgresql.org/wiki/Category:FAQ and you may find reading them interesting, even though some of those topics are covered in this chapter, too.

Bulk loading

There are two slightly different types of bulk data loads you might want to do. The first type, and the main focus of this section, is when you're initially populating an empty database. Sometimes you also need to do later bulk loads into tables that are already populated. In that case, some of the techniques here, such as dropping indexes and constraints, will no longer be applicable. And you may not be able to get quite as aggressive in tuning the server for better loading speed when doing incremental loading. In particular, options that decrease the integrity of the whole server, such as disabling fsync, only make sense when starting with a blank system.

Loading methods

The preferred path to get a lot of data into the database is by using the COPY command. This is the fastest way to insert a set of rows. If that's not practical and you have to use INSERT instead, you should try to include as many records as possible per commit, wrapping several into a BEGIN/COMMIT block. Most applications find that between 100 and 1,000 rows per commit gives the majority of the best performance possible in doing batch inserts, but it's still not going to be as fast as COPY.

From slowest to fastest, this is the usual ranking:

- Insert a single record at once.
- Insert larger blocks of records at one time.
- Use a single COPY at a time. This is what a standard pg_restore does.
- Multiple INSERT processes using larger blocks in parallel.
- Use multiple COPY commands at once. Parallel pg_restore does this.

Getting multiple processes doing INSERT or COPY at once can be harder than expected in some programming languages. Process or threading limitations of the programming language can end up being the bottleneck instead of the database itself.

Also, be aware that if you are using a regular programming language for this job, you may need to be very explicit about tuning off per-transaction autocommit in order to get proper batch insert behavior. It's also useful in some cases to use PREPARE to set up the INSERT statement, just to lower parsing overhead. Unlike a query, there's little potential for the plan to degrade when you do that.

External loading programs

Another thing to be aware of is that COPY will abort all its work if it finds any error in the input data. This can be frustrating if the bad row is near the end of a large input. If you're importing from an external data source (a dump out of a non-PostgreSQL database, for example), you should consider a loader that saves rejected rows while continuing to work anyway, like pgloader, (http://pgfoundry.org/projects/pgloader/). pgloader will not be as fast as COPY, but it's easier to work with on dirty input data and it can handle more types of input formats, too.

Another loader useful for some special cases is pg_bulkload. It can be even faster than straight COPY. This is due to very aggressive performance features, such as bypassing the WAL (which is possible in some cases, as covered later, with regular COPY), and it also has some features for handling bad data. pg_bulkload is a fairly invasive loader that requires loading custom functions into the database, and as such it's a little more intense to work with than the simpler, external-only pgloader. Which one makes more sense, or whether straight COPY is fine, really depends on the cleanliness of your data and exactly how fast you must have it loaded.

Tuning for bulk loads

The most important thing to do in order to speed up bulk loads is to turn off any indexes or foreign key constraints on the table. It's more efficient to build indexes in bulk and the result will be less fragmented. Constraint checks are much faster to check in bulk, too.

There are a few `postgresql.conf` values that you can set outside of their normal range specifically to accelerate bulk loads:

- `maintenance_work_mem`: Increase this to a much larger value than you'd normally run your server with. 1 GB is not unreasonable on a server with >16 GB of RAM nowadays. This speeds up `CREATE INDEX` and `ALTER TABLE ADD FOREIGN KEY`, presuming you've followed the advice mentioned earlier to do those in a batch after loading.
- `max_wal_size = 3 * checkpoint_segments * 16`: Much higher values than what would normally be safe are acceptable here, to spread out checkout I/O because crash recovery time and disk space aren't so important before the server goes live; 128-256 are common values for bulk loading. Similarly, increasing `checkpoint_timeout` can also be advisable, with values of 30 minutes being reasonable in this context.
- `autovacuum`: Having periodic `autovacuum` does little but get in the way of a standard bulk load. It's recommended to turn it off.
- `Wal_buffers`: This can easily turn into a bottleneck on a bulk load. Setting it to the practical upper limit of 16 MB is a recommended practice.
- `synchronous_commit`: If your bulk load is an all-or-nothing affair, there's little downside to turning off synchronous commits so that they are done in larger batches instead. If you crash and lose some transactions as a result, it's normally possible to just wipe out the last table being loaded and reload it from scratch.
- `fsync`: The only time that it's reasonable to consider turning off `fsync` is when doing the initial loading of a database. In that situation, the main downside of no `fsync`—a database crash can lead to corruption is normally not fatal. Just start over with the loading again. Disabling `fsync` was particularly valuable on PostgreSQL 8.2 and earlier, before `synchronous_commit` was available, and it is also valuable on hardware that doesn't include a non-volatile write cache. It can make the difference between only loading a hundred records per second and getting thousands instead.
- `vacuum_freeze_min_age`: Lowering this parameter to 0 is appropriate if you're going to manually do `VACUUM` of the database before putting it into production. It will maximize the amount of database cleanup that such a `VACUUM` can do.

Some of these presume that you're doing a fairly dumb loading routine. If your loading process involves any table cleaning procedure that does joins, you may need to keep autovacuum in particular ON in order for those to work efficiently. It might be beneficial to increase work_mem as well in that situation. All of these memory parameters can potentially be set to much higher values than normal during loading, so long as you're not allowing clients to connect while the loading is going on.

Skipping WAL acceleration

The purpose of the write-ahead log is to protect you from partially committed data being left behind after a crash. If you create a new table in a transaction, add some data to it, and then commit at the end, at no point during that process is the WAL really necessary. If the commit doesn't happen, the expectation is that the entire table is gone anyway. Accordingly, in recent PostgreSQL versions this particular case is accelerated. A bulk load is as follows:

```
BEGIN;
CREATE TABLE t ...
COPY t FROM ...
COMMIT;
```

It will not generate any WAL records by default, and therefore execute quicker. You can get the same acceleration with a table that exists if you use TRUNCATE to clear it out first.

However, if you have turned on the archive_command facility to feed WAL segments to a PITR standby, this optimization is disabled. The WAL is in that case the only way to get the data over to the standby system, so it can't be skipped. In PostgreSQL 9.0 and later, some settings of wal_level can disable this optimization, too. Since archiving is often off or can be delayed until after initial bulk loading of a database, this trick can still be useful in the early stages of a standby configuration.

Recreating indexes and adding constraints

Presuming you dropped indexes and constraints before loading data in, you'll now need to create them again. Index rebuild in particular can be very processor, memory, and disk intensive. If you have a large disk array, it's quite reasonable to consider running two or more such rebuilds in parallel. It's recommended that you have high values for shared_buffers, max_wal_size , checkpoint_timeout, and maintenance_work_mem to make indexing and constraint checking perform well.

Parallel restore

PostgreSQL 8.4 introduced an automatic parallel restore that lets you allocate multiple CPU cores on the server to their own dedicated loading processes. In addition to loading data into more than one table at once, running the parallel `pg_restore` will even usefully run multiple index builds in parallel. You just need to tell it how many *jobs* it can run at once, and once it has finished the basic table setup, it will try to keep that many things active at all times. You do have to use the custom database dump in just the right format for the parallel restore to use it.

`COPY` in PostgreSQL requires a pretty large amount of CPU to run, and it's actually quite easy to discover a single core is maxed out running it without keeping the disks busy. But it is possible that parallel restore may just turn disk bound and not see much of a speed increase. The magnitude of the improvement is proportional to how fast your disks are. Also, if the bulk of your loading time is spent dealing with one very large table, this won't benefit very much from a parallel load, either. The ideal case for it is where you have many similarly sized tables to load and/or index.

If you have a PostgreSQL 8.4 installation available, it's possible to use it to dump and restore against older database versions too. You might connect to an 8.2 server, dump in the format parallel restore expects, and then use parallel restore against an 8.3 server. All of the improved smarts here are handled on the client side; they don't require specific server support. There have been reports of this working fine, but since it's normally preferable to dump with the same client version you expect to restore, though it's a bit risky. Consider using parallel `pg_restore` against older versions, something you'll want to carefully test before you rely on it for a production quality migration.

Post-load cleanup

Your data is loaded, your indexes recreated, and your constraints active. There are two maintenance chores you should consider before putting the server back into production. The first is a must-do; make sure to run `ANALYZE` against all the databases. This will make sure you have useful statistics for them before queries start running.

You can also consider running a database-wide VACUUM if you can stand the additional downtime during the load. The reason for this is that it will set the hint bit data for each page of the database, as described later in the *Unexplained writes* section. You can even combine the two with VACUUM ANALYZE and get everything ready for good initial performance. It's possible to get autovacuum to chew away on that problem instead, but it will considerably slow the database until it has completed every table. Another potential improvement recommended here is making this wide VACUUM more aggressive about freezing old transactions, as the things you're loading are unlikely to get rolled back later. This is the spot when reducing the vacuum_freeze_min_age parameter in the postgresql.conf to 0 in order to make any manual post load VACUUM as aggressive as possible would be useful.

Once you've done as much of this maintenance as you can tolerate, make sure you also revert any loading specific optimizations you made to the postgresql.conf file before making the database live again. That may include turning autovacuum back on and changing your relative memory allocations to something tuned for clients, instead of loading.

Backup

PostgreSQL allows you to perform backups in a traditional way or through the continuous archiving and point-in-time recovery mode. Through the Point-In-Time Recovery (PITR), PostgreSQL is able to bring the database back to any point in the past.

pg_dump

pg_dump is a utility for backing up a PostgreSQL database. It makes consistent backups even if the database is being used concurrently. pg_dump does not block other users accessing the database (readers or writers). It only dumps a single database. To back up global objects that are common to all databases in a cluster, use pg_dump_all.

The dump can be made in a script or file formats. Script files are plain-text files containing the SQL commands required to reconstruct the database to the state it was in at the time it was saved. File formats can be used by pg_restore to rebuild the database.

To choose which format to use, you can select the output format using the `-F` option followed by:

- p: Plain—output a plain-text SQL script file (the default)
- c: Custom—output a custom-format archive suitable for input into `pg_restore`
- d: Directory—output a directory-format archive suitable for input into `pg_restore`
- t: Tar—output a tar-format archive suitable for input into `pg_restore`

A note for performance: Using the `-Fd` option, you can also add the `-j nbobs` option. This combination of options runs the dump in parallel by dumping `njobs` tables simultaneously.

You can find more info at `https://www.postgresql.org/docs/10/static/app-pgdump.html`.

Continuous archiving and point in time recovery

PostgreSQL has a native support for continuous archiving and PITR. In PostgreSQL, it is possible to perform these operations in a native way through simple SQL instructions (`https://www.postgresql.org/docs/10/static/continuous-archiving.html`); however, there are some tools that can simplify our life. Here are some examples:

- **Barman**: Barman (Backup and Recovery Manager) is an open source administration tool for disaster recovery of PostgreSQL servers written in Python. It allows your organization to perform remote backups of multiple servers in business critical environments and help DBAs during the recovery phase. More information is given at `https://www.pgbarman.org/`.
- **BART** : **EDB Backup and Recovery Tool (BART)** is a key component of an enterprise-level Postgres-based data management strategy. BART implements retention policies and point-in-time recovery requirements for large-scale Postgres deployments. Now available, Bart 2.0 provides block-level incremental backup. More info is given at `https://www.enterprisedb.com/products/edb-postgres-platform/edb-backup-and-recovery-tool`.

- **pgBackRest**: pgBackRest aims to be a simple, reliable backup and restore system that can seamlessly scale up to the largest databases and workloads. Instead of relying on traditional backup tools like `tar` and `rsync`, pgBackRest implements all backup features internally and uses a custom protocol for communicating with remote systems. Removing reliance on `tar` and X allows for better solutions to database-specific backup challenges. The custom remote protocol allows for more flexibility and limits the types of connections that are required to perform a backup which increases security. More information is given at `https://pgbackrest.org/`.

Common performance issues

Many performance issues come from bad designs or implementations that just don't fundamentally work well with PostgreSQL. There are a few areas where the problem is not so bad; it's more of a quirk with known workarounds. This section covers some of the more common problems new PostgreSQL users run into from this category.

Counting rows

It's not unusual to find an application that does the following to determine how many rows there are in a table:

```
SELECT count(*) FROM t;
```

In some databases other than PostgreSQL, this executes very quickly, usually because that information is kept handy in an index or similar structure. Unfortunately, because PostgreSQL keeps its row visibility information in the row data pages, you cannot determine a true row count without looking at every row in the table, one at a time, to determine whether they are visible or not. That's a sequential scan of the full table, and it's pretty slow; it even turns out to be an effective way to benchmark sequential read speed on a table to count its rows this way!

If your statement is fairly selective instead:

```
SELECT count(*) FROM t WHERE k>10 and k<20;
```

This form can execute quickly, presuming that the index scan on `k` is only returning a few rows. How fast a count runs is proportional to the number of rows returned.

If you need a row count and can't afford to wait that long, there are two alternate approaches. For situations that just need an approximate count without taking every last bit of row visibility information into account, one is computed each time ANALYZE is run, either manually or using autovacuum. You can find the row estimate it computes, which is usually quite accurate unless your rows vary wildly in size, like the following:

```
SELECT reltuples FROM pg_class WHERE relname='t';
```

If you might have more than one table with the same name but a different namespace, the following form is required:

```
SELECT reltuples
FROM pg_class C
LEFT JOIN pg_namespace N ON (N.oid = C.relnamespace)
WHERE c.relname='t' and nspname = 'public';
```

Again, these values are only as accurate as your last analysis, so make sure those happen regularly if you expect this form of count to be useful.

The other approach you can consider is adding a trigger onto the table that tracks the change in count each time a row is inserted or deleted, and then store the total that way. This total will always be exact, except for the usual fuzziness about whether the most recent transactions are visible or not. There is a list of code examples shown to build this into your own app at http://wiki.postgresql.org/wiki/Slow_Counting; they are worth looking at. At a somewhat higher level, maintaining a count can be considered a very simple materialized view, and some of the techniques useful for that can also be used here.

Unexplained writes

There are several situations where you can find yourself executing statements that only read against the database, yet find significant write volume happening on the database disk.

Parts of the buffer cache must be dirty before writes happen, so if any of that work is left hanging around, it could be involved. Flushing everything out with a manual checkpoint is one way to assure that it's not the cause of the writes.

A second small source of writes are the access time updates that many operating systems do every time you read from a file. It was suggested these get turned off in Chapter 4, *Disk Setup*, and the actual volume of writes from them is pretty low, anyway.

If the volume of writes is substantial and this data was recently created, what you most likely run into are updates to the hint bits in the database. Hint bits are two bits stored in each row that indicate whether that row's associated transaction has committed or rolled back. If they aren't set, the database's commit log data (in `pg_xact` and possibly `pg_subtrans`) has to be consulted to determine whether the row is visible. Once going though all that trouble, the row is then updated with the correct hint bit information so that an expensive computation doesn't have to be done again. The result is now a dirty page that needs to be written out again, even though all you did was read it.

Executing something that checks every row in a table—including a full table `SELECT`, `COUNT`, or running `VACUUM` against it—will perform this visibility check and write out final hint bits for each row. Until that has happened, expect some steady write activity consisting of hint bit updates any time you select against recently committed data. See `http://wiki.postgresql.org/wiki/Hint_Bits` for more information about the internals involved.

Don't forget about some simpler causes of writing when executing queries too. `autovacuum` running in the background after being triggered by recent activity might be writing things. And if your query is doing a sort operation or using temporary tables that spill over to disk, that will cause writes, too.

Slow function and prepared statement execution

A prepared statement is a valuable technique that rejects SQL injection into your applications as well as allows you to bypass regular query parsing in order to save overhead. You might use one like the following:

```
PREPARE getvals (int) AS SELECT * FROM t WHERE t.v=$1;
EXECUTE getvals(5);
```

This returns everything in the rows with a matching v value. The `PREPARE` saves the output from the query parsing and planning stage. You might think that this will always be a win over directly executing the query if it's being executed more than once, because that overhead will then be amortized over more statements.

This isn't necessarily true. When a statement is prepared, the query optimizer can only produce a generic query plan for it, not knowing anything about the actual values that are going to be requested. When you execute a regular query, the statistics about each column available to the optimizer can sometimes do much better than this. Consider the case where the value v=5 only appears in 1% of the rows in the table, which the optimizer could know based on the statistics collected about this table. Had you executed a regular statement using that restriction in a WHERE clause, the optimizer would have strongly considered an index scan to only retrieve that small number of rows. But in a prepared statement context, where it had to choose the query plan at preparation time, it could only choose a generic plan that couldn't take advantage of such detailed statistics; it didn't know the exact value to match against, yet.

In PostgreSQL 8.4, it's possible to use the new QUERY EXECUTE...USING syntax in order to get a newly planned query while still being safe from SQL injection. See `http://okbob.blogspot.com/2008/06/execute-using-feature-in-postgresql-84.html` for the background about this new feature. In older versions, you can construct statements as strings, quote_literal to resist SQL injection, and then manually do EXECUTE of those to work around this issue; see `http://blog.endpoint.com/2008/12/why-is-my-function-slow.html` for an example.

PL/pgSQL benchmarking

PostgreSQL 8.4 added a feature to allow track statistics on how long each database function written in PL/pgSQL and similar languages takes to execute. To enable this, edit your `postgresql conf`:

```
track_functions = all
```

The other option here is pl, which only tracks the pl/* language functions instead of all of them (that is, not the ones written in C). Once that's done, you've executed some functions, and you've waited a moment for those to show up in the statistics collector, the following query will show you what executed:

```
SELECT * FROM pg_stat_user_functions;
```

In earlier versions, it was possible to build your own test harness. If instead you'd like to figure out which individual statements are responsible for
the overhead, then instead of just finding out how long the entire function takes, you'll need something more like a profiling tool for that. EnterpriseDB has released a PL/pgSQL debugger that includes profiling features. It comes bundled with their PostgreSQL installer, and you may be able to install it separately on top of community PostgreSQL as well. There is also an interesting albeit intrusive way to build your profiling by hand described at `http://www.depesz.com/index.php/2010/03/18/profiling-stored-proceduresfunctions /`; that's applicable to any PostgreSQL install.

High foreign key overhead

When you commit a transaction, if there's a foreign key involved, that commit is fairly expensive. As a percentage of total processing time, this is particularly bad if you're doing updates one at a time. To help improve this situation for batch updates, you can mark foreign key constraints as `DEFERRABLE`, either during `CREATE TABLE` or in a later `ALTER TABLE` to adjust it. The default is `NOT DEFERRABLE`. Note that this only impacts foreign keys and similar constraints implemented as triggers. It doesn't do anything for `CHECK` and `UNIQUE` restrictions, which cannot be deferred and are instead always processed immediately, at least before PostgreSQL 9.0, that is. See the performance notes for 10.0 at the end of this chapter for more information about additional options available in that version.

For deferrable constraints, there are again two options. If the check is labeled `INITIALLY IMMEDIATE`, it still happens immediately rather than at the end of the transaction. You can also modify the constraint so the default is instead `INITIALLY DEFERRED`, making the check only at transaction end.

In the case where a check is `DEFERRABLE` and it's `INITIALLY IMMEDIATE`, you can alter what a particular session does using `SET CONSTRAINTS`. The standard practice for foreign keys is to make them deferrable but default to the more proactive immediate behavior, and then make batch updates process them in a deferrable transaction. like the following:

```
BEGIN;
SET CONSTRAINTS ALL DEFERRED;
[update or insert statements]
COMMIT;
```

This will batch all of the processing related to deferrable constraint checks into one block, which is much more efficient. There is a potential downside to be concerned about here though. If your batch size is large when using this technique, the COMMIT can block for quite some time while chugging through all that work. And it's easy for other transactions to get stuck behind it. Overall, large foreign key checks bunched together by deferring them are something to watch out for as a potential source of latency spikes in query activity.

Trigger memory use

If you've used some of the suggestions here to group your database commits into larger chunks, you might notice an expected downside to that: running out of memory at commit time. The issue is that if the table you're changing has an AFTER trigger on it, each statement due to trigger is inserted into an in-memory list. If there are a large number of them, perhaps due to a bulk loading job, it's possible to run out of the amount of memory on the system (or reach the limit for your user account) before the transaction can complete. Be careful when combining AFTER triggers with batch commits.

Transition tables for trigger

Starting from PostgreSQL 10, this feature is available. Transition tables for triggers are tables with old and new tuples, so your triggers can see what changed; they make the whole statement's changes available to you. Here is an example taken from the test suite at https://github.com/postgres/postgres/blob/a571c7f661a7b601aafcb12196d004cdb8b8cb23/src/test/regress/sql/plpgsql.sql:

```
CREATE TABLE transition_table_base (id int PRIMARY KEY, val text);

CREATE OR REPLACE FUNCTION transition_table_base_upd_func()
  RETURNS trigger
  LANGUAGE plpgsql
AS $$
DECLARE
  t text;
  l text;
BEGIN
  t = '';
  FOR l IN EXECUTE
        $q$
          EXPLAIN (TIMING off, COSTS off, VERBOSE on)
          SELECT * FROM oldtable ot FULL JOIN newtable nt USING (id)
        $q$ LOOP
    t = t || l || E'\n';
```

```
    END LOOP;

    RAISE INFO '%', t;
    RETURN new;
END;
$$;

CREATE TRIGGER transition_table_base_upd_trig
AFTER UPDATE ON transition_table_base
REFERENCING OLD TABLE AS oldtable NEW TABLE AS newtable
FOR EACH STATEMENT
EXECUTE PROCEDURE transition_table_base_upd_func();
```

Heavy statistics collector overhead

One of the background database processes that shouldn't occupy too much of your system is the statistics collector, which looks like this from the perspective of `ps`:

```
Postgres 32450 32445 0 13:49 ? 00:00:00 postgres: stats collector process
```

Under normal circumstances, the statistics collection shouldn't take more than a few percent of CPU time even under heavy activity. There are occasional versions of PostgreSQL where this is not true. For example, 8.2.0 through 8.2.3 had a serious bug where statistics wrote far too often. But even if you're running 8.2, you should never be using such an old minor release of it, anyway.

Sometimes, circumstances aren't normal enough and the statistics collector takes up a lot more time than it normally does to run. This is normally associated with the statistics collector file itself becoming very large; here's a small one:

```
$ ls -l $PGDATA/pg_stat_tmp
-rw------- 1 postgres postgres 28961 2010-06-01 13:49 pgstat.stat
```

If your statistics collector is running slowly, and particularly if that's accompanied by the `pgstat.stat` file being very large, you should try resetting your database statistics. It's hard to say what "large" implies here without knowing the size of your database; tracking the file size for a bit after reset may give you an idea of what's appropriate for your system. You might want to save interesting statistics, such as `pg_stat_user_tables`, before resetting, just so that cumulative data there isn't lost. Statistics are reset using the following command:

```
$ psql -c "select pg_stat_reset();"
```

And the file should be small again. It should grow for a while and then hit a steady-state size. If it continues to grow without bounds again, this is the behavior you can consider reporting to one of the PostgreSQL mailing lists, as it has been difficult to replicate the problem for some users recently.

Targeted statistics resets

Starting from PostgreSQL 9.0, it's also possible to reset the `pg_stat_bgwriter` view using the following command:

```
$ psql -c "select pg_stat_reset_shared('bgwriter');"
```

But this will never cause heavy statistics overload as it's not stored in a file that will get large. It's also possible to reset single statistics values in 9.0 using `pg_stat_reset_single_table_counters` and function stats with `pg_stat_reset_single_function_counters`, but if your issue is high statistics collector overhead, you should really reset the whole thing, instead.

Extended statistics

Starting from PostgreSQL 10, the following new commands are available:

- CREATE STATISTICS
- ALTER STATISTICS
- DROP STATISTICS

Using these commands, it is possible to create, modify, or delete objects that can monitor the statistics of a specific table, foreign table, or materialized view.

Also, you can refer to the following links:

- https://www.postgresql.org/docs/10/static/sql-createstatistics.html
- https://www.postgresql.org/docs/10/static/sql-alterstatistics.html
- https://www.postgresql.org/docs/10/static/sql-dropstatistics.html

Materialized views

One of the most effective ways to speed up queries against large datasets that are run more than once is to cache the result in a materialized view—essentially a view that is run and its output stored for future reference. Work on adding these into the core database is in progress but, like counting, it's possible to build them right now using features such as triggers. See `http://wiki.postgresql.org/wiki/Materialized_Views` for comments on the state-of-the-art stuff here, and pointers to code samples. If you have views derived from large tables in the database, few techniques are as effective as materializing those views and optimizing their updates for improving query performance.

Foreign data wrapper

Foreign data wrappers are a standardized way of handling access to remote objects from SQL databases. Using the foreign data wrapper module, you can connect PostgreSQL to different types of data sources.

All the foreign data wrapper modules for PostgreSQL are available at `https://wiki.postgresql.org/wiki/Foreign_data_wrappers`.

Some of these also allow the calculation of aggregates directly on the remote server, bringing only already calculated data to PostgreSQL; this feature is called **foreign data wrapper aggregate pushdown**.

The amcheck module

Starting from PostgreSQL 10, the `amcheck` module is available. The `amcheck` module provides functions that allow you to verify the logical consistency of the structure of indexes. If the structure appears to be valid, no error is raised. You can find it at `https://www.postgresql.org/docs/10/static/amcheck.html`.

With this module, you can check the following:

- Structural inconsistencies caused by incorrect operator class implementations
- Corruption caused by hypothetical undiscovered bugs in the underlying
- PostgreSQL access method code or sort code

- Filesystem or storage subsystem faults where checksums happen to be simply not enabled
- Corruption caused by faulty RAM, and the broader memory subsystem and operating system

Let's use it now:

```
pgbench=# create extension amcheck ;
CREATE EXTENSION

SELECT bt_index_check(c.oid), c.relname, c.relpages
FROM pg_index i
JOIN pg_opclass op ON i.indclass[0] = op.oid
JOIN pg_am am ON op.opcmethod = am.oid
JOIN pg_class c ON i.indexrelid = c.oid
JOIN pg_namespace n ON c.relnamespace = n.oid
WHERE am.amname = 'btree' AND n.nspname = 'pg_catalog'
-- Don't check temp tables, which may be from another session:
AND c.relpersistence != 't'
-- Function may throw an error when this is omitted:
AND i.indisready AND i.indisvalid
ORDER BY c.relpages DESC LIMIT 10;
```

bt_index_check	relname	relpages
	pg_depend_reference_index	51
	pg_depend_depender_index	45
	pg_proc_proname_args_nsp_index	33
	pg_description_o_c_o_index	24
	pg_attribute_relid_attnam_index	13
	pg_collation_name_enc_nsp_index	11
	pg_proc_oid_index	10
	pg_attribute_relid_attnum_index	10
	pg_collation_oid_index	7
	pg_amop_opr_fam_index	7

pgAdmin

pgAdmin is a graphical tool used for PostgreSQL administration; it is available on Linux, Windows and macOS X. You can download it from `https://www.pgadmin.org`.

With pgAdmin, you can do the following:

- Multiple connections
- Overview of the server status in real time
- Graphical explain and graphical explain analyze
- Create databases, schemas, tables, and so on
- Run queries

Take a view at the following figure for better understanding:

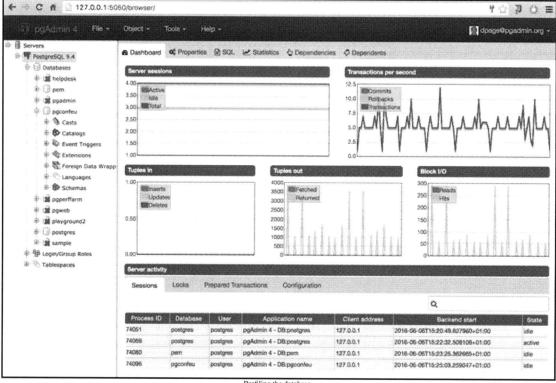

Profiling the database

Sometimes, figuring out why your code isn't working properly is best done by diving into the database itself and looking for bottlenecks in its code. There are a few techniques available for this.

gprof

The standard GNU profiler, gprof, is available for most Unix-like systems. If you compile the PostgreSQL server using the --enable-profiling option, it will produce a gmon.out file that can be given to gprof for verbose profiling of the server internals.

The main issue with gprof profiling and PostgreSQL is that it's known to have problems when tracing into functions in loadable libraries. Also, it's hard to combine the profiling information with a look at what the underlying operating systems is doing. These two limitations combine to make gprof only suitable for profiling fairly simple and pure database operations.

OProfile

OProfile is a venerable tool for profiling everything that happens on a Linux server. You need to have debugging information for your kernel, which can be tricky to obtain depending on your distribution. But the basic data collection is simple after that and contains everything from the OS to the highest level database operations.

OProfile is the preferred tool for many who work on PostgreSQL to find bottlenecks and hotspots in the code under Linux. An excellent introduction to it that covers additional tools to extend its analysis power is available at the link mentioned here:
http://wiki.postgresql.org/wiki/Profiling_with_OProfile.

Visual Studio

Starting with PostgreSQL 8.4, on Windows, the database can be built using Visual Studio. This means that it's possible to use Visual Studio tools, including the debugger and profiler in order to analyze the performance of the database code.

DTrace

Sun's Solaris 10 release in 2004 introduced DTrace, perhaps the most comprehensive toolkit for profiling available on any operating system. The probes required to instrument code with DTrace have minimal overhead when they are not enabled, and the way they're inserted makes it possible to instrument a production system very safely. Making this level of power available to regular user-level processes is also quite useful.

PostgreSQL must have been compiled with the `--enable-dtrace` option for its DTrace probes to be available. You could write an entire book just on how to use DTrace with PostgreSQL. The main PostgreSQL manual section at `http://www.postgresql.org/docs/current/interactive/dynamic-trace.html` covers all the probe points available as of the current version. Links to additional utilities and documentation are available at `http://wiki.postgresql.org/wiki/DTrace`.

The DTrace implementation on Apple's macOS X is also very complete, including surprisingly good details about what's happening in the operating system itself. In addition to the command-line tools, Apple provides a good GUI interface to the DTrace data named, *Instruments* as part of their XCode development tools.

DTrace on FreeBSD

As of the current FreeBSD 8.0, the DTrace implementation in the operating system has two major missing features. The probes into the operating system itself aren't very comprehensive, yet. And so far, only root can use DTrace. Both these limitations are being worked on, and FreeBSD may move closer to Solaris in terms of how capable it is for doing DTrace work in future releases.

Linux SystemTap emulation of DTrace

SystemTap is a Linux utility that allows dynamic tracing, similar to DTrace. Starting from SystemTap V0.9, it includes header files that expose the same user space capabilities that DTrace does. This means that on a Linux system with that version of SystemTap or later, you can compile PostgreSQL using `--enable-dtrace` and it will hook into SystemTap using the DTrace probes.

Support for SystemTap varies quite a bit based on Linux distribution. The Fedora Core versions starting with FC10 include support for the PostgreSQL DTrace probe emulation, and that support has been included as part of RHEL 6, too. These RedHat systems are the most reliable sources for SystemTap on Linux.

On Debian and Ubuntu, SystemTap with appropriate headers may be available, but support for the matching kernel debugging symbols has been very sporadic. It's not clear yet whether this will be considered a priority to resolve in future releases.

From a database administrator perspective, the amount of kernel level work required to make SystemTap install and instrument a running system makes it a less appropriate tool for use on a production server than DTrace. It just isn't as well designed for that purpose, particularly because it's easier to misuse in a way that's dangerous to the server.

Performance-related features by version

A guide to the major changes in each PostgreSQL version starting with 7.4 is available at the feature matrix page: `http://www.postgresql.org/about/featurematrix`.

Since many performance-related changes are more internal, you won't necessarily see them there. The details are only in the release notes, the latest version of which you can read at `http://www.postgresql.org/docs/current/static/release.html`.

This section will help you guide through features and settings that aren't available in older versions (or are removed from newer versions) of PostgreSQL in a more compact form, targeted specifically at performance-related ones. You will need to think first why digression is more important.

Aggressive PostgreSQL version upgrades

One habit some database deployments adopt, which is counterproductive with PostgreSQL, is that the version of the software used should be frozen forever once the system is validated as working. This is a particularly troublesome viewpoint to adopt for systems that run into performance issues. The performance increases that you'll find just from upgrading from older to newer PostgreSQL versions can be far larger than anything you can do just by tweaking the older version. Similarly, if you're running into a problem with how a specific query is executing, don't be surprised to find that it's fixed in a later version of PostgreSQL, and upgrading to it is really your only option to obtain that fix.

While major version upgrades like going from PostgreSQL 8.2 to 8.3 will introduce compatibility issues, you shouldn't expect that to be the case for minor version upgrades. If you're running 8.2.3 for example, merely because that's the version you originally tested your application on, your statistics collector process will write data at a quite active pace. I recall this particular bug as one that was crippling to the system I encountered it on. If you merely upgrade to the current 8.2 release (8.2.17 as this is being written), not only will that problem go away, but also you'll get a long list of other bug fixes—some of them resolve problems that might even lead to database corruption one day if left unfixed. Considering that only fixes for serious bugs are put into the minor version updates to PostgreSQL, not running the latest minor release available is a downright dangerous practice. A minor version upgrade like 8.2.3 to 8.2.17 is more like what some vendors refer to as a "fix pack" than a serious version upgrade. Avoid applying such fixes at your own peril.

Similarly, applying serious resources toward improving a system based on an old version of PostgreSQL is often the wrong move too. If you are suffering from really bad checkpoint spikes and you're on PostgreSQL 8.2 or earlier, there is no good substitute for upgrading to 8.3 or later to help improve those. If you're on PostgreSQL 8.3 and have queries that involve heavy group or sort operations, you would spend far more time trying to fix those queries than it would have taken you to upgrade to 8.4, where the hash-based implementation of those operations is available to vastly accelerate certain types of them.

There are a few reasons for the feature by version, listed later. One is to make you aware of what your version of PostgreSQL can and can't do from a performance perspective—information that can be hard to accumulate on your own (the release notes are not verbose). Knowing what was improved in a later version can be a clue as to what's wrong with earlier ones. And in cases where your problem sounds like something resolved in a later version, that should at least raise the possibility that a database version upgrade is worth considering.

To give a very real example of how this regularly plays out, there are people quite happily running PostgreSQL 7.4, a popular version because it shipped with RedHat Enterprise 4. And that version has continued to receive critical bug fixes and security patches up until very recently, even though it's 7 years old at this point. But if you're trying to optimize performance of a 7.4 installation, something the PostgreSQL community regularly sees people trying to do with little success, that's the time you're probably wasting. Your effort would be better spent upgrading to a newer version. The same thing is true for PostgreSQL 8.0, and even 8.1 and 8.2 look pretty slow from the perspective of the current version at this point.

Please note the following updates for 8.1:

- The shared buffer cache used to hold database data was redesigned for better concurrent use. This change is the major reason 8.1 is the earliest PostgreSQL version with good scalability.
- Bitmap scans allow combining multiple single-column indexes for queries that reference more than one column. This decreases the need to create computationally expensive multi-column indexes on tables.
- `autovacuum`, formerly a module that had to be explicitly loaded, was integrated into the main server (but not started by default).
- Table partitioning is improved to allow skipping partitions that can't possibly satisfy a query.
- Indexes are automatically used for `MIN()` and `MAX()` queries.

Please note the following updates for 8.2:

- Memory settings in the `postgresql.conf` file can be specified in standard units such as 1 MB, instead of simply raw integers whose settings depends on the server units.
- Indexes can be created concurrently, without blocking writes to the table.
- You can watch the `autovacuum` daemon work in `pg_stat_activity`, and it records what it has done in views such as `pg_stat_user_tables`.
- Tables and indexes can have a `FILLFACTOR` that allows better clustering when inserting data out of order.
- The `seq_page_cost` configuration parameter was added, allowing easier fine tuning of how expensive the query planner thinks sequential and random I/O are.
- Several features were improved allowing more useful warm-standby server setups for disaster recovery failover.
- `COPY` can dump the results of an arbitrary query out, allowing that high-performance output path more targeted data replication capabilities. A faster binary `COPY` was also added.
- Initial support for DTrace was added. The number of things you can monitor with it is limited in this version, though.

Please note the following updates for 8.3:

- **Heap-Only Tuples (HOT)** allow quicker reuse of the dead space left behind when a row is updated or deleted, as long as that doesn't touch its indexed columns.
- `autovacuum` is turned on by default, and multiple `autovacuum` processes can run at once.
- You can turn off `synchronous_commit` in order to speed up database commits, at the expense of introducing some potential for lost transactions.
- Checkpoints can be spread over a longer period of time, adjusted using the `checkpoint_completion_target` setting.
- The background writer in earlier versions was easy to configure so that it decreased performance instead of improving it. The new just-in-time background writer in this version is largely automatic and has less parameters to configure.
- `pg_stat_bgwriter` allows monitoring both the background writer and the writes done by the spread checkpoints.

- Sequential scans use an improved scheme that reduces their memory footprint, so that they're less likely to eject useful pages from the buffer cache as they execute. And if multiple scans are executing against the same table, they will synchronize in order to reduce duplication of reading. This is another reason to make sure you explicitly ORDER things that need to be sorted because when synchronized scans kick in the second client joining the scan will get rows starting with wherever the first one happens to be reading against.

- Read-only transactions are allocated virtual transaction ID numbers instead of real ones, reducing their overhead. The rate of transaction use and associated snapshot information can be inspected using a set of added functions that include `txid_current()` and `txid_current_snapshot()`.

- Temporary files can be moved using the `temp_tablespaces` parameter.

- Several types of activity that can correlate with performance issues can be more easily logged: `autovacuum`, checkpoints, and temporary file usage.

- All log activity can also be saved in the **Comma Separated Values (CSV)** output format, which makes them easier to process with external tools.

- If you comment out a previously set parameter in the `postgresql.conf`, starting in this version that will return it to the default; in earlier ones that just left it unchanged.

- Live and dead tuples (a tuple is essentially what most people think of as a row) are tracked in `pg_stat_user_tables`.

- Long-running transactions are easier to find in `pg_stat_activity`.

- The `archive_mode` parameter makes it easier to toggle on and off saving write-ahead log segments for a standby server.

- The CLUSTER command has improved to a point where it's a viable way to clean up after some situations where VACUUM FULL was the only alternative before.

- The performance of the Windows port has been improved by building it and using memory in a more efficient manner for that platform.

- The `pg_buffercache` module can now display page usage counts, allowing more useful introspection of the buffer cache.

- The `pgbench` utility now saves latency information with a full timestamp for each transaction, enabling analysis such as graphing of the results.

- Indexing of NULL values is greatly improved, including the ability to control where they are placed relative to the rest of the table (beginning or end).

Please note the following updates for 8.4:

- The FSM used to track space that used to belong to now-deleted data is tracked on disk instead of in shared memory, which removes any limits on how large it can be. This removes the need to worry about the `max_fsm_pages` and `max_fsm_relations` parameters, which are removed in this version. It also makes it much less likely that systems that are not being vacuumed frequently enough will end up in a situation where it's difficult to recover from that situation.

- The default value of the `default_statistics_target` parameter was increased from 10 to 100. This makes query planning time longer, and is responsible for a significant portion of the sometimes measured degradation in performance between 8.4 and 8.3 seen in many benchmarks. This mainly impacts trivial queries however. In more real-world ones, having improved statistics to work with will improve performance by making it less likely the query planner will pick a particularly bad execution plan. It's always possible to reduce this parameter for 8.4 systems that don't need to plan more complicated queries.

- In earlier versions, queries running against partitioned tables would only know how to limit their search to individual partitions if the `constraint_exclusion` parameter was changed from its default value because that overhead would otherwise apply to every query. A new `partition` setting for this parameter, now the default, allows partitioned queries to be supported without impacting the performance when a partition isn't involved.

- Bitmap index scans, often used when combining multiple relevant indexes used by a query, can do read-ahead set by the `effective_io_concurrency` parameter to improve performance. This feature was tested mainly on Linux. It can have a significant benefit on systems that support more than one disk operation at once, such as when a striped RAID volume is available.

- SQL `WINDOW` functions allow writing new types of queries far more efficiently than before, such as queries that need an idea of what the contents of nearby rows are.

- `WITH` clauses, such as `WITH RECURSIVE` allow **common-table expression (CTE)** programming. A common use of CTEs is to execute recursive query programs, which greatly simplifies and speeds up handling structures such as trees stored in the database.

- pg_restore can now do some operations in parallel to improving loading speed on systems that are limited there by CPU speed instead of disk throughput.
- The auto_explain feature makes it easy to log EXPLAIN output only for queries that take longer to run.
- A new pg_stat_statements add-in module allows tracking execution statistics of all SQL statements executed by a server. This replaces several situations where parsing the database log files was needed to gather statement profiling information needed for query tuning.
- User-defined functions can be monitored using pg_stat_user_functions.
- EXPLAIN VERBOSE gives a more useful set of information than before.
- SQL standard LIMIT and OFFSET queries are now supported, and they can use subselects.
- autovacuum parameters can now be easily adjusted per table using the CREATE TABLE and ALTER TABLE storage parameter mechanism.
- VACUUM is more likely to make progress on systems with really long-running transactions. Partial VACUUM was also added, which allows the processing to skip those sections of a table that it knows cannot have anything to clean up left in them.
- It's possible to adjust some of the server block size parameters at build time using parameters passed to the configure script, instead of needing to edit the source code.
- The database statistics file, which is both written too often and not necessarily critical for all situations, can be run against a different location, such as a RAM disk, using the stats_temp_directory parameter. When this is enabled, a normal startup/shutdown procedure will save the data changes to disk, but some statistics could be lost in an unplanned crash.
- More DTrace probes were added, and now they work on platforms other than Solaris (such as macOS X).
- pgbench can be run for a period of time instead of just for a number of transactions. The names of the tables it uses now are all prefixed with pgbench_ to avoid confusion with real user tables.
- Much smaller sizes of data might be compressed using the TOAST scheme.

Version 9.0

The individual items in the lists were previously sorted approximately by the expected impact on your system. But there were so many changes in 9.0 that they're being broken up by category for this section. As with all the version summaries here, this focuses on performance-related features, which represent only a fraction of the changes made in this version. Some major areas renovated in 9.0, such as big changes to database function languages PL/pgSQL, PL/Perl, and PL/Python, are completely excluded here. The goal here is to provide a quick (compared to the release notes at least) summary of the big performance-related pieces in only a few pages.

Replication

Asynchronous master/slave streaming replication is built into the database, without requiring external scripts to be configured.

Replicated systems can be set up as Hot Standby ones that allow read-only queries to execute against them.

The control over WAL archiving has been split. In addition to the existing `archive_mode` and `archive_command` settings, a new `wal_level` setting allows fine-tuning of how much information is written to the WAL.

Monitoring of the replication progress made by a standby server that accepts HOT Standby queries can be done using the `pg_last_xlog_receive_location()` and `pg_last_xlog_replay_location()` functions.

A new tool for removing older WAL archive files has been provided as `contrib/pg_archivecleanup`. This is expected to be called when using the new `archive_cleanup_command` parameter to maintain standby archive log directories. The program is always written so that it can be copied to and compiled for earlier PostgreSQL versions too, where this problem already existed and was usually handled with less robust techniques than this program uses.

Queries and EXPLAIN

EXPLAIN plans can be output in XML, JSON, or YAML formats, to make it easier to analyze them with external tools (or to write such tools yourself). EXPLAIN (BUFFERS) allows monitoring of the actual I/O done by a particular query, instead of just showing its costs. EXPLAIN output shows more information about how the increasingly useful hash nodes in query plans.

Window functions have some new options, such as PRECEDING, FOLLOWING, and starting with CURRENT ROWS, all of which allow writing some new types of windowed queries. Outer joins that reference tables not actually used to satisfy the query can now be removed from the query plan to improve their performance. Queries with that issue are commonly created by **object-relational mapper (ORM)** software. This can happen when queries use only part of the data in a complicated view, too.

Each tablespace can be assigned its own sequential and random page costs via ALTER TABLESPACE. This allows tweaking those settings for disks known to be particularly fast or slow relative to others. SSD and similar memory-based storage where random page lookup is nearly as fast as sequential are an example.

The statistics for how many distinct values are in a column can be manually adjusted using ALTER TABLE, to improve cases where they've been estimated badly. Queries using IS NOT NULL can now use indexes to help compute their results. This particularly accelerates MIN() and MAX() lookups when your index has many NULL values.

The **Genetic Query Optimizer (GEQO)** can now be forced to use a fixed random seed value. While query plans will still be random, any given query will always get the same optimizer plan. This makes reviewing and troubleshooting bad GEQO plans much easier to do. Before, it was impossible to be sure how a query using this feature was optimized and executed if you didn't log it at the time.

Estimations for values using greater or less than comparisons are improved, particularly for situations where data is constantly inserted into a table at one end of a column's range. This is common for time series and many other types of data. If the relevant statistics histogram bucket for the comparison is the first or last one available, and there is an index available, it's cheap to determine the true minimum or maximum value of that column. That min/max will be used instead of what's in the histogram bucket to find the left or right edge of the values in the column—instead of the possibly out-of-date information that ANALYZE last put into the relevant histogram bucket.

The query optimizer is much more aggressive about using `Materialize` nodes when it plans queries, if it believes that will perform better than earlier approaches for executing that plan. This may result in queries to use a higher multiple of `work_mem` than they did before as a result, to hold those Materialize nodes. This feature can be disabled by turning off the `enable_material` parameter. Like any new optimizer feature, this is useful for troubleshooting whether the implementation is working as expected when you see more of these nodes appear in query plans.

GIN indexes are created using self-balancing red-black trees, which particularly improves their performance when data is inserted in index order, a situation particularly common when loading a database.

Database development

The PL/pgSQL language used for writing many types of functions is now installed in all databases by default. It can still be removed if desired. Triggers can be attached specifically to a column, eliminating unnecessary calls to trigger function that aren't needed unless specific columns are altered. It's also possible to restrict when a trigger fires using a WHEN clause, further cutting down on unnecessary calls to the trigger function.

The LISTEN/NOTIFY mechanism for passing messages between database clients is faster and allows sending a "payload" string message. This allows building some better cross-client messaging systems using the database itself than was possible before. Applications can set an `application_name` parameter, which is shown in the `pg_stat_activity` information the database displays. Consistent use of this feature allows better monitoring of activity based on what the application is doing. In older versions, assigning dedicated user roles to certain application functions was normally done to approximate tracking at this level. While that still works too, this mechanism gives a more fine-grained way to track what the application is doing.

The error message when a constraint uniqueness violation occurs now includes the value involved. This makes it much easier to figure out what caused the problem. Constraint checks can now be marked as DEFERRABLE. Previously constraints were checked on a per row basis. This new approach allows checking for constraint violations only at the end of a statement or transaction. Some types of changes that were previously difficult to execute, such as mass renumbering of the primary key in a table, are much easier to execute if you defer all key checking until commit of every change.

A new class of constraints similar to uniqueness ones are available, called exclusion constraints. These allow constraints to enforce things such as ranges that must not overlap, instead of just checking for duplicate values. This can be particularly useful for applications that work with date ranges. A simple example is preventing items on a calendar from overlapping.

The `contrib/hstore` module, which adds a relatively low overhead key/value store type, has been upgraded to be faster and more capable. It's much more practical to add a high performance simple key/value store to a PostgreSQL database using this module now. This sometimes allows for a more practical storage approach to be combined with traditional relational queries, using whichever of the two is more appropriate for each type of data you need to store.

Configuration and monitoring

Server parameters can be adjusted per user/database combination. When the `postgresql.conf` file is reloaded via `pg_ctl reload` or sending the server a `SIGHUP` signal, the server log file notes which parameters were changed as a result. Background writer statistics can now be reset using `pg_stat_reset_shared('bgwriter')`.

Table and function counters can be individually reset using the `pg_stat_reset_single_table_counters()` and `pg_stat_reset_single_function_counters()` functions. The `log_temp_files` parameter is now specified in kilobyte units and its documentation is corrected. The description in earlier versions was misleading.

The `log_line_prefix` option can now track the `SQLSTATE` value set for messages such as errors, allowing logs to be more carefully analyzed by their exact error codes. The somewhat confusing relation size functions include new variations named `pg_table_size()` and `pg_indexes_size()`, which don't require knowing as much about database storage trivia to interpret usefully.

Tools

`pgbench` can now run multiple benchmarking processes/threads at once. Earlier versions could easily become limited by the speed of the `pgbench` client coordination part of the program itself instead. The `contrib/auto_explain` output displays the query being executed, in addition to its plan.

Query log data collected by `contrib/pg_stat_statements` includes counts for how much buffer cache activity was associated with each statement.

Internals

A utility named `contrib/pg_upgrade` allows upgrading to `9.0` from either version `8.3` or `8.4` without needing to dump and reload the database, which is normally referred to as *in-place upgrade*. A 64-bit Windows version was released, which allows the server to use more memory than earlier versions. It's still not expected that extremely large settings for `shared_buffers` will be useful on that platform. But this does allow you to be more aggressive with settings like `work_mem` than you were able to before.

`VACUUM FULL` has been changed to use the same rebuild mechanism that `CLUSTER` uses in earlier versions. This requires more disk space, but is normally faster and it avoids the index bloat issues that `VACCUM FULL` used to introduce in many situations. You can use `CLUSTER` on any system catalog tables that are per database, but still not ones that are shared by all databases. However, shared system catalogs can now have `REINDEX` executed on them safely. Previously, that was only possible in the special database maintenance standalone mode, and even there it was dangerous.

Some variations of `ALTER TABLE` require making a whole new copy of the table that includes the added/changed information, in a way similar to how `CLUSTER` rewrites a table. Since the copy in progress is not important unless it is complete, the block changes to create it are not longer written to the WAL. This is the same way that new and truncated tables avoid WAL logging when you write to them in a transaction that clears them. If the transaction doesn't complete, the partial copy is just destroyed. In this new case, as with the older `CREATE TABLE`/`TRUNCATE` ones, if you have WAL archiving enabled to send data to a standby server this optimization can't be used.

When compiling the database, the default is now to include the feature that used to require requesting `--enable-thread-safety`. That option allows multi-threaded client programs to be compiled using the database client libraries and run safely. In earlier versions, this was disabled by default and required recompiling the database to fix.

The database has a better idea on how to deal with the Linux **out of memory (OOM)** killer process. With the appropriate matching changes to server startup scripts, this allows making the main database server process resistant to the killer. Individual clients will, instead, be targeted if their memory usage goes out of control. In earlier versions, it was usually the main server process that was killed in that situation.

Several commands now allow a new syntax where options can be passed using a list in a `()` block instead of more traditional SQL syntax. `EXPLAIN`, `COPY`, and `VACUUM` all have this alternate syntax available for some parameters. In some cases, it's the only way to use newer features added to those commands.

Summary

One of the advantages of an open source community like the one surrounding PostgreSQL is that it's easy to see what other people struggle with. Watch enough of that, and some trouble spots that aren't too difficult to avoid become obvious. Some of the biggest problems people run into are quite fundamental to PostgreSQL: getting `VACUUM` to work properly, making sure your application acquires locks properly—there's a long list of major things you need to get right. But sometimes the little details can trip you up, instead. The tips covered in this chapter, from bulk loading to profiling might provide the right background information to make your use of the database simpler when dealing with smaller problems, too. And sometimes the answer to your problem is solved simply by using a newer version of PostgreSQL, where it's been engineered out of the database.

Bulk loading works well using `COPY`, but alternate techniques such as bulk inserts or even add-on tools may be appropriate when dealing with less-than-perfect input data. You should also consider tuning your database server a bit differently when running a bulk load than you would for regular operation. PostgreSQL doesn't have any reliable way of knowing how many rows are visible in a table, in order to accelerate counting them. Applications that expect this to be fast may need to use an alternative approach.

After transactions are updated, a vacuum processing step called hint bit updating can cause unexpected writes even when doing simple reads from a table. Statements that are prepared or executed from functions can get generic query plans that don't take into account all the table statistics available. You may benefit from executing these differently so that proper query optimization takes place.

Foreign key processing can be deferred to commit time for better efficiency. But if you batch up too many of those at once, you should make sure that deferral doesn't itself cause an activity spike. Directly profiling functions and other activities in the database, including snooping into what the operating system is doing under the hood, can find unexpected performance issues that no simpler analysis can locate.

The performance and features of PostgreSQL have increased so much in recent versions that time spent trying to optimize an older version might be better spent planning an upgrade. Minor PostgreSQL releases focus on bug fixes, and can be effective at removing performance issues caused by bugs, too.

Other Books You May Enjoy

If you enjoyed this book, you may be interested in these other books by Packt:

Mastering PostgreSQL 10
Hans-Jürgen Schönig

ISBN: 978-1-78847-229-6

- Get to grips with the advanced features of PostgreSQL 10 and handle advanced SQL
- Make use of the indexing features in PostgreSQL and fine-tune the performance of your queries
- Work with stored procedures and manage backup and recovery
- Master replication and failover techniques
- Troubleshoot your PostgreSQL instance for solutions to common and not-so-common problems
- Learn how to migrate your database from MySQL and Oracle to PostgreSQL without any hassle

Learning PostgreSQL 10
Salahaldin Juba, Andrey Volkov

ISBN: 978-1-78839-201-3

- Understand the fundamentals of relational databases, relational algebra, and data modeling
- Install a PostgreSQL cluster, create a database, and implement your data model
- Create tables and views, define indexes, and implement triggers, stored procedures, and other schema objects
- Use the Structured Query Language (SQL) to manipulate data in the database
- Implement business logic on the server side with triggers and stored procedures using PL/pgSQL
- Make use of advanced data types supported by PostgreSQL 10: Arrays, hstore, JSONB, and others
- Develop OLAP database solutions using the most recent features of PostgreSQL 10
- Connect your Python applications to a PostgreSQL database and work with the data efficiently
- Test your database code, find bottlenecks, improve performance, and enhance the reliability of the database applications

Leave a review - let other readers know what you think

Please share your thoughts on this book with others by leaving a review on the site that you bought it from. If you purchased the book from Amazon, please leave us an honest review on this book's Amazon page. This is vital so that other potential readers can see and use your unbiased opinion to make purchasing decisions, we can understand what our customers think about our products, and our authors can see your feedback on the title that they have worked with Packt to create. It will only take a few minutes of your time, but is valuable to other potential customers, our authors, and Packt. Thank you!

Index

Made in the USA
Middletown, DE
26 September 2019